THE COMPLETE
— BOOK OF —
mother &
baby care

Elizabeth Fenwick

THE COMPLETE
— BOOK OF —
mother &
baby care

NEW FULLY UPDATED EDITION

DK

LONDON, NEW YORK, SYDNEY, DELHI,
PARIS, MUNICH, and JOHANNESBURG

THIS REVISED EDITION

Produced for Dorling Kindersley Limited by
Design Revolution, Queens Park Villa,
30 West Drive, Brighton, East Sussex BN2 2GE
Senior Art Editor Becky Willis

Project Editor Julie Whitaker

ORIGINAL EDITION

Senior Art Editor Carole Ash

Project Editors
Sarah Pearce
Pregnancy and Birth Tanya Hines
Health Care Claire Le Bas

Art Editors
Pregnancy and Birth Rowena Alsey
Health Care Tina Hill

Production Manager Michel Blake

Editorial Direction Daphne Razazan

Main Photographers
Antonia Deutsch, Dave King, Susannah Price

CONSULTANTS

Professor R. W. Taylor, MD, FRCOG, Head of
Department of Gynaecology, The United Medical Schools
of Guy's and St Thomas's Hospitals, London
Professor Jon Scopes, MB, PhD, FRCP, Department
of Paediatrics, St Thomas's Hospital, London
Christine Williams, RGN, HV, FWT, Health Visitor
and Family Planning Nurse
Janice Leighton, RGN, RM, Community Midwife
Alan McLaughlin, RGN, Department of Clinical
Neurology, St Thomas's Hospital, London

Published in Great Britain by Dorling Kindersley Limited
80 Strand, London WC2 ORL
A Penguin Company

10 9 8 7 6 5 4 3 2

Publisher's note
Throughout this book, the pronouns "he" and "she" refer to both
sexes, except where a topic applies specifically to a boy or a girl.

A CIP catalogue record for this book is
available from the British Library.

ISBN 0-7513-01515

Reproduced by Colourscan, Singapore
Printed in Slovakia by Neografia

D.L.TO:1042-1996

See our complete catalogue at www.dk.com

INTRODUCTION

Every pregnancy, and every baby, is special. Even though it's an experience that has happened countless times, to countless couples, it will still be momentous for you. Having a baby opens up a new and exciting world – but it can seem a dauntingly unfamiliar world too. This book guides you through your pregnancy stage-by-stage, showing you how to make it a happy, healthy time for yourself, and give your baby the best possible start in life.

Most of us know very little about pregnancy and babycare at first and we may assume that there is a "right" or a "wrong", way of doing things. There seldom is. But there's often an easy way. So what we have tried to do in this book is to show you what parents have found works best, and what makes life easiest, by offering practical solutions to common problems.

Since the first edition of this book was published I have become a grandmother and been reminded all over again of what parenthood actually means, of the highs and lows, the hard work, the anxieties, the exhaustion, as well as the moments of sheer joy and wonder. Over the last decade our ideas about how a family works have been changing too. More women are trying to find ways of combining work and family responsibilities. More are having to cope alone with bringing up a family. And more fathers are involved in their children's care, sometimes indeed as the child's primary carer. But parental anxieties do not change much over the years. What all parents want is their children's health and happiness.

I hope you will quickly discover that parenthood, for all its responsibilities, can be fun. You don't have to aim to be perfect parents, just the parents who are right for your baby. A baby is a personality in his or her own right almost from the moment of birth. Perhaps one of the harder tasks of parenthood is to accept each child as an individual in its own right, and to tolerate and encourage your children's differences from you and from each other. If you feel you need a philosophy to see you through the next few years, you cannot do better than to remember the words of psychologist Anthony Storr: "Children develop most satisfactorily if they are loved for what they are, not for what anyone thinks they ought to be".

Elizabeth Fenwick

CONTENTS

PREGNANCY AND BIRTH
8–73

CARING FOR YOUR BABY
74–177

YOUR CHILD'S HEALTH

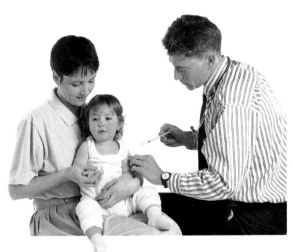

PREGNANCY
AND BIRTH

An illustrated guide to a healthy and happy
pregnancy, incorporating practical self-help
advice for labour and birth.

THINKING ABOUT PREGNANCY

There are a number of steps you can take to increase your chances of conceiving and giving birth to a normal, healthy baby. Ideally, you and your partner should plan for pregnancy at least three months before you conceive. It is in the first few weeks, when you may not even know you are pregnant, that the baby's development can be most easily affected. Keeping fit and eating well will ensure you have done as much as possible to nourish and protect your unborn baby. There may also be hazards at work that could affect the baby, or maybe you have not been vaccinated against German measles. Planning your pregnancy gives you the time you need to consider these kinds of risks and, if necessary, to do something positive about them.

CHECKLIST FOR PREGNANCY

Use these questions as a checklist if you want to have a baby or find that you are pregnant. A few may not apply to you, but it's important to ask yourself all of them. Talk to your partner too, as some of the questions relate directly to him. If you feel worried by any of the points, see your doctor.

Are you immune to German measles?

German measles, or rubella, can cause serious defects to the baby if you develop it in pregnancy, especially early pregnancy, when the baby's internal organs are developing. So, before you become pregnant, ask your doctor for a blood test to make sure that you are immune from the disease. If you are not, your doctor can give you a vaccination. Have the test in plenty of time as you shouldn't try to become pregnant for at least three months afterwards.

Have you or your partner a family history of inherited disease?

Some medical conditions, such as haemophilia and cystic fibrosis, are inherited. If either you or your partner has a close relative with an inherited disease, there is a chance that it might be passed on to your baby. See your doctor before trying to become pregnant, and if necessary he can refer you to a genetic counsellor who can assess the level of risk that you will be taking. It's reassuring to know that, in most cases, only if both partners carry the gene that causes the disease, does the child run a real risk of inheriting it.

Do you have a long-standing medical condition?

If you have a medical disorder, such as diabetes or epilepsy, you should talk to your doctor before trying to become pregnant. Your doctor may want to change your drug treatment, either because the drugs you are on might affect the baby, or because they might make it more difficult for you to conceive.

"What is generally the best age to have a baby?"

Q&A

This is probably in your twenties, although more women are deciding to start a family at a later date, when they feel emotionally and financially ready for a baby. Risks of a difficult pregnancy do increase when the mother is over 35 years old, but they are reduced if you have a fit and healthy lifestyle. You are also more likely to have a Down's syndrome baby if you are over 35. Women under 18 run a greater risk of having a stillbirth or low-birthweight baby, but regular visits to the clinic and keeping healthy minimize this.

Are you, or have you been, on the pill?

It is best to stop taking the pill well before you want to conceive, to allow your body time to return to its normal cycle. Wait until you have had three menstrual periods before trying to become pregnant (you can use a condom or cap during this time). If you conceive before the regular rhythm of your periods has been established again, it makes it more difficult to predict the delivery date of your baby.

Does your work bring you into contact with any risks?

Your employer has a responsibility to make sure that you are not exposed to any risks in your work that might affect your chances of conception, or put your baby at risk. VDUs (visual display units) are now believed to cause no harm to the baby. One rare infection, *Chlamydia psittaci*, which causes miscarriage, can be caught from sheep at lambing time. Therefore, if you work on a farm, you should not help with lambing during your pregnancy, or come into contact with newborn lambs, or milk ewes that have recently given birth.

How much do you weigh?

Ideally, your weight should be normal for your height for at least six months before conceiving, so if you are seriously over- or under-weight, see your doctor for advice on attaining the right weight. Unless you have a serious weight problem, never diet in pregnancy, as you may deprive your body of vital nutrients.

Are you eating healthily?

Your chances of conceiving, and of having a healthy baby, increase if you eat a healthy balanced diet.

Do you smoke or drink?

You should both stop smoking and drinking as soon as you want to become pregnant, as tobacco and alcohol can affect fertility in men as well as women. Smoking and drinking can also harm the growing baby both before and after birth.

Are you taking folic acid?

Start taking folic acid (a vitamin that prevents birth defects such as spina bifida) before you start trying to conceive. Take 400 micrograms each day for the first 12 weeks of pregnancy.

FOLIC ACID

From the time you stop using contraception until the 12th week of pregnancy you should take a folic acid supplement. Folic acid, also called folate or folacin, is one of the B vitamins. It is one of the few nutrients that is known to prevent neural tube defects (NTDs) such as spina bifida or anencephaly. The neural tube, which goes on to form the baby's spine, develops very soon after conception – probably even before you realize that you are pregnant. Without sufficient folic acid, the neural tube may fail to fuse completely along its length, exposing the spinal cord and resulting in the condition known as spina bifida. Infants with anencephaly die shortly after birth because most or all of the brain is absent.

SOURCES OF FOLIC ACID

Research has shown that an increased intake of folic acid can prevent up to 70 per cent of cases of spina bifida.

Good natural food sources of folic acid include dark green leafy vegetables (spinach and broccoli), some fruits (particularly citrus fruits), legumes (kidney beans, chick peas), wheatgerm, yeast, and egg yolks. Try to eat vegetables lightly steamed or raw. Some foods have also been fortified with folic acid. These include grain products such as bread, rice, pasta, and breakfast cereals.

However, you should not depend on food sources alone. To be on the safe side, you should start to take a folic acid supplement as soon as you decide to stop using contraception. Multivitamin tablets often contain some folic acid, but not enough to protect your baby. To reduce the risk of spina bifida you need to take one 400 microgram folic acid tablet every day. Tablets can be bought over the counter without a prescription, from any pharmacy or health food shop, and most supermarkets. If you have had one child with a neural tube defect, you have a higher risk of having a second child with the same defect. In this instance, your doctor will advise you to take a higher dose (4 milligrams) of folic acid each day.

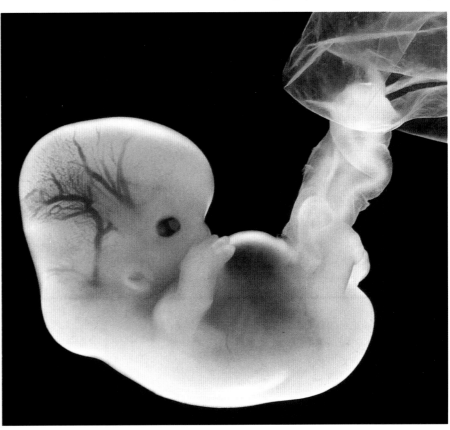

The developing embryo
Your unborn baby will stand a better chance of developing normally if you take a folic acid supplement. This should be taken before conception and during the first 12 weeks of pregnancy.

A PREGNANCY CALENDAR

This month-by-month calendar charts the progress of one woman's pregnancy. It shows the physical and emotional changes you may experience, and follows the baby's development from conception to the last days in the womb. There is advice on what to do at each stage, as well as reassuring answers to questions and worries you might have. Each month has at least one additional feature on a relevant aspect of pregnancy, such as options for antenatal classes. Every pregnancy varies, so don't be surprised if some of the changes described don't happen to you at exactly the same time. The calendar counts day one of pregnancy as the first day of your last menstrual period, so two weeks after conception, you are four weeks pregnant.

BECOMING PREGNANT

If you are thinking of becoming pregnant, check that your lifestyle involves nothing that might harm the baby. All the major organs of his body are formed during the first three months, and it is now that his health can be harmed most easily. Once you have conceived, you will probably know or suspect that you are pregnant because of a number of changes, such as heavy breasts, or feeling sick. Most of these changes are set off by the increase in hormone levels during the early weeks, as your body prepares to nurture the baby.

EARLY SIGNS OF PREGNANCY

One or more of these changes can signify that you are pregnant. You may not notice any of them at first, but still instinctively know you are pregnant because you "feel" different.
★ A missed period (amenorrhoea). This is usually one of the first signs of pregnancy, but if your periods are normally irregular, or you are anxious, busy, or ill, or are under-weight, this may not be a reliable guide. It is also possible to have slight bleeding around the time you would normally expect your period, after you have become pregnant.
★ Your breasts may become enlarged and tender, and perhaps tingle a little. The veins over the surface of the breasts may become more prominent.
★ A strange metallic taste in the mouth.
★ A feeling of deep tiredness, not just in the evening, but also during the day.
★ Feeling faint, and perhaps dizzy.
★ You may experience an increase in normal vaginal discharge.
★ Nausea and perhaps vomiting; this may happen at any time of day. Certain odours may make you feel nauseous, particularly cooking smells.

★ Some foods may taste different from normal, and you may develop a strong dislike of some things, such as alcohol, coffee, and cigarette smoke, and a craving for others.
★ Feeling unusually emotional. This is due primarily to the changes in your hormones.
★ A frequent need to pass water, although this may be only in very small quantities.

CONFIRMING THE PREGNANCY

Two weeks after conception a pregnancy hormone, hCG (human chorionic gonadotrophin), appears in your urine. As soon as you have missed a period, a test of the urine will confirm whether or not you are pregnant. Your GP or family planning clinic will give you a free test, and many pharmacies and pregnancy advisory services will also do a test for a small fee.

HOME PREGNANCY TESTING KITS

If you would rather do the pregnancy test yourself, buy a testing kit from a chemist. All kits contain a chemical solution, which you must mix with a few drops of urine. The first urine that you pass in the morning is used, as it contains the most hormone. Modern testing kits are very accurate; if you get a positive result, you can safely book your first antenatal appointment.

CALCULATING YOUR DELIVERY DATE

Pregnancy lasts about 266 days from conception to birth. The most likely time of conception is when you ovulate. In a normal 28-day cycle, this happens about 14 days before the next period is due, so to calculate your approximate delivery date, count 280 days (266 plus 14) from the first day of your last period. Remember, this is only a guide. Although the average pregnancy is 40 weeks, a normal pregnancy can be anything from 38 to 42 weeks.

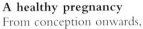

A healthy pregnancy
From conception onwards, it is important to avoid ingesting any substance that could harm your unborn baby.

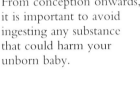

WHAT TO AVOID

Avoid smoking, alcohol, and any form of medication unless confirmed as safe by your doctor, throughout pregnancy, but especially in the first three months when the baby's organs are forming.

Smoking

This deprives the baby of oxygen. Babies of mothers who smoke are more likely to be premature and have a low birthweight. Smoking also increases the chances of having a miscarriage, a stillbirth, a malformed baby, or a baby that dies after birth. The more you smoke, the greater the risk, so stop smoking completely. If you really can't give up, switch to a low-tar brand, ration the cigarettes you smoke, don't inhale, and stub out your cigarette when you've smoked half of it. Doctors believe that passive smoking could be a factor in causing cot death, so avoid smoky atmospheres when pregnant. Protect your baby from inhaling other people's cigarette smoke.

Alcohol

A glass of wine once or twice a week won't do you or your baby any harm. But drinking two or more units of alcohol every day (one unit is equivalent to a small glass of wine or half a pint of beer) can seriously affect your baby. "Binge drinking" is particularly harmful.

Medication

Many drugs can have harmful or unknown effects on your unborn baby, so avoid taking medication in pregnancy, unless it is prescribed by a doctor who knows that you are pregnant. This includes many of the remedies you would normally take for minor complaints, such as aspirin. If you require medication to control an existing condition such as diabetes, your doctor may have to alter your dose.

Other risks

Cats' and dogs' faeces, and raw or undercooked meat, may contain a parasite called toxoplasma, which can seriously harm the unborn baby. Wash your hands after handling raw meat, and don't eat undercooked meat.
Avoid emptying cat litter trays (if you must, wear rubber gloves and then wash your hands). Wear gloves for all gardening jobs and wash all fruit and vegetables well before eating to remove any soil.

THE START OF LIFE

During the first eight weeks of pregnancy, the baby develops from a single cell at conception to a fetus approximately 2.5cm (1in) long that is starting to look human.

CONCEPTION TO WEEK FOUR

1 Ovulation

Around day 14 of your menstrual cycle, a ripe egg is released from one of your ovaries, and fertilization becomes possible. The egg is caught by the fingers at the end of the Fallopian tube, and drawn into it. The egg can survive for up to 24 hours; if it isn't fertilized, it passes out of the vagina with the lining of the womb in your next monthly period.

The swim of the sperm

During orgasm, a man may ejaculate between 200 and 400 million sperm into a woman's vagina. Many spill out again, or are lost along the way, but some swim through the mucus secreted by the cervix (the neck of the womb), which becomes thin and stretchy around ovulation, and cross the womb into the Fallopian tube. If an egg hasn't been released, the sperm can survive in the tube for up to 48 hours.

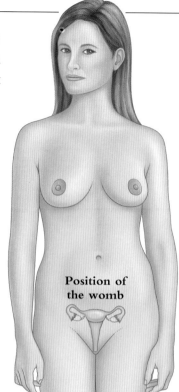

Position of the womb

5 Implantation

The fertilized egg begins to embed itself in the soft, thick lining of the womb at about the end of week three. This is called implantation. When the egg is securely attached to the lining of the womb, conception is complete.

Sponge-like fingers from the outer cells of the embryo start to burrow into the lining, to link up with the mother's blood vessels. These later form the placenta. Some of the cells also develop into the umbilical cord, and the membranes that protect the baby. The inner cells divide into three layers, which develop into the different parts of your baby's body.

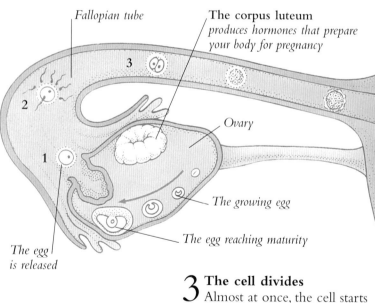

Fallopian tube

The corpus luteum *produces hormones that prepare your body for pregnancy*

Womb

Ovary

The growing egg

The egg reaching maturity

The egg is released

The embryo *embeds itself deep into the womb lining*

The cervix *becomes soft and stretchy around ovulation, so that sperm can pass through it more easily*

2 Fertilization

Sperm carry a substance that can dissolve the outer covering of the egg, so that one of them can penetrate it. As soon as the successful sperm enters the egg, no other sperm can get through. The sperm loses its tail and its head begins to swell. It fuses with the egg, forming a single cell.

3 The cell divides

Almost at once, the cell starts to divide. It carries on dividing into more and more cells, as it travels down the Fallopian tube.

4 Reaching the womb

On about the fourth day after fertilization, the egg reaches the cavity of the womb. It has developed into a ball of about 100 cells with a hollow, fluid-filled centre, but it is still too small to be seen by the naked eye. For the next few days it floats about in the womb cavity.

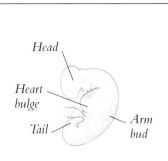

Head

Heart bulge

Tail

Arm bud

About week six

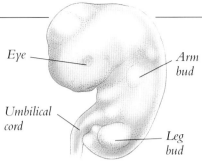

Eye

Arm bud

Umbilical cord

Leg bud

About week seven

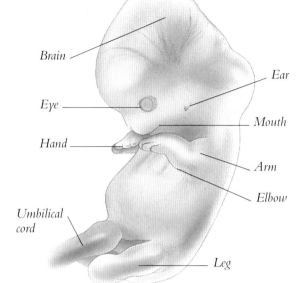

Brain

Ear

Eye

Mouth

Hand

Arm

Elbow

Umbilical cord

Leg

About week eight

WEEKS FIVE TO SIX

★ The embryo is floating in a fluid-filled sac.

★ It has a simple brain, spine, and central nervous system.

★ Four shallow pits have appeared on the head, which will later become the baby's eyes and ears.

★ The embryo has the beginnings of a digestive system, and of a mouth and a jaw.

★ The stomach and chest are developing. The heart can be seen as a large bulge at the front of the chest; by the end of the week it will start beating.

★ A system of blood vessels is forming.

★ Four tiny limb buds have developed.

WEEK SEVEN

★ The head looks large and is bent on to the chest. A face is forming, though the eyes are on the sides of the head and still sealed. Black pigment can be seen under the skin overlying the eyes.

★ The arms and legs are clearly visible, with clefts at the end, which become fingers and toes.

★ The heart starts to circulate blood around the embryo's body.

★ The outline of the baby's nervous system is already nearly complete.

★ Bone cells are beginning to develop.

★ The embryo has lungs, an intestine, a liver, kidneys, and internal sex organs, but all are not yet fully formed.

WEEK EIGHT

★ The embryo can now be called a fetus, which means "young one".

★ All the major internal organs have developed, although they are still in a simple form, and may not be in their final position.

★ A face is recognizable: the nose seems to have a tip, the nostrils have formed, and the two sides of the jaw have joined to make a mouth. There is a tongue already.

★ The inner parts of the ears, responsible for balance and hearing, are forming.

★ The fingers and toes are becoming more distinct, though they are joined by webs of skin.

★ The arms and legs have grown longer, and shoulders, elbows, hips, and knees are detectable.

★ The baby moves around quite a lot, though you can't feel him yet.

Length: The embryo is now 6mm ($\frac{1}{4}$ in), about the size of an apple seed.

Length: The embryo is now 1.3cm ($\frac{1}{2}$ in), about the size of a small grape.

Length: The fetus is now 2.5cm (1in), about the size of an average strawberry.

TWINS

About one in 80 pregnancies results in twins. If twins run in your family, your chances of having them are greater.
Fraternal twins occur when two separate eggs are fertilized by two separate sperm. They are three times as common as identical twins. The twins each have their own placenta, may or may not be the same sex, and are no more alike than any other brothers or sisters.
Identical twins are produced when the egg is fertilized and divides into two separate halves, each of which developes into an identical baby. The twins share a placenta, are always of the same sex, and have the same physical characteristics and genetic make-up.

"Can I do anything to influence the baby's sex?"

The baby's sex is determined by the man's sperm, which can be either male or female. Research suggests that male sperm swim faster but survive less long than female sperm, so you may increase your chances of having a boy if you make love when you are most fertile (about 14 days before your period is due); and of having a girl if you have intercourse up to three days before you next expect to be fertile.

15

WEEK

12

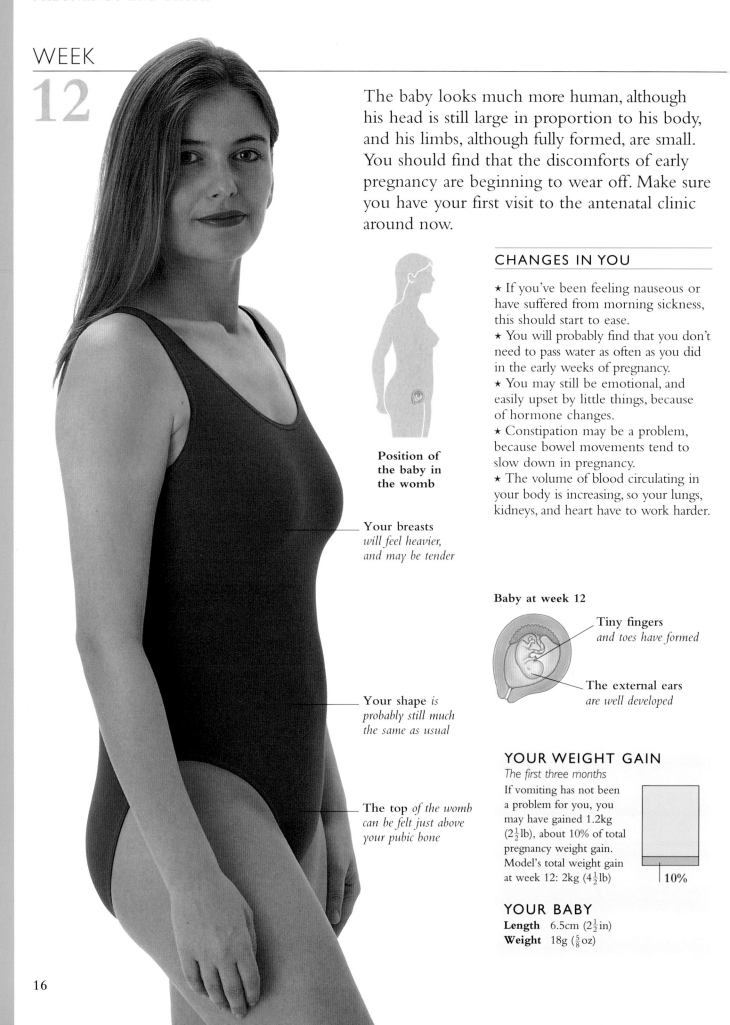

The baby looks much more human, although his head is still large in proportion to his body, and his limbs, although fully formed, are small. You should find that the discomforts of early pregnancy are beginning to wear off. Make sure you have your first visit to the antenatal clinic around now.

Position of the baby in the womb

Your breasts *will feel heavier, and may be tender*

Your shape *is probably still much the same as usual*

The top *of the womb can be felt just above your pubic bone*

CHANGES IN YOU

★ If you've been feeling nauseous or have suffered from morning sickness, this should start to ease.
★ You will probably find that you don't need to pass water as often as you did in the early weeks of pregnancy.
★ You may still be emotional, and easily upset by little things, because of hormone changes.
★ Constipation may be a problem, because bowel movements tend to slow down in pregnancy.
★ The volume of blood circulating in your body is increasing, so your lungs, kidneys, and heart have to work harder.

Baby at week 12

Tiny fingers *and toes have formed*

The external ears *are well developed*

YOUR WEIGHT GAIN
The first three months
If vomiting has not been a problem for you, you may have gained 1.2kg (2½lb), about 10% of total pregnancy weight gain. Model's total weight gain at week 12: 2kg (4½lb)

10%

YOUR BABY
Length   6.5cm (2½in)
Weight   18g ($\frac{5}{8}$oz)

WHAT TO DO

★ Buy a bra that will support your breasts well.
★ Check that you are eating a varied diet of fresh foods.
★ Guard against constipation by drinking plenty of water and including high-fibre foods in your diet.
★ Make an appointment with your dentist for a check-up.
★ Tell your employer that you are pregnant, so that you can take paid time off work to go to the antenatal clinic.
★ Visit the clinic for your first antenatal check-up.
★ Ask at the clinic how to claim for free dental treatment and prescriptions during pregnancy.
★ Practise antenatal exercises regularly. Go swimming.
★ Enrol for antenatal exercise classes if you want to.
★ Find out about other antenatal classes in your area.

YOUR GROWING BABY

★ All of the internal organs are formed, and most are working, so the baby is far less likely to be harmed by infections or drugs.
★ The eyelids have developed, and are closed over the eyes.
★ The baby has earlobes.
★ The limbs are formed, with fingers and toes. Miniature fingernails and toenails are growing.
★ Muscles are developing, so the baby moves much more. He can curl and fan his toes. He can make a fist.
★ He can move the muscles of his mouth to frown, purse his lips, and open and close his mouth.
★ He can suck. He swallows the fluid that surrounds him and he passes urine.

see also:
Antenatal clinic *pages 34–6*
Antenatal exercises *pages 45–7*
Eating healthily *pages 50–3*
Frequent urination *page 41*
Morning sickness *page 41*
Pregnancy bra *page 23*
Protecting your back *page 44*

ANTENATAL CLASSES

Start thinking about the type of class that will best suit you and your partner. Often you can go to introductory classes now – on ways to keep healthy in pregnancy, for example – and the classes themselves start eight to ten weeks before the baby is due. Antenatal exercise classes may continue throughout your pregnancy.

CHOOSING A CLASS

Different classes emphasize different subjects, so select a class that is going to cover in most detail the topics that concern you. There are three main types of classes, and you may want to go to more than one. All of these classes cover labour and birth.

Hospital classes

These free classes are an invaluable source of information on the procedures and routines followed in the hospital where you are having your baby, and you will probably go on a tour of the delivery room and maternity wards. The only drawback is that the classes are usually large, and they may take the form of lectures with films, so it can be hard to ask questions.

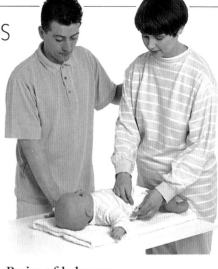

Basics of babycare
It's fun and helpful to learn how to look after your baby at the classes.

Local classes

Ask your doctor where these classes are held. They are also free, but are usually smaller and more friendly than hospital classes. You will meet the people who will look after you and your new baby, as well as other prospective mothers.

The classes emphasize how to care for your new baby; labour and birth will be covered, too. If you are having a hospital birth, you may be able to go on a tour of the hospital where you are having your baby. Your partner will be invited to some classes.

Other classes

These are run by organizations such as the National Child-birth Trust (NCT), and a fee is usually charged, with exemptions. The classes concentrate on antenatal exercises, as well as techniques such as relaxation, to help you cope with labour and birth, and are a good place to meet other mothers in your area. Your partner will be encouraged to attend, too.

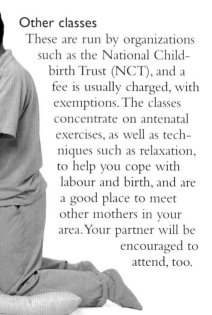

Tips for labour
Massage is one of the techniques you and your partner may be taught to help you cope with labour.

WEEK

16

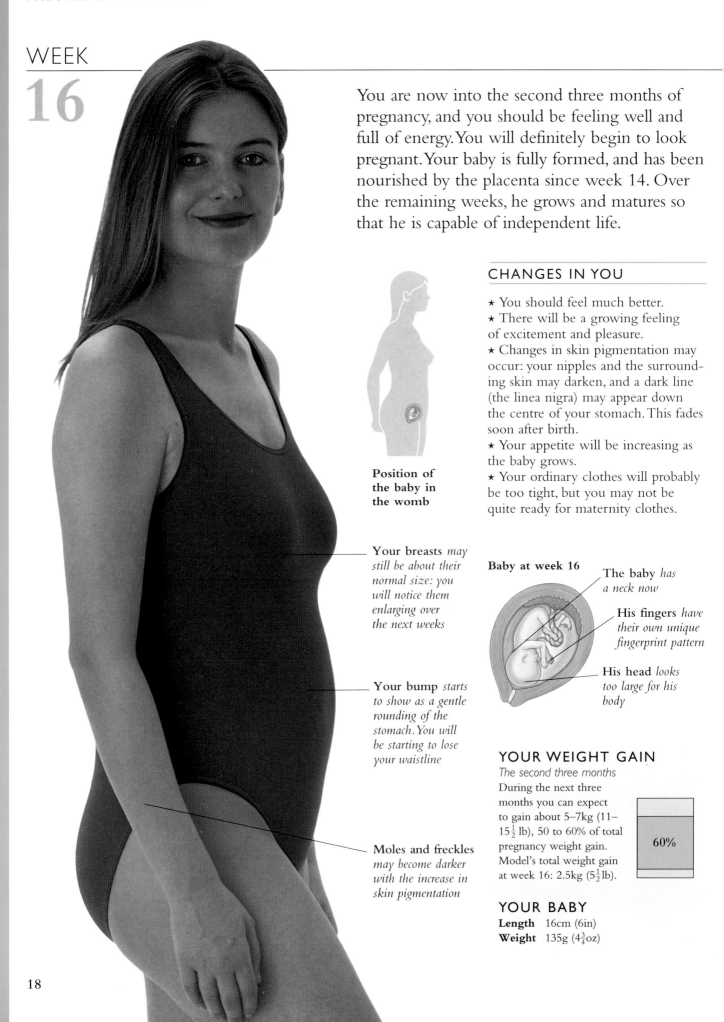

You are now into the second three months of pregnancy, and you should be feeling well and full of energy. You will definitely begin to look pregnant. Your baby is fully formed, and has been nourished by the placenta since week 14. Over the remaining weeks, he grows and matures so that he is capable of independent life.

Position of the baby in the womb

CHANGES IN YOU

★ You should feel much better.
★ There will be a growing feeling of excitement and pleasure.
★ Changes in skin pigmentation may occur: your nipples and the surrounding skin may darken, and a dark line (the linea nigra) may appear down the centre of your stomach. This fades soon after birth.
★ Your appetite will be increasing as the baby grows.
★ Your ordinary clothes will probably be too tight, but you may not be quite ready for maternity clothes.

Your breasts *may still be about their normal size: you will notice them enlarging over the next weeks*

Baby at week 16

The baby *has a neck now*

His fingers *have their own unique fingerprint pattern*

Your bump *starts to show as a gentle rounding of the stomach. You will be starting to lose your waistline*

His head *looks too large for his body*

YOUR WEIGHT GAIN

The second three months
During the next three months you can expect to gain about 5–7kg (11–15½ lb), 50 to 60% of total pregnancy weight gain. Model's total weight gain at week 16: 2.5kg (5½ lb).

60%

Moles and freckles *may become darker with the increase in skin pigmentation*

YOUR BABY

Length 16cm (6in)
Weight 135g (4¾oz)

WHAT TO DO

★ Give up smoking if you have not already done so. Encourage your partner to do the same.
★ Don't use the increase in your appetite as an excuse to eat the wrong kinds of foods; eat healthily and watch weight gain.
★ Start to take iron supplements, if prescribed by your doctor.
★ After the first trimester you can stop taking folic acid.
★ Visit the antenatal clinic for the second time. You will probably be offered an ultrasound scan and a serum screening test. Amniocentesis is also done around now if there is a chance of the baby having an abnormality.

YOUR GROWING BABY

★ The eyebrows and eyelashes are growing, and the baby has fine downy hair on his face and body (lanugo).
★ His skin is so thin that it is transparent; networks of blood vessels can be seen underneath.
★ Joints have formed in his arms and legs and hard bones are beginning to develop.
★ His sex organs are sufficiently mature for his sex to be evident, but this is not always detectable by an ultrasound scan.
★ The baby makes breathing movements with his chest.
★ He can suck his thumb.
★ He moves around vigorously, but you probably won't be able to feel him yet.
★ His heart is beating about twice as fast as your own; the doctor or midwife can hear it with a sonicaid (a special listening device) after week 14.
★ The baby grows rapidly this month.

see also:
AFP test *page 37*
Amniocentesis *page 37*
Eating healthily *pages 50–3*
Relaxation and breathing *pages 48–9*
Skin colour *page 21*
Smoking *page 13*
Supplements *page 52*
Ultrasound *page 37*

MIXED FEELINGS

You and your partner are bound to have mixed emotions about the pregnancy, so don't be surprised if as well as feeling elated and excited, you sometimes feel low. Try to tolerate and understand any negative feelings; they will probably fade after the birth.

COMMON WORRIES

The best way to dispel any worries that you may have about the baby or parenthood is to talk about them frankly with each other. It also helps to find out as much as you can about pregnancy, so you understand the changes taking place.

You

It's only natural for your feelings of excitement and anticipation to be sometimes clouded by more negative thoughts. You may worry about loving the baby, but once he's born and you get to know each other, love will grow. You may also feel depressed about your changing shape, and even resent the baby for putting your body through such strains. But most adverse bodily changes disappear after birth, and with some gentle exercising your shape will return.

Your partner

The baby becomes a reality when you see him for the first time on the ultrasound screen. Up to now you may have felt left out, and perhaps jealous of all the attention the baby is receiving, but you should now start to feel positive and excited. If you're worried about whether your income will be enough to support you all, try to plan and budget.

Both of you

It's normal to feel excited about the new baby, yet to worry that you're not yet ready for parenthood. If you're anxious about labour and birth, find out about them, and practise techniques, such as good breathing, so you feel more confident and in control when the time comes.

"How can I be sure the baby will be all right?"

Q & A

The chances of the baby being abnormal are very small. Most abnormalities occur in the first weeks, and end in an early miscarriage. By week 13 the baby is fully formed and very little can go wrong. If you check that your lifestyle involves nothing that could harm him, you can reduce the risk still further.

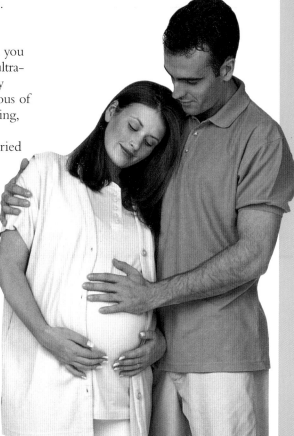

WEEK
20

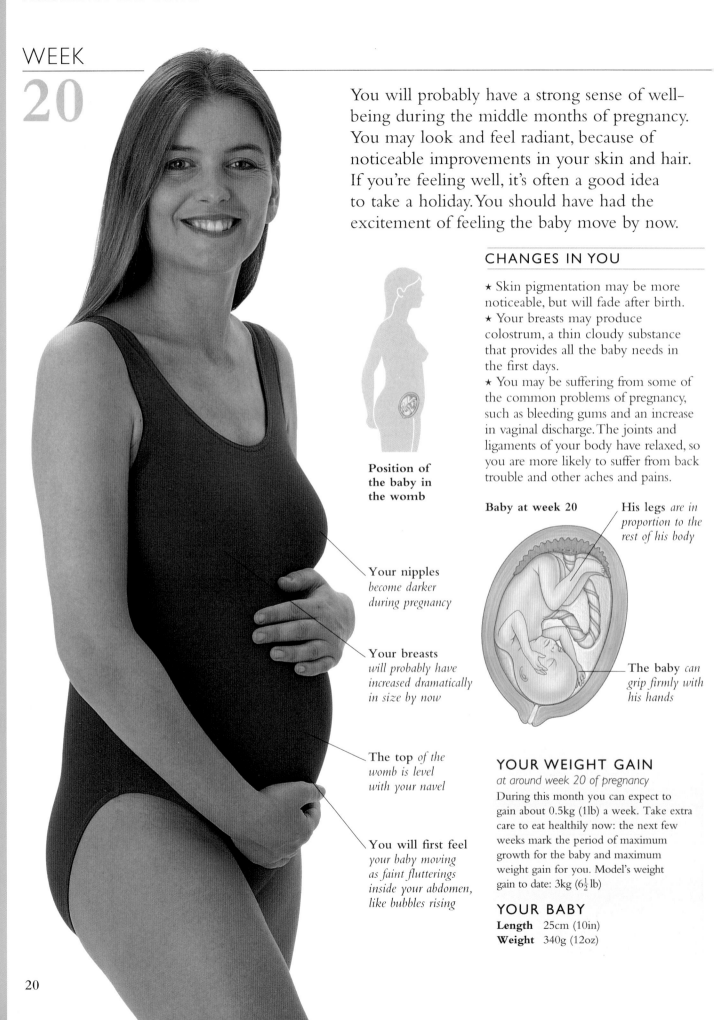

You will probably have a strong sense of well-being during the middle months of pregnancy. You may look and feel radiant, because of noticeable improvements in your skin and hair. If you're feeling well, it's often a good idea to take a holiday. You should have had the excitement of feeling the baby move by now.

Position of the baby in the womb

CHANGES IN YOU

★ Skin pigmentation may be more noticeable, but will fade after birth.
★ Your breasts may produce colostrum, a thin cloudy substance that provides all the baby needs in the first days.
★ You may be suffering from some of the common problems of pregnancy, such as bleeding gums and an increase in vaginal discharge. The joints and ligaments of your body have relaxed, so you are more likely to suffer from back trouble and other aches and pains.

Baby at week 20

His legs *are in proportion to the rest of his body*

The baby *can grip firmly with his hands*

Your nipples *become darker during pregnancy*

Your breasts *will probably have increased dramatically in size by now*

The top *of the womb is level with your navel*

You will first feel *your baby moving as faint flutterings inside your abdomen, like bubbles rising*

YOUR WEIGHT GAIN
at around week 20 of pregnancy
During this month you can expect to gain about 0.5kg (1lb) a week. Take extra care to eat healthily now: the next few weeks mark the period of maximum growth for the baby and maximum weight gain for you. Model's weight gain to date: 3kg ($6\frac{1}{2}$ lb)

YOUR BABY
Length   25cm (10in)
Weight   340g (12oz)

WHAT TO DO

★ Make sure you are holding yourself well, and that you avoid straining your back. Wear low-heeled shoes.
★ Take the practical steps suggested on pages 40–2 to relieve any other discomforts that you may have.
★ Start to think about essential clothes and equipment for the baby, such as a carrycot.

"Is a long journey advisable?"

There's usually no reason why you shouldn't travel in pregnancy, but preferably not on your own, especially on a long car journey. Wear loose, comfortable clothes, and break the journey up by walking around for a few minutes at least every two hours, to help your circulation. Always remember to take your notes card with you.

YOUR GROWING BABY

★ Hair appears on the baby's head.
★ Teeth are developing.
★ Vernix, the white greasy substance that protects the baby's skin in the womb, forms.
★ The baby's arms and legs are well developed.
★ Protective substances may be transferred to the baby through your blood to help him resist disease in the first weeks.
★ The baby is very active; you should have felt his movements for the first time as a faint fluttering. He may even react to noises outside the womb, but don't worry if he doesn't move around much; it's fairly common for babies to have a quiet period now.

see also:
Common complaints *pages 40–2*
Eating healthily *pages 50–3*
Essentials for the baby *page 27*
Protecting your back *page 44*

LOOKING GOOD

You may look and feel your best during the middle months of pregnancy, with lustrous hair, rosy cheeks, and healthy skin. But not everyone blooms; the high hormone levels can have less flattering effects on your skin, nails, and hair, though any adverse changes usually disappear after birth.

HAIR

Thick, shiny hair is often a bonus of pregnancy. However, not all hair improves, and greasy hair may become more oily, and dry hair, drier and more brittle, so that you may seem to lose more hair than usual. Facial and body hair also tends to darken.

Have *your hair cut into a style that is easy to look after*

What to do

If your hair is dry and splits easily, use a mild shampoo and conditioner, and don't brush it too often or too vigorously. Wash greasy hair frequently to keep it shiny. As hair is so unpredictable during pregnancy, avoid perms or having your hair coloured.

Your skin *may become smooth and blemish free*

SKIN TEXTURE

Your skin will probably improve in pregnancy: blemishes disappear, and skin texture becomes smooth and silky. However, you may find that your skin becomes very dry, or greasy, and perhaps spotty. **What to do** Cleanse your skin thoroughly. If it is dry, gently rub moisturizer over the dry areas, and add bath oil to your bath water. Use as little soap as possible.

NAILS

You may notice that your nails split and break more easily than usual. **What to do** Wear gloves for household chores and gardening.

SKIN COLOUR

An increase in skin pigmentation is normal during pregnancy. Moles, birthmarks, scars, and especially freckles usually darken and grow in size, and a brown line often appears on the stomach. You may also notice a brownish patch, or "butterfly mask", across your face and neck. Don't worry, as this disappears soon after the birth. **What to do** Avoid strong sunlight as this makes pigmentation worse, but if you have to go out in the sun, use sun-cream with a strong filter. Don't try to bleach the mask; if you want to disguise it, you can use a skin-blemish covering stick.

WEEK
24

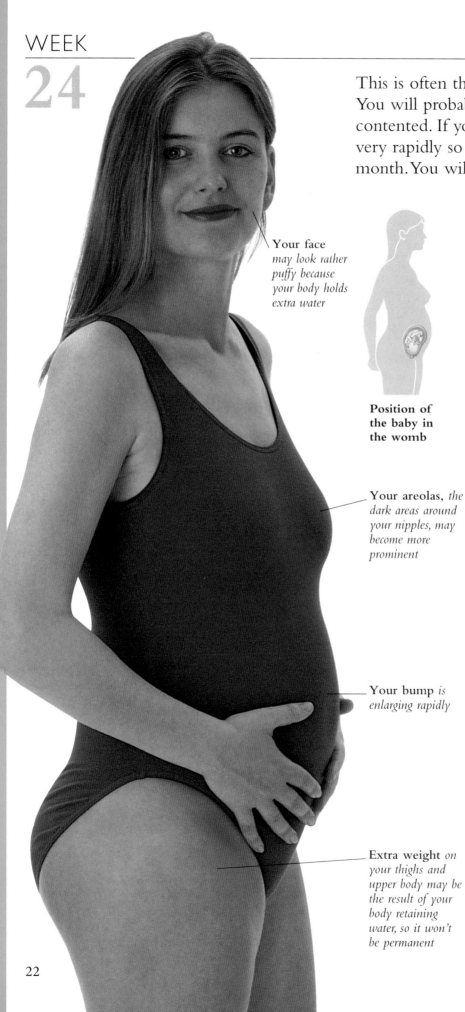

This is often the best month of pregnancy. You will probably look well, and feel happy and contented. If you have not been gaining weight very rapidly so far, you may put on a lot this month. You will start to appear visibly pregnant.

Your face *may look rather puffy because your body holds extra water*

Position of the baby in the womb

Your areolas, *the dark areas around your nipples, may become more prominent*

Your bump *is enlarging rapidly*

Extra weight *on your thighs and upper body may be the result of your body retaining water, so it won't be permanent*

CHANGES IN YOU

★ It's quite common to put on a spurt of weight around this month or the following one.
★ You may find that loose-fitting, unrestricting clothes are more comfortable from now until the end of your pregnancy.
★ Sweating may be a problem because you tend to feel the heat more. Make sure that you drink plenty of water, and try to avoid wearing any man-made materials.

Baby at week 24

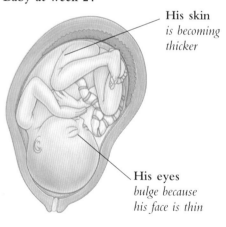

His skin *is becoming thicker*

His eyes *bulge because his face is thin*

YOUR WEIGHT GAIN
at around week 24 of pregnancy
You will probably continue to gain weight at the rate of about 0.5kg (1lb) a week, although if you were underweight when your pregnancy began you might gain at a faster rate than this. Model's weight gain to date: 4.5kg (10lb)

YOUR BABY
Length 33cm (13in)
Weight 570g ($1\frac{1}{4}$lb)

WHAT TO DO

★ If you have flat or inverted nipples, and you want to breast-feed, you should be able to do so; talk to the midwife.
★ Put your feet up as much as possible in the day.
★ Continue to exercise gently, but regularly. Practise relaxation and breathing exercises.
★ If you have been working during the past year, ask at the clinic for your maternity certificate, so that at week 26 you can apply for either maternity pay or maternity allowance.

Q&A

"What is the best kind of bra?"

To give your breasts the support they need in pregnancy, choose a bra (preferably cotton), with a deep band under the cups, broad shoulder straps, and an adjustable back. Check your size regularly, as your breasts will continue to swell throughout pregnancy. By the end, you might fit a cup size two sizes larger than usual. If your breasts become very heavy, wear a lightweight bra at night.

YOUR GROWING BABY

★ No fat has been laid down yet, so the baby is still lean.
★ Sweat glands are forming in the skin.
★ Arm and leg muscles are well developed, and the baby tries them out regularly. He has periods of frenzied activity, when you feel him moving around, alternating with periods of calm.
★ The baby can cough and hiccup; you may feel the hiccups as a knocking movement.

see also:
Antenatal exercises *pages 45–7*
Pregnancy clothes *page 25*
Relaxation and breathing *pages 48–9*

THE BABY IN THE WOMB

While the baby is developing physically, he is also becoming an aware, responsive person with feelings. He lies tightly curled up in the womb, cushioned by the bag of waters that surrounds him, entirely reliant on your placenta for food and oxygen, and for the disposal of his waste products. However, he looks and behaves much the same as a baby at birth.

SIGHT
His eyelids are still sealed, but by week 28, they become unsealed, and he may see, and open and close his eyes.

HEARING
He can hear your voice, and if he's asleep can be woken by loud music. He may prefer some types of music, and show this by his movements. He jumps at sudden noises.

FACIAL EXPRESSIONS
He frowns, squints, purses his lips, and opens and closes his mouth.

LIFE-SUPPORT SYSTEM
The baby is nourished by the placenta and protected by warm amniotic fluid, which can change every four hours. It regulates the baby's temperature, and protects against infection and sudden bumps.

MOVEMENTS
He kicks and punches, and sometimes turns somersaults. He can make a fist.

SLEEPING PATTERNS
He sleeps and wakes randomly, and will probably be most active when you are trying to sleep.

PERSONALITY
The part of the brain concerned with personality and intelligence becomes far more complex over the seventh month, so his personality may soon be developing.

SUCKING, SWALLOWING, AND BREATHING
He sucks his thumb, and swallows the warm water (the amniotic fluid) that surrounds him, passing it out of his body as urine. Sometimes he drinks too much of the fluid and hiccups. He makes breathing movements with his chest, practising for life outside the womb.

TASTE
His taste buds are forming, and by week 28 he can respond to sweet, sour, and bitter tastes.

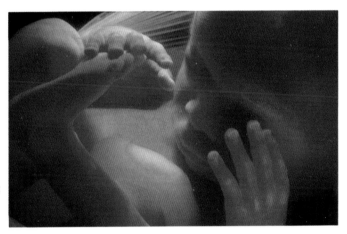

The placenta supplies all the nutrients the baby needs; almost anything entering your body, good or bad, is filtered through to him.

The umbilical cord, a rope of three blood vessels, links the placenta to the baby

23

WEEK
28

You are now entering the home straight, with only three months of pregnancy left to go. You will be starting to feel large and clumsy, and perhaps forgetful. During the last months, the baby lays down fat stores. He is very active, and you may see him moving around. If he were born now he could survive, given special care.

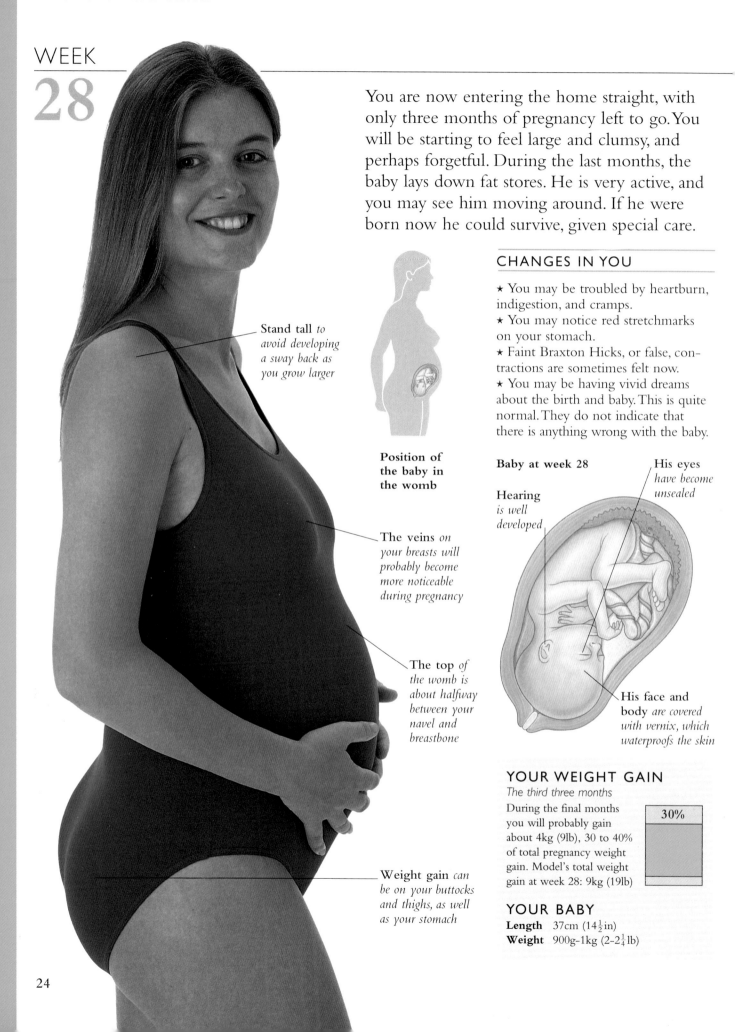

Stand tall *to avoid developing a sway back as you grow larger*

Position of the baby in the womb

The veins *on your breasts will probably become more noticeable during pregnancy*

The top *of the womb is about halfway between your navel and breastbone*

Weight gain *can be on your buttocks and thighs, as well as your stomach*

CHANGES IN YOU

★ You may be troubled by heartburn, indigestion, and cramps.
★ You may notice red stretchmarks on your stomach.
★ Faint Braxton Hicks, or false, contractions are sometimes felt now.
★ You may be having vivid dreams about the birth and baby. This is quite normal. They do not indicate that there is anything wrong with the baby.

Baby at week 28

His eyes *have become unsealed*

Hearing *is well developed*

His face and body *are covered with vernix, which waterproofs the skin*

YOUR WEIGHT GAIN
The third three months
During the final months you will probably gain about 4kg (9lb), 30 to 40% of total pregnancy weight gain. Model's total weight gain at week 28: 9kg (19lb)

30%

YOUR BABY
Length 37cm (14$\frac{1}{2}$in)
Weight 900g–1kg (2–2$\frac{1}{4}$lb)

WHAT TO DO

★ Make sure you are getting enough rest in the day, and have as many early nights as possible. If you are still at work, put your feet up during the lunch hour and rest when you come home.

★ Let your employer know in writing when you intend to stop work, and if you want to return to your job after the baby is born. Give at least three weeks' notice. You are legally entitled to claim maternity pay from week 29, but depending on your type of work, how far you have to travel, and your budget, you may want to remain working for a while longer.

★ Visit the antenatal clinic every two weeks from now until week 36. The baby's heartbeat can be heard from now on, using either a fetal stethoscope or a Doppler ultrasound device.

YOUR GROWING BABY

★ His skin is red and wrinkled, but fat is starting to accumulate beneath it.

★ There have been dramatic developments in the thinking part of the brain, which becomes bigger and more complex. A seven-month-old baby can feel pain, and responds in much the same way as a full-term baby.

★ The baby has far more taste buds than he will have at birth, so his sense of taste is acute.

★ His lungs are still not fully mature, and need to develop a substance called surfactant, which stops them collapsing between each breath.

★ Your partner can feel the baby move if he puts his hand on your stomach, and he may even see the shape of a foot or bottom as the baby kicks and turns.

see also:
Common complaints *pages 40–2*
Protecting your back *page 44*
Stretchmarks *page 42*

YOUR PREGNANCY WARDROBE

Up to five or even six months of your pregnancy, many of your normal clothes may be wearable if they fit loosely or you use a little creativity. However, a few new outfits may greatly improve your morale and you don't have to buy special maternity wear. Look for clothes that are attractive, comfortable, and easy to care for from the standard selection in the shops.

Comfortable tops
Go for stretchy fabrics in soft natural fibres. Some days you may feel happier wearing a baggy sweatshirt.

Loosen *the cord as the bulge gets larger*

Choose *a style with plenty of room across the chest to accommodate your growing breasts*

Loose-fitting bottoms
Trousers with a drawstring are comfortable and unrestricting; they are convenient because they can be adjusted to fit your expanding waistline.

A versatile fabric *will stretch to fit your changing shape*

Dressing up
A simple dress can look casual, but is also easy to dress up. Check that there's enough length in the hem so the dress hangs evenly as you grow larger. Maternity dresses are usually 2.5cm (1in) longer at the front to allow for this.

WHAT TO CHOOSE

You tend to feel the heat more during pregnancy, so look for lightweight, loose-fitting clothes, made of cotton or other natural fibres. If it's cold, put on layers. Avoid anything that is tight around the waist or that restricts blood flow in your legs, such as tight knee-high socks.

Comfortable, low-heeled shoes are essential, although completely flat heels are best avoided. You probably won't be able to wear lace-ups soon, as you will have difficulty tying them.

WEEK
32

You need all the rest you can get, so try to lie down in the middle of the day. You will be feeling very bulky, and probably weary of your pregnant state. Now is the time to start going to parentcraft classes, which will run until the end of your pregnancy.

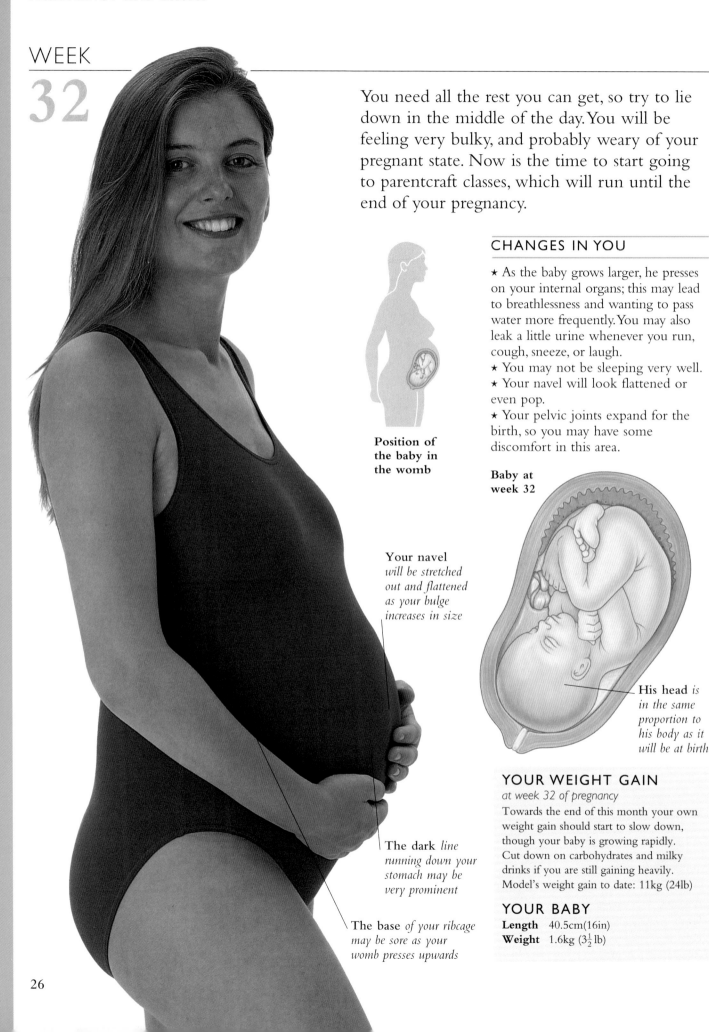

Position of the baby in the womb

CHANGES IN YOU

★ As the baby grows larger, he presses on your internal organs; this may lead to breathlessness and wanting to pass water more frequently. You may also leak a little urine whenever you run, cough, sneeze, or laugh.
★ You may not be sleeping very well.
★ Your navel will look flattened or even pop.
★ Your pelvic joints expand for the birth, so you may have some discomfort in this area.

Baby at week 32

Your navel *will be stretched out and flattened as your bulge increases in size*

His head *is in the same proportion to his body as it will be at birth*

The dark *line running down your stomach may be very prominent*

The base *of your ribcage may be sore as your womb presses upwards*

YOUR WEIGHT GAIN
at week 32 of pregnancy
Towards the end of this month your own weight gain should start to slow down, though your baby is growing rapidly. Cut down on carbohydrates and milky drinks if you are still gaining heavily. Model's weight gain to date: 11kg (24lb)

YOUR BABY
Length 40.5cm(16in)
Weight 1.6kg ($3\frac{1}{2}$ lb)

WHAT TO DO

★ Break up the day by putting your feet up for an hour or two.

★ If you have difficulty sleeping, practise relaxation techniques before going to bed, and try sleeping on your side, with one leg bent and supported on a pillow. Try not to worry if you still can't sleep; it's very normal to be wide awake at night during this stage of pregnancy.

★ Keep up with your pelvic floor exercises; this is especially important if you are suffering from leaking urine.

★ Start attending antenatal classes if they haven't begun already.

★ Have another blood test at the clinic to check for anaemia and, if necessary, for rhesus problems.

Q&A

"I'm worried about harming the baby during intercourse. Is there any danger of this?"

This is a common worry, but an unnecessary one if your pregnancy is normal. The baby is protected and cushioned by the bag of fluid surrounding him, so he cannot be harmed when you make love. The doctor or midwife will say if there are any dangers, such as a low-lying placenta.

YOUR GROWING BABY

★ The baby looks much the same as at birth, but his body still needs to fill out more.

★ He can now tell the difference between light and dark.

★ Because there is less room in the womb, he will probably have turned into a head-down position by now, ready for birth.

see also:

Antenatal classes *page 17*

Breathlessness *page 40*

Frequent urination *page 41*

Pelvic floor *page 45*

Relaxation techniques *pages 48–9*

ESSENTIALS FOR YOUR BABY

Buy the following basic items of equipment and clothing for your new baby, then add anything else when he's born.

EQUIPMENT

Buy new equipment if you can. Second-hand items may not comply with safety regulations. You will need:

★ a carrycot, cot, or Moses basket

★ a front carrying pack

★ appropriate bedding

★ a soft cellular blanket

★ an infant car seat, if you have a car; this can double as a chair

★ a baby bath

★ two soft towels

★ changing mat

★ nappies and changing equipment

★ bottle-feeding equipment (if you are going to bottle-feed).

CLOTHES

Babies grow quickly, so buy only the minimum of first-size (newborn) clothes. Three or four nighties, stretchsuits, and wide or envelope-necked vests, plus two cardigans should see you through the first few weeks. Babies lose heat easily from their heads, so a soft-knit hat is essential.

ENJOYING SEX

Making love is often particularly enjoyable during pregnancy because you become aroused more easily as a result of the increase in hormone levels, and there are no worries about contraception.

OTHER WAYS OF LOVING

There may be times when you lose interest in sex, especially in the first and last weeks. This doesn't mean that you have to stop showing your loving feelings for each other. Even if you feel too tired or heavy to make love, find other ways of showing your affection, such as kissing, cuddling, stroking, and touching.

A CHANGE OF POSITION

In the last weeks of pregnancy, you may find the traditional man-on-the-top position rather uncomfortable. Experiment with other positions; perhaps sitting on your partner's lap, kneeling with him behind, or both lying side by side.

WEEK
36

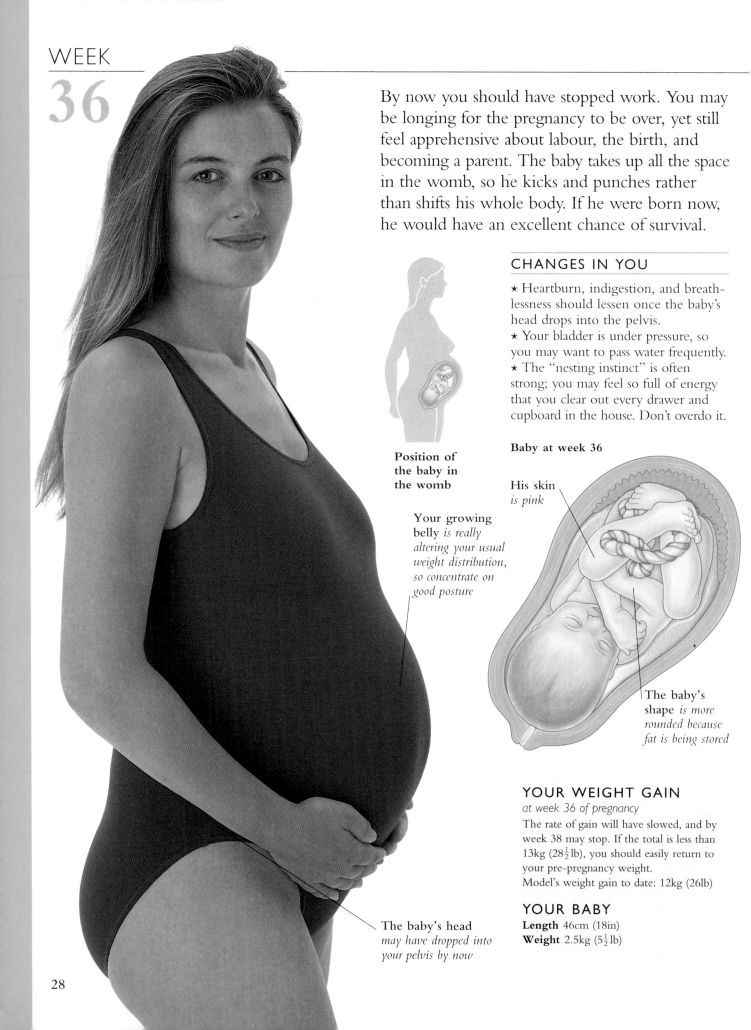

By now you should have stopped work. You may be longing for the pregnancy to be over, yet still feel apprehensive about labour, the birth, and becoming a parent. The baby takes up all the space in the womb, so he kicks and punches rather than shifts his whole body. If he were born now, he would have an excellent chance of survival.

CHANGES IN YOU

★ Heartburn, indigestion, and breathlessness should lessen once the baby's head drops into the pelvis.
★ Your bladder is under pressure, so you may want to pass water frequently.
★ The "nesting instinct" is often strong; you may feel so full of energy that you clear out every drawer and cupboard in the house. Don't overdo it.

Position of the baby in the womb

Baby at week 36

His skin *is pink*

Your growing belly *is really altering your usual weight distribution, so concentrate on good posture*

The baby's shape *is more rounded because fat is being stored*

YOUR WEIGHT GAIN
at week 36 of pregnancy

The rate of gain will have slowed, and by week 38 may stop. If the total is less than 13kg (28½lb), you should easily return to your pre-pregnancy weight.

Model's weight gain to date: 12kg (26lb)

YOUR BABY
Length 46cm (18in)
Weight 2.5kg (5½lb)

The baby's head *may have dropped into your pelvis by now*

WHAT TO DO

★ Put your feet up whenever you can to guard against swollen ankles and varicose veins.
★ Visit the clinic every week from now.
★ If you are having your baby in hospital, make sure you have a tour of the delivery room and maternity wards.
★ Buy your nursing bras.
★ Stock the food cupboards and the freezer for when you are in hospital, and for your return.
★ Pack your suitcase for hospital; if you are having a home birth, assemble all the things you need.
★ Check that everything is ready for the baby.

"Should I have my partner with me during labour?"

Most hospitals actively encourage this. Labour can be a long process, and a rather lonely one unless you have someone close to share it with, and a natural choice is your partner. But if he really doesn't want to be there, it's unfair to put too much pressure on him. It's quite acceptable to have a relative or a good friend as a labour companion instead.

YOUR GROWING BABY

★ If this is your first baby, his head will have probably descended into the pelvis ready for birth.
★ Soft nails have grown to the tips of his fingers and toes.
★ In a boy, the testicles should have descended.
★ The baby will gain about 28g (1oz) every day from now onwards.

see also:
Essentials for the baby *page 27*
Frequent urination *page 41*
Preparing for the birth *pages 54–5*
Protecting your back *page 44*
Relaxation techniques *pages 48–9*
Swollen ankles *page 42*
Varicose veins *page 42*

RESTING IN LATER PREGNANCY

During the last weeks, you will probably become tired very easily. You may not be sleeping as well as usual, and you will also feel exhausted by the extra weight you have been carrying around. It's important not to fight this tiredness, but to rest and relax as much as possible.

TO AVOID TIRING YOURSELF

Put your feet up whenever you need to during the day. Think of quiet things to do while you rest: practise gentle relaxation exercises, listen to soothing music, read a book or magazine, or perhaps knit something for the baby. It also helps if you try to do things at a slower pace than usual, so that you don't become overtired.

YOUR NURSING BRA

If you want to breastfeed, you will need at least two plain cotton nursing bras with firm support straps. To make sure these are the right size, it's best to buy them no earlier than week 26.

WHAT TO LOOK FOR

There are two main types of bra: one has flaps, which open to expose the nipple and some of the surrounding breast; the other fastens at the front, so you can expose the whole breast. The front opening kind is best, as it allows the baby to feel and fondle the breast while he's sucking. It also allows the milk to flow freely.

MEASURING UP
Take the measurements while wearing one of your ordinary pregnancy bras.

1 Measure around your body below your breasts. Add 12cm (5in) to get your final chest measurement.

2 Measure around the fullest part of your breasts. If this equals your chest measurement, you need an A cup. If it is 2.5cm (1in) more, you need a B cup. If it is 5cm (2in) more, you need a C cup.

WEEK
40

By this stage, you will feel very ungainly, and will be bumping into objects because of your size. You will be most impatient to give birth, but also excited and relieved that you are nearly there. Rest as much as possible, and enjoy these last baby-free days.

CHANGES IN YOU

★ You will have a feeling of heaviness in your lower adbomen.
★ Your cervix will be softening in preparation for labour.
★ Braxton Hicks contractions may be so noticeable that you think you are in labour, but they won't be regular.

YOUR WEIGHT GAIN
at week 40 of pregnancy
In the final two weeks you may actually lose a little weight. This is a sign that your baby is fully mature, and you can expect labour to start within 10 days. Model's weight gain as at week 36

YOUR BABY
Length 51cm (20in)
Weight 3.4kg ($7\frac{1}{2}$ lb)

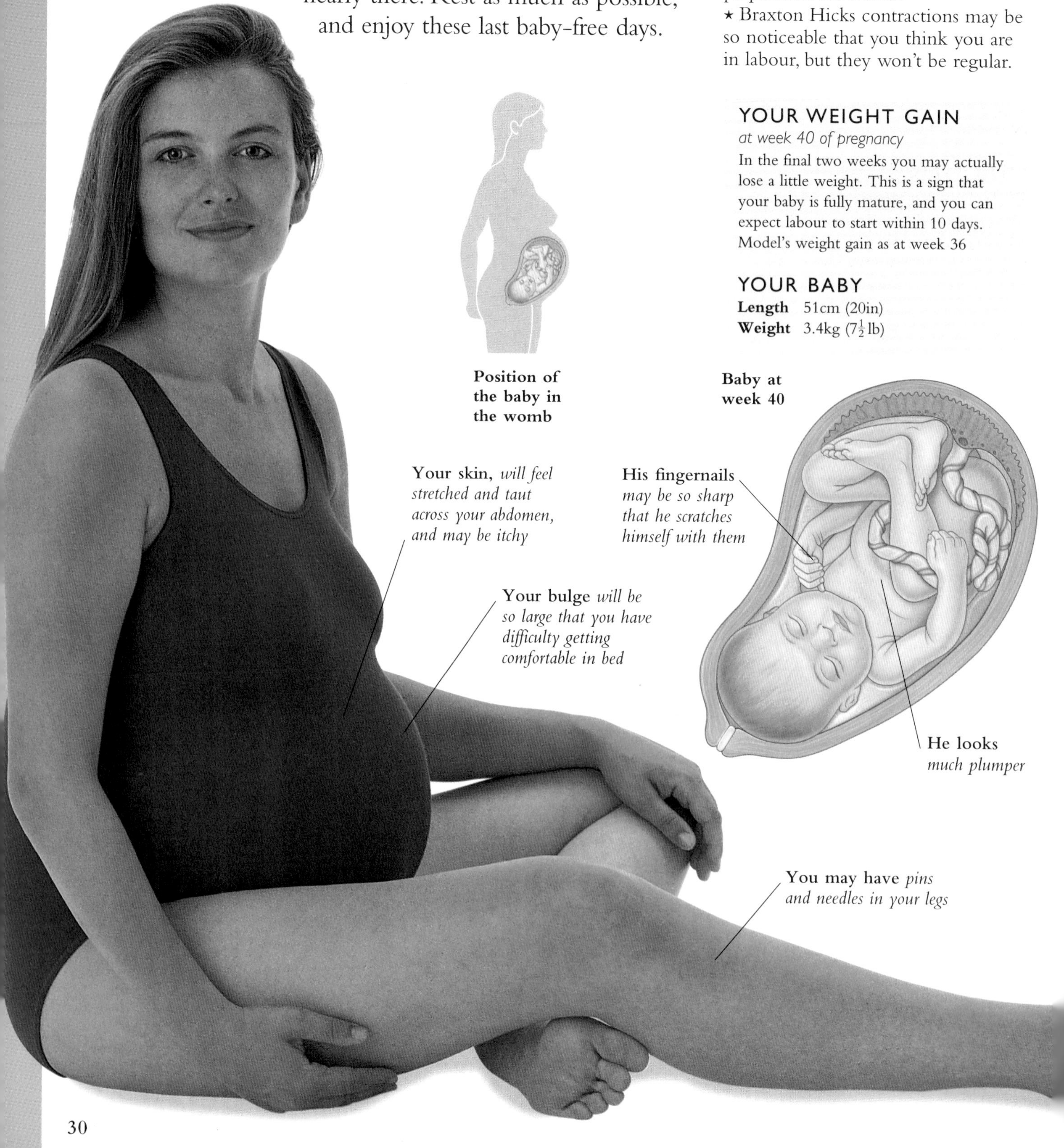

Position of the baby in the womb

Baby at week 40

Your skin, *will feel stretched and taut across your abdomen, and may be itchy*

Your bulge *will be so large that you have difficulty getting comfortable in bed*

His fingernails *may be so sharp that he scratches himself with them*

He looks *much plumper*

You may have *pins and needles in your legs*

WHAT TO DO

★ If you don't feel at least ten movements from your baby in the day, ask your midwife to check his heart rate, as he may be distressed.
★ If the Braxton Hicks contractions are noticeable, practise your breathing.
★ Don't worry if your baby doesn't arrive on time; it's perfectly normal for a baby to be born two weeks either side of the expected delivery date.

TOTAL WEIGHT GAIN

The average amount of weight gain during pregnancy varies between 10 and 12kg (22–27lb), but you may put on more or less weight. The total weight gain is made up as follows:

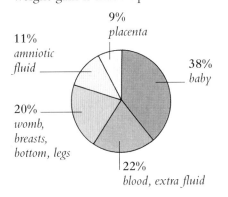

9%
placenta

11%
amniotic fluid

38%
baby

20%
womb, breasts, bottom, legs

22%
blood, extra fluid

YOUR GROWING BABY

★ Most of the lanugo hair has disappeared, though there may still be a little over his shoulders, arms, and legs.
★ He may be covered in vernix, or just have traces in skin folds.
★ A dark sustance called meconium gathers in the baby's intestines; this will be passed in his first bowel movement after birth.
★ If this is your second or later baby, his head may engage now.

see also:
Braxton Hicks contractions *page 56*
Breathing techniques *page 49*

BECOMING A MOTHER

After all the weeks of preparation and planning, you can now hold your baby in your arms. You will probably feel overwhelmingly protective towards this tiny person, who is dependent on you for everything.

THE FIRST WEEKS

Life in the early weeks following the arrival of your baby revolves round her and her needs, whether she needs feeding, nappy changing, or comforting. But once you get to know each other, and you become more adept at handling your baby and understanding what she requires, she will become more settled, and life will fall into some sort of routine once again.

ANTENATAL CARE

Having a baby nowadays is very safe. This is largely because of the availability of antenatal care, a system of checks and tests at regular intervals throughout pregnancy, designed to confirm that all is well with you and the baby. It is also designed to ensure that, as far as possible, you have a trouble free labour and birth. If there are any problems,

they can be spotted early and dealt with effectively. It is important for your antenatal care to start early in pregnancy, as the first set of checks and tests provides a baseline for assessing any changes later on. Ask your doctor about the available choices as soon as possible after the pregnancy is confirmed, and he can make the arrangements.

WHERE TO HAVE YOUR BABY

One of the first decisions you will need to make is where to have your baby. Most babies today are born in hospital, in a unit headed by a consultant.

In some areas, you may be able to choose to have your baby in a small maternity unit. It is also possible to have your baby at home.

HOSPITAL BIRTH
A hospital has all the equipment and expertise available for giving pain relief, for monitoring the baby's progress, for intervening in the birth to help you and the baby, if necessary, and for providing emergency care for you both. After the birth, a few days in hospital may give you the rest you need from coping at home; the average stay is about 48 hours, but you may have the option of staying as long as ten days. If you are a first-time mother, you may also find the support of staff and other mothers reassuring.

However, because the hospital staff is a team, there is no guarantee that you will see the same doctor at each antenatal clinic. Neither can you be sure which midwife will deliver your baby, so you don't have a chance to build up a relationship with them before labour.

It can be very noisy in a hospital ward, as well as

daunting to be in unfamiliar surroundings. But most hospitals hold antenatal classes (see page 17), and if you go along to these, you will be encouraged to look round the delivery room and maternity wards in advance to familiarize yourself with them.

SMALL MATERNITY UNITS
These units, which are usually run by midwives or family doctors, are not usually available in large towns or cities. However, if you live in a small town or a rural area, there may be one nearby. These small units do not have the full medical facilities of a hospital.

DOMINO CARE
Under the domino scheme you will be able to give birth in hospital, cared for by a midwife who has looked after you during your pregnancy. You will be able to go home about six hours later.

HOME BIRTH
If you are healthy, have had a normal pregnancy, and feel you would be more relaxed and able to cope during labour in your own familiar surroundings, you may be able to have your baby at home. If there are complications, though, and you have to go into hospital, it will take longer for you and your baby to get emergency treatment. If your doctor is unwilling to deliver your baby at home, the Supervisor of Midwives at your local hospital may be able to provide you with a midwife. A few independent midwives specialize in home births. Otherwise, ask your Community Health Council or Family Practitioner Committee to suggest another GP in your area who specializes in obstetrics.

WHERE TO GO FOR ANTENATAL CARE
Your doctor or midwife will make arrangements for your antenatal care.
★ If you are having your baby on a hospital consultant unit, you will either have "full care" at a hospital antenatal clinic or "shared care", with a few appointments at a hospital clinic and most at your GP's surgery or local health centre.
★ If you are having your baby under the domino scheme or at home, your doctor or midwife will provide all or most of your antenatal care, with possibly some hospital visits for tests.

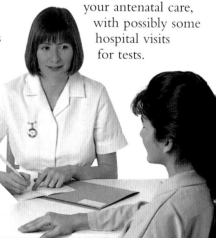

QUESTIONS TO ASK

Hospital policies vary, so discuss any issues that are important to you with the staff at the clinic. It's natural to have pre-conceived ideas about labour and birth, but the reality is often quite different. However sure you are, for example, that you don't want pain relief, do try to keep an open mind and ask for it if you need it. This list covers some of the questions you might like to ask.

ABOUT LABOUR

Can my partner or a friend stay with me all through labour?
Will he or she ever be asked to leave the delivery room?
Will I be able to move around as I please during labour?
What is the hospital policy on pain relief, routine electronic monitoring, and induction (see pages 64, 65, and 66)?
What kind of pain relief will I be offered; are epidurals or TENS (see pages 64 and 65) available?

ABOUT THE BIRTH

Can I give birth in any position I choose to? Are chairs, large cushions, and birth stools available?
Will I be able to use a birthing pool? (see page 58)
What is the hospital policy on episiotomies, Caesareans, and syntometrine (see pages 66, 67, and 63)?

AFTER THE BIRTH

How long will I stay in hospital after delivery?
Will I be able to have my baby with me all the time, including nights?
Is there free visiting for my partner?
Is there a special care baby unit? If not, where will my baby be taken if he needs treatment?

YOUR MATERNITY RECORDS

The results of the clinic tests, and any other details about your pregnancy, are usually recorded on a co-op card or patient-held records, which you are given at your first visit. Keep this on you at all times; if you have to see another doctor, the card provides a record of everything he or she will need to know. Some hospitals give you your own notes instead. In either case, make sure that you understand what is written down, and if anything is unfamiliar, ask.

AA	Hepatitis test.
AFP	Alpha fetoprotein.
Alb	Albumin (a protein) found in urine.
BP	Blood pressure.
Br	The baby is bottom down.
C/Ceph or Vx	The baby is in the normal (head down) position.
CS	Caesarean section.
E/Eng	The baby's head has engaged.
EDD/EDC	Estimated date of delivery/confinement.

Fe	Iron supplements prescribed.
FH	Fetal heart.
FHH/H or √	Fetal heart heard.
FHNH	Fetal heart not heard.
FMF	Fetal movements felt.
Fundus	Top of the womb.
Hb	Haemoglobin levels in the blood (to check for anaemia).
H/T	High blood pressure.
LMP	Last menstrual period.
MSU	Mid-stream urine sample.
NAD or nil or √	Nothing abnormal discovered in urine.
NE	The baby's head has not engaged.
Oed	Oedema (swelling).
Para O	A woman who has had no other children.
PET/PE	Pre-eclampsia.
Presentation	Which way up and round the baby is.
Primigravida	First pregnancy.
Relation of PP to brim	Relation of the part of the baby to be born first to the brim of the pelvis.

SFD	Small for dates.
TCA	To come again.
TBA	To come into hospital.
Tr or +	A trace found.
U/S	Ultrasound.
VE	Vaginal examination.
WR/KAHN	Test for syphilis.

Abbreviations are used to describe the way the baby is lying in the womb. These are some of the positions:

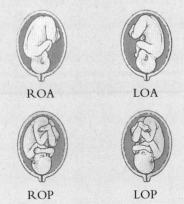

ROA   LOA

ROP   LOP

A VISIT TO THE CLINIC

Your first visit to the clinic takes place at about 12 weeks, and you will be asked to go once a month until 28 weeks. Visits become more frequent after this; every two weeks until you are 36 weeks pregnant, and every week in the last month. Routine tests are carried out by the doctor and midwife at every visit, to check that the pregnancy is progressing normally. Write down any questions you have beforehand.

BLOOD TESTS *first visit*
Some blood will be taken from your arm to check:
★ your main blood group and your rhesus blood group (see page 38)
★ that you are not anaemic (see page 38); your blood will be tested for this again at about 32 weeks
★ that you are immune to German measles (see page 10)
★ that you do not have a sexually transmitted disease, such as syphilis, which must be treated before week 20 if it is not to harm the baby
★ for sickle cell trait, if you and your partner are of West Indian or African descent, and thalassaemia, if your families come from the Mediterranean, or the Middle and Far East. These forms of anaemia are inherited, and could put the baby's health at risk.

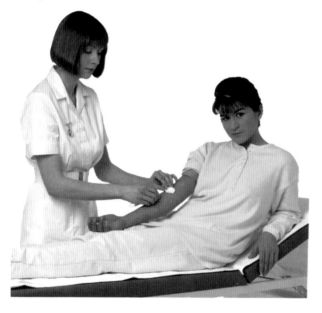

GENERAL EXAMINATION
first visit
The doctor or midwife will examine you physically, and listen to your heart and lungs. Your breasts will be checked for lumps and inverted nipples (see page 23). You will probably be asked about your dental health, and encouraged to go for a check-up.

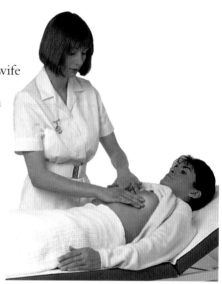

URINE SAMPLE *every visit*
Most clinics test a sample of urine at your first visit and, from the 28th week onwards, at each visit. This will be tested for:
★ traces of sugar
★ traces of protein, which, if found in the urine sample in late pregnancy, could be a sign of pre-eclampsia (see page 38).

WEIGHT *every visit*
You will be weighed at your first visit. Don't worry if you lose weight during the first three months because of morning sickness, as this is usual. If you gain weight suddenly in late pregnancy, this can be a sign of pre-eclampsia (see page 38).

INITIAL TALK
At the first visit, the doctor or midwife will ask some questions about you and your partner, to find out whether there is anything that could affect the pregnancy or your baby. Clinic routines vary from place to place, but you can expect to be asked about:
★ personal details, such as your date of birth, and what work you and your partner do
★ your country of origin, as some forms of anaemia are inherited and affect only certain ethnic groups (see above)
★ your health: any serious illnesses or operations you may have had, whether you are being treated for any disease, and whether you have any allergies, or are taking any drugs
★ your family's medical history: whether there are twins or any inherited illnesses in your or your partner's family
★ the type of contraceptives you used before you became pregnant, and when you stopped using them
★ your periods: when they began, whether are regular, when the first day of your last period was, and how long your cycle is
★ any previous pregnancies, including miscarriages and terminations.

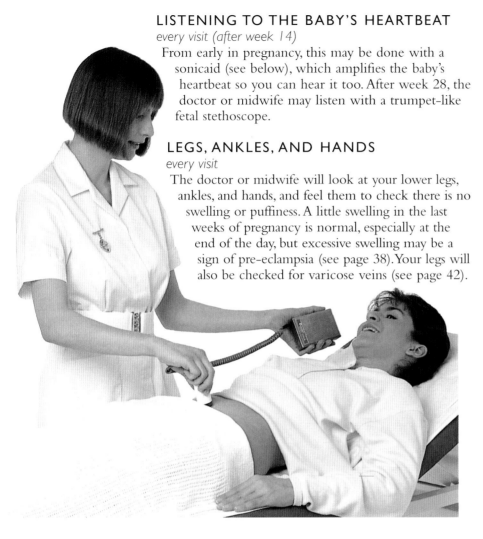

LISTENING TO THE BABY'S HEARTBEAT
every visit (after week 14)

From early in pregnancy, this may be done with a sonicaid (see below), which amplifies the baby's heartbeat so you can hear it too. After week 28, the doctor or midwife may listen with a trumpet-like fetal stethoscope.

LEGS, ANKLES, AND HANDS
every visit

The doctor or midwife will look at your lower legs, ankles, and hands, and feel them to check there is no swelling or puffiness. A little swelling in the last weeks of pregnancy is normal, especially at the end of the day, but excessive swelling may be a sign of pre-eclampsia (see page 38). Your legs will also be checked for varicose veins (see page 42).

BLOOD PRESSURE *every visit*

Your blood pressure is slightly lower in pregnancy, and it is measured regularly to detect any sudden rises and keep them under control. Normal blood pressure is about 120/70, and there will be cause for concern if your blood pressure rises above 140/90. Raised blood pressure can be a sign of a number of problems, including pre-eclampsia (see page 38).

HEIGHT *first visit*

This will be measured as a guide to the size of your pelvis; a small pelvis can mean a difficult delivery. If you are over 152cm (5ft) tall, you are unlikely to have difficulties.

FEELING THE ABDOMEN
every visit

The doctor or midwife will gently feel your abdomen to check the position of the top of the womb, which gives her a good idea of the rate of the baby's growth. Later in your pregnancy, checks will be made to ensure that your baby is turning the right way round (head first), and, in the final weeks, that the head is dropping into your pelvis (engaging).

SCREENING AND DIAGNOSTIC TESTS IN PREGNANCY

During your pregnancy you will probably be offered tests to look for conditions that might cause your baby to have a disability. Some of these tests are offered as a routine part of antenatal care. Others are offered only in special circumstances, usually when it is thought that there is a small chance of a baby being abnormal.

The object of the tests is to detect any serious problem as early as possible. If the problem is detected early enough, the pregnancy can, if you wish, be safely terminated. But, the most likely outcome is that they will give you the reassurance every parent wants, that your baby is normal.

You don't have to have any of these tests if you don't want to, and indeed you may prefer not to if you are certain that, whatever the outcome, you would never consider terminating the pregnancy. Even so, you might want to be prepared for a baby with a disability before the birth and, if the condition is treatable, to discuss and plan the treatment in advance.

TYPES OF TESTS THAT YOU MAY BE OFFERED
Screening tests
A screening test will not detect any abnormality. It will only show whether you are **more likely** to have a baby with a particular disability. If the results show you are in a "high risk" group ("screen positive") you will be offered a diagnostic test, but this does not mean there is anything wrong with your baby.

Diagnostic tests
If a screening test shows you are "high risk", you may be offered a diagnostic test that will give you a firm answer and show whether or not your baby has a particular disability. All diagnostic tests except "anomaly" ultrasound scan involve taking samples from inside your uterus, and they carry an increased risk of miscarriage.

ULTRASOUND SCAN

An ultrasound scan is a test you will be offered routinely at some stage of your pregnancy. Your first ultrasound scan, when you actually see your baby on the screen, turns your pregnancy into a fascinating reality. Ultrasound is a safe and painless procedure. A thin layer of oil is rubbed over your stomach and a hand-held instrument, a transducer, is passed gently over it. This beams and receives sound waves that are built into an image of your baby on the screen.

Unless the scan is performed late in pregnancy, you will be asked to drink plenty of water and arrive with a full bladder, so that the womb is lifted up and can be seen more easily.

Early scan

If you have a history of miscarriage, or have had any pain or bleeding, you may be offered a very early scan, at 6–11 weeks. This will confirm that the pregnancy is safely established, and also detect an ectopic pregnancy. If you have a very early scan, the transducer may be placed in your vagina, but there is no risk that this will cause a miscarriage.

Booking in scan

Some hospitals offer a scan between 11 and 16 weeks, to help date the pregnancy accurately.

18–20 week anomaly scan

This scan is offered routinely to confirm the date of the pregnancy, to make sure the baby's growth is normal, and that his heart, brain, other organs and limbs are all developing normally. It will also show any condition that might complicate the delivery, such as a low-lying placenta.

Further scans

You may be offered additional scans later in pregnancy if you are expecting twins, or if your doctor thinks that your baby is not growing properly. A scan within the last 6 weeks of pregnancy may be offered to check on the "lie" of the baby and the position of the placenta.

NUCHAL TRANSLUCENCY SCAN (11–14 weeks)

In some areas you may be offered a special scan to help calculate the risk of Down's syndrome. Only a few hospitals offer this scan, which measures fluid accumulation at the back of the baby's neck. All babies have some fluid there between 11 and 13 weeks, but most babies with Down's have an increased amount. This test result, combined with the mother's age and the results of blood-screening, will help calculate the risk of Down's, and to decide whether the mother should be offered a diagnostic test.

DOPPLER ULTRASOUND SCAN (as necessary)

A Doppler scan is a special ultrasound scan that is used to examine the blood flow to the baby through the umbilical cord. If a baby is not growing at the expected rate, a Doppler scan may be given to check that the placenta is working properly and the baby is getting enough oxygen. During labour it may also be used to monitor the baby's heart rate.

Ultrasound scan

SERUM SCREENING TEST
(16–18 weeks)

You may be offered one of several different blood tests to assess your risk of having a baby with Down's syndrome or an open neural tube defect such as spina bifida.

The alphafetoprotein (AFP) test

This measures the level of AFP in the blood, and indicates the risk of a neural tube defect.

The triple (Barts) test

This measures three blood chemicals, AFP, uE3 (estriol), and hCG (human chorionic gonadotrophin). It is used to assess the risks of a neural tube defect, Down's syndrome, and other chromosomal abnormalities. Some hospitals measure only two of these markers (the double test).

HIV TESTING (11–13 weeks)

You may also be offered a test for HIV (the Human Immunodeficiency Virus). HIV can be transmitted to your baby during pregnancy, at the birth, or even during breast-feeding. Your baby can be infected even if you have no symptoms. However, if your doctor knows that you are HIV+ve, precautions can be taken to minimize the risk of the infection being passed to your baby during the birth. So it is worth having the test even if you do

Having an ultrasound
The first time you see your baby on the ultrasound screen will be an experience you'll never forget.

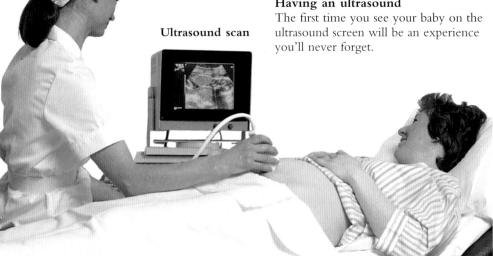

not think that you or your partner are particularly at risk.

TOXOPLASMOSIS

Toxoplasmosis is an infection that may cause mild flu-like symptoms, but often produces no symptoms at all. The parasite that causes the infection is found in raw meat and cat faeces. If you are infected during your pregnancy, it can cause serious harm to your baby. However, once you have had the disease, you can't be infected again. A blood test can show whether you are immune to the disease, but this is not given routinely in the UK. You may be offered one if there is a high risk that you have been exposed to the infection.

AMNIOCENTESIS (weeks 15–20 but usually at week 16)

Amniocentesis can be used to detect some abnormalities in the baby, such as Down's syndrome and spina bifida. It is not offered routinely, as there is a risk of miscarriage in about one woman in 100. You may be offered the test if:
★ you are over 37, when there is a higher risk of a Down's baby
★ you have a family history of inherited disease, such as spina bifida
★ your screening test was "screen positive".
An ultrasound scan is done to check the position of the baby and the placenta. A hollow needle is inserted through the wall of the stomach into the womb, and a sample of the fluid that surrounds the baby, and contains some of his cells, is taken. The cells are then tested for abnormality. The test results can take three weeks.

CHORIONIC VILLUS SAMPLING (CVS) (from week 11)

Some inherited disorders can be detected by examining a small piece of the fingers of tissue that form part of the placenta. The sample can be obtained either through the entrance to the womb, or by inserting a needle directly into the womb through the abdominal wall, guided by an ultrasound scan. The test carries a slightly greater risk than amniocentesis.

TABLE OF SCREENING AND DIAGNOSTIC TESTS

Time	Test	What for	Disadvantages
From 11 weeks	Chorionic villus (CVS) (diagnostic test)	Down's syndrome Blood disorders Baby's sex	You may find the procedure painful and worrying. Increased risk of miscarriage – about 2%.
11–13 weeks	HIV test (screening test)	The presence of antibodies to the HIV virus	
11–14 weeks	Nuchal scan (screening test)	Down's syndrome	New technique whose accuracy is not yet known. Does not identify all affected babies.
16–18 weeks	AFP blood test (screening test)	Spina bifida	You may suffer unnecessary anxiety by being told you are "high risk". A few "low risk" women will have affected babies.
15–20 weeks	Double, triple, or quadruple blood tests (screening tests)	Down's syndrome Chromosome abnormalities Spina bifida	A "high-risk" result may cause unnecessary anxiety. A few "low-risk" women will have affected babies.
14–16 weeks and sometimes later	Amniocentesis (diagnostic test)	Down's syndrome Chromosome abnormalities Spina bifida	The procedure may be worrying and can be a bit painful. Increased risk of miscarriage (0.5–1%).
18–20 weeks	Ultrasound fetal anomaly scan (diagnostic test)	Confirms dates of pregnancy Checks for fetal abnormality	How much it shows depends on skill of radiographer, how good the equipment is, and how the baby is lying.
20 weeks	Fetal blood sampling (cordocentesis) (diagnostic test)	Chromosomal and blood disorders	Only done in specialist centres. Carries risk of miscarriage of 1–2%. Results take 3–4 days.

SPECIAL CARE PREGNANCIES

Nearly all pregnancies are normal and straightforward, but there may be circumstances that make your doctor think there is a greater risk of complications, and so you need to be monitored closely during pregnancy. This could be because you have a general medical condition, or perhaps you are expecting twins. Sometimes symptoms develop that also warn the doctor that special care is needed.

ANAEMIA
Many women are slightly anaemic before pregnancy, and this is usually due to an iron deficiency. It's important to correct this, in order to cope with the increased demands of pregnancy, and any bleeding during labour. **Treatment** Try to prevent the problem by eating a varied diet, with plenty of iron-rich foods. However, you should avoid liver and liver products in pregnancy (see page 52). If blood tests at the clinic show you are anaemic, the doctor can prescribe iron supplements; some doctors do as a matter of course to all pregnant women. Take iron tablets directly after a meal, with fluid, as they can cause constipation, diarrhoea, or nausea.

Anaemia Eating foods that are a good source of iron, such as spinach and red meat, will help to guard against the problem.

DIABETES
Diabetes must be carefully controlled during pregnancy and your blood sugar level constantly monitored. If this is done, there's no reason why the pregnancy shouldn't be staightforward.
Treatment It's imperative that your blood sugar level remains stable, so the doctor may adjust your insulin intake for the pregnancy, and you should pay special attention to diet. You will also need to visit the antenatal clinic more often. Some women find a mild form of the disease appears for the first time during pregnancy. This nearly always disappears soon after delivery.

INCOMPETENT CERVIX
In a normal pregnancy, the cervix (neck of the womb) stays closed until the beginning of labour. But if miscarriages frequently occur after the third month of pregnancy, it could be because the neck of the womb is weak, and so it opens up, expelling the baby.
Treatment Your doctor may suggest a small operation to stitch the cervix firmly closed at the beginning of pregnancy. The stitch is then removed towards the end of pregnancy, or as labour starts.

PRE-ECLAMPSIA
This is one of the more common problems in late pregnancy. Warning signs are: raised blood pressure above 140/90; excessive weight gain; swollen ankles, feet, or hands; and traces of protein in the urine. If you develop any of these symptoms, the doctor will monitor you very carefully.

If blood pressure rises untreated, it could progress to the extremely dangerous condition of eclampsia, where fits may occur.
Treatment At the moment there is no effective way to prevent pre-eclampsia. If your blood pressure is raised, you may be given a drug to lower it. Bed rest isn't necessary. If the signs are severe you will be admitted to hospital even though you might be feeling perfectly well. Labour may be induced (see page 66).

RHESUS NEGATIVE MOTHER
Your blood is tested at the first clinic visit to see if it is rhesus positive or rhesus negative. About 15 per cent of people are rhesus negative, and if you are one of these, you will only have a problem in pregnancy if you give birth to a rhesus positive baby. Your blood groups will be incompatible, and although this won't harm a first baby, you could have problems with later pregnancies.
Treatment If your first baby is rhesus positive, and you're a rhesus negative mother, you will probably be given a protective vaccination called anti-D soon after birth. This will almost always prevent problems with any future pregnancies. The anti-D vaccination may be given during pregnancy in some hospitals.

EMERGENCY SIGNS

Call for emergency help immediately if you have:
- ★ a severe headache that won't go away
- ★ misty or blurred vision
- ★ severe, prolonged stomach pains
- ★ vaginal bleeding
- ★ a leakage of fluid, which suggests your waters have broken early
- ★ frequent, painful urination (drink plenty of water in the meantime).

Consult your doctor within 24 hours if you have:
- ★ swollen hands, face, and ankles
- ★ severe, frequent vomiting
- ★ a temperature of 38.3°C (101°F)
- ★ no movement, or fewer than ten kicks, from your baby for 12 hours after week 28.

MISCARRIAGE

A miscarriage is the ending of a pregnancy before 25 weeks, and this may happen in about one pregnancy in five. Most miscarriages occur in the first 12 weeks, often before the woman even knows she is pregnant, and usually because the baby is not developing normally. Bleeding from the vagina is usually the first sign. You should call your doctor straight away. Bed rest is often advised, but there is no evidence that it helps prevent a miscarriage.

Threatened abortion

If the bleeding is mild and painless and occurs around the time of a missed period the pregnancy can often be saved. You will probably be given an ultrasound scan (see page 37), which will show whether the fetus is alive, and predict whether the pregnancy is likely to continue safely.

True miscarriage

If the bleeding is heavy and you are in pain, it probably means that the baby has died. You may have to go into hospital, so that your womb can be cleaned out under general anaesthetic.

Your feelings

Even if you lose the baby early in pregnancy, you will feel an intense sense of loss. Other people don't always understand that you need to mourn your baby, and to come to terms with losing it. Worrying about whether you can ever have a normal, healthy baby is common. You may feel guilty too, though don't blame yourself; it really isn't your fault. It's quite safe to try for another baby as soon as you like, although some doctors suggest waiting until at least three menstrual cycles have passed. Unless you have had a string of miscarriages, there is no reason at all why you shouldn't experience a successful pregnancy the next time.

VAGINAL BLEEDING

If you notice bleeding from your vagina at any time in pregnancy, call your doctor without delay. Before 28 weeks, it can be a sign of an impending miscarriage. After this time, it may mean that the placenta is bleeding. This can happen if the placenta has started to separate from the wall of the womb (placental abruption) or if the placenta is too low down in the womb and covers, or partially covers, the cervix (placenta praevia).

Treatment The placenta is the baby's lifeline, so if the doctor thinks that there is any risk to it, you will probably be admitted to hospital straightaway, where the position of the placenta can be checked. You may stay in hospital until after the birth. If you have lost a lot of blood, you may be given a blood transfusion, and the baby will probably be delivered as soon as possible, by induction or Caesarean section (see pages 66 and 67). But if bleeding is only slight and occurs several weeks before the baby is due, the doctor may decide to wait for you to start labour naturally, while observing you closely.

"SMALL FOR DATES" BABIES

A baby who doesn't grow properly in the womb and is small at birth is called a "small for dates" baby. This may happen because the expectant mother smokes or eats a poor diet, or because the placenta doesn't work properly (usually when the mother has a general medical condition, for example, diabetes).

Treatment If tests show your baby is small, you will be monitored very closely throughout pregnancy, to check his health, and whether the flow of blood to the placenta is adequate. If the baby stops growing, or appears to be distressed, then he will be delivered early, either through induction or Caesarean section (see pages 66 and 67).

TWINS

Your pregnancy and labour will progress normally, although you will have two second stages in labour, and there is greater chance that you may go into labour prematurely. There's a greater likelihood of complications such as anaemia, pre-eclampsia, and of the babies lying abnormally in the womb. You may also find that all the common disorders of pregnancy are exaggerated, especially in the last few months.

Treatment Regular visits to the antenatal clinic are essential if you are expecting twins, so that any complications can be spotted immediately. A multiple pregnancy puts greater strain on your body than usual, so watch your posture and rest as much as possible, especially in the last few weeks. To avoid problems with your digestion, eat smaller amounts of fresh, unprocessed food often.

Twins You may find this position comfortable to rest in.

COMMON COMPLAINTS

You may suffer from a variety of discomforts in pregnancy, which, although worrying at the time, are perfectly normal. Many are caused by hormonal changes, or because your body is under extra pressure. A few symptoms, however, should be taken very seriously, so call the doctor if you have any of the complaints that have been highlighted in the box on page 38.

COMPLAINT	SYMPTOMS	WHAT TO DO
Bleeding gums 1 2 3 The gums become softer and more easily injured in pregnancy. They may become inflamed, allowing plaque to collect at the base of the teeth. This can lead to gum disease and tooth decay.	Bleeding from the gums, especially after brushing your teeth.	★ Floss and brush your teeth thoroughly after eating. ★ See your dentist. Treatment is free during pregnancy, but you shouldn't have X-rays or general anaesthetic.
Breathlessness 3 Late in pregnancy, the growing baby puts pressure on the diaphragm, and prevents you breathing freely. The problem is often relieved about a month before the birth, when the baby's head engages. Breathlessness can also be caused by anaemia.	Feeling breathless when you exert yourself, or even when you talk.	★ Rest as much as possible. ★ Try crouching if there's no chair around and you feel breathless. ★ At night, use an extra pillow. ★ If the problem is severe, consult your doctor or midwife.
Constipation 1 2 3 The pregnancy hormone progesterone relaxes the muscles of the intestine, which slows down bowel movements, making you more likely to become constipated.	Passing hard, dry stools at less frequent intervals than usual.	★ Eat plenty of high-fibre foods and drink lots of water. Go to the lavatory whenever you need to. ★ Exercise regularly. ★ Take any iron supplements you have been prescribed on a full stomach, with plenty of fluid. ★ See your doctor if the problem persists. ★ Avoid laxatives. ★ Chamomile, fennel, and ginger herbal supplements may help.
Cramps 3 May be caused by a calcium deficiency.	Painful contractions of muscles, usually in the calves and the feet, and often at night. Commonly started by a leg stretch with the toes pointed down.	★ Massage the affected calf or foot. ★ Walk around for a moment or two once the pain has eased to improve your circulation. ★ See your doctor who may prescribe calcium and vitamin D supplements. ★ Eat plenty of calcium-rich foods, and include garlic in your diet.
Feeling faint 1 3 Your blood pressure is lower in pregnancy, so you are more likely to feel faint.	Feeling dizzy and unstable. Needing to sit or lie down.	★ Try not to stand still for too long. ★ If you suddenly feel faint, sit down and put your head between your knees until you feel better. ★ Get up slowly from a hot bath, or when sitting or lying down. Turn on to one side first, if lying on your back.

The numbers in **bold** after each complaint relate to the third of pregnancy in which you are most likely to suffer from the problem.

Backache see page 44
Skin pigmentation see page 21

Breathlessness
Crouching helps if you suddenly feel out of breath halfway up the stairs. Hold on to the bannister.

Cramps
Pull your foot up towards you with your hand, and massage the calf vigorously, to help relieve painful cramps.

COMPLAINT	SYMPTOMS	WHAT TO DO
Frequent urination 1 3 Caused by the womb pressing on the bladder. The problem is often relieved in the middle months of pregnancy.	You need to pass water often.	★ If you find yourself getting up in the night to go to the lavatory, try drinking a little less in the evenings. ★ See your doctor if you feel any pain as you could have an infection.
Heartburn 3 The valve at the entrance to your stomach relaxes in pregnancy because of hormone changes, so stomach acid passes back into the oesophagus (the tube leading to your stomach).	A strong burning pain in the centre of the chest.	★ Avoid large meals, highly spiced, or fried foods. ★ At night, try a warm milk drink, and raise the head of the bed or use extra pillows. ★ See your doctor, who may prescribe a medicine to treat stomach acidity. ★ Chamomile or peppermint tea may give relief.
Leaking urine 3 Caused by weak pelvic floor muscles (see page 45), and the growing baby pressing on your bladder.	Leakage of urine whenever you run, cough, sneeze, or laugh.	★ Pass water often. ★ Practise your pelvic floor exercises regularly. ★ Avoid constipation and heavy lifting.
Morning sickness 1 Often one of the first signs of pregnancy, which can occur at any time of day. Tiredness can make the problem worse. Nausea usually disappears after week 12, but sometimes returns later.	Feeling sick, often at the smell of certain foods or cigarette smoke. Most women find there is a particular time of day when this happens.	★ Eat a couple of plain biscuits before getting up in the morning. ★ Avoid foods and smells that make you feel sick. ★ Have small, frequent meals throughout the day. ★ Drink an infusion of ginger or chamomile tea.
Piles 2 3 Pressure from the baby's head causes swollen veins round the anus. Straining to empty the bowels will make the problem worse. Mild piles usually disappear, without treatment, after the baby is born.	Itching, soreness, and possibly pain or bleeding when you try to pass stools.	★ Avoid constipation. ★ Try not to stand for long periods. ★ An ice pack (frozen peas tied in a polythene bag) held against the piles may ease any itching. ★ If piles persist, tell the doctor or midwife who may give you an ointment. ★ Try chamomile, dandelion root, nettle, and licorice herbal supplements.
Rash 3 Usually occurs in women who are overweight and who perspire freely. Can be caused by hormone changes.	Red rash, which usually develops in sweaty skin folds under the breasts or in the groin.	★ Wash and dry these areas often. Use unperfumed soap. ★ Soothe the skin with calamine lotion. ★ Wear loose, cotton clothes.
Sleeping difficulty 1 2 3 You may have a problem because the baby is kicking, you keep on needing the lavatory, or the size of the bulge makes it difficult to get comfortable in bed. Your doctor will be reluctant to prescribe sleeping pills.	Having trouble going to sleep in the first place, and finding it hard to get to sleep after waking. Some women find they have very frightening dreams about the birth or the baby. Don't worry about dreams; they do not reflect what will happen.	★ Reading, gentle relaxation exercises, or a warm bath before bedtime may help. ★ Experiment with extra pillows. If you sleep on your side, put a pillow under the top thigh. ★ Drink a glass of honey and apple cider vinegar in warm water before bed-time.

Heartburn and sleeplessness
This arrangement of pillows is comfortable if you suffer from heartburn or are unable to sleep.

Morning sickness
To counteract nausea, try eating a dry biscuit, toast, or fruit. Ginger biscuits or ginger beer can be helpful, too, as can mineral water.

COMPLAINT	SYMPTOMS	WHAT TO DO
Stretchmarks 2 3 These form if your skin stretches beyond its normal elasticity. Excess weight gain can also cause them. The marks seldom disappear altogether, but they may fade to thin silvery streaks.	Red marks that sometimes appear on the skin of the thighs, stomach, or breasts in pregnancy.	★ Avoid putting on weight too rapidly. ★ Rubbing moisturizer into the skin may feel cool and soothing, although creams and ointments won't prevent or heal stretchmarks. ★ Try a light massage of lavender and neroli essential oils in a carrier oil.
Sweating 2 3 Caused by hormone changes, and because blood flow to the skin increases in pregnancy.	Perspiring after very little exertion, or waking up in the night feeling hot and sweaty.	★ Wear loose cotton clothes. ★ Avoid manmade materials. ★ Drink plenty of water. ★ Open a window at night.
Swollen ankles and fingers 3 Some swelling (oedema) is normal in pregnancy, as the body holds extra water. This is usually no cause for concern.	Slight swelling in the ankles, especially in hot weather and at the end of the day. This shouldn't cause pain or discomfort. You may also notice stiff, swollen fingers in the morning, and that your rings don't fit.	★ Rest with your feet up often. ★ Try gentle foot exercises. Hold your hands above your head; flex and stretch each finger. ★ See your doctor or midwife. More marked swelling could be a warning sign of pre-eclampsia (see page 38). ★ Try dandelion tea; it is a mild diuretic.
Thrush 1 2 3 Hormone changes of pregnancy increase the chances of getting thrush. It is important to treat this before the baby is born, as it can affect his mouth and make feeding difficult. Washing with soap can worsen the problem.	A thick white discharge and severe itching. There may also be soreness and pain when you pass water.	★ Stop using soap if you are sore. ★ Insert a little plain yogurt into the vagina with your finger. ★ Avoid all nylon underwear, tight trousers, and vaginal deodorants. ★ See your doctor who will probably prescribe cream or pessaries. ★ Add a few drops of tea tree oil to a cup of cool water and apply to the vaginal area.
Tiredness 1 3 Caused by the extra demands that pregnancy makes on your body. Sometimes the result of worry.	Feeling weary, and wanting to sleep in the day. Needing to sleep longer at night.	★ Rest as much as possible and practise relaxation exercises. ★ Go to bed earlier. ★ Don't over-exert yourself. ★ Olive Bach Flower Remedy is good for general exhaustion.
Vaginal discharge 1 2 3 You may notice some increase in the amount of mucus produced by the vagina because of the hormone changes of pregnancy.	Slight increase in clear or white discharge, without soreness or pain.	★ Avoid vaginal deodorants and perfumed soap products. ★ Wear a light sanitary pad. ★ See your doctor if you have any itching, soreness, coloured or smelly discharge.
Varicose veins 1 2 3 You are more likely to have them in a later pregnancy, if you are overweight, or they run in your family. Standing for too long, or sitting cross-legged, can worsen the problem.	Aching legs; the veins in the calves and the thighs become painful and swollen.	★ Rest with your feet up often. Try raising the foot of your bed with pillows under the mattress. ★ Support tights may help. Put them on before getting up in the morning. ★ Exercise your feet. ★ Apply a witch hazel compress to the legs.

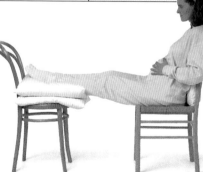

Swollen ankles and varicose veins
Gently circle your ankles and feet to improve circulation.

Varicose veins
Rest with your feet well raised up on at least two cushions if you suffer from this problem. Tuck another cushion into the small of your back.

KEEPING FIT AND RELAXED

Pregnancy, labour, and birth will make great demands on your body, so the more you can prepare yourself physically, the better you will feel. You will also find it easier to regain your normal shape after the birth. Relaxation exercises are just as important; they will help you cope far more effectively during labour, and they are invaluable for relieving stress and for increasing blood flow to the placenta. Try the exercises on the following pages. They are specially designed to make your joints and muscles more supple, in preparation for labour and the birth. Begin exercising as soon as the pregnancy is confirmed, or earlier if you wish. Practise at home or go to an antenatal exercise class. Don't worry, though, if you are well into pregnancy by the time you begin; it's never too late to start. Build up gradually at first, until you are exercising for at least 20 minutes every day.

EXERCISING SENSIBLY

If you have always enjoyed sport, you can usually carry on in pregnancy. But there are provisos.

★ Pregnancy is not the time to launch into a fitness blitz; just continue with what your body is used to. If you want to keep on going to your dance or exercise class, make sure that the teacher knows you are pregnant.

★ Don't exercise to the point where you get very tired or out of breath.

★ Avoid any sports where there is a danger of hurting your abdomen, such as riding, skiing, and water-skiing.

★ Be extra careful in the first weeks, or towards the end of pregnancy, as you may overstretch your ligaments.

Swimming
This is excellent and perfectly safe; the water supports your body.

LOOKING AFTER YOUR BODY

During pregnancy, it's important to hold yourself well and avoid strain on your back. You're far more likely to suffer from backache; the weight of the baby pulls you forwards, and so there is a tendency to lean slightly backwards to compensate. This strains the muscles of the lower back and pelvis, especially towards the end of pregnancy.

Be aware of your body, whatever you are doing. Avoid heavy lifting, and try to keep your back as long as possible. Wear low heels, as high heels tend to throw your weight even further forwards.

PROTECTING YOUR BACK

To avoid back trouble, it's equally important to be aware of how you use your body when going about everyday activities such as gardening, lifting a child, or carrying heavy bags. The hormones of pregnancy stretch and soften the muscles of the lower back, and so they are more easily strained if you bend over, get up too suddenly, or lift something the wrong way.

STANDING WELL

You can check that you are standing the right way in front of a full-length mirror. Lengthen and straighten your back, so that the weight of the baby is centred and supported by your thighs, buttocks, and stomach muscles. This will help prevent bakcache, and tone up your abdominal muscles, making it easier for you to regain your figure after the birth.

Drop *your shoulders and keep them back*

Hold *your back straight*

Lift *your chest and ribs*

Tighten *your stomach muscles*

Tuck in *your bottom*

Bend *your knees slightly*

Stand *with your feet a little way apart*

Bad Posture
This is common during pregnancy. As the baby grows, its weight throws you off-balance, so you may over-arch your back and thrust your abdomen forwards.

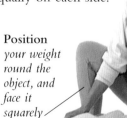

Working at a low level
Do as much as you can at floor level, kneeling down to garden, clean, make a bed, or dress a child instead of bending over.

Lifting and carrying
When lifting an object, bend your knees and keep your back as straight as possible, bringing the object close in to your body. Try not to lift something heavy from up high, as you may lose your balance. If you're carrying heavy bags, divide the weight equally on each side.

Keep *your back straight*

Position *your weight round the object, and face it squarely*

Getting up from lying down
Always turn on your side when you have been lying down. Then move into a kneeling position. Use the strength of your thighs to push yourself up; keep your back straight.

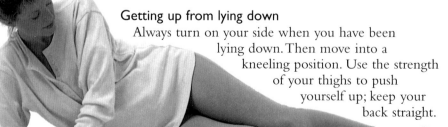

THE PELVIC FLOOR

This is a hammock of muscles that supports the bowel, bladder, and womb. During pregnancy, the muscles go soft and stretchy, and this, together with the weight of the baby pushing down, weakens them, making you feel heavy and uncomfortable. You may also leak a little urine whenever you run sneeze, cough, or laugh. To avoid these problems it's essential to strengthen the pelvic floor.

The pelvic floor
This forms part of the pelvis, cradling and protecting the baby in the womb. The baby passes though it at birth.

STRENGTHENING THE PELVIC FLOOR

Practise this exercise often – at least three or four times a day. Once you've learned it, you can do it anytime, anywhere, lying down, sitting, or standing. You will also find it useful in the second stage of labour, when knowing how to relax the muscles can reduce the risk of a tear, by easing the passage of the baby through the pelvis. Lie on your back, with your knees bent and your feet flat on the floor. Now tighten the muscles, squeezing as if stopping a stream of urine. Imagine you are trying to pull something into your vagina, drawing it in slightly, then pausing, then pulling, until you can go no further. Hold for a moment, then let go gradually. Repeat ten times.

Practise the exercise standing

Practise *the exercise sitting*

DO THIS WHEN:
★ waiting for a bus or train
 ★ ironing or cooking
  ★ watching TV
  ★ having intercourse
  ★ you have *emptied* your bladder.

PELVIC TILT

This exercise helps you move the pelvis with ease, which is good preparation for labour. It also strengthens the stomach muscles and makes the back more flexible. The pelvic tilt is especially helpful if you suffer from backache. You can do the tilt in any position; remember to keep your shoulders still.

1 Kneel on the floor on your hands and knees. Make sure that your back is flat (at first it helps to use a miror to check this).

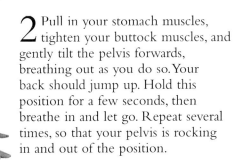

2 Pull in your stomach muscles, tighten your buttock muscles, and gently tilt the pelvis forwards, breathing out as you do so. Your back should jump up. Hold this position for a few seconds, then breathe in and let go. Repeat several times, so that your pelvis is rocking in and out of the position.

DO THIS WHEN:
★ lying on your back
★ standing
★ sitting
★ kneeling
★ dancing to music.

TAILOR SITTING

Tailor sitting strengthens the back and makes your thighs and pelvis more flexible. It will also improve the blood flow in the lower part of the body, and will encourage your legs to flop apart during labour. The main position below is far easier than it appears. This is because your body becomes more supple during pregnancy.

SITTING WITH CUSHIONS

If you find tailor sitting difficult, put a cushion under each thigh, or sit against a wall for support. Remember to keep your back straight.

Straighten *your back*

Stretch *your inner thighs by pressing outwards with your elbows*

SITTING WITH CROSSED LEGS

You may find it more comfortable to sit like this. Make sure you change the front leg occasionally.

THIGH STRENGTHENER

Sit with your back straight, the soles of your feet together, and your heels close to your body. Grasp your ankles, and press your thighs down with your elbows. Hold them there for 20 seconds. Do this several times.

Keep *your feet close to your body*

WARNING

When you are doing any exercises, remember these guidelines.
* Don't push yourself beyond your own limits or exhaust yourself.
* If you feel any pain, stop.
* Try not to lie flat on your back in late pregnancy.

SQUATTING

Squatting makes your pelvic joints more flexible, and strengthens the back and thigh muscles. It can also protect your back, if you squat down instead of bending over, and is comfortable if you experience backache. Squatting is also a good position to take up during labour.

You may find it difficult to do a full squat at first, so try holding on to a firm support, such as a chair or window ledge, and place a rolled-up rug or blanket under your heels. Get up slowly, or you may feel slightly dizzy.

Clasp *your hands*

Press *your elbows against your thighs*

Lengthen and straighten *your back*

Try to keep *your heels flat on the ground*

WITH A CHAIR

Stand facing a chair with your feet slightly apart. Keeping your back straight, open out your legs, and squat down, using the chair to support you. Stay in this position as long as it is comfortable to do so. If you find it difficult to keep your feet flat on the ground, place a folded blanket under your heels.

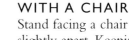

DO THIS WHEN:
★ breathless on the stairs
★ picking up an object
★ taking something from a low drawer
★ on the telephone
★ there's no chair around.

UNSUPPORTED

Keeping your back straight, open out your legs and squat down, turning your feet out slightly. Try to keep your heels flat on the ground and stretch your inner thighs by pressing outwards with your elbows. Stay in this position as long as you find it comfortable.

Turn *your feet out slightly*

RELAXATION AND BREATHING

These relaxation and breathing exercises are among the most beneficial that you can learn. They are invaluable during labour, when knowing how to breathe properly and relax the muscles of your body will help you cope with painful contractions and conserve vital energy. Practise these exercises regularly so that they become a natural response during labour. Relaxation will also help you unwind any time you feel tense or anxious.

HOW TO RELAX
At first it's best to practise this exercise in a warm room where you won't be disturbed. Later you should find it easy to relax anywhere.

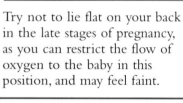

Relax your body
Make yourself comfortable, lying on your back, well propped up by pillows, or on your side, with one leg bent and supported on cushions. Now, tense and relax the muscles of each part of your body in turn, starting with the toes and working upwards. After doing this for eight to ten minutes, let your body go limp. Try to feel heavy, as though you are sinking into the floor.

Lying on your side
You may be more comfortable, especially during later pregnancy, lying on your side with one leg bent and supported on cushions. Don't place too many pillows under your head, because this is bad for your spine.

> ### WARNING
> Try not to lie flat on your back in the late stages of pregnancy, as you can restrict the flow of oxygen to the baby in this position, and may feel faint.

Tilt *your head from side to side, then hold still*

Screw up *your eyes, open, then close*

Pull in *your stomach muscles, then relax*

Arch *the small of your back, then let go*

Clench *your hands, then open*

Squeeze *your buttock muscles, then let go*

BREATHING FOR LABOUR

Practise the different levels of breathing with a partner or friend on a regular basis in the weeks leading up to labour. Controlled breathing will help you to remain relaxed and calm during labour, and can even control your body during contractions.

Light breathing

This level of breathing will help you at the height of a contraction. Breathe in and out of your mouth, taking air into the upper part of your lungs only. A partner or friend should put her hands on your shoulder blades and feel them move. Practise making the breaths lighter and lighter, but take an occasional deeper breath when you need one.

Deep breathing

This has a calming effect, helpful at the beginning and end of contractions. Sit comfortably and as relaxed as possible. Breathe in deeply through the nose, right to the bottom of your lungs. Your partner or friend should place her hands just above your waistline and feel your ribcage move. Now, concentrate on breathing slowly and gently out. Let the next in-breath follow naturally.

Panting

After the first stage of labour, you will want to push, even though the cervix may not be fully opened. You can resist this by taking two short breaths, and then blowing a longer breath out: say "huff, huff, blow" to yourself.

Tighten *your thigh muscles, then let the tension go*

Bend *your feet at the ankles, then let go*

Relax your mind

While relaxing your body, try to calm and empty your mind. Breathe slowly and evenly, sighing each breath out gently. Do not breathe too hard. Alternatively, repeat a word or sound silently to yourself, or concentrate on some pleasant or peaceful image. Try not to follow any thoughts that arise.

Tense *your calf muscles, then relax*

Curl *your toes, then relax*

EATING FOR A HEALTHY BABY

A baby has only one source of food – you. During pregnancy, more than at any other time, it is essential that you have as varied and balanced a diet as possible. You do not need to plan this specially, nor do you have to eat for two. All you have to do is eat a variety of fresh, unprocessed foods from the selection below, to ensure that you get all the nutrients you need. Once you are, or know you want to become, pregnant, think about how many healthy foods you eat regularly. Do you eat or drink anything that might harm the baby? Increase your intake of raw vegetables and fresh fruit, and cut down on sugary, salty, and processed foods.

ESSENTIAL NUTRIENTS

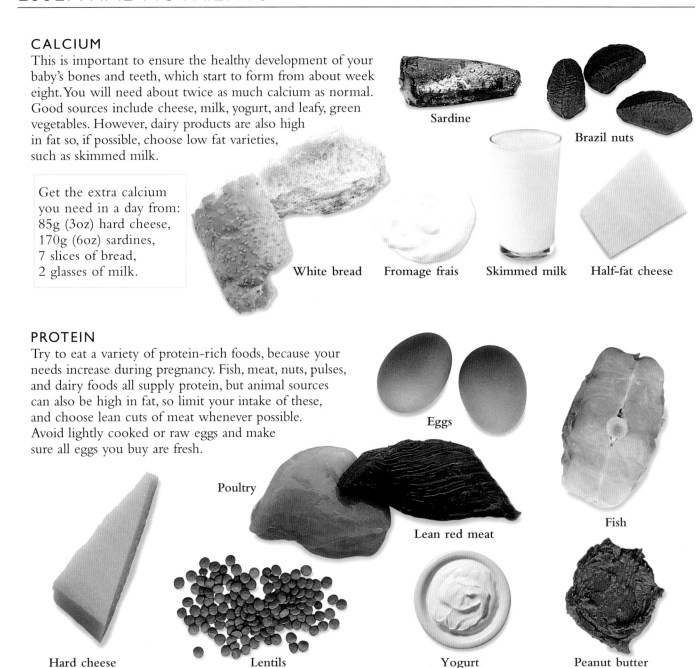

CALCIUM

This is important to ensure the healthy development of your baby's bones and teeth, which start to form from about week eight. You will need about twice as much calcium as normal. Good sources include cheese, milk, yogurt, and leafy, green vegetables. However, dairy products are also high in fat so, if possible, choose low fat varieties, such as skimmed milk.

Get the extra calcium you need in a day from:
85g (3oz) hard cheese,
170g (6oz) sardines,
7 slices of bread,
2 glasses of milk.

Sardine

Brazil nuts

White bread   Fromage frais   Skimmed milk   Half-fat cheese

PROTEIN

Try to eat a variety of protein-rich foods, because your needs increase during pregnancy. Fish, meat, nuts, pulses, and dairy foods all supply protein, but animal sources can also be high in fat, so limit your intake of these, and choose lean cuts of meat whenever possible. Avoid lightly cooked or raw eggs and make sure all eggs you buy are fresh.

Eggs

Poultry

Lean red meat

Fish

Hard cheese   Lentils   Yogurt   Peanut butter

VITAMIN C

This will help to build a strong placenta, enable your body to resist infection, and aid the absorption of iron. It is found in fresh fruit and vegetables, and supplies of the vitamin are needed daily, as it cannot be stored in the body. A lot of vitamin C is lost by prolonged storage and cooking, so only eat fresh produce, and steam green vegetables or eat them raw.

Red, yellow, and green pepper

Savoy cabbage

Brussels sprouts

Cauliflower

Potato

Tomatoes

Orange

Grapefruit

Strawberries

FIBRE

Foods rich in fibre should form a large part of your daily diet since constipation (see page 40) is common in pregnancy and fibre will help prevent this. Fruit and vegetables are important sources as you can eat a lot of them every day. Don't rely too heavily on bran because it can hinder the absorption of other nutrients; there are plenty of better sources.

Mixed nuts

Raspberries

Wholewheat pasta

Garden peas

Dried apricots

Wholemeal
bread

Brown rice

Raisins

Leeks

FOLIC ACID

Folic acid is a B vitamin that is needed for the development of the baby's central nervous system, especially in the first few weeks. During the first three months of pregnancy you need three times as much folic acid as normal. Folic acid is destroyed by over-cooking, and by prolonged storage, but not by freezing. So, if you can't buy fresh vegetables daily, buy frozen ones instead. Look out for bread and cereals fortified with folic acid. They will be endorsed by the Health Education Authority. A product labelled "with extra folic acid" will provide 100 mcg of folic acid in an average portion – a quarter of your daily need. If it is simply labelled "contains folic acid", an average portion will provide 30 mcg. But you cannot get enough folic acid from even the healthiest diet alone – it's essential to take a folic acid supplement as well.

Foods high in folic acid (50-100 mcg/serving): cooked black-eyed beans, brussels sprouts, beef extract, yeast extract, cooked kidney, kale, spinach, granary bread, spring greens, broccoli, green beans, wholemeal bread, hazelnuts.

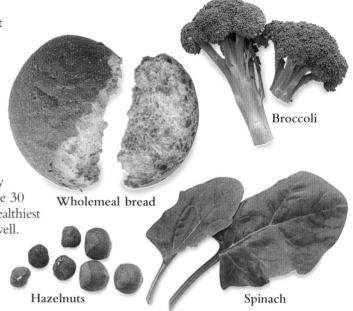

Broccoli

Wholemeal bread

Hazelnuts

Spinach

IRON

Lean red meat and oily fish such as sardines are the most easily absorbed sources of iron. Baked beans, spinach, black-eyed beans, wholemeal bread, cereals and pulses are all iron-rich too, though they are not quite as readily absorbed. Iron is absorbed more easily in the presence of vitamin C, while tea and coffee inhibit iron absorption. So, try to avoid drinking tea or coffee with iron-rich foods, especially if you are a vegetarian and cannot eat the most easily absorbed sources of iron – drink blackcurrant or orange juice instead.

Tuna fish

Spinach

Lean red meat

Dried apricots

VEGETARIAN DIET

If you eat a variety of protein-rich foods and fresh fruit and vegetables every day, you should provide the baby with all that he needs. The only nutrient you may lack is iron; the body has great difficulty absorbing iron that comes from plant sources, so you may be given supplements of the mineral to compensate. If you are vegan, and don't eat any dairy foods, you may also be prescribed calcium, and vitamins D and B12.

SALT

Pregnant women used to be advised to restrict the amount of salt in their diet, as it was believed that too much salt was related to problems such as excess swelling and pregnancy-induced high blood pressure. But it is now thought that there is little evidence to justify such advice.

FLUID

This is essential during pregnancy for keeping your kidneys healthy and avoiding constipation. Water is best.

TOP TEN FOODS

These ten types of food are excellent sources of at least one nutrient. Try to eat some of them once a day:
★ Cheese, milk, yogurt: calcium, protein.
★ Dark green, leafy vegetables: vitamin C, fibre, folic acid.
★ Lean red meat: protein, iron.
★ Oranges: vitamin C, fibre.
★ Poultry: protein, iron.
★ Raisins and prunes: iron.
★ Sardines: calcium, protein, iron.
★ White fish: protein.

★ Wholemeal bread: protein, fibre, folic acid.
★ Wholewheat pasta and brown rice: fibre.

TAKING SUPPLEMENTS

Folic acid supplements are recommended from the time you stop using contraception until the 12th week of pregnancy. Iron supplements may be prescribed if you are anaemic. If you eat a varied diet with lots of fresh foods, these are probably the only supplements you will need.

PROTECTING YOUR BABY

As the nutrients from your food can cross the placenta to the baby, so can many harmful substances that we regularly eat and drink.

PROCESSED FOODS

Avoid processed convenience foods, such as canned foods and packet mixes. Processed foods often have sugar and salt added, and they may contain a lot of fat, as well as preservatives, flavourings, and colourings. Read the labels carefully and choose additive-free products.

COOK-CHILL FOODS

Avoid hot canteen foods, pre-cooked supermarket meals, and ready-to-eat poultry (unless served piping hot). These foods may contain bacteria that can be passed to the baby and put his life at risk.

CHEESE

Unpasteurised milk and dairy products, and soft matured cheeses, such as Brie made from both pasteurized and un-pasteurized milk, can be harmful because of the risk of listeria infection, so it's best to avoid them.

COFFEE, TEA, AND HOT CHOCOLATE

Caffeine, a substance that is found in all these drinks, has a harmful effect on the digestive system. Reduce your intake to no more than three cups of caffeine-containing drinks a day, and, if possible, cut them out altogether. Drink plenty of mineral water instead.

HERBAL TEAS

If you want to drink herbal teas in pregnancy, it is sensible to check first with a pharmacist who sells herbal teas, or a herbalist. Most pre-packaged teas won't harm the baby, but some may have unwanted effects. Raspberry leaf tea is a traditional remedy to ease labour.

SUGAR

Sugary foods, such as cakes, biscuits, jam, and fizzy drinks, are low in essential nutrients, and can make you put on excess weight during your pregnancy. Try to get your energy from starchy carbohydrates, such as wholemeal bread and pasta, and cut down on sweet things.

CRAVINGS

It's common in pregnancy to find that you suddenly develop a taste for certain foods, such as pickled onions or ice cream. If you long for a particular food, go ahead and indulge yourself within reason, provided it isn't fattening, and doesn't cause indigestion.

ALTERNATIVES TO ALCOHOL

Any alcohol that you drink during pregnancy is passed through the placenta into your baby's bloodstream, and can be harmful. So it's best to cut out alcohol altogether and make your own soft drinks. Even beers, lagers, and wines that claim to be alcohol free or low in alcohol are not necessarily free from harmful additives and chemicals; some contain high levels of these substances, which may have unknown effects on your baby's health.

ESSENTIAL FATTY ACIDS

Long chain, polyunsaturated fatty acids (LCPUFAs) are vital for the development of your baby's brain, nervous system, and retina. The fetus can't manufacture these for itself, and relies on an efficient supply from the mother across the placenta and, after birth, from breast milk. Oily fish such as salmon and mackerel are by far the richest source of LCPUFAs. Nuts, seeds, wholegrain cereals, and dark green leafy vegetables are other sources.

GENETICALLY MODIFIED FOODS

At present there is not enough evidence to be certain that genetically modified foods are safe. Neither is there enough evidence to show that they could be harmful for either you or your baby.

Genetic engineering is not a precise process. No-one can be sure that the inserted gene will not interact with other genes or that it will have precisely and solely the action it is expected to have. For example, many vegetables, including potatoes and tomatoes, have poisonous ancestors. The fact that the modern potato is not poisonous does not necessarily mean that it has lost the toxic gene, only that the gene is not at present being expressed. There is at least a theoretical possibility that genetic engineering of a potato might re-activate a dormant ancestral gene for toxicity.

It is likely to be some time before there is evidence to prove conclusively whether or not GM foods are safe, so if you are at all concerned the best thing is to play safe and avoid them.

PRACTICAL PREPARATIONS

About a month before your delivery date, check that everything is ready for the baby, and buy in food and other essentials to make life easier after the birth. Now is the time to pack for hospital, or to think about what you need if you are having a home birth. Some hospitals provide a list of what to take with you, and even some of the items on it, so check with your hospital first.

HELPFUL THINGS FOR LABOUR

All the items below may be useful in labour and immediately after birth. Pack them separately, as you will probably need them in a hurry.

Deodorant

Small natural sponge
Moisten it, and suck on it if your mouth is dry.

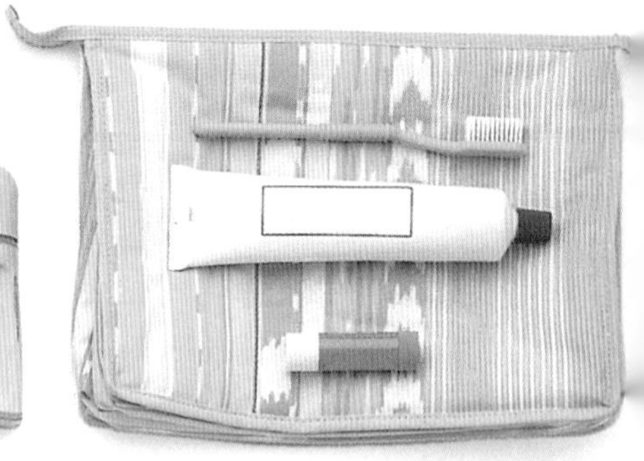

Talcum powder
This will smooth back massage.

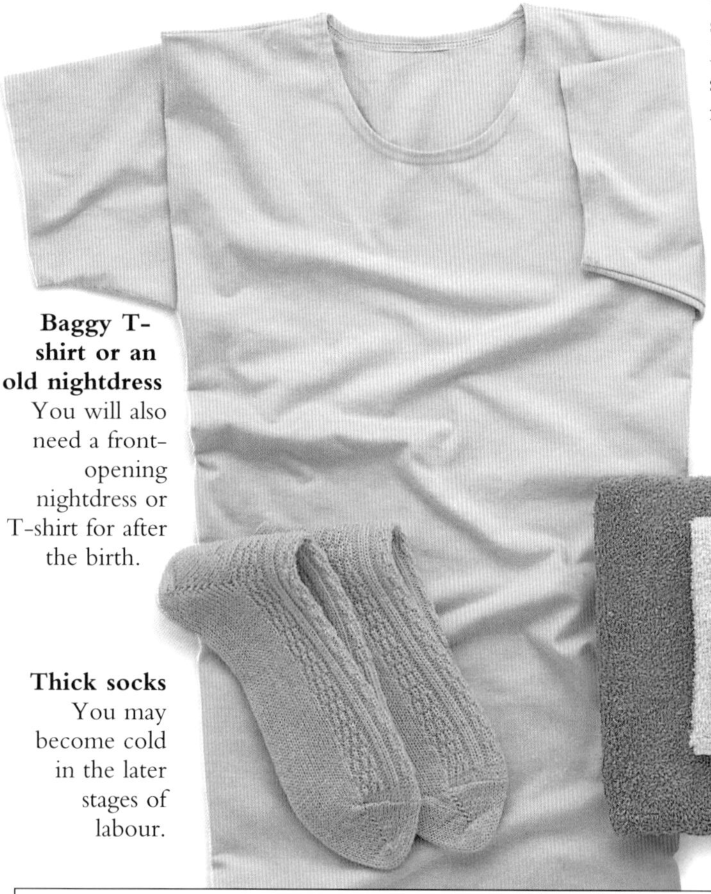

Spongebag, toothbrush and paste, lipsalve

Also:
★ a hot-water bottle
★ books, magazines, camera, a personal stereo
★ food and drink for your partner
★ phone numbers of relatives and friends
★ coins for the telephone
★ anything else that you have practised with at antenatal classes and would like to use during labour, such as a bean bag. Check with your hospital first.

Dark-coloured towel, two face flannels, soap

Baggy T-shirt or an old nightdress
You will also need a front-opening nightdress or T-shirt for after the birth.

Thick socks
You may become cold in the later stages of labour.

HOME BIRTH

There are several preconditions for a home birth, and you should talk to your midwife if you are thinking about one. These include a warm room, with easy access to hot water, a lavatory, and a telephone. You should also live somewhere an ambulance could reach.

What you will need:
★ bed with a firm mattress (put a board under the mattress, if necessary)
★ two clean surfaces nearby, one for equipment, the other for the midwife's examination of the baby after birth
★ clean towels, sheets, and blankets
★ plastic sheet
★ one medium-sized plastic bowl
★ large rubbish bags
★ two packets of stick-on sanitary pads, one superabsorbent
★ baggy T-shirt or nightdress

★ front-opening nightdress, bra, and pants
★ nappy, vest, stretchsuit or nightie, and blanket for the baby.

Making the bed
Put a clean undersheet on the bed. Cover this with a plastic sheet and another clean undersheet, which can be taken off after birth, leaving the bed freshly made underneath.

FOR AFTER THE BIRTH

You will need a few essentials after the birth, but your partner can bring these along later if you go into labour unexpectedly. The hospital will probably provide all you need for the baby during your stay.

Brush, comb, shampoo, towel

Also:
★ tissues
★ hairdryer, for drying your hair, as well as your stitches
★ big plastic bags for dirty washing.

Breast pads
Slip these inside your bra to absorb leaking milk. Shaped ones are best.

Nipple cream
This relieves sore nipples.

One packet
should be superabsorbent for the first few days

Two packets of stick-on sanitary pads

Front opening,
to allow your baby to feel as much as possible of your breast; one cup unzips at a time

Wide
support straps

Two to three nursing bras
Take the bras that you have been wearing throughout pregnancy, if you are not breast-feeding.

Choose *large ones, with plenty of air holes*

6 pairs of pants
Buy either cotton pants in a dark colour, or, better still, disposable pants.

Two to three machine-washable nightdresses and a dressing gown
These should be made of cotton or polycotton as the ward may be hot.

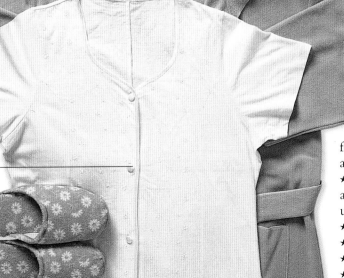

Front opening,
with buttons that undo well below the breasts, if breast-feeding

Low-heeled slippers

COMING HOME
You will need to leave out a set of clothes for your partner to bring when it's time for you to leave hospital. Don't choose anything too tight fitting; you will not be back to your pre-pregnancy size. The baby needs clothes for coming home in, too, so set aside these things:
★ two nappies (don't forget a pin and plastic pants if you're not using disposables)
★ vest
★ stretchsuit or nightie
★ cardigan and hat
★ blanket (for cold weather).

LABOUR AND BIRTH

At last the weeks of waiting are over and labour is beginning. You will feel excited, yet apprehensive, about how your labour will progress. You will feel more confident if you have prepared yourself well so that you understand what is happening to your body at each stage of labour. Giving birth can be an immensely fulfilling experience, and if you are calm and relaxed, you are far more likely to enjoy it. Practise your relaxation and breathing techniques beforehand, to help you stay calm during the contractions and cope with the pain, and don't be disappointed if your labour doesn't turn out quite as you expected.

KNOWING YOU ARE IN LABOUR

You may worry that you won't recognize labour when it comes. This is most unlikely. Although it is possible to confuse the first labour contractions with the contractions that may occur in the last weeks of pregnancy, you will probably be able to tell if labour is imminent, as it is heralded by a number of signs.

SIGNS OF LABOUR
A show
The plug of thick, blood-stained mucus that blocks the neck of the womb in pregnancy usually passes out of the vagina, either before or during the early stages of labour.
What to do The show may happen a few days before labour starts, so wait until you have regular pains in your stomach or back, or your waters break, before ringing the hospital or midwife.

Your waters break
The bag of fluid that surrounds the baby can break at any time during labour. It may be a sudden flood, but it's far more common to notice a trickle of fluid, as the baby's head has often engaged; this stems the tide.
What to do Call the hospital or midwife at once. You need to go to hospital even if you don't have any contractions, as there is a risk of infection. In the meantime, wear a sanitary towel to absorb the flow.

Contractions
These may start off as a dull backache, or you may have shooting pains down your thighs. As time goes on, you will probably have contractions in your stomach, rather like bad period pains.
What to do When the contractions seem to be regular, time them. If you think you are in labour, call the hospital or midwife. Unless contractions are coming very frequently (every five minutes), or are very painful, there is no need to go into hospital immediately. A first labour usually lasts about 12 to 14 hours, and it is often better to spend several hours of this time at home. Move gently around, resting whenever you need to. Perhaps relax in a warm bath, if your waters haven't broken, or eat a light snack. The hospital will probably suggest you wait until the contractions are quite strong and occurring every five minutes or so before you leave home.

FALSE STARTS
Throughout pregnancy, the womb contracts. In the last weeks, these Braxton Hicks contractions become stronger so you may think you are in labour. But true labour contractions occur very regularly, and grow stronger and more frequent, so you should be able to tell when the real thing begins. Occasionally contractions start, and then die away. Keep moving; in time they will get going again.

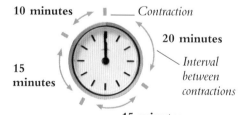

TIMING CONTRACTIONS

10 minutes — *Contraction*

20 minutes

15 minutes

Interval between contractions

15 minutes

Time contractions over an hour, noting when each one starts and ends. They should become stronger and more frequent, and last for at least 40 seconds as labour becomes established. The diagram shows the kind of intervals between contractions you may have in early labour.

THE FIRST STAGE

During this stage, the muscles of your womb contract to open up the cervix (neck of the womb) to allow the baby to pass through at birth. It takes an average of ten to twelve hours for a first baby.

Don't be surprised if at some time in the first stage you suddenly feel panic-stricken. However well-prepared you are, the feeling that your body has been taken over by a process that you can't control can be frightening. Stay as calm as possible and try to go with your body. It is now that you will most appreciate having your partner or a good friend by your side, especially if they know about labour, and have gone to antenatal classes.

After admission
When the checks are over, you can have a bath or shower.

ADMISSION TO HOSPITAL

Once you reach hospital, you will see a midwife who carries out several routine admission procedures. Your partner can stay with you while she does this. If you are having the baby at home, your community midwife will probably prepare you for the birth in much the same way.

The midwife's questions
The midwife will check your notes and co-op card and ask you if your waters have broken and if you have had a show. She will also want to know about your contractions: when they started, how frequent they are, what they feel like, and how long each one lasts.

Checking you
After you have changed into the hospital gown or your own clothes for the birth, the midwife will take your blood pressure, temperature, and pulse, and may give you an internal examination to check how far the neck of the womb has opened.

Checking the baby
The midwife will check the baby's position by feeling your abdomen, and she will listen to his heartbeat with a fetal stethoscope or a sonicaid. She may attach a microphone to you for 20 minutes or so, to record the baby's heartbeat. This helps her to be sure that he is getting enough oxygen during contractions.

Group B streptococcal infection
About 10 per cent of women are carriers of Group B streptococcus, a bacterium that can cause serious infection in new-born infants, particularly those whose birthweight is low. The risk of infection is increased if the membranes rupture before contractions have begun. If you are a known carrier, or if you go into premature labour, or your membranes rupture before labour begins, you may be given an antibiotic during labour to protect you and your baby from infection.

INTERNAL EXAMINATIONS
The midwife may give you regular internal examinations to check the position of the baby and how much the cervix is dilating (opening up). Ask if you are not told; it is encouraging to find that the cervix is widening, but this may not happen at a steady rate.

The examination is usually done between contractions, so tell the midwife if you feel one coming. Try to relax as much as possible, to minimize any discomfort. You can also use the gas and air inhaler.

THE CERVIX IN LABOUR
This is normally kept closed by a ring of muscles. Other muscles run from the cervix up and over the womb. These contract during labour, drawing the cervix into the womb, and then stretching it so it is wide enough for the baby's head to pass through.

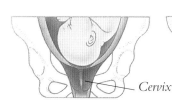

Cervix

1 The tough cervix is gradually softened by hormone changes.

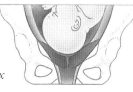

2 Gentle contractions then efface (thin) the cervix.

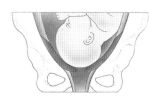

3 Once it is fully effaced, stronger contractions dilate it.

POSITIONS FOR THE FIRST STAGE

Try a variety of positions during the first stage of labour, as different positions will probably be comfortable at different times. Practise these positions beforehand, so that you can follow your body's natural cues with ease.

Staying upright

During early contractions, support yourself on a nearby surface, such as a wall, chair seat, or the hospital bed. Kneel down if necessary.

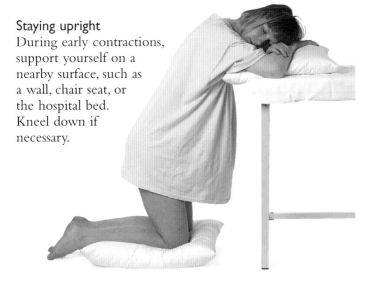

Sitting forwards

Sit facing the back of a chair, and lean over it on to a cushion or pillow. Rest your head on your folded arms.

WHAT YOUR PARTNER CAN DO

★ During contractions give her plenty of praise, comfort, and support. Don't worry if she becomes annoyed with you; you are important.
★ Remind her of the relaxation and breathing techniques she has learned.
★ Mop her brow, give her sips of water, hold her hand, massage her back, suggest a change of position, or do anything else that helps. Learn what sort of touch and massage she likes beforehand.
★ Act as a mediator between your partner and the hospital staff. Stand by her wishes, for example on pain relief.

WATER BIRTHS

Immersion in water at body-heat can help you to relax and ease pain during labour. Some hospitals provide birthing pools, and it is also possible to hire a portable pool for a home birth. If you want to use a birthing pool in labour, it is essential for you to have a midwife with water-birth experience.

YOUR BIRTH PARTNER

If you do not have a partner, or if he cannot to be at the birth, choose your mother, sister, or a female friend to be with you.

Massage *her lower back*

Resting
As you move around in early labour, you may like to lean against your partner during contractions. He can massage your lower back, or stroke your shoulders.

Kneeling forwards

Kneel down with your legs apart, and relax forwards on to a pile of cushions or pillows, or a bean bag. Try to be as upright as possible. Sit to one side between contractions.

On all fours

Kneel down on your hands and knees on the floor (you may find a mattress more comfortable), and tilt you pelvis to and fro. Do not arch your back. Between contractions, relax forwards and rest your head in your arms.

BACKACHE LABOUR

When the baby is facing towards your abdomen, instead of away from it, his head tends to press against your spine, causing backache. To relieve pain:
★ during contractions, lean forwards with your weight supported, such as on all fours, to take the baby's weight off your back, and rock your pelvis to and fro, move around between contractions
★ ask your partner to massage your back, or hold a hot-water bottle to the base of your spine between contractions.

BREATHING FOR THE FIRST STAGE

At the beginning and end of a contraction, breathe deeply and evenly, in through the nose and out of the mouth. When the contraction peaks, try a lighter, shallower kind of breathing. Both in and out breaths should be through your mouth. Don't do this for too long, as you will feel dizzy.

WAYS TO HELP YOURSELF

★ Keep moving between contractions; this helps you cope physically with the pain. During contractions, take up a comfortable position.
★ Try to stay as upright as possible, so the baby's head sits firmly on the cervix, making your contractions stronger and more effective.
★ Concentrate on your breathing, to calm you and take your mind off a contraction.
★ Relax between contractions (see pages 48 to 49) to save energy for when you need it.
★ Sing, or even moan and groan, to release pain.
★ Look at a fixed spot or object to help take your mind off a contraction.
★ Take one contraction at a time, and don't think about the contractions to follow. Perhaps see each contraction as a wave, which you have to ride over to reach the baby.
★ Pass water often, so your bladder doesn't get in the way of the baby.

Lower back massage

This will relieve backache, and calm, and reassure you. Your partner should massage you at the base of the spine, using the heel of his hand to make firm, circular movements. Talcum powder will help prevent friction.

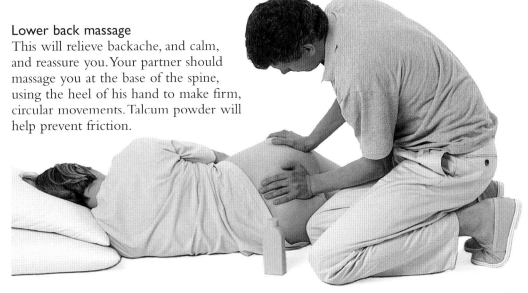

TRANSITION

The most difficult time in labour is often at the end of the first stage, when contractions are strongest. They last about a minute, and may be only a minute apart, so there is little time to rest after one before the next is upon you. This phase, which often lasts about half an hour, is known as transition. You will be tired, and may feel disheartened, tearful, excitable, or just bad-tempered. You will probably lose all sense of time and doze off between contractions. Nausea, vomiting, and shivering are common, too.

Eventually, you may have a strong urge to push. If you do this too early, the cervix can become swollen. Tell the midwife you are ready to push. She may examine you to determine whether your cervix is fully dilated.

To stop yourself pushing
If the midwife says you are not fully dilated, say "huff, huff, blow" (see above, right) in this position. You may also find gas and air useful (see page 64).

Kneel down, and lean forwards, resting your head in your arms; stick your bottom in the air. This reduces the urge to push, and also makes pushing more difficult.

THE SECOND STAGE

Once the cervix has dilated and you can push, the second stage of labour has begun. You can now add your own efforts to the powerful contractions of the womb, and help push the baby out. If the baby is lying in a slightly different position, you may not feel this urge to push, but the midwife will guide you so that you push when it is most needed. She will also help you find the most comfortable position in which to push. Even though the contractions are stronger, they don't feel as bad as before. Pushing is hard work but satisfying; each effort brings your baby's birth closer. This stage usually lasts about an hour for a first baby.

BREATHING FOR TRANSITION

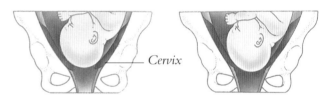

Short breaths   Short breaths   Short breaths
IN

OUT
Blow   Blow   Gently out

If you want to push too early, say "huff, huff, blow" to yourself, taking two short in- and out-breaths, and blowing a longer breath out. When the need to push fades, give a slow, even breath out.

WHAT YOUR PARTNER CAN DO
★ Try to relax her, encourage her, and wipe away any perspiration; if she doesn't want to be touched, stay back.
★ Breathe with her through contractions.
★ Put thick socks on her legs if they start to shake, and hold them still.
★ If she feels an urge to push, call the midwife immediately.

THE CERVIX IN LABOUR

Cervix

At 7cm ($2\frac{3}{4}$ in), the midwife feels the cervix quite well stretched out round the baby's head.

When the midwife can't feel the cervix (at about 10cm/4in), you are fully dilated.

BREATHING FOR THE SECOND STAGE

Deep breaths   Deep even breaths   Even breaths
IN

Push   Push

OUT

When you want to push (this may happen several times during a contraction), take a deep breath and hold it for a short time as you bear down, if this helps the push; it's important to do what your body tells you. Between pushes, take a few deep calming breaths. Relax slowly as the contraction fades.

POSITIONS FOR DELIVERY

Try to be as upright as possible when you are pushing during the second stage of labour, so you are working with gravity, rather than against it.

Sitting upright

A common delivery position is to sit on the bed propped up by pillows, a bean bag, or a wedge. Keep your chin down, and grip under your thighs as you push. Between contractions, try to relax back on the pillows.

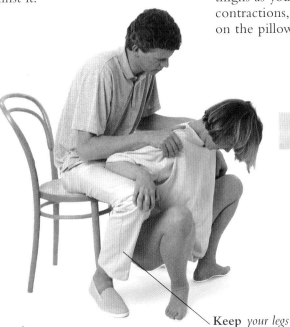

Keep *your legs comfortably apart*

WAYS TO HELP YOURSELF

★ Push smoothly and steadily during a contraction.
★ Try to relax the muscles of your pelvic floor, so you feel as if you are letting go completely.
★ Keep your face relaxed.
★ Don't worry about trying to control your bowels, or about any leakage of water from the bladder.
★ Rest as much as possible between contractions, so you save all your energy for pushing.

Squatting

This is an excellent position for delivery, because it opens the pelvis wide and uses gravity to help push out the baby. But unless you have practised it beforehand (see page 47), you may find it tiring after a while. If your partner sits on the edge of a chair, with his legs apart, you can squat between his knees, resting your arms on his thighs for support.

Kneeling

This may be less tiring than squatting, and is also a good position to push from. A helper on each side will make you feel more stable. You may also find kneeling down on all fours comfortable; keep your back straight.

WHAT YOUR PARTNER CAN DO

★ Try to relax her between the contractions, and continue to give encouragement and support.
★ Tell her what you can see as the baby's head emerges, but don't be surprised if she doesn't notice you during the birth.

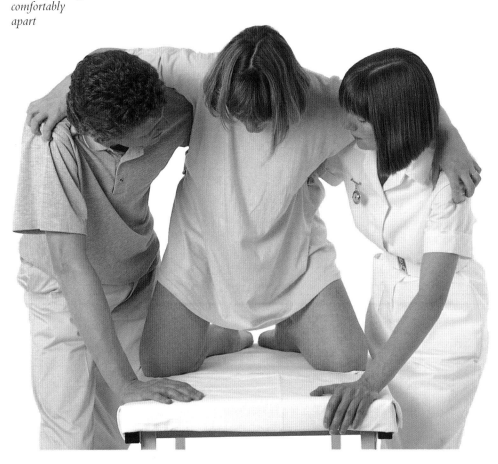

THE BIRTH

The climax of labour has now arrived, and your baby is about to be born. After all your hard work, you can actually touch your baby's head for the first time as it emerges, if you want to.

Your partner's company may calm you and give you confidence during the long hours of labour and delivery. If you have both been to childbirth classes, you have trained together for this moment. Your partner can coach and support you and remind you of breathing and relaxation techniques. The sheer force of the muscular contractions can make you feel that your body has been taken over and rendered powerless. You experience physical sensations that are completely new to you. Your partner can rub your back, sponge your brow, and count you through the contractions so that you can push with them. His involvement will help him to feel that he is a more integral part of the birthing process. If your partner is not able to be there, you will appreciate the help of a close friend or relative.

You will hold your baby very soon and will probably feel a great sense of physical relief, but there may also be wonder, emotional tears of joy, or perhaps a feeling of great tenderness towards your baby. Exhausting, painful, and emotionally overwhelming, the birth of your baby will certainly be one of the most memorable and extraordinary experiences of your life.

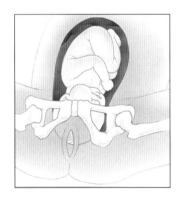
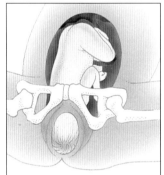
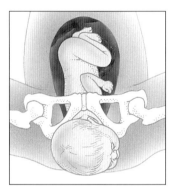
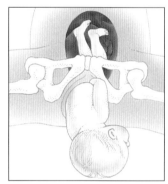

1 The baby's head moves nearer the vaginal opening, until eventually your partner will be able to see the bulge where it is pressing against the pelvic floor. Soon the head itself will be seen, moving forwards with each contraction, and perhaps slipping back slightly as the contraction fades. Don't be discouraged if this happens; it is perfectly normal.

2 When the head "crowns" (the top is visible), the midwife will ask you not to push, because if the head is born too quickly, your skin might tear. So, relax, and pant like a dog for a few seconds. If there is a risk of a serious tear, or the baby is distressed, you will have an episiotomy (see page 66). As the head widens the vaginal opening, there will be a stinging feeling, but this only lasts for a short while, and is soon followed by numbness because the tissues have been stretched so much.

3 The head is born face down. The midwife will probably check the umbilical cord, to make sure it isn't looped around the baby's neck (if it is, the cord can usually be slipped over the head when the body is delivered.) Then, the baby turns her head to one side so that it is in line with her shoulders. The midwife cleans her eyes, nose, and mouth, and, if necessary, sucks out any fluid from her upper air passages through a tube.

4 The body comes sliding out within the next two contractions. The midwife will usually lift the baby up under her armpits and deliver her on to your stomach, still joined to the cord. Your baby will probably look rather blue at first. She may be covered in vernix, and have streaks of blood on her skin. She may be crying. If she is breathing normally, you can hold her at once, and put her to the breast. Otherwise, the midwife may clear her airways again and, if necessary, give her oxygen.

Q&A **"I'm very worried about permanently damaging myself during the birth of my baby. Is there any danger of this occurring?"**

You won't damage yourself as you push. The vaginal walls are elastic, and made of folds, so they can stretch to allow the baby through.

Q&A **"Should I breast-feed my baby immediately after the birth?"**

Try offering your baby the breast and leave the decision up to her. Although there won't be any milk yet, a newborn baby's urge to suck is often quite strong, and your baby will find the sucking comforting.

THE APGAR SCORE

Immediately after birth, the midwife will assess the baby's breathing, heart rate, skin colour, movements, and response to stimulation, and give her an Apgar score of between 0 and 10.

Most babies score between 7 and 10. The test is done again about five minutes later, so even if the score was initially low, it should have improved the second time around.

THE THIRD STAGE

During, or just after, the birth, you will probably be given an injection of a drug call syntometrine in your thigh, which makes the womb contract strongly, and delivers the placenta almost immediately. You may lose more blood and there is a risk of haemorrhaging if you wait for the placenta to be expelled naturally. Talk to the midwife beforehand.

To deliver the placenta, the midwife puts her hand on your stomach, and gently pulls the umbilical cord with her other hand to help the placenta come away. Afterwards, the midwife checks the placenta to ensure it is complete.

AFTER THE BIRTH

You will be cleaned up, and stitched if necessary. The midwife will weigh and measure the baby, and quickly check all is well.

The baby may be given a vitamin K injection to prevent a rare bleeding disorder. The umbilical cord will probably be clamped and cut soon after the delivery, especially if syntometrine has been given.

Becoming a family
After birth, you can relax and spend a few quiet moments alone with your new baby.

PAIN RELIEF

Although labour is not usually pain free, the pain does have a purpose; every contraction brings you one step nearer the birth of your baby. However determined you may be now not to have pain relief, do try to keep an open mind. Whether you need it or not depends very much on your labour and your ability to deal with pain. You may be able to cope using the self-help methods on pages 59 and 61; pain is always worse if you try to fight it. But if the discomfort is more than you can bear, ask for pain relief, and don't feel a failure.

Gas and air
You regulate the gas that you breathe, and can move around freely.

Hold *the mask firmly against your face*

EPIDURAL

An epidural is an anaesthetic that relieves pain by temporarily numbing the nerves in the lower body. It can be especially good in a backache labour. Not all hospitals offer epidurals.

The epidural must be timed very carefully, so its effects have worn off by the second stage. Otherwise, you will take longer to push the baby out, and this increases the likelihood of having an episiotomy and a forceps delivery.

What happens
An epidural takes about 20 minutes to set up. You will be asked to tuck your knees up under your chin, so that your back is rounded. The anaesthetic is injected through a tube into your lower back. This is left in place, so that you can be given top-ups as necessary; the anaesthetic wears off in about two hours. You will have a drip in your arm, and be monitored continually. Movement may be restricted but some hospitals offer an epidural that allows you to walk around.

Effects
You If the epidural works properly, you should feel no pain, and remain fully aware of what is happening. Some women feel faint, and have a headache that may last for a few hours afterwards. Your legs may feel rather heavy for several hours.
The baby None.

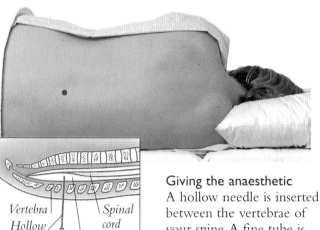

Giving the anaesthetic
A hollow needle is inserted between the vertebrae of your spine. A fine tube is passed through the needle, and local anaesthetic fed directly into this.

Vertebra
Hollow needle
Spinal cord
Epidural space

ENTONOX *(gas and air)*
A mixture of oxygen and nitrous oxide, entonox gives good pain relief to most women.

What happens
You inhale the gas through a hand-held mask, so you control it. It takes about half a minute to reach a peak so you need to breathe deeply when a contraction starts.

Effects
You May not provide enough pain relief with entonox. You may feel light-headed or sick while inhaling the gas.
The baby None.

PETHIDINE
Given by injection early in first stage of labour. Pethidine doesn't actually decrease pain but it will help to calm and relax you during labour.

What happens
Pethidine will probably be given by injection in your buttock or thigh. It takes about 20 minutes to work and its effects last about two to three hours.

Effects
You It makes some women feel out of control or "high", others relaxed and drowsy. You may experience vomiting.
The baby If given too close to the birth, can slow baby's breathing and make him sleepy.

MEPTID *(meptazinol)*
This is a drug similar to pethidine, but with the advantage that it has less effect on the baby and so can be given at any stage of labour. You can control the dose yourself via a system that delivers it into your arm. Like pethidine, it may make you sick.

TENS

This treatment lessens pain and stimulates the body's natural system of pain relief through small impulses of electric current on your back. It helps to practise with the TENS machine in the last month before the birth. So, if your hospital doesn't have one to lend you, ask your local branch of the NCT if they can help.

What happens

Four pads containing electrodes are stuck on to your back, over the nerves that supply the womb. These pads are joined by wires to a hand-held control, with which you regulate the strength, frequency, and length of time of the electric current to suit yourself.

Effects

You TENS can lessen the pain considerably for some women, especially if used from early labour. Others say it is no help at all. If labour is very painful, TENS probably won't be sufficient.
The baby None.

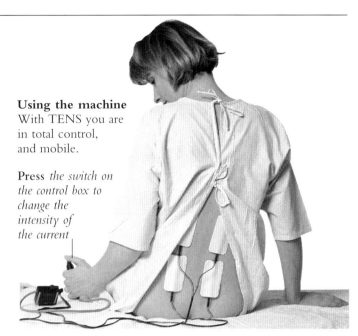

Using the machine
With TENS you are in total control, and mobile.

Press *the switch on the control box to change the intensity of the current*

MONITORING

Throughout labour your baby's heartbeat will be monitored so that any signs of distress can be detected as early as possible. This will be done either with a hand-held fetal stethoscope, a sonicaid, or an electronic monitor.

FETAL STETHOSCOPE OR SONICAID

The midwife places the instrument on your stomach at regular intervals throughout labour to listen to the baby's heartbeat.

ELECTRONIC FETAL MONITORING *(EFM)*

This is a way of recording the baby's heartbeat and your contractions using sophisticated electronic equipment. Some hospitals routinely monitor women throughout labour, others only at intervals unless:
★ your labour is induced (see page 66)
★ you are having an epidural
★ you have a problem or condition that puts you or the baby at risk
★ the baby is distressed at any time.
  EFM is not painful, but it does restrict your freedom to move

around, which may make your contractions more uncomfortable. The procedure is perfectly safe for both you and your baby, and if your doctor or midwife suggests continual monitoring it is probably because they believe it is in the best interests of your baby.

What happens

You will probably be asked to sit or lie on the hospital bed with your trunk well supported by pillows, and small pads will be strapped to your abdomen, to monitor the baby's heartbeat and measure your contractions. These appear on a paper print-out attached to the monitor. Later in labour, when your waters have broken, the baby's heartbeat can be measured directly by clipping an electrode to his head. This is the most accurate kind of monitoring, but it may be uncomfortable.

  A few hospitals use a remote-control system of monitoring by radio waves, called telemetry. The advantage of this is that you are not attached to a large machine, so you can move about freely during labour. Enquire at the hospital if this is available.

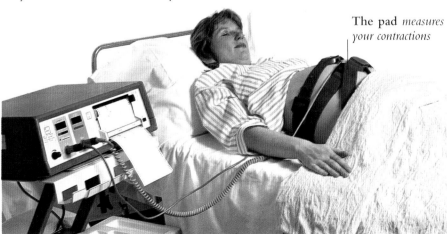

The pad *measures your contractions*

SPECIAL PROCEDURES

EPISIOTOMY	ASSISTED DELIVERY	INDUCTION
This small cut widens the vaginal opening and prevents a tear. Some hospitals perform episiotomies more often than others, so speak to an approachable midwife about the trends in your hospital. To avoid an episiotomy or a tear: ★ learn how to relax your pelvic floor muscles (see page 45) ★ stay upright during the delivery.	Sometimes the baby has to be helped out with forceps or by suction. Forceps are used only when the cervix is fully dilated, and the baby's head has engaged, although suction may be used occasionally before full dilation if labour is prolonged.	If you are induced, labour has to be started artificially. Some of the methods may be used to speed up labour if it is going slowly. Hospital policies on induction vary from place to place, so find out from your hospital how long you can wait before being induced.
When used An episiotomy may be needed if: ★ the baby is breech, premature, distressed, or has a big head ★ you have an assisted delivery ★ you are having difficulty controlling your pushing ★ the skin around your vaginal opening hasn't stretched enough.	**When used** You may have an assisted delivery if: ★ you cannot push the baby out, perhaps because he has a big head ★ you or the baby shows signs of distress during the labour ★ your baby is breech or premature; the forceps protect his head from pressure in the birth canal.	**When used** Labour may be induced if: ★ it is more than a week past the baby's due date, and he shows signs of being distressed or the placenta starts to fail ★ you have high blood pressure, or another problem or condition that puts you or the baby at risk.
What happens Your pelvic floor area will probably be numbed with an injection of local anaesthetic, and a small cut is made from the bottom of the vagina, usually slightly out to one side, at the peak of a contraction. Sometimes there is no time for an injection, but the stretching of the tissues also numbs them, so you shouldn't feel any pain. Stitching up after an episiotomy or a tear may take some time, as the different layers of skin and muscle have to be carefully sewn together. It can be painful, too, so ask for more anaesthetic if you need some. The stitches are soluble and do not have to be removed.	**What happens** ★ **Forceps** You will probably be given an injection of local anaesthetic into your pelvic floor area, and an episiotomy. The doctor positions the forceps on either side of the baby's head and gently pulls to deliver the head. You can help by pushing. The rest of your baby's body is delivered normally. **Forceps** These form a cage around the baby's head, protecting it from pressure and damage. ★ **Vacuum** A small plastic cup, connected to a vacuum pump, is passed into the vagina and attached to the baby's head. The baby is gently pulled through the birth canal, as you push.	**What happens** Induction is always planned in advance, and you will probably be asked to go into hospital the night before. Labour may be induced in three ways: **1** Inserting a pessary into the vagina containing a hormone that softens the cervix. This is done in the evening or very early morning. You may go into labour within an hour or so, but the pessary is not usually very effective on its own in a first pregnancy. **2** Breaking your waters. If labour still has not started within 8 to 12 hours, the doctor makes a small hole in the bag of waters surrounding the baby. Most women don't feel any pain. Contractions nearly always start soon afterwards. **3** Giving you a hormone, which makes the womb contract. This is fed through a drip in your arm at a controlled rate. Ask for the drip to be inserted into the arm you use least.
Effects Some discomfort and soreness is normal after an episiotomy, but the pain can be quite severe, especially if an infection develops. The wound should heal within 10 to 14 days, but if you are sore after this time, go to see your doctor. There is usually less pain with a natural tear.	**Effects** ★ If forceps are used to deliver your baby, they may leave pressure marks or bruises on either side of the baby's head. However, these are harmless and will disappear within a few days of the birth. ★ The vacuum cup will cause slight swelling, and later a bruise, on the baby's head. This gradually subsides.	**Effects** Induction by pessary is preferable, as you avoid having your waters broken and you will still be able to move around freely. With the drip especially, your contractions may be stronger and more painful, with shorter intervals between them than in labour that has started naturally. Your mobility is restricted,

CAESAREAN SECTION

BREECH BIRTH

A breech baby is born bottom first. In a breech birth, the baby's head will be more vulnerable to pressure as it passes along the birth canal. This is because the birth canal has not been sufficiently stretched by the buttocks. About four in 100 births are breech.

As the largest part of the baby (the head) is born last, this is usually measured by ultrasound towards the end of pregnancy, to check that it is small enough to fit through your pelvis.

Labour with a breech baby can be more prolonged and more difficult than a head down presentation and must always take place in hospital. You will need an episiotomy, and forceps are commonly used. Occasionally a Caesarean will be necessary if you have a breech baby, and it is the policy of some hospitals to deliver all breech babies like this.

TWINS

It is essential to have twins in hospital. Forceps delivery or a Caesarean section may be necessary and the babies may be small and need special care. You will probably be advised to have an epidural (see page 64) too.

There is only one first stage, but you will have two second stages as you push first one baby out, and then the other. The second twin is usually born 10 to 30 minutes after the first.

With a Caesarean birth, the baby is delivered abdominally. You may know you are going to have a Caesarean in advance, or it may be an emergency operation because of problems in labour. If a Caesarean is planned, you can have it under an epidural (see page 64), so you are awake throughout and can hold your baby straight away. This may also be possible if you are told in labour you need the operation, but sometimes a general anaesthetic is necessary.

It's only natural to feel disappointed, and perhaps cheated of a normal delivery, if you need a Caesarean. But these feelings can be minimized if you prepare yourself thoroughly. Ask your hospital if your birth partner can be with you throughout.

WHAT HAPPENS

Your pubic hair will be shaved, a drip will be put in your arm, and a tube inserted into your bladder. You will be given the anaesthetic. If you are having an epidural, a screen is often set up between you and the surgeon. The cut is usually made horizontally, and the surgeon drains away the amniotic fluid. The baby is lifted out, sometimes with forceps. You can hold him as the placenta is delivered. The start of surgery to the birth usually takes about five minutes. A further 20 minutes or so are spent stitching you.

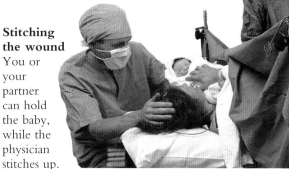

Stitching the wound
You or your partner can hold the baby, while the physician stitches up.

The incision
The "bikini" cut is usually made horizontally, just above the pubic hairline, and it is almost invisible when it heals.

AFTER THE OPERATION

You will be encouraged to walk soon after the birth. The incision will be painful for a few days, so ask for pain relief. Moving around won't open it up. Stand tall, and cup your hands over the wound. By about two days after the operation, begin gentle exercise (see page 72), and a day or so later, when the dressing is removed, you can have a bath. The stitches will be removed five days after birth, unless soluble, and you will feel much better after a week. Avoid straining yourself for at least six weeks. The scar fades, usually in three to six months.

How to breast-feed
Support your baby on one or two pillows beside you, so he is not resting on the wound.

YOUR NEW BABY

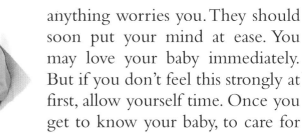

Your baby will probably look very different from what you expected. He will probably seem smaller than you imagined, and very vulnerable. The shape of his head may seem rather strange, and you are bound to notice spots, blotches, and changes of colour, all of which are perfectly normal. Ask your doctor or midwife if anything worries you. They should soon put your mind at ease. You may love your baby immediately. But if you don't feel this strongly at first, allow yourself time. Once you get to know your baby, to care for him and cuddle him, when you find that he responds to you and is soothed by the sound of your voice, love will grow naturally.

FIRST IMPRESSIONS

Don't be dismayed if your baby doesn't look perfect – few babies do at birth. You may notice some red marks and other blemishes, but most of these will disappear by the time the baby is about two weeks old.

HEAD
A strange shape is usually caused by the pressure of birth. The head should look normal in two weeks.
On the top of the head is a soft spot (fontanelle), where the bones of the skull have not yet joined together. They should fuse by the time the child is 18 months.

EYES
These are usually blue at birth. True eye colour may not develop until the baby is about six months old.
Puffy eyelids are usually caused by the pressure of birth, but ask the doctor or midwife to check your baby's eyes, as there is sometimes an infection.
Squinting is common. The baby may look cross-eyed at times in the first months.

TONGUE
This may seem anchored to the floor of the mouth, so that the tip looks slightly forked when the baby sticks it out. The tip will grow forwards in the first year.

HANDS AND FEET
These may be bluish because the baby's circulation is not working properly. If you move your baby into another position, they should turn pink.
The fingernails are often long at birth; carefully trim using special baby scissors.

BREASTS
Your baby's breasts may be swollen and even leak a little milk. This is perfectly normal in both sexes. The swelling should go down within two days; do not squeeze the milk out.

GENITALS
These look large on both male and female babies.
A baby girl may have discharge from her vagina. This is caused by the mother's hormones and will soon disappear.
The testicles of a baby boy are often pulled up into his groin. If worried, see your doctor.

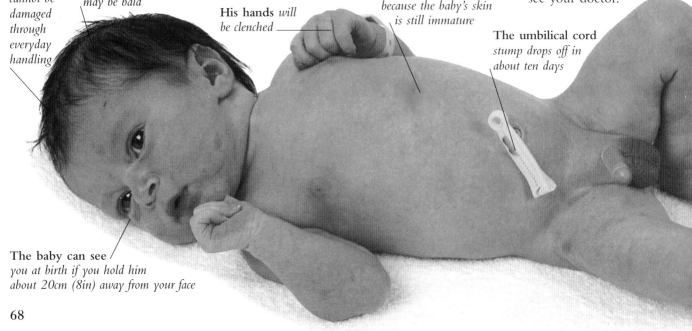

The fontanelle *cannot be damaged through everyday handling*

Your baby *may have a good head of hair, or he may be bald*

His hands *will be clenched*

Red marks *are caused by pressure from the birth, or because the baby's skin is still immature*

The umbilical cord *stump drops off in about ten days*

The baby can see *you at birth if you hold him about 20cm (8in) away from your face*

CHECKS ON THE BABY

SKIN

Spots and rashes are very common, and should vanish of their own accord.

Peeling skin, especially on the hands and feet, should go in a couple of days.

Downy body hair (lanugo) may be noticeable, especially if the baby was born early. This rubs off within two weeks.

Greasy white vernix is the substance that protects the baby's skin in the womb, and may cover him completely. It can be easily wiped off.

Birthmarks usually vanish. These include:
★ red marks (stork bites), often found on the eyelids, forehead, and at the back of the neck; they take about a year to go
★ strawberry birthmarks, which can be worrying as they gradually increase in size; they usually disappear by the time the child is five
★ blue patches (Mongolian blue spots), often found on the lower backs of babies with dark skin
★ port wine stain, a bright-red or purple mark, which is permanent.

STOOL

At birth, the baby's bowel contains a dark, sticky substance called meconium. Once he starts to feed, the stool changes colour.

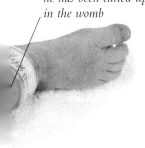

The baby's legs
often look bowed because he has been curled up in the womb

Your baby will be examined several times in the first week. The midwife will weigh him regularly, and check him daily for any problems or signs of infection. She also does one other test (the Guthrie test, see below) when the baby is about six days old. In addition, the baby will be thoroughly examined by a doctor at least once in the first few days. This is a good time to discuss any worries that you may have.

GENERAL EXAMINATION
The doctor will check the baby from head to toe to ensure there is nothing abnormal.

1 The doctor may measure the head, and looks for any abnormalities. He checks the fontanelle, and feels the roof of the mouth to make sure it is complete.

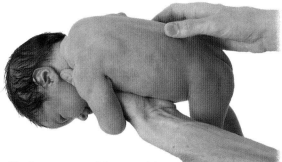

2 He listens to the heart and lungs to see if they are normal. Heart murmur is common among newborn babies, and does not usually indicate a defect.

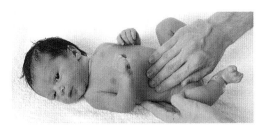

3 By putting his hand on the baby's tummy, the doctor checks that the abdominal organs are the right size. He also feels the pulses in the baby's groin.

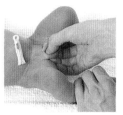 

4 The genitals are checked for abnormality. If you have a boy, the doctor will be looking to see if both testicles have descended.

5 He gently moves the baby's limbs to and fro, and checks that the lower legs and feet are in alignment, that the legs are the right length, and that the baby doesn't suffer from club foot.

6 The doctor checks the hips for any dislocation, by bending the baby's legs up and gently circling them.

THE GUTHRIE TEST
This test is usually done at home by the midwife six or seven days after birth. A blood sample taken via a small prick on the baby's heel is tested for PKU (a rare cause of mental handicap), thyroid deficiency, and other blood disorders.

7 He runs his thumb down the baby's back, making sure that all the vertebrae are in place along the spine.

BABIES NEEDING SPECIAL CARE

Some babies need special care after birth. This is usually because they are premature (babies born before 37 weeks), or small for dates (see page 39). These babies are more likely to have problems with breathing, feeding, and maintaining their temperature, and so need special treatment and monitoring. The time that your baby has to spend in special care is bound to be difficult for you. Not only will you be separated from her before you have got to know her, but you will have to become used to seeing her surrounded by the intimidating array of equipment that is keeping her safe. This can seem quite frightening at first, but it helps if you ask the staff to explain what the equipment is for.

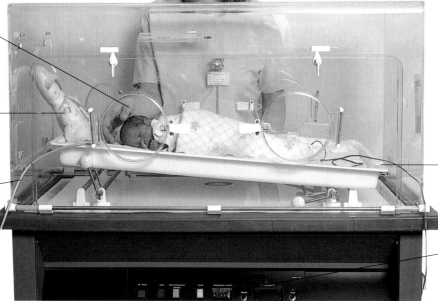

Portholes, *so you can touch your baby and talk to her*

You may like *to bring along a soft toy for your baby*

Feeding tube, *which passes into the baby's stomach; you can express your own milk to be fed to the baby*

The baby in the incubator
Your baby needs just as much love and attention as any normal healthy baby.

Tilting tray, *to help with respiration and feeding*

Control, *to regulate the temperature inside the incubator*

GETTING TO KNOW YOUR BABY
It's important to spend as much time with your baby as possible; many hospitals have special rooms you can stay in, so you are near to your baby and can take part in her daily care. At first, she may look so small and vulnerable that you worry about touching her. But, all babies respond to loving handling, and even if she can't be taken out of the incubator and cuddled, which some babies can, you can still talk to her and stroke her through the portholes in the side. You may even be able to help with changing her nappy and dressing her.

ASKING QUESTIONS
Ask the doctor or nursing staff about anything that worries you. Often parents don't ask questions, because their baby looks so frail that they are afraid of the reply. But with modern intensive care, even babies born before 28 weeks can survive.

FEEDING
If the baby can suck, you may be able to feed her normally. Otherwise, she will be fed through a tube, which is passed through her nose or mouth and down into her stomach.

JAUNDICE
Many newborn babies develop very mild jaundice about three days after birth, which turns their skin and the whites of the eyes slightly yellow. This happens because a baby's liver is still immature, and a pigment called bilirubin accumulates in the blood faster than the liver can dispose of it.

Jaundice usually clears up in a few days of its own accord, although the baby may be more sleepy than usual, so wake her up often, and encourage her to feed. It also helps if her cot is near a window so she is exposed to sunlight. Sometimes jaundice has to be treated with a special light (phototherapy). This can usually be done on the postnatal ward, and only in a few severe cases is the baby taken into special care.

STILLBIRTH
Very rarely, a baby is born dead. What makes this so hard to bear is that you never knew your child. It's probably a good idea to see him after birth; by holding him, and giving him a name, you can grieve for him as a person, and you need to do this. You will probably feel angry, and want to know what went wrong, and find something or someone to blame. Shame and guilt are also quite common. Ask your doctor to put you in touch with a group of people who have had a stillbirth.

GETTING BACK TO NORMAL

For the first week after delivery, try to rest whenever you can. Don't be tempted to use your spare time to catch up on all the things you haven't had time to do. The midwife will visit you at home until the baby is at least ten days old. She will check your womb, breasts, and any stitches, and will help you with your new baby. You may be rather dismayed when you see your body after birth. Your bump will be gone, but your tummy won't be flat yet. Your breasts will be large, and the tops of your legs will feel heavy. But if you practise your postnatal exercises from the first day after birth, you should soon look and feel better.

HOW YOU WILL FEEL

You will probably have some discomfort, and even pain, in the first days after birth. Ask the midwife if anything worries you.

AFTER PAINS
You may feel cramping pains in your stomach, especially when breast-feeding, as the womb contracts back to its pre-pregnant size. This is a good sign that your body is returning to normal. The pains may last several days. **What to do** If contractions are severe, a mild pain-killer such as paracetamol may ease them.

BLADDER
It's normal to pass more water in the first days, as the body loses the extra fluid gained in pregnancy.

What to do Urinating may be difficult at first, because of soreness, but try to do so as soon as possible after birth.
★ Get up and about to encourage the flow.
★ Soak in a warm bath. Don't worry if you pass urine into the water, as urine is sterile; wash yourself well afterwards.
★ If you have stitches, try pouring warm water over them as you pass urine to stop your skin stinging.

BLEEDING
You may have vaginal bleeding for anything from two to six weeks. This usually stops more quickly if you are breast-feeding. The bright-red discharge is heavy at first, but over the next few days it gets less and gradually becomes brownish. Often the discharge continues until the first menstrual period.
What to do Wear sanitary pads to catch the flow; don't use internal tampons, they can cause infection.

BOWELS
You may not need to empty your bowels for a day or more after the birth.
What to do Get mobile as soon as possible: this will start your bowels working.
★ Drink plenty of water and eat high-fibre foods to stimulate your bowels.
★ When you want to open your bowels, do so at once, but don't strain or push.
★ It is most unlikely that any stitches will tear when you move your bowels, but holding a clean sanitary pad against the area while you do so may feel good and give you confidence.

STITCHES
These may be very sore for a day or two. Most dissolve in about a week.
What to do The following suggestions will help.
★ Practice pelvic floor exercises as soon as possible after birth to speed up healing.
★ Keep stitches clean by relaxing in a warm bath. Dry the area thoroughly afterwards.
★ Soothe soreness by applying an ice-pack to the area.
★ Lie down to take pressure off the stitches, or sit on a rubber ring.

COPING WITH THE BLUES
Many women feel low a few days after delivery, usually when the milk comes in. One cause is the sudden change in hormone levels, another is the feeling of anti-climax that inevitably occurs after birth. These postnatal blues usually vanish. If you feel depressed for more than four weeks, or your depression is very severe, see your doctor or talk to your health visitor.

Thinking positively
The sheer pleasure and delight of having your newborn baby will probably more than compensate for the after-effects of birth.

SHAPING UP AFTER BIRTH

With some gentle exercising every day, your figure can return to normal again in as little as three months after the birth, although your stomach muscles may not be as firm as before. Build up your exercise programme slowly at first, as your ligaments are still soft and stretchy, and always stop straight away if you feel pain or tiredness. It's best to exercise little but on a regular basis.

WEEK ONE
You can begin to strengthen the stretched, and possibly weakened, muscles of your pelvic floor and stomach from the first day after birth. The pelvic floor and foot pedalling excercises are also good if you have had a Caesarean.

PELVIC FLOOR EXERCISE *from day one*
Practise gentle squeezing and lifting exercises (see page 45) as often as possible every day to stop yourself leaking urine involuntarily. It's important to do this before you go on to the exercises in week two. If you have had stitches, strengthening the pelvic floor will help them to heal.

FOOT PEDALLING *from day one*
This will guard against swelling in the legs and improve circulation. Bend your feet up and down at the ankle. Practise hourly.

STOMACH TONER *from day one*
A gentle way to strengthen these muscles is to pull them in as you breathe out, hold them in for a few seconds, then relax. Try to do this as often as possible.

From day five after birth, if you feel all right, practise the following exercise twice a day, too:

1 Lie on your back, with your head and shoulders supported on two pillows, and your legs bent and slightly apart. Cross your arms over your stomach.

2 Lift your head and shoulders, and as you do this, breathe out and press gently on each side of your stomach with the palms of your hands, as if pulling the two sides together. Hold this position for a few seconds, then breathe in, and relax. Repeat three times.

WEEK TWO
After about a week, try the following exercises as a daily routine, and continue for at least three months. Repeat each exercise as many times as is comfortable. Begin with the curl downs, and when you can do these easily, move on to the other exercises. If you find the new exercises strain you, practise the curl downs for a few days longer. Remember to keep practising the exercise for your pelvic floor.

CURL DOWNS
1 Sit up, with your legs bent and slightly apart, and your arms folded in front of you.

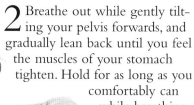

2 Breathe out while gently tilting your pelvis forwards, and gradually lean back until you feel the muscles of your stomach tighten. Hold for as long as you comfortably can while breathing normally. Then breathe in and sit up straight.

SIDE BENDS

1 Lie flat on your back with your arms by your side, and the palms of your hands resting on the outsides of your thighs.

2 Lift your head slightly, and bending to the left, slide your left hand down your leg. Lie back and rest for a moment, then repeat on your right side. As this becomes easy, try bending to each side two or three times before you lie back and rest.

CURL UPS

1 Lie flat on your back on the floor, with your knees bent and your feet slightly apart. Rest your hands on your thighs.

2 Breathe out, and lift your head and shoulders, stretching forwards to touch your knees with your hands. Don't worry if you can't reach far enough at first, you will with practise. Breathe in and relax.

WHEN THIS IS EASY, TRY:

★ lifting yourself up more slowly and holding the position for longer
★ placing your hands on your chest as you lift your head and shoulders
★ clasping your hands behind your head as you lift yourself up.

CHECKING YOUR PELVIC FLOOR

By three months after birth, these muscles should be strong again. Test them by skipping. If any urine leaks, practise the pelvic floor exercises for another month and try again. If leaking is still problem after four months, see your doctor.

HOW YOUR BODY RECOVERS

Your body won't be fully recovered for at least six months after the birth of your baby. However, by the time you visit your GP or the hospital for your six-week check-up, your body should be getting back to normal. Your womb may have shrunk back to its pre-pregnant size and you may have started your periods again. If you have been practising your postnatal exercises regularly, your muscles should be in far better shape.

THE SIX-WEEK CHECK-UP

About six weeks after the birth you will have a check-up at the hospital or at the doctor's surgery. It is a good time to discuss any worries with the doctor or nurse who gives the check-up.

What happens

★ Your blood pressure, weight, and a sample of urine will be checked.
★ Your breasts and stomach will be examined. The doctor will check that any stiches have healed.
★ You will have an internal examination to check the size and position of the womb, and may be given a cervical smear test.
★ The doctor will discuss contraception; you can be fitted with a cap or coil.

YOUR PERIODS

The first period after the birth is often longer and heavier than usual. When it arrives depends on how you are feeding your baby. If you are breast-feeding, your periods may not start until after your baby is weaned. If you are bottle-feeding, the first period usually comes four to six weeks after the birth.

Q&A "When can we resume our sex life?"

The best time to start making love again is when you are both ready. You may feel too sore and tender to resume sex until after the post-natal check-up, or you may want to try sooner – it's up to you.

When you resume your sex life, take it slowly. Relax as much as you can, and use extra lubrication, as your vagina may be slightly drier then normal.

Q&A "I'm breast-feeding my baby; do we still have to use contraception?"

Even if you are breast-feeding or haven't started your periods again, you need to use contraception. The doctor or midwife will discuss this with you soon after the birth. If you want to go on the pill, make sure the doctor knows you are breast-feeding; if you previously used a cap, you must have a new one fitted as your cervix will have changed shape.

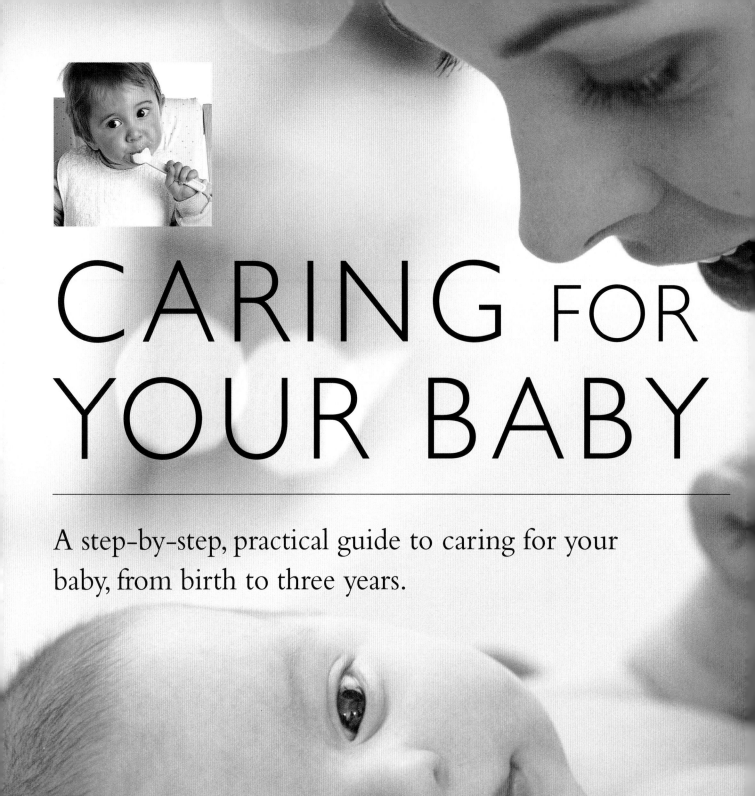

CARING FOR
YOUR BABY

A step-by-step, practical guide to caring for your
baby, from birth to three years.

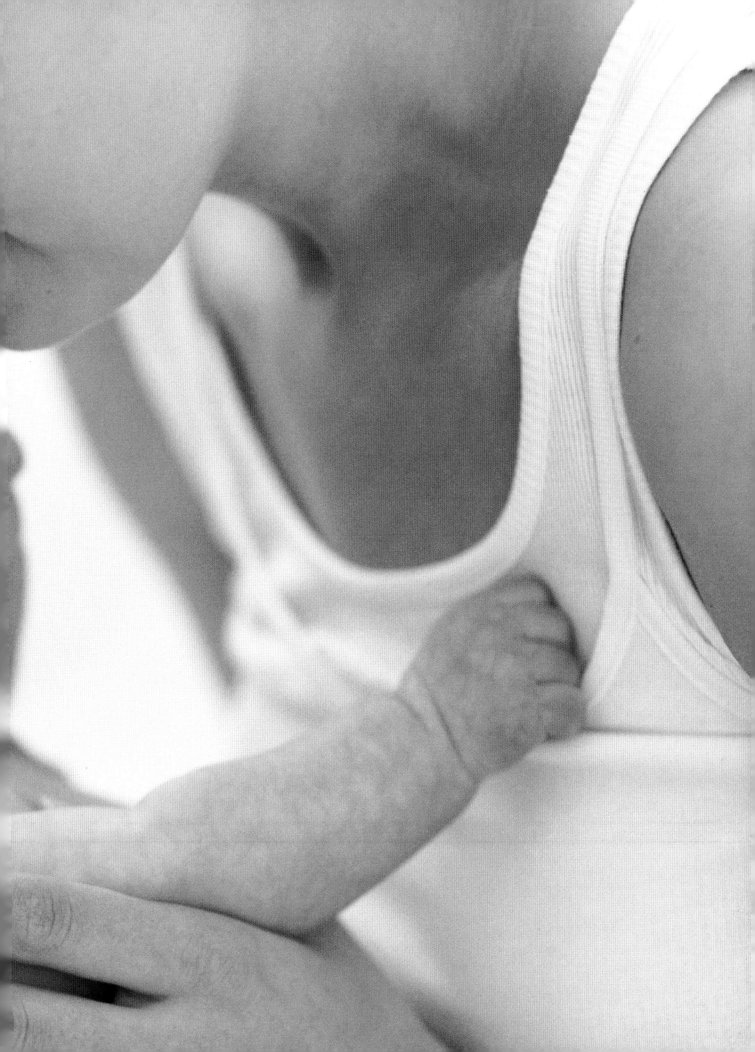

THE FIRST WEEKS OF LIFE

Nothing can really prepare you for the reality of having a child. The first weeks of your baby's life seem like a chaotic whirlwind of new experiences and sensations, as you get to know this new person in your lives and adapt to being a parent. You have so much to learn: how to feed and nourish your baby, how to dress her and care for her skin, what she likes and what she doesn't. Looking after a new baby involves a combination of warmth, attention, and responsiveness, and although some of this will be instinctive, some has to be learnt – by both of you. You'll learn new skills too: before long, eating one-handed while your baby feeds will be second nature. But the early phase of adjustment and·chaos won't last long. This chapter tells how one couple and their new baby Amy coped in the first few weeks.

"The first weeks weren't easy. You think you're a capable, confident person, then you have a helpless baby to look after and you feel like jelly!"

First days at home
Life with your new baby will take you by surprise. Her apparent vulnerability produces powerful feelings within you, while a turmoil of emotions makes you burst into tears for no known reason or become distressed by, say, the television news. Don't fight your feelings; concentrate on the new life that you are nurturing.

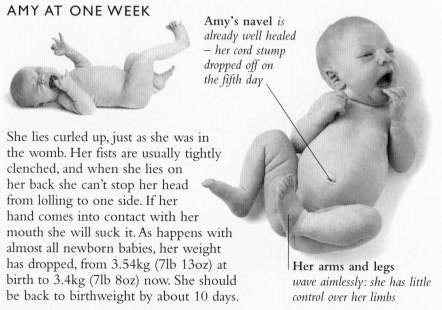

AMY AT ONE WEEK

Amy's navel is already well healed – her cord stump dropped off on the fifth day

She lies curled up, just as she was in the womb. Her fists are usually tightly clenched, and when she lies on her back she can't stop her head from lolling to one side. If her hand comes into contact with her mouth she will suck it. As happens with almost all newborn babies, her weight has dropped, from 3.54kg (7lb 13oz) at birth to 3.4kg (7lb 8oz) now. She should be back to birthweight by about 10 days.

Her arms and legs *wave aimlessly: she has little control over her limbs*

Amy asleep
Newborn babies sleep an average of 16 hours a day, but Amy sometimes slept as little as 10 or 11 hours in total, with a long, stormy period from late afternoon to late at night when she only dozed for very short periods. During her times of deep sleep Amy was oblivious to her surroundings. Within five weeks Amy had adopted a more sociable sleep pattern, with a longer sleep during the night and an earlier bedtime.

BECOMING A FAMILY

Now there are three of you, and everything changes. Your partner is no longer just your lover, he's your companion and ally in this new adventure of parenthood – and she's as much his baby as yours. Your tried and tested family relationships will subtly change too: you're not just a son or a daughter any more, you're a parent, with a new life depending on you. No matter how topsy-turvy your life seems at this time, try to make time for your partner. Often it's the new father who is most shell-shocked in the days immediately following the birth, and he needs your support as much as you need his. Talk to each other about your feelings and let him share in the care of the baby: he may be more nervous than you of handling her floppy little body, but he will soon grow more confident.

"The first days were such a tangle of conflicting feelings – elation and overwhelming pride at being a father, anxiety about Ruth, exhaustion from the round-the-clock demands of our new baby, even a tiny regret that our happy, carefree life together seemed to be at an end."

AMY'S DAY

"Amy seemed insatiably hungry. Ruth was good at expressing her milk, so in the evenings when Amy would cry inconsolably for hours at a stretch, I could take over with a bottle. I took over the nappy-changing too, to give Ruth a break. I was surprised to find I even loved that – it was one way Amy and I built a closeness together. We would play little games, or I would pull funny faces, or introduce her to her feet and hands."

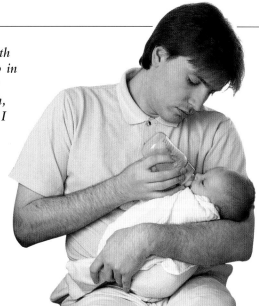

Building a loving relationship

Right from the beginning, your relationship with your new baby is an intense, two-way one that will grow into a real and lasting love. As you bring her up close to talk and coo to her, she will gaze raptly at your face – and eye contact plays a big part when you are falling in love. She will reward your efforts to calm her by quietening at the sound of your voice. And when she's miserable, she wants you to comfort her.

A TYPICAL DAY AT AROUND THREE WEEKS OF AGE

9am	**Ruth is woken** by Amy crying next to her in the bed: she had a feed there at 5am, and they both fell asleep together. Amy has another feed now.	**1pm**	**Amy cries** for a feed, and afterwards they doze off together on the sofa.
10am	**Ruth takes Amy** into the bathroom to change her nappy and clothes, and top and tail her. Then she puts Amy in the carrycot and chats to her while she dresses herself.	**3.30pm**	**The health visitor's** ring on the doorbell wakes Ruth. She has some advice on how to relieve Ruth's sore nipples, then wakes Amy to examine her.
11am	**Amy falls asleep.** Ruth puts the washing in the washing machine and tidies up, then she puts her feet up, but doesn't sleep.	**4pm**	**The health visitor** leaves, but Amy is cross from being woken, so Ruth feeds her to soothe her.
12.30pm	**Ruth has** some lunch.	**5.30pm**	**Ruth puts Amy** in the carrycot and clips it to its wheels, then she walks to the station to meet Tim. The movement puts Amy to sleep.

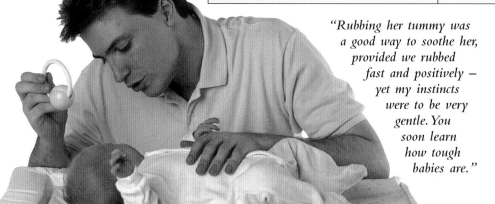

"Rubbing her tummy was a good way to soothe her, provided we rubbed fast and positively – yet my instincts were to be very gentle. You soon learn how tough babies are."

Amy crying
Crying is your baby's way of expressing her need for love and comfort. Always respond – don't leave her.

Amy wakeful
Held against your shoulder
your baby has a good view
of the world, and will
enjoy her wakeful times.

*"I was astonished at how
difficult it was to get any
small job finished during the day.
Once Tim got home from
work it was down to him
to get the supper ready –
sometimes I wouldn't
even be dressed! It was
odd for me to be so
disorganized, I wasn't
used to having so little
time for myself."*

6.15pm	**Home again**, and Amy starts to cry. Ruth feeds Amy, changes her, then rocks her in her arms. Feeding is the only thing that really soothes Amy at this time of day, but Ruth is sore, so it's painful. Tim snatches some sleep.	10pm	**Amy is still crying;** she will be soothed for a while, then cry again. Tim and Ruth let her suck, walk her around, push her to and fro in her pram.	
8.30pm	**Tim wakes up** and he and Ruth take turns to carry Amy around and prepare some food. Amy dozes off for a few minutes at a time, then wakes and cries – so supper is interrupted by short feeds at the breast and on a bottle of expressed milk.	2am	**Amy falls asleep** at last. Tim and Ruth, exhausted, go to bed.	
		4am	**Amy wakes** and cries, so Ruth takes her into bed for a feed. Tim wakes up too and helps to rock Amy back to sleep again after her feed.	
		7am	**The alarm goes off** and Tim gets up to go to work – he's had four hours' sleep plus two in the evening.	

Involving other family members
Your parents, sisters, brothers, and
other members of your family will all
be extremely keen to meet the new
baby; but don't feel guilty about
limiting visitors if you want to.

Getting plenty of rest
Every new mother has to
learn how to cope with too
little sleep. Plenty of rest
whenever you can snatch it is
the only answer – and this is
especially important if you're
breast-feeding your baby. Rest
whenever your baby is asleep,
even if you don't go to sleep
yourself. Your body isn't strong
enough yet for strenuous
work, and the housework can
go undone for now.

SIX WEEKS OLD

"By six weeks Amy was a real person – nothing like the greedy, screaming bundle of only weeks before. She responded to each of us in her own way: her first, crooked smiles were just for me, usually when I changed her, but at times only Ruth would do. We were lucky, Amy was very perky and she helped us to love her; and you certainly learn fast when you have a new baby reliant on you for every need."

PREMATURE BABIES

Your baby's first six weeks at home may be especially difficult if she was born prematurely. She may cry incessantly and refuse to be comforted; or be very sleepy and reluctant to feed. In addition to your natural anxiety about your new baby, you may feel rejected by her: she doesn't make you feel that she loves you, so it's that much harder to love her in return. Your pre-term baby will need extra care from you: she loses heat quickly, so you need to keep your home warm for her, especially when bathing or changing her, and she will need frequent feeding to help her grow. Even though she may have a small appetite and be a troublesome feeder, offer her a feed as often as every three hours, letting her take as much as she wants at each feed. Concentrate on giving the care she needs: in time your baby will grow more responsive to you, and you will learn to understand your baby better.

AMY AT SIX WEEKS

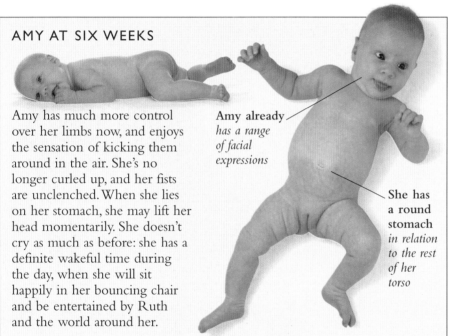

Amy already *has a range of facial expressions*

She has a round stomach *in relation to the rest of her torso*

Amy has much more control over her limbs now, and enjoys the sensation of kicking them around in the air. She's no longer curled up, and her fists are unclenched. When she lies on her stomach, she may lift her head momentarily. She doesn't cry as much as before: she has a definite wakeful time during the day, when she will sit happily in her bouncing chair and be entertained by Ruth and the world around her.

AMY'S SIX-WEEK CHECKUP

The six-week check-up is the first of the major development checks for a new baby. Your doctor or local baby clinic will perform the check in a friendly, informal atmosphere.

1 General assessment The doctor discusses Amy's general well-being and demeanour with Ruth. She wakes Amy and talks to her to assess how she responds to the stimulus of a new face. The doctor is looking for that magical early smile, a sure sign that Amy is developing a normal, sociable personality. She checks Amy's sight by moving a rattle across her field of vision. Amy follows it with both eyes, demonstrating healthy eyesight with no sign of a squint.

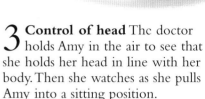

Amy already *has some control over her neck muscles*

2 Limbs and muscle tone
The doctor undresses Amy herself, so she can observe her muscle tone and how she moves her limbs.

3 Control of head The doctor holds Amy in the air to see that she holds her head in line with her body. Then she watches as she pulls Amy into a sitting position.

4 Grasp reflex A baby at birth can grasp hold of a finger put into her palm and hold on strongly. By six weeks it's normal for her birth reflexes to begin to disappear, as Amy's have.

5 Head circumference Amy has her head measured, to check for normal growth. Her head is now 15in (38cm).

6 Heartbeat The doctor listens to Amy's heart with a stethoscope: about 120 beats a minute is normal for the first year.

7 Internal organs A good feel around Amy's stomach reassures the doctor that her liver, stomach, and spleen are all growing normally, and none is too big or the wrong shape.

9 Weighing Amy has been weighed in her nappy at weekly intervals up to now, and she will be weighed at every visit to the baby clinic, or whenever Ruth requests: normal weight gain usually means a healthy baby. Amy's weight chart will be an important record for years to come.

8 Hip check Hip dislocation is a possibility still, so the doctor tests the action of the joints with her middle fingers, as she manipulates Amy's legs.

Amy's weight ___ *is recorded on her personal chart*

HANDLING YOUR BABY

From an early age, your baby needs closeness and comfort as well as food, warmth, and sleep. Talk to your baby as you handle him – your voice is familiar and reassuring. Remember that until he is about eight weeks old, he cannot control his head or muscles. You need to support his body all the time. Your normal, careful handling won't hurt him; even the soft fontanelle on his head has a tough membrane to protect it. But you may startle him if you pick him up suddenly, making him fling his limbs out. It won't be long before you're much more confident of each other. As he gains control over his muscles, your baby may enjoy boisterous games – at five months he may love to be swung above your head or perched high on your shoulders. If he's timid, respond by handling him gently until he is more outgoing.

PICKING UP AND PUTTING DOWN A NEWBORN BABY

Always put your baby on his back to sleep. He will run a much lower risk of cot death than if he sleeps on his tummy, and no more risk of choking. Side sleeping is not as safe as sleeping on the back, but much safer than front sleeping. However, when he is awake, he should spend some time each day lying on his front.

1 To pick up your baby, slide one hand under his lower back and bottom, the other under his head and neck.

2 Lift him gently and slowly, so that his body is supported and his head can't loll back.

3 Carefully transfer his head to the crook of your elbow or your shoulder, so that it is supported.

PUTTING YOUR BABY DOWN

1 Put one hand underneath his head and neck, then hold him under the bottom with the other. Lower him slowly, gently supporting him until the mat or mattress is taking his weight.

2 Slide your nearest hand out from under his bottom. Use this hand to lift his head a little so you can slide out your other hand, and lower his head down gently. Don't let his head fall back on to the surface, or jerk your arm out quickly.

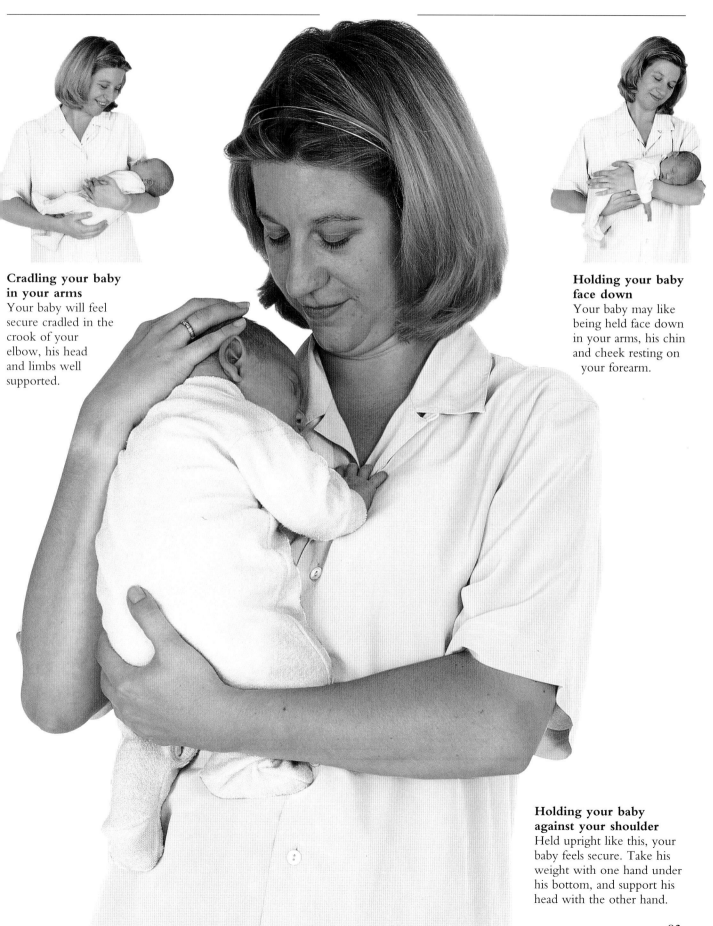

Cradling your baby in your arms
Your baby will feel secure cradled in the crook of your elbow, his head and limbs well supported.

Holding your baby face down
Your baby may like being held face down in your arms, his chin and cheek resting on your forearm.

Holding your baby against your shoulder
Held upright like this, your baby feels secure. Take his weight with one hand under his bottom, and support his head with the other hand.

83

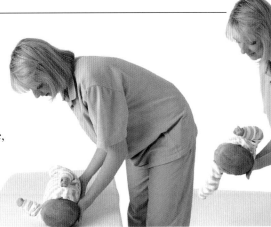

PICKING YOUR BABY UP FROM HER SIDE

1 When asleep, your baby is safest lying on her back. But if she is awake and on her side, pick her up by sliding one hand under her neck and head, the other under her bottom.

2 Scoop your baby into your arms, making sure her head doesn't flop. Lift her slowly and gently.

3 Hold her against your body, then slide your forearm under her head.

4 Now her head is supported in your elbow, and she feels secure.

SAFETY FIRST

You will often want to lay your baby down for a few moments, either for her own amusement or because you need to do something. Whether in your own home or visiting family or friends, follow these simple precautions to ensure that your baby keeps safe and sound at all times:

★ Never place your baby's chair, basket, or carry cot on a raised surface – only the floor will be completely safe.

★ Never put your baby next to a radiator, fire, or open window. She may burn herself or overchill.

★ Never leave your baby alone with a dog, cat, or other animal.

★ Never place your baby within reach of unstable furniture or other heavy objects. She may pull them over and hurt herself.

★ Never leave your baby unsupported on a bed, sofa, or chair – always use a pillow to prevent her rolling off.

★ Favourite toys will keep your baby entertained – but take care not to leave anything sharp in her reach. Avoid toys that are small enough to fit into her mouth, or heavy enough to hurt her.

PICKING YOUR BABY UP FROM HER FRONT

1 If your baby is lying awake on her tummy, lift her by sliding one hand under her chest, so your forearm supports her chin, the other under her bottom.

2 Lift her slowly, turning her towards you. Bring her up to your body and slide the arm supporting her head forwards, until her head nestles comfortably in the crook of your elbow. Put your other hand under her bottom and legs, so she is cradled and secure.

USING A SLING

A sling is an excellent way of carrying your baby around in the first three months. The contact with your body and the motion as you walk will soothe and comfort her. An added advantage is that it leaves your arms free. It's not difficult to put the sling on when there's no one to help you; take it off using the same method in reverse.

PUTTING A SLING ON

1 Slip the sling straps over your shoulders so that the two metal rings hang down at the front.

2 Attach the padded triangular section by snapping the circular fasteners on the straps into place.

3 Close one side of the sling by feeding the toggle through the ring and snapping it securely closed.

4 Hold your baby so that she faces you. If she is very young, support her head with your hand. Feed her leg through the hole on the fastened side of the sling. Keep your arm around her on the open side to ensure that she doesn't fall.

5 Support your baby in the seat of the sling with one hand while you fasten the toggle and snap under her arm with the other.

A padded back *supports your baby's head*

6 Close the top fasteners so that an arm hole is created on each side. The back flap supports a younger baby's head and neck.

WEARING THE SLING

After three months, your baby may prefer to face forwards. Follow the same sequence, but start with your baby facing forwards. With the front flap folded down, she can get a better view of the world around her.

Wide shoulder straps *are the most comfortable*

A machine-washable fabric *is a good idea*

HANDLING AND PHYSICAL PLAY

LET HER FACE FORWARDS

Your alert three-month-old has a good view of the world facing forwards. Put one hand between her legs, the other round her chest. She doesn't need you to support her head any more.

PLAY BOUNCING GAMES ON YOUR LAP

Your four-month-old baby will love the feeling of being jogged up and down by your knees, in time to a favourite rhyme. Hold his arms in case he jerks backwards.

LET HER KICK

It's best not to let your baby become too dependent on being held. Let her spend some time kicking on the floor – and get down to her level instead.

SIT HIM ON YOUR SHOULDER

Sit your six-month-old on your shoulder so he's taller than you are: he will be exhilarated by this new perspective.

EYE-TO-EYE CONTACT

Your baby will love you to swing her up high. Your face is always the best entertainment of all.

PLAY ROCKING GAMES

Rock her to and fro, going higher and higher if she likes the game. This type of rocking motion is a good way to soothe her too.

WINDING DOWN

However boisterously you play with your baby, have a few minutes of gentle, quiet cuddles afterwards. Always take your cue from your baby, and forget the rough-housing for today if he's not responding with his usual giggles of pleasure.

FEEDING YOUR BABY

One of the first decisions you will have to make is whether to breast-feed or bottle-feed your baby. Breast milk meets his needs perfectly and is digested easily; but your baby won't suffer if you do bottle-feed. If you think you would prefer to bottle-feed, it's a good idea to delay the decision until after your baby is born. There's no substitute for the colostrum that your breasts produce in the first few days, and feeding your baby this will

provide him with valuable antibodies to help him fight infection in the early months. It's difficult, but not impossible, to make the switch from bottle- back to breast-feeding because without the stimulation of your baby sucking, your breasts will have stopped producing milk. Whichever method you opt for, remember that your love, cuddling, and attention are all just as important to your baby as the milk you give him.

BREAST OR BOTTLE

You may know how you want to feed your baby. If you want to breast-feed, then with good professional help you should almost certainly succeed. But even if you're sure bottle-feeding is the method for you, it's worth considering the advantages and disadvantages, and listening to the comments other mothers make. It's a decision that will affect you, your partner, and your baby for months to come.

"I knew that by breast-feeding I was giving him the best possible milk he could have. I could tell he was digesting it easily, and I knew it had exactly the right blend of nutrients."

Breast milk contains substances that help protect your baby from disease until his own immune system has matured, and protects against allergies – which is important if there is allergy in your family. Formula milk can't provide either protection.

"I loved the convenience of breast-feeding my baby: the milk was always there, always sterile, always at the temperature she liked."

"The sheer enjoyment of breast-feeding took me by surprise. It's so intimate, so physically satisfying: her little hand used to come up and stroke my breast, and I could feel her face against my skin. It got better and better, too, as the first year went on."

"The breast was always the best method of soothing my baby when he cried. He wasn't necessarily hungry, he just needed the comfort of sucking."

"The health visitor told me that the reason I slimmed back to my pre-pregnancy figure so quickly was because I persevered with breast-feeding. So that was an unexpected benefit of listening to her advice."

Breast-feeding is more time-consuming in the early weeks, partly because a breast-fed baby feeds more frequently, partly because he likes to suck – in fact sucking is a need and a pleasure quite distinct from the need for food. However, preparing and sterilizing bottles also takes a lot of time, and will soon become a chore when you've done it for several months; while breast-feeds become less frequent and quicker as your baby gets older.

"I had always been convinced that I couldn't breast-feed – my bust was so small. But I sailed through. I had plenty of milk, and my baby certainly didn't mind my small breasts."

Travelling is easier if you breast-feed: there's no bottle to warm, and no danger of storing the made-up formula at too high a temperature.

"The only thing I didn't like about breast-feeding was the night feeds. I didn't much enjoy expressing milk, so the whole burden of those nocturnal sessions fell on me. But it was only for a few weeks of our lives."

"I felt that my decision to bottle-feed was the right one when I saw how much my husband enjoyed feeding our baby: they built a very strong relationship right from the start as a result."

"With a bottle, I could always see how much milk my baby had taken – and that was very reassuring after so many miserable weeks trying to get the hang of breast-feeding."

Tiredness, illness, or stress, which can reduce a breast-milk supply, won't affect the bottle-fed baby's feeds.

You may find it harder to trust your baby's own appetite when bottle-feeding, so it is easier to overfeed him and encourage him to be overweight.

A bottle-fed baby is more at risk of picking up micro-organisms that could cause diarrhoea and vomiting.

ESSENTIALS OF FEEDING

DEMAND FEEDING

Feeding on demand simply means giving your baby a feed whenever he is hungry, not following a timetable.

Hunger is a new sensation for your young baby. In the uterus he was being continually "topped up", but once he is born your baby has to go long periods without food. His digestive system is too immature to cope with large meals at infrequent intervals; little and often must be the rule at first.

There is nothing to be gained by keeping your baby waiting for a feed once he has cried to be fed – he will only get so distressed that he refuses to suck. You will have to comfort and calm him until he'll settle to a feed. You're not spoiling your baby by answering his needs. In the early weeks his empty stomach is the usual reason for waking and crying: as his digestive system matures and his stomach grows, he'll take more at each feed and the intervals between feeds will become longer.

How often will he demand food?

Your baby will demand food whenever he needs it, and to begin with this will be often. Newborn babies will have no discernible pattern of feeding. By day three or four, feeds will be about every two or three hours, and there may be eight or so feeds a day with a lot of short feeds during the evening. At night, you may be feeding your baby two or three times, because few babies under the age of six weeks are able to sleep more than five hours at a stretch without waking with hunger. Breast-fed babies usually need more frequent feeds than bottle-fed babies, because breast milk is more easily and quickly digested than formula milk.

By three months your baby will probably be settling to a roughly four-hourly feeding routine, with five feeds a day plus one or two at night. If you are bottle-feeding, you will probably be able to establish a four-hourly routine more quickly.

SPECIAL CASES

Premature babies Your pre-term baby may have a small appetite but he will need frequent feeds. Pre-term babies tend to sleep a lot, and may not wake and demand food even though they need it, so wake your baby every three hours and offer a feed.

If you have managed to express milk for your baby while he's been in hospital, you will be able to breast-feed once you get him home. It isn't always easy for a baby to adapt to taking milk from a human nipple. To help him, express a little milk before a feed (see page 94) so that the nipple stands out, and rub breast milk over it to give him the taste.

Twins It's perfectly possible to breast-feed twins successfully. Feed them one at a time to begin with, then when you've got more confidence, you'll find it's easy to feed them both at the same time, their legs tucked under each arm, and their heads lying in your hands.

WIND AND WINDING

Whether your baby is breast- or bottle-fed, give him the chance to burp up any swallowed air when he pauses for a rest; the wind may be making him feel full. If he doesn't burp after about half a minute, give up: he probably doesn't need to bring up any air at that feed.

Protect your clothes *with a clean fabric nappy*

Hold her face down

At any age, holding your baby face down across your lap or in your arms may help her bring up wind.

Rub or pat her back *gently but rhythmically*

Your newborn

To help a very young baby bring up wind, put her against your shoulder and rub her back, or lean her forwards on your lap, supporting her floppy head under the chin. She's very likely to bring some milk up too (known as possetting), so have a clean fabric nappy handy.

Your older baby

By three months, when your baby can sit up for short periods, jiggling him gently on your lap while you rub his back will help him burp up swallowed air.

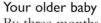

"Our feeding times were relaxing, calm, and deeply emotional for both of us."

BREAST-FEEDING YOUR BABY

Breast-feeding can be a supremely rewarding aspect of caring for your baby, and you'll be giving her the best nourishment nature can provide – so don't be deterred if you encounter a few problems in the early days. You and your baby have to learn this new skill together, so if at first she doesn't seem to know how to suck, or doesn't suck for very long, be patient with her. She doesn't need a lot of food just after the birth. If breast-feeding seems difficult at first, your midwife or health visitor will be able to help you, and there will be plenty of friends and relatives to offer you advice. Several breast-feeding associations provide breast-feeding support. It's worth persevering. Once you're over the first week or so, you can look forward to months of successful and satisfying feeding.

Settle yourselves comfortably: you may be there for up to an hour. Take a deep breath and relax your shoulders: the more relaxed you feel to your baby, the easier she will settle to feed. Give her plenty of opportunity for skin contact. If you're in private, take your top off: with no clothes in the way, you might find it easier to get her "latched on" – that is, properly positioned on your breast and sucking efficiently.

GETTING COMFORTABLE

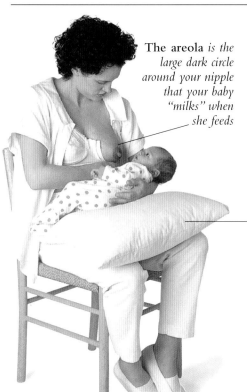

The areola *is the large dark circle around your nipple that your baby "milks" when she feeds*

Your young baby's early feeds
Sit comfortably in an upright position with your back supported. A low chair without arms is ideal, or sit up in bed with plenty of pillows propping your back. Your baby should be turned towards you, held close, chest to chest. Lift the baby up to your breast, rather than bending low over him.

A pillow *takes the weight of your baby's body*

Make sure your *baby has a hand free to touch and stroke your breast*

Your older baby's feeds
Once you're both adept at feeding, you will find you can nurse in almost any relaxed position. Sitting cross-legged on the bed or floor is excellent, especially if you can prop your back against pillows or furniture.

FINDING THE NIPPLE

1 Your baby has an instinctive reflex that makes her search for your nipple to find food – this is the "rooting" reflex. Until about her tenth day of life, alert this reflex by stroking the cheek nearest to you: she will turn towards your breast and search for your nipple.

2 If your baby doesn't turn her head instinctively, try gently squeezing just behind your areola until a few drops form on your nipple. Touch her lips with this to encourage her to open her mouth.

YOUR FIRST BREAST-FEEDS

LATCHING ON

3 Bring her head up close to your breast, so her chin is against it and her tongue is underneath your nipple. Guide your breast in.

1 Once latched on, your baby doesn't just suck, she "milks" the breast with her jaws by pressing on the reservoirs of milk at the base of the areola. If your baby just sucks on the nipple, you will get sore and she won't get any milk. If you feel a momentary piercing pain, breathe deeply to help you relax.

2 From your viewpoint, your well latched-on baby will have her jaws open very wide and her mouth full of your breast. You can tell she is feeding properly when you see her temples and ears moving, showing her jaw muscles are working hard.

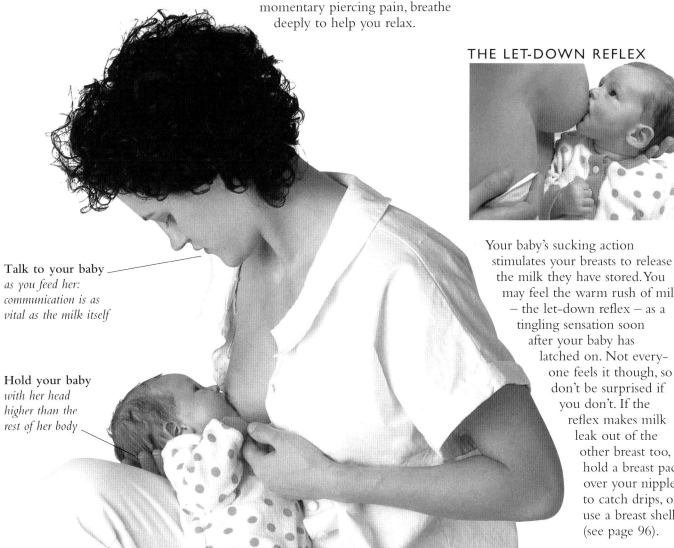

Talk to your baby *as you feed her: communication is as vital as the milk itself*

Hold your baby *with her head higher than the rest of her body*

THE LET-DOWN REFLEX

Your baby's sucking action stimulates your breasts to release the milk they have stored. You may feel the warm rush of milk – the let-down reflex – as a tingling sensation soon after your baby has latched on. Not everyone feels it though, so don't be surprised if you don't. If the reflex makes milk leak out of the other breast too, hold a breast pad over your nipple to catch drips, or use a breast shell (see page 96).

TAKING YOUR BABY OFF THE BREAST

1 Let your baby feed for as long as she wants at the first breast, so she drains it – your breast will look smaller, and feel lighter, when all the milk has gone. Your baby will often pause during her feed and just suck for a while. After several minutes when she doesn't take any milk, remove her from the breast to wind her. Don't pull your nipple away – this will hurt. Slip a finger between her jaws to break the suction.

Use your clean *little finger to break your baby's suction*

2 Slip a tissue into your bra on the side your baby has emptied. At the next feed put her on the other side to begin with, so both breasts get equal stimulation. Sit your baby up to wind her.

OFFER THE OTHER BREAST

1 After a burp or two, perhaps a short sleep, offer your baby the other breast. She may be hungry enough to drain this one, too, or she may just suck for comfort – which is as much a need as the milk.

2 When your baby's had enough, she will fall fast asleep in your arms and let your nipple slip from her mouth. Don't worry if you don't think she's taken enough milk; you can trust your baby to know how much she wants and needs at any time.

HOW YOUR BREASTS PRODUCE MILK

In the first days after the birth your breasts produce colostrum, a protein-rich food that supplies your baby with valuable antibodies against infection. Once you begin to produce milk on around the fourth day, your baby will naturally stimulate your body into producing a plentiful supply.

The key to a good milk supply is feeding your baby when she wants to be fed – and in the early days that means feeds at two- or three-hourly intervals. Breast milk production works on a supply and demand system: the more often your baby nurses, and the more she

takes, the more your breasts will produce. Supplementary bottles of formula milk will undermine this system: if your baby's hunger is satisfied by a bottle, she won't be eager to suck and your breasts won't get the stimulation they need.

Breast milk isn't all the same. At the beginning of the feed your baby takes foremilk, which is watery and thirst-quenching. Then she gets to the hindmilk, rich in calories and more satisfying. This is why it's important to let her suck for at least 10 to 15 minutes on one breast at each feed: otherwise she will soon be hungry again.

What you need to do

All *you* need to do to produce enough milk is to eat a good, balanced diet with plenty of protein, to drink whenever you are thirsty – have a glass of juice or milk on hand while you feed – and rest as much as you can. Your baby's natural appetite will do the rest.

You need a lot of energy to produce breast milk, so this is not the time to diet – you will only feel run down and exhausted. Follow your appetite, and make sure you get the extra calories you need from fresh, vitamin-rich foods rather than "empty" carbohydrates.

WHEN YOUR MILK COMES IN

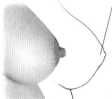

Normal breast

Engorged breast

The areola is swollen, so it may be hard for your baby to grasp; and the nipple is flattened

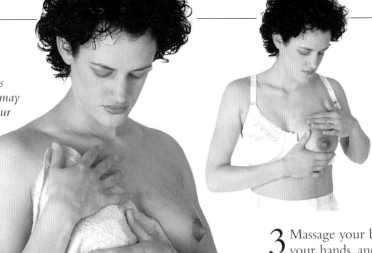

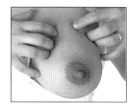

Draw your fingertips down towards the areola

1 On about the fourth day of breast-feeding your breasts start to produce mature milk, rather than the colostrum that you've fed your baby up to now. You may wake up to find your breasts big and hard, and they can be quite uncomfortable. This is engorgement, and it may last for up to 48 hours. Your baby will find it hard to latch on because the nipple isn't sticking out, but is flattened by the swollen areola. The following tips should help her to feed, so clearing the engorgement and easing your discomfort.

2 Before you try to breast-feed your baby, soften your breasts by laying warm flannels over them for several minutes. Or, you may prefer to stand in the shower and splash warm water over your breasts.

3 Massage your breasts gently with your hands, and try to express some milk to relieve the swelling and help your baby get the nipple in her mouth (see page 94). Don't worry if you can't get the hang of expressing at this stage, you will soon.

4 When you put your baby to the breast, put your free hand on your ribcage under your breast and push gently upwards: this should help the nipple to protrude so your baby can get the areola in her mouth. Her sucking will quickly relieve the engorgement and discomfort.

"My baby son cries a great deal; could it be that he isn't getting enough milk from me to satisfy his hunger?"

When you are breast-feeding, you can't actually see how much milk your baby takes, so it's natural sometimes to worry that he's not getting enough. However, as long as you offer a feed whenever your baby cries, and he is gaining weight normally with occasional spurts, you have no need to worry. Remember that your baby will probably lose a little weight during the first days of life, and won't regain his birthweight until he is about ten days old.

"Will breast-feeding alter my figure for life?"

Your breasts may be slightly smaller after you've weaned your baby from the breast, because some of the fatty tissue in the breast has been replaced by milk glands. Otherwise, you will probably regain your pre-pregnancy figure more quickly if you breast-feed. This is because the hormones released encourage the uterus to shrink back to normal quickly, and the fat reserves that your body laid down during your pregnancy are used in the production of breast milk. Your waistline, too, will contract sooner.

"Do I have to be as careful about the drugs and medications I take when I am breast-feeding as when I was pregnant?"

What you eat and drink can be passed on to your baby through your milk, so it's still vital that you tell your chemist or doctor that you are breast-feeding before they prescribe any medicines for you. It's sensible to avoid stimulants such as alcohol and caffeine too. If your baby won't sleep well, it may be worthwhile cutting coffee and tea out of your diet for a few weeks to see if the situation improves – the caffeine may be keeping him awake.

EXPRESSING MILK BY HAND

The ability to express your own milk gives you considerable flexibility. You can freeze the milk (keep it for up to one month), and someone else can give it to your baby when you're out: see pages 98–107 for bottle-feeding advice. Expressing by hand is easy and painless. Sterilize the equipment and wash your hands. Encourage the flow of milk by having a warm bath, or hold warm flannels over your breasts. Make yourself comfortable at a high surface, with the bowl in front of you.

YOU WILL NEED
Sterilizing equipment (see page 100)
Large bowl
Bottle and teat
Plastic funnel

HAND EXPRESSING

Use your whole hand to massage the breast

1 Support your breast in one hand and start to massage, working downwards from above the breast.

2 Work your way all round the breast, including the underside. Complete at least ten circuits: this helps the flow of milk through the ducts.

3 Stroke downwards towards the areola with your fingernails several times. Avoid pressing on the breast tissue.

4 Apply gentle downward pressure on the area behind the areola with your thumbs and fingers.

5 Squeeze thumbs and forefingers together, at the same time pressing backwards: the milk should spurt out through the nipple. Keep this up for a couple of minutes, then do the other breast.

EXPRESSING MILK USING A PUMP

Expressing by pump can be quicker and less tiring than hand expressing, but you may find it harder to get a good quantity of milk – and it may be painful. (If it is, express by hand.) The "syringe" type of pump is generally more efficient than the bulb type. Choose one with an outer cylinder that converts into a bottle. Or ask your health visitor about hiring an electric pump, or buy a battery-operated one. You can also buy bags for storing breast milk.

2 Keep a good seal and draw the outer cylinder away from you: the suction draws milk from your breast.

1 Sterilize all the equipment as before, and wash your hands. Assemble the pump. Soften your breasts in warm water and massage them as when expressing by hand. Place the funnel of the pump over the areola so that it forms an airtight seal: it needs to press on the milk ducts just as your baby's jaws do.

3 Put the cap on tightly and refrigerate or cool and freeze the milk until it is needed.

PUMPS

Manual pumps These type of pumps are hand-operated and have a bulb or other similar device that needs to be squeezed to create suction. They can be quite hard work.

The funnel
should fit snugly over the breast

Squeeze the
rubber bulb with one hand

Funnel

Inner cylinder

Outer cylinder

Battery

Battery pump
Suction tends not to be as powerful with battery operated pumps as an electric pump, but they are useful if you have a good, well-established milk supply. Some come with an adaptor so that they can be operated by mains electricity.

DIOXINS IN BREAST MILK

Recent studies have shown that dioxins – widespread environmental pollutants – are present in breast milk and can pose a variety of risks to humans and animals. Research on animals has shown that they can act like hormones and affect sperm production. While the precise nature of the risk to humans remains controversial, accumulating evidence suggests that exposure to dioxins may affect the developing reproductive organs and immune system. Babies are particularly susceptible to these toxic effects because of their dependence on breast milk for food, the high degree of absorption of substances found in milk, and the unique sensitivity of certain biological processes in early development. However, the important advantages of breast-feeding must be weighed against a baby's susceptibility to dioxins. In almost all cases, the proven benefits will exceed the risks.

BREAST-FEEDING PROBLEMS

Get professional help quickly if you have any problems with breast-feeding: struggling on alone is discouraging, and something minor like a blocked duct can lead to mastitis if it doesn't clear. Don't stop feeding if you encounter the problems below: you will only become engorged with milk, and make any problem worse. Take good care of your breasts. Wear a comfortable nursing bra, both day and night for the early weeks: don't wear one that is too tight, it may constrict the milk ducts. Be gentle when you massage your breasts too. Let the air get to your nipples as often as possible, and wash them with water, not soap as it dries the skin. Dry thoroughly.

LEAKING BREASTS

Your breasts may leak copiously between feeds in the early weeks.
Treatment Breast pads inside your bra will absorb some drips, but change the pads frequently as wetness near your skin may make you sore. If you leak a lot, try using a plastic breast shell.
Prevention None, but leaking breasts are proof of a good milk supply, and help prevent engorgement. The leaking will diminish as your milk supply matches demand.

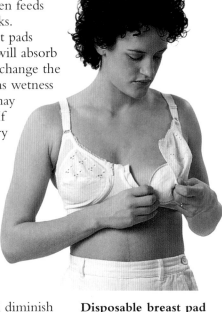

Disposable breast pad
A breast pad will absorb drips and small leaks.

BLOCKED DUCT

A small, hard, tender, red lump in the breast usually means that one of the milk ducts has become blocked.
Treatment Bathe the breast in hot water and massage it gently, then put your baby to the breast. You may get a moment's intense pain, but the duct should clear. If the duct doesn't clear, see your doctor that day.
Prevention Make sure your bra is not too tight, and take care not to press hard on your breast tissue when you feed or express.

MASTITIS

A blocked milk duct may become infected, produ-cing flu-like symptoms. *Seek medical help urgently*: if untreated, mastitis may lead to a breast abscess, which may need surgery.
Treatment Your doctor will prescribe antibiotics, and you must finish the course. Continue to feed your baby from both breasts as normal.
Prevention Regular feeding from both breasts will help prevent mastitis. Never let a tender lump in your breast go longer than a day without treatment.

SORE OR CRACKED NIPPLES

Sore nipples are usually the result of your baby not latching on properly, which is due to poor positioning. Your skin will be red, and it will be painful to feed. The best way to prevent sore nipples is to make sure that your baby is correctly positioned at the breast and that he has the whole nipple in his mouth while he is feeding.

If you have a cracked nipple, you will probably experience a sharp, shooting pain in your breast as your baby sucks. However, the crack will generally heal within a few days.
Treatment Try the following suggestions:
★ Dry your nipples thoroughly after a feed: use a hairdryer on a cool setting.
★ Let the air get to your nipples for several hours a day. Put a tea strainer with the handle cut off or a breast shell over your nipple inside your bra. This will allow some air to circulate and help the nipple to heal.
★ Change the position that your baby feeds in, so pressure is applied to different parts of the areola.
★ Express from the worst breast for a day.
★ Don't let your baby suck for more than a couple of minutes after she's emptied the breast.
Prevention Make sure that your baby takes the areola into her mouth. Keep your nipples dry between feeds.

Nipple cream
A calendula-based cream or antiseptic spray may help to relieve the soreness.

YOUR EMOTIONS AND LET-DOWN

Your let-down reflex is strongly associated with your emotional state of being. When you are embarrassed, irritated, exhausted, or anxious, your breast milk doesn't always appear like magic. A few minutes of quiet cuddling with your baby in private should help to relax both of you and make you and your baby ready to nurse.

FEEDING THROUGHOUT THE FIRST YEAR

Until the age of approximately four months, you will be feeding your baby on milk alone. But how will your breast-feeding routine change once you start to introduce solid food to your baby? How long should you keep giving her some breast-feeds a day? During the second half of her first year, your baby will need less and less milk from you, and be more willing to take drinks straight from a training beaker. Betweeen the ages of nine months and one year your baby will, in all likelihood, wean herself off the breast quite happily, and with no prompting from you: she has reached an age when she's getting her nourishment and her comfort from other sources.

How will my routine develop?
A typical routine for a fully breast-fed baby might be:
★ three months: five feeds a day plus night feeds
★ four/five months: four or five feeds a day plus some solid food
★ six months: two breast-feeds a day: early morning and bedtime
★ nine months: bedtime feed only.

Going back to work
It is perfectly possible to return to work and continue breast-feeding. But it means planning ahead. While you are away, your baby will have to take milk from a bottle or, if she is over six months, from a trainer cup with a soft spout. Whichever method you chose, it will take time for your baby to get used to a different way of feeding. So, before you return to work, get her used to taking an occasional bottle of expressed milk from somebody else.

If you want her to have breast-milk only, you will need to express milk during the day at work to keep your milk supply stimulated. Or you may want her to have formula milk during the day but continue to breast-feed during the evenings and nights when you are at home. Your milk supply will respond to your baby's changing needs.
★ Build up a stock of expressed milk in your freezer for a few weeks before you go back to work. You can buy special poly-bags to store it in and it will keep for up to three months. Thaw or warm the milk by putting the container in a bowl of warm water (not a microwave).
★ At work you will need sterile equipment and a private place to express milk during the day, plus access to a fridge to store it. Transport the milk in an insulated cool box.
★ If necessary, boost your milk supply by giving extra feeds during the evening and night.
★ Ask your baby's carer to delay the late afternoon feed so your baby will be ready for a breast-feed when you get home.
★ For everybody's peace of mind, leave formula ready to be made up in case your baby demands an extra feed.

When should I stop?
You can continue to breast-feed well into your baby's second year if you both want to; or you can gradually wean your baby off the breast at any time in the first year. She may give up the breast of her own accord between nine months and a year. Biting your breast is not a reason for you to give up feeding: tell your baby sharply that it hurts, and she will soon learn to stop biting you.

Never give up breast-feeding abruptly. It's important to let your production of milk reduce gradually over a period of weeks, by letting your supply-and-demand system work in reverse. Drop one feed at a time, waiting at least three days before dropping another (see page 106). Don't express to relieve the full feeling: the milk will be gradually re-absorbed in a few days.

Giving up the final feed
Most babies usually settle more happily at night after a comforting "sucking" feed, so this is usually the last breast-feed to be dropped.

Towards the end of the first year, gradually reduce the length of this feed. Then drop it altogether, and give plenty of attention and love for a few days to make up. Give her a drink in a beaker at bedtime.

What do I give my baby instead of breast milk?
If you give up breast-feeding before six months, you will need to feed your baby formula milk from a bottle. If you are happy to breast-feed until your baby is at least six months, you can wean her straight on to a beaker (see page 113); give formula milk until one year, then full cream cow's milk. She may settle better at night with a comfort suck on a bedtime bottle.

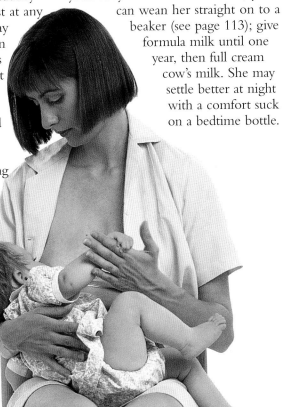

BOTTLE-FEEDING YOUR BABY

If you decide that you would prefer to bottle-feed your baby, then you will have two main advantages over the breast-feeding mother. Firstly, you don't have to do all the feeding yourself, so your partner can take a share too; and secondly, you can see how much milk your baby is taking. The big disadvantage is that you must be very vigilant about protecting your baby from bacteria that might cause stomach upsets or diarrhoea. You will need to suppress your own milk supply too. If you decided to bottle-feed because you thought you couldn't supply enough milk, you may be surprised at how full and uncomfortable your breasts feel once you go over to bottle-feeding. Your health visitor will watch your bottle-fed baby's weight carefully. If he is putting on too much weight, it may be because you are over-feeding. Always follow the manufacturer's instructions carefully when making up a feed, as a feed that is too concentrated is harmful to your baby.

EQUIPMENT FOR BOTTLE-FEEDING

For a fully bottle-fed baby you will need at least eight full size (250ml/8oz) bottles. Buy extra teats, and keep them ready for use in a sterile jar in case a teat gives an inadequate flow of milk (see page 106).

Some bottles are used with throw-away plastic liners, which can reduce the amount of air your baby swallows with his milk: the bag collapses as he sucks milk out, so the teat doesn't flatten and halt the flow.

BOTTLES AND OTHER EQUIPMENT

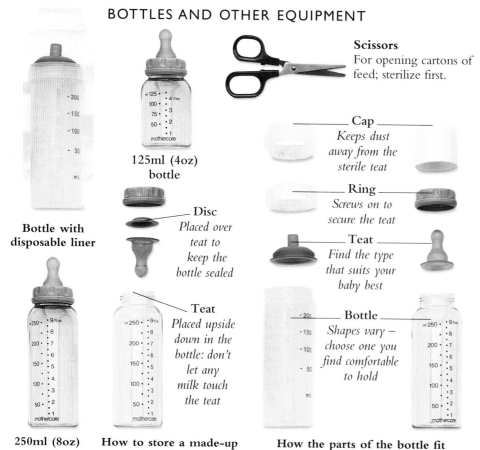

Bottle with disposable liner

125ml (4oz) bottle

Disc *Placed over teat to keep the bottle sealed*

Teat *Placed upside down in the bottle: don't let any milk touch the teat*

250ml (8oz) bottle

How to store a made-up feed in the fridge

Scissors For opening cartons of feed; sterilize first.

Cap *Keeps dust away from the sterile teat*

Ring *Screws on to secure the teat*

Teat *Find the type that suits your baby best*

Bottle *Shapes vary – choose one you find comfortable to hold*

How the parts of the bottle fit together when in use

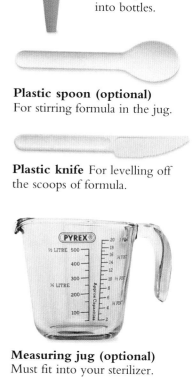

Plastic funnel (optional) Useful for pouring made-up formula into bottles.

Plastic spoon (optional) For stirring formula in the jug.

Plastic knife For levelling off the scoops of formula.

Measuring jug (optional) Must fit into your sterilizer.

TEATS

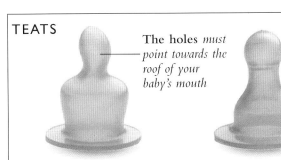

The holes *must point towards the roof of your baby's mouth*

Valve in rim *lets air under the teat and into the bottle*

Teats for young *babies have a short nipple*

Natural-shaped teat
This teat most closely mimics the sucking action of feeding from your breast, so encourages proper development of your baby's palate and jaws. The teat must go into your baby's mouth with the holes facing upwards, so that the milk sprays over the roof of his mouth.

Universal teat
The standard shape of teat gives a sucking action that is not really like sucking from your breast. Teats are sold with different rates of flow, but check at each feed: there should be two or three drops of milk a second. A cross-cut hole gives a better flow of milk than a pinhole.

Anti-colic teat
An anti-colic teat lets air into the bottle as your baby sucks milk out. This stops the teat collapsing, so enabling him to get a steady stream of milk and helping him not to gulp air. Silicone teats, shown above, last up to a year: latex teats deteriorate after about one month.

Wide-based teat
This type is not interchangeable amongst different makes of bottle. As your baby sucks, his lips push against the squashy base and the nipple moves in and out in his mouth, rather like a human nipple. Fit teat and ring together before assembling the bottle ready for filling.

WASHING YOUR BABY'S FEEDING EQUIPMENT

Your baby's teats, bottles, and other feeding equipment must be kept scrupulously clean. They can be cleaned either by hand or you can put them into your dishwasher. For babies under one year old, it will also be necessary to sterilize all equipment before use.

USING A DISHWASHER
An efficient way to wash your baby's feeding equipment is to put it in your dishwasher and then make sure it goes through the hot drying cycle. The high heat is usually sufficient to kill any bacteria. But be careful – teats may have to be boiled separately on the cooker because dishwashers can turn them into unusable sticky blobs.

Dishwasher-proof teats *should be put upwards within the cutlery compartment*

HAND-WASHING

1 Put all the rinsed out bottles, teats, caps, rings, discs, jug, funnel, spoon, and knife into hot soapy water, and wash them thoroughly.

2 Scrub inside the bottles with the bottle brush to remove all traces of milk. Make sure you also scrub carefully around their necks, and the screw thread.

3 Caked-on formula can be removed by rubbing a little salt inside the teat. BUT if you do this it is important to rinse well to remove every trace of salt.

4 Make sure that you rinse the bottles, teats, and any other equipment thoroughly under running water. Use a pin to clear the holes in the teats.

GOOD HYGIENE AND STERILIZING

Formula, when it is warm or held too long at room temperature, is an ideal breeding ground for the bacteria that cause vomiting or diarrhoea. Vomiting and diarrhoea, though not so serious in an older child, can be life-threatening in a young baby. Before filling your baby's bottle, make sure that your hands are absolutely clean. Until your baby is at least six months old, sterilize the bottle and everything that comes in contact with it either by boiling or using chemical sterilizing tablets. You can also buy a steam sterilizer or microwave steam unit specially designed for sterilizing bottles. Store bottles of made-up formula in the body of the fridge (not the door) and use within 24 hours.

EQUIPMENT FOR STERILIZING

Sterilizer Must incorporate a float to keep the items fully submerged.

Microwave unit
This unit works as a steam sterilizer in the microwave.

Steam Sterilizer
You can sterilize a large number of bottles at once.

Sterilizing tablets
You can use tablets to sterilize your equipment.

STERILIZING YOUR BABY'S FEEDING EQUIPMENT

Sterilize all your baby's feeding equipment either by boiling or by using sterilizing tablets.

If using the boiling method, wash the equipment and boil for five minutes. Use tongs to remove the hot bottles and leave them until they are quite cold before filling.

If using tablets, fill the sterilizing tank with cold water and add the tablets. When they have dissolved, put the equipment in, filling the bottles so they can't bob up. Leave for at least the minimum time, then take out items as needed and rinse in boiled water. Drain on kitchen paper.

All items
must be fully submerged during the boiling period

The boiling method

Sterilizing with tablets

PROTECTING YOUR BABY FROM AN UPSET STOMACH

If you take the precautions below, you should be able to protect your baby from the bacteria that cause stomach upsets or gastro-enteritis.

★ Sterilize all feeding equipment before use, even if brand new.

★ If you have no fridge, make up each feed only when you need it.

★ If your baby doesn't finish his bottle at a feed, throw the milk away: don't save it for next time, because his saliva will have contaminated it.

★ Throw away any milk warmed for your baby, even if he doesn't touch it; the process of warming the milk encourages bacteria to grow.

★ Store bottles of made-up feeds in the main part of the fridge, not in the door, which is at a lower temperature. Don't keep for longer than 24 hours.

★ Leave the bottles in the sterilizing solution until you need them (it's effective for 24 hours) – then they can't be contaminated by bacteria in the air. Take the teats out after the minimum time, drain on kitchen paper then store in a sterile jar.

★ Don't drain sterilized equipment on your draining board, or dry it on a teatowel. Drain on kitchen paper, and dry the knife only, using kitchen paper.

★ Wash your hands before touching sterile equipment.

TAKING CARE OF TEATS

Your baby can only feed happily if the teat allows him to suck out milk at the right rate. When you tip the bottle up you should see two or three drops a second: too small a hole will mean that your baby gets frustrated in his efforts to suck out enough milk; too large and the milk will gush out. Teats do deteriorate and the holes clog up. Have some spare sterile teats stored in a jar, so you can just swap an imperfect teat for a fresh one. Throw away teats if the holes are too large; holes that are too small can be enlarged with a needle. Check the flow again afterwards.

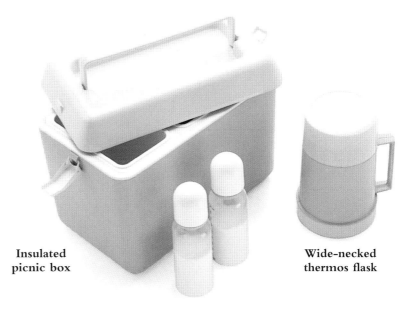

Insulated picnic box

Wide-necked thermos flask

When away from home

If you're going out for more than a couple of hours, make up a batch of feeds as normal and chill in the fridge. Pack the ice-cold bottles into an insulated picnic box with some ice packs, and keep for up to eight hours. Then take a thermos filled with hot water, and warm your baby's bottle in this when needed. Never carry a warm feed in a thermos: bacteria will grow and may cause a stomach upset. Cartons of made up feed are even more convenient when away from

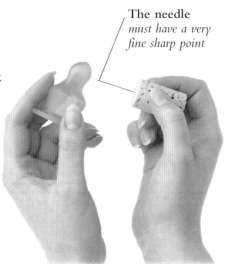

The needle
must have a very fine sharp point

Enlarging a hole that is too small
Push the eye of a needle into a cork. Heat the point in a flame until hot, then push into the hole.

home: the milk has been ultra-heat treated (UHT), so needs only to be stored in a cool place to stay safe. Take sterile bottles and teats with you in a plastic bag, and pour out a feed as your baby asks for it.

FORMULA: WHAT'S IN IT?

Have you tasted your baby's formula? It's sweeter than cow's milk and as close in composition to breast milk as manufacturers can make it. That's because cow's milk is not well suited to your baby's needs; it doesn't contain all the nutrients she must have for growth, and it can be difficult for her to digest because of the concentrations of protein and fat. Most infant form-ulas are adapted from a cow's milk base but are supplemented with other ingredients. Vegetable oils are added to replace cow's butter fat, and lactose is used to sweeten the mixture. Some formulas come with additional iron, clearly marked on the tins. Some formulas are based entirely on soy. If your baby vomits after a bottle; has diarrhoea, cramps, or excessive wind; wheezes; develops a rash; or is generally irritable, call your doctor immedi-ately and discuss the problem. Babies can dehydrate quickly.

MAKING UP YOUR BABY'S FEED

In the early weeks you need to have a supply of feeds ready in the fridge so that whenever your baby cries, wanting to be fed, you can respond quickly and easily. Until your baby is at least one year old, give him an infant formula milk, which is modified cow's milk: your health visitor will help you choose a brand. You can upset your baby by switching brands, so never do so without professional advice. Do not give cow's milk until your child is one year old.

Making up a powder formula

Infant formula is most commonly and cheaply available as powder in tins, which you mix up as needed.

The instructions on the tin should tell you the correct number of level, loosely filled scoops to add to each measure of water. It is very important to maintain these proportions exactly. If you add too much formula, the feed will be dangerously concentrated: your baby may gain too much weight, and his kidneys may be damaged. If you consistently add too little powder, he may gain weight too slowly. Once the milk is made up correctly, let your baby take as much as he wants at each feed.

Always use fresh, cold, mains water to make up your baby's feeds, and boil it once only. Some types of water should never be used:
★ water that has been repeatedly boiled, or left standing in the kettle
★ water from a tap with a domestic softener attached – the extra sodium (salt) can damage your baby's kidneys
★ water from a tap with a domestic filter attached – these filters can trap harmful bacteria
★ mineral water – the sodium and minerals may be harmful.

There are two methods of making up your baby's feed: mixing the formula directly in the bottles, or mixing it in a jug first. Use the jug method if you use bottles with disposable liners.

Ready-mixed infant milk

Some brands of infant milk are also available ready-mixed in sealed cartons containing 250ml (8fl oz). You need add no water to the milk. If the brand formula you are feeding your baby comes in this form, then you have a very convenient – but expensive – option.

The milk in the carton has been ultra-heat treated (UHT). Store unopened cartons in a cool place, and do not use after the "best before" date.

Once opened, the milk can be stored in the fridge for up to 24 hours, either in a sterile, sealed bottle, or in the carton. But unless you can be sure that you won't forget when you put the carton in the fridge, it's probably safer to pour all the milk out when your baby wants a feed, and throw away any he doesn't drink.

How much will my baby want?

Babies' appetites vary from day to day. During the first weeks of life put 100ml (4fl oz) of feed into each of six bottles, and see how that matches your baby's appetite. As he gains weight, he will often cry for more at the end of a feed, so gradually increase the amount you put into each bottle. By the time he is six months old you will be making up feeds of 200ml (7fl oz). As a rough guide, your baby needs about 150ml of milk per kilogram of body weight ($2\frac{1}{2}$ fl oz per 1lb) every 24 hours.

Should I give anything else?

After six months on infant formula, your baby may benefit from supplements of iron or vitamins A, C, and D, or may need to be put on a follow-up milk: your health visitor will advise you. Never add anything, not even baby rusk, to your baby's feed. Because formula is modified cow's milk it can very rarely set off an allergy. Go back to breast-feeding if you can but if this isn't possible see your doctor. Infant soya milk may be prescribed, but must be used only under medical supervision. Goat or sheep milks are no less likely to cause allergies than cow's milk. Consult your doctor if you suspect an allergic reaction.

THE RIGHT MILK TO GIVE YOUR BABY		Birth	6m	9m	12m	18m
Type of milk		**Birth**	**6m**	**9m**	**12m**	**18m**
Infant formula	Cow's milk modified to resemble human breast milk. From six months your baby may need supplements of iron and vitamin D.					
Follow-up formula	Optional. Modified cow's milk, intended for babies of six months or over. Contains iron and vitamin D, so supplements are not needed.					
Whole cow's milk	Introduce as main milk drink from 12 months; extra iron and vitamin D may be needed. Can be given mixed with cereal from 6 months.					

MAKING UP POWDER FORMULA IN THE BOTTLES

YOU WILL NEED
Tin of powder formula
Bottles and teats
Knife
Kitchen paper

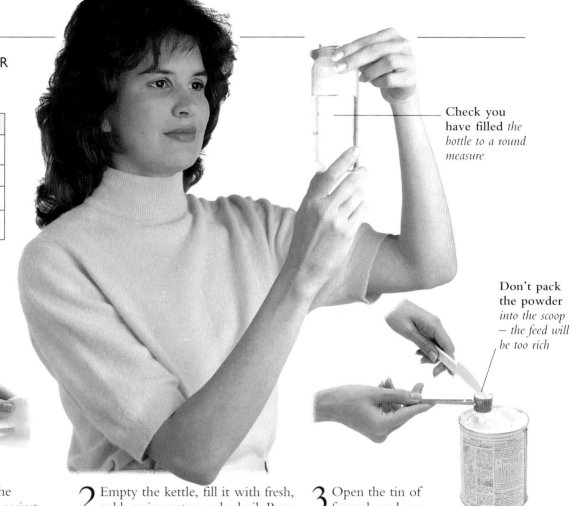

Check you have filled *the bottle to a round measure*

Don't pack the powder *into the scoop – the feed will be too rich*

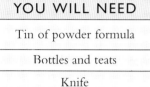

1 Boil the kettle to rinse the sterilized equipment: it's easiest if you drain the sterilant out of the sterilizer, then pour boiled water all over the equipment. Wash your hands, take everything out, and put to drain on kitchen paper; dry the knife only.

2 Empty the kettle, fill it with fresh, cold, mains water, and reboil. Pour the boiling water into the bottles, filling them to a suitable measure (see opposite). Check at eye level: the measure must be exact to mix the feed to the right concentration.

3 Open the tin of formula and use the special scoop inside to scoop up some powder. Level each scoop off with the back of the sterilized knife: do not heap the scoop, nor pack the powder down inside it.

STORING THE MILK

Adjust the amount *you make up according to your baby's appetite*

4 Drop each scoop of powder into the bottle. Add **only** the number of scoops recommended for that amount of water, and no more. The powder will dissolve quickly in the hot water.

5 Put the disc and ring on the bottle – not the teat at this stage – and screw on tightly to make a seal. Shake the bottle well to mix the formula.

Don't let the teat *touch the milk*

1 Take the disc and ring off. Put the teat in upside down, but don't let it dip in the milk: empty some out if necessary. Replace the disc and ring.

2 Fill all the bottles and put the caps on. Store in the fridge (but not in the door) for no longer than 24 hours; stand them on a tray if they fall over.

MAKING UP FORMULA USING A JUG

YOU WILL NEED
Tin of powder formula
Bottles and teats
Knife
Kitchen paper
Measuring jug
Spoon
Plastic funnel

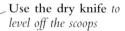

Use the dry knife to level off the scoops

Be very careful *to get the milk powder level – not heaped or packed in*

1 Rinse and drain equipment, drying the knife only on kitchen paper.

2 Boil fresh, cold, mains water in the kettle. Fill the jug to an exact full measure. Use the scoop inside the tin of formula to scoop up some powder. Level each scoop off with the back of the knife: do not heap the scoop, nor pack the powder down.

3 Add scoops of powder to the jug, counting carefully so you add only the number recommended for that amount of water, and no more.

4 Stir the formula well with the sterilized spoon until all the powder dissolves – the hot water will help the powder mix in.

5 Pour into bottles through the sterile funnel. Put the teat in upside down – pour milk out if the teat touches the milk – cover with the disc and screw the ring on. Make up fresh jugfuls until the bottles are full, then store as before.

Add as much *milk or as little as your baby seems to want (see page 102)*

USING READY-MIXED FORMULA

YOU WILL NEED
Carton of infant milk
Bottles and teats
Scrubbing brush
Scissors

Scrub well all around the cutting line

1 Rinse a bottle from the sterilizer in boiled water. Put to drain on kitchen paper. With a clean brush, scrub the top of the carton under running water.

2 Cut the top corner off. Don't touch the raw edges of the carton – you may contaminate the milk.

3 Empty the whole carton into the bottle (but see page 102 for storing this type of milk).

USING DISPOSABLE LINERS

YOU WILL NEED
Tin of powder formula
Bottles and teats
Disposable liners
Knife
Kitchen paper
Measuring jug
Spoon
Plastic funnel

Touch the outside *of the liner only*

1 Make up a jugful of powder formula, or if you prefer, scrub and cut open a carton of ready-to-feed formula (see opposite). Then wash your hands thoroughly. Take the teats and rings from the sterilizer, and rinse in boiled water. Clip the teat into the ring without touching the nipple end of the teat. Tear a pre-sterilized disposable liner off its roll.

2 Fold the liner in half lengthways and place in the "bottle" – it's not a real bottle, but a plastic sleeve that supports the liner, teat, and ring.

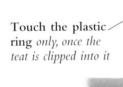

Touch the plastic ring *only, once the teat is clipped into it*

3 Make sure the liner folds well down all round the rim – otherwise milk will spill out.

4 Hold the liner firmly in place so the weight of the milk can't pull it down, and pour milk in through the funnel. Add as much as your baby seems to want.

5 Screw on the ring with the teat clipped in – this will hold the liner securely. Pull off the perforated tabs and dispose of them immediately, so older children can't get hold of them. Put the cap over the teat and store the bottles in the fridge.

USING DISPOSABLE BOTTLES

1 Make up a jugful of powder formula, or open a carton of ready-mixed feed, as shown opposite. Wash your hands. Unwrap the disposable parts of the bottle, but not the teat. The plastic sleeve "bottle" is re-usable, and needs only to be washed.

2 Straighten out the bag and put it inside the plastic sleeve, locking the holder on securely.

3 Pour in formula. Unwrap the teat and clip into position without touching the nipple with your fingers. Put the cap on.

Unwrapping the teat

Press hard *with your thumbs all round the base of the teat*

YOU WILL NEED
Disposable bottle and teat
Tin of powder formula
Disposable liners
Knife
Kitchen paper
Measuring jug
Spoon
Plastic funnel

GIVING YOUR BABY A BOTTLE

Feeding your baby is the most important thing you can do for her – but don't make the mistake of thinking that the milk in the bottle is all she needs, or that "anyone" can feed her. Your love, your cuddling, and attention are just as important to your baby as the milk itself. Always hold her close and cuddle her against you, smile and talk to her – just as you would if you were breast-feeding. Never leave your baby alone with her bottle, she may choke.

Right from the beginning, give your baby as much control over feeding as you can. Let her set the pace, pausing to look around, touch the bottle, or stroke your breast if she wants to – the feed may take as long as half an hour if she's feeling playful. Above all, let her decide when she's had enough milk.

Make yourself comfortable, put a bib on her, and have a muslin nappy to hand for when you wind her.

Sharing feeds
Your partner can feed your baby, too. As she gets older, she will want to control her feed herself.

FROM BREAST- TO BOTTLE-FEEDING

If you have to change over to bottle-feeding from breast-feeding for any reason, remember that the transition needs a gradual approach and professional help. Replacing one breast-feed every third day is the best method – or you can go more slowly. Start by replacing a lunchtime breast-feed with a bottle. If your baby won't take it, try again at the same feed the next day – you could offer a different type of teat, or moisten the teat with a few drops of breast milk to encourage him. After three days with one bottle-feed, replace a second daytime feed with a bottle, and wait another three days before tackling a third feed. Carry on like this until eventually your baby has a bottle for his night-time feed.

GETTING THE BOTTLE READY

1 Take a bottle from the fridge and turn the teat right way up. Warm in warm water. Don't use a microwave oven, because the milk may get very hot although the bottle still feels cool on the outside.

2 Check the flow of milk: it should be two or three drops a second. Too small a hole will make sucking hard, too large will let the milk gush out. If the teat isn't right, swap it for another sterile teat and test the flow of milk again.

"My baby never seems to finish her bottle: is she getting enough milk?"

Poor feeding could be a sign of illness, or of a serious underlying defect that needs medical attention. Check to see how much milk your baby should have for her weight (see page 102), and see if that matches what she actually takes. If you are at all concerned, talk to your health visitor about the problem and make sure your baby is weighed regularly at the clinic, where her weight will be plotted on a growth chart. Poor feeding, if combined with inadequate weight gain, is always a cause for concern.

3 Test the temperature by tipping a few drops on to the inside of your wrist – it should feel tepid. Cold milk is safe, but your baby may prefer it warm.

4 Unscrew the ring so that it just stays on the bottle, to let air in as your baby sucks milk out. This will stop the teat collapsing and halting the flow.

GIVING YOUR BABY HER BOTTLE

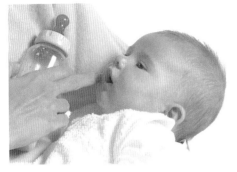

1 For the first ten days or so of life, alert your baby's sucking reflex: stroke the cheek nearest you, and she should turn and open her mouth. If she doesn't, or is older, let some drops of milk form on the teat, then touch her lips with it to give her the taste.

2 As your baby feeds, hold the bottle firmly so that she can pull against it as she sucks, and tilt it so that the teat is full of milk, not air. If the teat collapses, move the bottle around in you baby's mouth to let air back into the bottle.

3 When your baby has finished all the milk, pull the bottle firmly away. If she wants to continue sucking, offer her your clean little finger: she will soon let you know if she wants more milk.

IF SHE WON'T LET GO

If your baby doesn't want to let go of the bottle even after a long suck, slide your little finger between her gums alongside the teat.

It's easier *for your baby to swallow if she lies in a semi-upright position*

SLEEPING DURING A FEEDING

If she dozes off during her feed, she may have wind, which is making her feel full. Sit her up and wind her for a couple of minutes, then offer her some more milk.

Put a bib *on your baby before you begin*

INTRODUCING SOLID FOOD

From the age of four months, your baby will be ready to try some solid food. You will notice that even after a full feed she still seems hungry; she may even demand an extra feed a day. She will gradually take more and more solid food at each mealtime, until eventually, sometime after her first birthday, she no longer needs the breast or bottle for nourishment. Introduce her to as many new foods as you can, so she is used to a varied diet and not suspicious of unfamiliar tastes and textures – you may help to avoid a "faddy" phase when she gets older. Let her own appetite dictate how much she eats, and avoid confrontations: let her enjoy her food. Mealtimes are an important part of family life, and if you include your baby in family meals from an early age you will be helping her learn essential social skills.

EQUIPMENT FOR FIRST SOLIDS

A clean plastic spoon, a bowl, and a bib are the only essentials for feeding your baby her first tastes. Soon you will need beakers for drinks, and once she's sitting up steadily you will need a highchair. You don't need to sterilize equipment for solid food, just wash it well in very hot water, rinse, drain, and dry on kitchen paper.

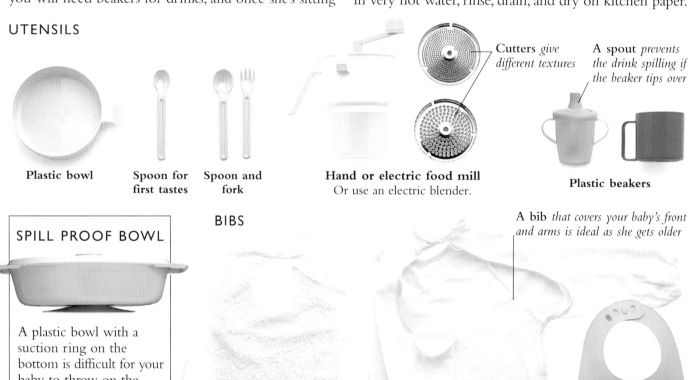

UTENSILS

Plastic bowl

Spoon for first tastes

Spoon and fork

Cutters give different textures

Hand or electric food mill
Or use an electric blender.

A spout prevents the drink spilling if the beaker tips over

Plastic beakers

SPILL PROOF BOWL

A plastic bowl with a suction ring on the bottom is difficult for your baby to throw on the floor. This bowl usually has three food compartments as well as a double shell with a stoppered hole, so that you can fill the cavity with hot water to keep food warm for a slow eater.

BIBS

Plastic-backed terry bib
This is the best type in the early months. Plastic backing and ties at the sides ensure that your child's clothes are protected.

A bib that covers your baby's front and arms is ideal as she gets older

Bib with sleeves

Plastic bib

CHAIRS

Some chairs have reclining seats for infants

Make sure *the tray can be wiped clean*

A rim **around the edge** *of the tray will stop at least some food from falling on the floor*

An easy-care seat cover *is advisable, because food will go everywhere*

The frame must *lock rigid, so your child's fingers can't get pinched*

A restraining strap *or bar is important to stop your baby from slipping down between tray and seat*

A chair that folds *up is useful in a small kitchen*

Highchair
Your baby needs a highchair from the age of about six months, or from when she can sit up steadily; before that feed her on your lap and then in her bouncing cradle or car seat. Always strap her into her highchair with a safety harness, and never leave her in it unsupervised. Put the chair on a plastic sheet, and involve your child in family mealtimes by setting it next to the table. The chair should conform to British Standard number BS5799.

Clip-on chair
A seat that screws on to a table is excellent when you're away from home – but follow the manufacturer's guidelines carefully, because there are several types of table on which this chair must not be used. Use a safety harness, and protect the floor underneath.

Booster seat
From the age of about 18 months to two years, your child can reach the level of the table with a booster seat strapped securely to an ordinary chair. Adjust the height by turning the seat over. It's harder to fall off a booster seat than a cushion.

WHY WAIT TO FEED YOUR BABY SOLIDS?

Babies used to be fed puréed foods from a very early age. But we now know that the digestive system of a very young baby isn't ready for solid foods. The gut and kidneys can handle formula or breast milk, but not much else. Allergies, indigestion, constipation, and diarrhoea are less likely if you wait till your baby is at least four months old (six months if there is a family history of allergy) before giving solids.

Very young infants cannot easily move food from the front to the back of their mouth, and have such poor head control that it is difficult to hold them in a position where they can be fed and easily swallow semi-solid foods. By four months, most can sit supported in a chair, by five, a baby can easily swallow food from a spoon, and by six, he can chew. A seven-month baby will turn his head away to indicate that he has had enough.

Food tastes and preferences
Food smells, tastes, and feels different from breast or formula milk and it comes in mouthfuls rather than a continuous stream. Don't worry if your baby refuses food or spits it out at first. Let him play with his food, and once he is six months, give finger foods he can hold himself. All this will encourage your baby to experiment with this strange new way of feeding.

WHAT TO FEED YOUR BABY

The best foods to give your baby are fresh foods that you prepare and cook yourself.

Texture Gear the texture of the food to what she can happily cope with. It's normal to see occasional chunks of whole food on her nappy, but if they appear regularly, go back to mashing for a few weeks longer. Make her food wet and easy to swallow. Moisten puréed, mashed, or minced foods with boiled water, breast milk, formula, the cooking liquid (if unsalted), fruit juice, or yogurt (from six months).

Temperature Always let the food cool to lukewarm.

Introducing a new food If there is a family history of allergy, offer each new food on its own, and wait 24 hours before giving it again to see how your child reacts. If diarrhoea, sickness, or a rash follows, don't offer it again for several months.

Seasoning Don't use any: salt can damage young kidneys, and your baby won't mind bland flavours.

What to avoid Until she is at least four, avoid nuts and any salty, processed, or fatty foods: salami, bacon, salt fish, Jersey milk, cream, and tandoori foods are not suitable. Don't give soft cheese or honey under one year. Use fresh eggs and always cook them well. Avoid citrus fruits, spinach, turnip, and beetroot before six months.

4–6 MONTHS

Texture Give semi-liquid purées, bland and smooth and without any lumps.

Preparation

★ peel carefully
★ cook: steam or boil
★ remove pips and strings
★ purée or sieve

Other good foods

Peas, marrow, well-cooked green beans, cauliflower.

Baby rice **Puréed carrot** **Puréed apple** **Puréed potato**

6–8 MONTHS

Texture Foods can be minced or mashed to the texture of cottage cheese, adding liquid or yogurt. Give plenty of finger foods that are easy for her to pick up herself, for example: sticks of raw vegetables, pieces of peeled fruit.

Preparation, fruit/vegetables

★ peel carefully
★ remove pips and strings
★ purée or sieve.

Preparation, meat/fish

★ trim fat and skin off
★ cook: grill or poach
★ remove all bones
★ mince finely.

Other good foods

Wheat cereals, parsnip, tomato (remove skin first, and sieve), sweet corn, soaked, dried apricots.

Foods to avoid Biscuits, cake, ice cream, pastry, fried foods. Don't give whole egg before eight months.

Minced chicken **Minced white fish** **Mashed egg yolk** **Plain yogurt** **Finger foods**

HOW TO STORE YOUR BABY'S FOOD

Have nutritious, home-cooked food for your baby always on hand by making up batches of purées and freezing them. Purée fruits and vegetables separately, and cool them quickly by standing the bowl in cold water. Pour the purée into ice-cube trays, cover with plastic wrap, and freeze. When frozen, empty the cubes out and store in sealed freezer bags, one type of food per bag. Label with the name and date, and don't keep for longer than one month.

Half an hour before a mealtime, put some cubes in a bowl to thaw – one or two will be enough at first. Stand the bowl in hot water to heat the purée, then transfer the purée to your baby's bowl.

You can keep a prepared food for your baby in the fridge for up to 24 hours; always cover it first. After your baby has finished her meal, throw away any food that your baby's spoon has been dipped into, including commercial baby foods if you have fed her straight from the jar.

8–9 MONTHS

Texture Introduce your child to chunkier textures now, so chop food rather than mashing it. Give plenty of finger foods to encourage feeding skills. Stay nearby when she is eating finger foods in case she chokes.

Preparation, fruit/vegetables
* peel carefully
* remove pips and strings
* give in slices or sticks or grate, if raw
* chop or mash, if cooked: leave plenty of lumps.

Preparation, meat/fish
* trim fat and skin off
* cook: grill, stew, or poach
* mince lumpily.

Other good foods Toast, red meat, home-cooked dishes, e.g. lasagne, soup, or shepherd's pie (cooked without salt).

Lean minced beef or lamb **Pasta** **Mashed lentils** **Brown rice**

Finger foods

10–12 MONTHS

Texture Your child is eating almost everything the family eats, chopped into bite-sized pieces. Continue to avoid salt in your cooking; you can salt your own food at the table.

Preparation, fruit/vegetables
* peel carefully
* remove pips and strings
* if cooked, steam whenever possible.

Preparation, meat/fish
* trim fat and skin off
* cook: grill, stew, or poach
* chop up small.

Other good foods Pork (if thoroughly cooked), stronger-flavoured green vegetables, for example, cabbage, green pepper, whole peeled tomato.

Foods to avoid Spicy, fatty, or salty foods, sugary foods, fruit squashes, soft unpasteurized cheeses.

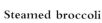
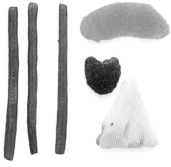

Steamed broccoli **Green beans** **Fruits**

Tinned tuna

DEVELOP A WATER HABIT

Many children never drink plain water, but have fruit juices or squashes instead. Some derive as much as a third of their daily calorie requirements from these drinks, which reduce their appetite but give no real nutrients. If they are sweetened, these drinks contribute to tooth decay too. Offer water when your child is thirsty between meals so she doesn't develop a "fruit juice habit". Colas and similar fizzy drinks aren't suitable for young children, neither are "diet" soft drinks, which may contain high levels of artificial sweeteners.

IRON AND VITAMINS

The best way to make sure your baby gets the nourishment she needs is to offer her a wide range of foods. The store of iron she was born with will begin to run out when she is about six months old. Good sources of iron include: red meat, liver, dried fruit, breakfast cereals, lentils, egg yolk, and green vegetables such as peas and spinach. Your baby will be able to absorb more iron if she eats foods containing vitamin C (found in fruit and vegetables) at the same time. Don't give tea – it will reduce the amount of iron she absorbs from her food.

WARNING

Never give a pre-school child peanuts. It's easy for a small child to inhale a fragment accidentally, and if this happens the oil the peanuts contain can cause severe irritation in the lungs.

INTRODUCING FIRST TASTES

At four months your baby is probably ready to try small amounts of solid food, but you can wait until five or six months if she seems happy and content on milk alone. Remember that for the first weeks you're simply introducing her to the idea of eating solid food from a spoon; breast or formula milk is still providing her with all the nourishment that she needs. Start at the breakfast or lunchtime feed, avoiding teatime because of the possibility of a food upsetting her and giving you both a disturbed night's sleep. She will most likely be more co-operative if you let her partially satisfy her hunger first, so "sandwich" a teaspoon of baby rice or fruit purée between two halves of her normal breast- or bottle-feed. The whole process might take as long as an hour.

YOU WILL NEED
Bib
Small plastic bowl or eggcup
Small plastic spoon
About a dessertspoonful of fresh apple or pear purée, or baby rice
Damp tissue or facecloth

COMMERCIAL BABY FOODS

Baby foods in jars, cans, or packets can be useful, especially when you're away from home or in a hurry. But your baby will be better off if you can keep them to a minimum in her diet, because their flavours are so dull and uniform: home-made food has greater variety of texture and taste. If you want to keep some commercial food in store, avoid those whose list of ingredients includes sugar, dextrose, sucrose, or salt, or shows water as the first item – this means that it's the largest ingredient, so the food may not be as nutritious as your home-made equivalent. Always check the sell-by date and packaging.

GIVE A FEED FIRST

Sit down comfortably with your baby's bowl of food within reach. Put a bib on her, then give her half her usual breast- or bottle-feed: let her empty one breast, or give her half her bottle. Help her bring up any wind. She will go on needing her milk feeds for several months to come.

GIVING YOUR BABY HER FIRST TASTES

1 With her still on your lap, scoop a little food on to the spoon – enough to coat the tip. Put the spoon between your baby's lips so that she can suck the food off. Don't try to push the spoon in, she will gag if she feels food at the back of her tongue. She may be surprised at the taste and sensation at first, so be patient and talk to her encouragingly.

2 She may quickly discover that she enjoys this new experience. If she pushes the food out, scrape it up and put the spoon between her lips again. When she's had about a teaspoonful of purée or rice, wipe her mouth and chin and resume her milk feed.

IF SHE FUSSES AT THE SPOON

Dip the tip of a clean finger into the food and let your baby suck that. If she still protests, she may not like the taste of that food; try another next time.

HOW TO WEAN YOUR BABY

How you wean your baby off breast- or bottle-feeds and on to solid food will depend very much on her temperament. Don't try to rush her. Take one step at a time, and let her adjust before taking the next. The chart below is just one way you might approach weaning: it assumes you start at about four months, and that you would prefer to make lunch the first solids-only meal. You might want to go a great deal slower than shown below, or you may prefer to concentrate on freeing yourself from feeding at breakfast-time first. Remember that if you are breast-feeding, your milk production system needs to wind down gradually. Drop one feed at a time, and leave at least three days before dropping another.

A STAGE-BY-STAGE GUIDE TO WEANING							
Stage/age	**What to do**	**Drinks**	**Meals and feeds**				
			EARLY AM	BREAK-FAST	LUNCH	TEA	BED-TIME
Weeks 1 and 2 Age 4 months (ages are guide-lines only)	Give small tastes of baby rice or fruit or vegetable purée at lunchtime, halfway through the breast- or bottle-feed. Give the same food for three days to accustom your baby to it.	If you are bottle-feeding, offer your baby occasional drinks of cooled boiled water.	■	■	■ ■■	■	■
Weeks 3 and 4 Age 4½ months	Introduce solid food at breakfast, halfway through the feed: baby rice or other gluten-free cereal (no wheat, barley, oats, or rye) is ideal. Increase the amount of solid food at lunchtime to 3–4 teaspoonfuls.	Offer cooled boiled water or diluted fruit juice in a bottle. Don't worry if she doesn't want any.	■	■■■	■■■	■	■
Weeks 5 and 6 Age 5 months	Introduce solid food at teatime, halfway through the feed. A few days later, offer two courses at lunch: follow a vegetable purée with a fruit one, giving 2–3 teaspoonfuls of each.	Introduce a trainer beaker, but don't expect her to be able to drink from it yet – it's just a toy.	■■■	■■■■	■■■	■	
Weeks 7 and 8 Age 5½ months	Offer solid food as the first part of lunch, then give breast or bottle to top up. She can have two courses at teatime now, a sandwich and a piece of banana, for example. At breakfast and tea, continue giving the feed first. She may eat 5–6 dessertspoonfuls of solid food at each meal now.	You can start to give your baby drinks in her beaker, but hold it for her as she drinks from it.	■■■	■■■	■■■■	■	
Weeks 9 and 10 Age 6 months	After lunch solids, offer a drink of formula milk from a beaker instead of the feed. After a few days with no lunchtime feed, offer solid food as the first part of tea.	Offer formula milk in a beaker at each meal and cooled boiled water or diluted juice at other times.	■■■	■■	■■■	■	
Weeks 11 and 12 Age 6½ months	Offer your baby a drink of formula milk in a beaker instead of a full feed after her tea. You may find she often refuses her topping-up feed after her breakfast solids now.	As before.	■■	■■	■■	■	
Week 13 onwards Age 7 months	Offer a drink in a beaker instead of the feed before breakfast: now your baby is having solids at three meals a day. Breast or formula milk should be the main milk drink until one year. She can have cow's milk from twelve months.	As before. Your baby may possibly be able to manage her own beaker now.	■	■■	■■	■	
			Key ■ feed ■ solid food				

HOW YOUR BABY LEARNS TO FEED HERSELF

Your baby will be keen to try and feed herself long before she's able to do so efficiently. However messy an experience this is – be prepared for food to end up all over her face and clothes, into her hair (and yours!) and on the floor – and however long-drawn-out it makes mealtimes, try to encourage her as much as you can, it is her first real step towards independence. Try to keep a calm and relaxed attitude at meal times and don't rush your baby: if your baby finds them interesting and enjoyable occasions, you are less likely to encounter problems over food and eating in the future.

AT SEVEN MONTHS
Your baby may be making determined efforts to feed herself by this age, but she won't be co-ordinated enough to get all the food she needs into her mouth. Feed her yourself, but don't stop her from playing with her food. Smearing it over her face may be messy, but it's the first step in learning to feed herself; have a clean facecloth to wipe her with when she's finished. Give her plenty of different finger foods, too. They're easy to handle, so she will gain in confidence and dexterity.

1 She will be hungry at the start of the meal. Keep the bowl out of her reach and spoon-feed her.

2 Once you've satisfied her initial hunger, let her join in but continue feeding her yourself.

Your baby *won't be very skillful yet, but will love the challenge*

TIPS TO HELP
★ If she grabs your spoon, use two spoons at the same meal. Fill one and put it in her bowl so she can pick it up. Fill the other one and keep it ready for when her spoon turns over on the way to her mouth. When this happens, pop your full spoon in, and fill hers so she can try again.
★ Have clean spoons ready for when she drops hers on the floor.

3 Your baby may get so absorbed in the pleasure of dabbling her fingers in her bowl and pushing the food into her mouth that she will lose interest in you feeding her with a spoon. If she's still hungry, she may cry and wriggle out of frustration because she can't get the food in quickly enough, so offer some more spoonfuls. Otherwise let her practise her feeding skills: feeling "I can do it myself" is important to her. She knows when she's had enough.

4 Solid food may make her thirsty, so offer formula and tip the beaker for her – she won't be able to hold it herself yet. Introduce cow's milk from one year.

"How much food should I offer my baby?"

Let your baby decide how much food she wants at each meal. At six months, start with no more than four tablespoons of food in her bowl, and offer more if she eats it all. With her pudding, start with about two tablespoons. Some days she will eat voraciously, others hardly anything. If she is gaining weight normally, there's no need to worry that she's not getting enough.

"My child will only eat cheese sandwiches. What can I do?"

Food fads are extremely common in young children, and thankfully usually don't last more than a couple of weeks. Don't stop offering your child other things at meal times, but don't worry or get frustrated with him if he won't eat them; he won't suffer unless the fad goes on for several weeks. If you are concerned that he is missing vital nutrients, ask your health visitor about vitamin drops.

"Should I make him eat things he doesn't seem to like?"

Respect your child's opinions. If he doesn't like something, don't mix it with something he does like, he will only end up disliking both. Try varying the form in which you give a particular food. For example, if he doesn't like vegetables, he might eat them raw or liquidized in soup; or egg custard might be a good alternative to hard-boiled eggs, if he always refuses to eat those.

FIFTEEN MONTHS

Your child will be making a good attempt to feed himself with a spoon or fork with rounded prongs, so cut his food into bite-sized pieces. He may need your help on some days.

EATING AND YOUR OLDER CHILD

Around the age of two years your child will probably be ready to graduate out of his highchair and join the rest of the family at the meal table. Mealtimes are extremely important social occasions, and learning how to participate as a member of the family is a vital part of your child's continuing social development. What he eats is obviously important as well, but as long as you provide your child with enough nutritious food, you can leave it up to him whether he eats it or not. Your child won't starve himself, and he knows best how much food he wants at any particular time.

A healthy snack
An apple is always a good source of fibre and vitamins. Wash it well first, or peel it.

Avoiding mealtime problems
The secret of avoiding mealtime problems is to keep your own attitude relaxed and friendly. From the beginning, make your child feel that eating is a pleasurable way to satisfy his hunger. It is always a mistake to join battle over eating – you will end up more upset than your child, and he will refuse more strongly next time. Instead, keep the eating issue in perspective for both of you, for it should be an enjoyable experience:
★ Give your toddler a varied diet, and give him some choice over what he eats. He will soon make his likes and dislikes clear.
★ Don't punish him for not eating a particular food, and don't reward him for eating something either. "Eat up your carrots and you can play on your tricycle" will make any child think there must be something rather nasty about carrots if he has to be rewarded for eating them.
★ Don't spend a great deal of time preparing food especially for him: you will only feel doubly resentful if he doesn't eat it.
★ If he dawdles over his food, don't rush him to finish it. He's bound to be slower than you. If you would expect him to stay at the table while you finish your meal, then you must do the same and wait for him to finish when he's being slow.
★ Don't persuade him to eat more than he wants. Let him decide when he has had enough. He won't starve, and if he's growing normally, you know he's eating enough.

The right diet
Variety is the keynote of a good diet: if you offer many different foods throughout the week, you can be reasonably sure that your child is getting the nutrients he needs. His diet will only be unhealthy if for long periods he eats too much of some kinds of food – perhaps biscuits and cakes, or highly processed foods such as sausages or bought hamburgers – to the exclusion of others.

Snacks and sweets
Your child will often need a snack to give him energy between meals. Rather than biscuits, offer him healthy, nutritious snacks such as a

---

WAYS TO IMPROVE YOUR FAMILY'S DIET
A healthy diet is one that includes a wide variety of foods. Although a low fat diet is healthiest for adults, a child should be given full-fat foods until the age of five.
★ Use fresh rather than processed foods – they will contain more nutrients and less salt and sugar.
★ Use vegetable margarine and oil instead of butter.
★ Eat chicken or fish instead of red meat at least three times a week.
★ Steam vegetables rather than boil them to preserve nutrients, or serve them raw.
★ Buy wholemeal bread rather than white.

---

piece of wholemeal bread, an apple, a carrot, or a banana. If he's not very hungry at the next meal, he won't have missed out nutritionally.

Sweets can be a battleground, but it's up to you to make the rules, and stick to them. Certainly it's not fair or realistic to ban sweets altogether; he may learn to covet them even more. But sweets provide few nutrients other than calories, and they are very destructive for your child's teeth.

Control your child's love of anything sweet by keeping sugary and sweetened foods to a minimum:
★ Provide fruit or unsweetened yogurt for pudding at most meals. Cheese is excellent too, because it neutralizes the acid that forms in the mouth and attacks tooth enamel.
★ When you do let your child have sweets, give them at the end of the meal, not between meals.
★ Choose sweets that can be eaten quickly, rather than sucked or chewed for a long time.
★ Give pure, diluted fruit juices rather than squashes, and give them only at meals; offer milk or water as drinks at other times.
★ Don't use sweets as your main way of rewarding or punishing your child: they will become intensely valuable to him, so harder to control.
★ Make brushing with fluoride toothpaste a routine at least after breakfast and before bed (see pages 144-5).

CRYING AND YOUR BABY

Your baby is bound to cry a great deal during his first year. To begin with, it's his only means of communicating his need for food and comfort, but from around three months you will see a change. Instead of spending much of his waking time crying, he will use that time to learn about the world around him. When your baby cries, your instinct will be to pick him up and cuddle him; you need not worry that by doing so you are spoiling him, or encouraging him to cry more. Your baby needs to know that he can rely on you. However, constant bouts of crying are exhausting for you. If you find your baby cries so much that you are fast losing patience, seek help from your health visitor.

WAYS TO SOOTHE YOUR NEWBORN

The important thing when your baby cries is to respond quickly, without making a lot of anxious fuss: leaving him to cry will agitate him more.

SEVEN WAYS TO SOOTHE YOUR CRYING BABY

Offer a feed In the first months hunger is the most likely reason for your baby crying, and offering a feed the most effective way to soothe her – even if that means frequent feeds day and night. If your baby is bottle-fed and sucks hungrily at her bottle with short gaps between feeds, try offering cooled boiled water in a sterile bottle: she may be thirsty.

Cuddle her Very often this will be just the sort of loving contact your baby needs to calm down and stop crying. If she quietens when you hold her upright against your shoulder, or face down in your arms (see page 83), it may have been wind that was making her cry. If she has been passed around for relatives and friends to hold, she may just want a few quiet moments being cuddled by a familiar parent.

Rock her rhythmically Movement often comforts a fractious baby, and may send her off to sleep. Rock her in your arms, and if she doesn't quieten try rocking faster – perhaps 60 to 70 rocks per minute. Or just jig her up and down by shifting from foot to foot, perhaps with your baby in a sling on your tummy (see below). Or rock with her in a rocking chair, if you have one. Or put her in her carrycot and push her to and fro; if you can take her round the block, the gentle bumping over the pavements will often soothe her.

Carry him Very often you will be able to soothe your baby simply by putting him in the front pack and carrying him around with you. This leaves your hands free, and your baby will be soothed both by the close physical contact with you and the motion as you move around. If your baby is crying because of something you've had to do to him – changing his nappy, bathing, or dressing him for example – this may be the best way to calm him, and probably even send him off to sleep.

Pat her Rhythmically patting and rubbing her back or tummy will often calm her down, and may help her to bring up wind. The feel of your hand will often comfort her when you first put her down to change her nappy, too.

Give him something to suck Almost all babies are soothed by sucking. Your clean little finger will probably work like magic, pacifying him and sometimes sending him to sleep. He may well suck his own fist from an early age. If you want to try giving him a dummy, use a natural-shaped one, and sterilize it before every use (see page 124).

Distract your baby Something to look at may make your baby forget why he was crying, at least for a while. Bright, colourful patterns may fascinate him: he will often gaze intently at postcards, wallpaper, or your clothes. Faces and mirrors are also excellent distractions, and a walk round the house to look at photographs or at himself in a mirror may calm your crying baby.

SEVEN REASONS YOUR BABY MIGHT BE CRYING

Often you won't really know why your young baby is crying or why he stopped. If you've tried the simple remedies such as feeding and a cuddle, and you've tried the soothing tactics that usually work (see previous page), all without success, there may be another reason. Listed below are some other possible causes of his crying.

Illness may be making your baby cry, particularly if his crying sounds different from normal. Always call your doctor if your baby shows any symptoms that are unusual for him. A blocked nose from a cold may stop him feeding or sucking his thumb, so he can't comfort himself in the way he's used to, even though he may not be very ill. Your doctor can prescribe nose drops to help him breathe easily. (See pages 180–81.)

Nappy rash or a sore bottom may make your baby cry. Take his nappy off, clean him thoroughly, and, leave him without a nappy for the rest of the day: just lay him on a towel or terry nappy. Take steps to stop the rash worsening (see page 150).

Colic, often called three-month or evening colic, is characterized by a pattern of regular, intense, inconsolable screaming at a certain time each day, usually the late afternoon or evening. The pattern appears at about three weeks, and continues until 12 or 14 weeks. The crying spell may last as long as three hours. Always ask for medical advice the first time your baby screams inconsolably. Colic isn't harmful, but you might misdiagnose it and miss other, serious symptoms.

His surroundings may make your baby cry. He might be too cold: your baby's room temperature should be about 18–20°C (65–68°F), a temperature comfortable for lightly clothed adults. Avoid over-heating – don't pile on too many bed-clothes. If the back of your baby's neck feels warm and damp, he's probably too hot; remove some bed-clothes and undo some clothes to help him cool off. If he is sweating, a towel under the crib sheet may make him more comfortable. Bright lights can make him cry too: make sure an overhead lamp above his changing mat, or the sun, isn't shining in his eyes.

Activities he hates can't always be avoided, however loudly he voices his dislike. Dressing and undressing, bathing, having eye or nose drops are all common dislikes in a new baby, but all you can do is get them over with as quickly as possible, then give your baby a cuddle to calm him down.

Your own mood may be a reason for your baby's distress. Perhaps it's evening and you're feeling tired; perhaps your baby's tetchiness is making you irritable. Knowing that your baby is often just reacting to your own emotions may help you to be calmer with him.

Too much fussing can sometimes make an upset baby cry all the more. Passing him between you, changing a nappy unnecessarily, offering a feed again and again, discussing his crying in anxious voices, may all make him more agitated. If there's no obvious reason for his crying, don't keep trying to find one: he probably just wants a calming cuddle.

COPING WITH COLIC

All you can do if your baby has evening colic is learn to live with it, in the certain knowledge that he isn't ill or ab-normal, and that the colic won't last. Don't suffer alone: this will be a difficult three months for you, your partner, and your baby. Remember these three points:
★ Try any of the methods on the previous page to try to soothe your baby. But as long as you are confident nothing is wrong with the baby it can help to put him in his cot for a few minutes.
★ Don't resort to medicines. Colic can't be cured. Gripe water is harmless and comforts some babies. Talk to your health visitor or midwife; they will reassure you that this is just a normal, passing phase.
★ Try to have an evening out. Leave your partner or a relative in charge.

YOUR CRYING OLDER BABY

From the age of about three months, you may notice a real change in your baby. He's now much more aware of what goes on around him, he's responsive and interested in everything – much more of a person altogether. He'll still cry a lot, and will continue to do so for many months to come, but by now you'll have a much better idea of why he is crying.

SIX REASONS WHY YOUR OLDER BABY MIGHT BE CRYING

Hunger is still an obvious reason for your baby to cry. As his first year progresses and he becomes mobile and moves on to solid food, he will often get tired and fractious between meals – his life is a busy one. A snack and a drink may restore his energy and cheer him up.

Anxiety will be a new reason for crying from the age of seven or eight months, because by then your baby will have discovered his unshakable attachment to you. You are his "safe base"; he'll be happy to explore the world, provided he can keep you in sight. He may cry if you leave him, or if he loses sight of you. Be patient with him, and let him get used to new people and situations gradually.

Pain, from bumps as he becomes mobile, will be a frequent cause of tears. Often it will be the shock that makes him cry, rather than any injury, so a sympathetic cuddle and a distracting toy will usually help him forget it quickly.

Wanting to get her own way will often be a cause of friction and tears, particularly from the age of two. It's worth asking yourself if you're frustrating her unnecessarily, or perhaps trying to assert your own will; but sometimes she will need to be checked for her safety. If she gets so angry that she throws a tantrum, don't shout at her, or try reasoning with her, or punish her afterwards. It's best to ignore the tantrum completely. Wait until the fit of temper has passed, then continue with whatever you were going to do (see also page 176).

Frustration, as your baby tries to do things that are beyond her capabilities, will be a more and more common reason for crying. You can't avoid this although you can make life easier for her by, for example, putting her things where she can reach them. Distraction is the best cure: introduce a new game or toy and her tears may soon be forgotten. Or help her if she's struggling, but don't take over completely.

"Every new tooth my toddler cuts is preceded by days of crying. What can I do to help him?"

The first teeth shouldn't cause your baby any trouble, but the back teeth, which are usually cut during the second year, can be painful. Your child will probably dribble a lot and have a red cheek for a couple of days. There are ways you can help him:
★ Rub his gums with your little finger.
★ Give him something firm to chew on: a carrot is ideal, chill it in the fridge first. Make sure that he does not bite off a piece and choke on it.
★ If you use a water-filled teething ring, put it in the fridge, not the freezer: frozen rings can cause frostbite.
★ Avoid giving repeated doses of medications or teething gels.

Overtiredness will show itself in whininess, irritability, and finally tears. By the end of her first year your child's life is so full of new experiences that she can run out of energy before she's run out of enthusiasm. She needs you to help her relax enough to get the sleep she needs. A quiet time sitting on your lap listening to a story may work, and a calming, enjoyable bedtime routine (see pages 124–25) that you stick to every evening will help too.

SLEEP AND YOUR BABY

Broken nights and lack of sleep for you will be a fact of life for many weeks until your baby settles into a routine that coincides more closely with yours. At around nine months, new problems may develop. She may be very reluctant to let you leave her, or she may settle into a pattern of night waking. Careful handling at bedtime from around the middle of your baby's first year can help to avoid problems later: a relaxing bedtime routine, that takes place in exactly the same way every night, will give her the sense of security she needs. Until at least the age of two-and-a-half, and probably much longer, some daytime sleep will be essential. Your toddler's life is an active, exciting one, and she will need a reviving nap to prevent her getting overtired and irritable.

EQUIPMENT FOR SLEEP

What you buy for your baby to sleep in will be a significant investment, so shop around. You will also need plenty of machine-washable bedding. Duvets should not be used for infants under one year. Cotton sheets and cellular blankets are good as you can add or remove them and so prevent your baby getting cold or too hot. Until your baby is a year, tuck the bottom end of the top sheet and blankets well under the end of the mattress, so that the top ends come only half way up the cot. You can then put your baby to sleep so that she is lying half way down the cot, with her feet near the end of the cot. In this position she is unlikely to slip down beneath the bedclothes and overheat or suffocate.

WHAT TO SLEEP IN

Cot Your baby will be sleeping in this from around three months to around three, so it's worth investing in a sturdy, well-made one. Safety is paramount: choose a cot that conforms to British Standard number BS1753.

Carrycot For your young baby, a carrycot that you clip to a wheeled chassis is a good buy: it provides somewhere for her to sleep day or night, and a good way to transport her outdoors. If you buy a carrycot, you won't need a Moses basket or a crib. The carrycot you buy should conform to British Standard number BS3881.

Watch for *any sharp edges: sand them down if necessary*

A fitted sheet *in 100% cotton is easy to put on and comfortable for your baby*

Handles *enable you to transport your baby easily while she's asleep*

YOUR BABY'S BEDDING

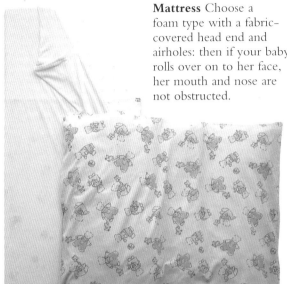

Mattress Choose a foam type with a fabric-covered head end and airholes: then if your baby rolls over on to her face, her mouth and nose are not obstructed.

Fitted sheet and duvet Light and warm, a duvet is suitable for a baby over a year old. For your newborn baby, however, choose a brushed cotton sheet and cellular blankets so you can regulate her temperature and avoid overheating.

Cot bumper This cushions and cuts out draughts, but should not be used for very young babies. Cut the bumper's ties to no longer than 18cm (7in) as soon as you buy it.

Cellular blanket Cellular cotton blankets are best for very young babies.

TOYS FOR THE COT

Mobile Hanging just out of reach above your baby's cot, a colourful mobile will amuse her.

Teddy bear

YOUR BABY'S ROOM

★ Keep the room warm: 15–20°C (65–68°F) is ideal. At this temperature a sheet plus three layers of blankets is enough for your baby.
★ Install a dimmer switch or nightlight, so you can check on your baby while she's asleep without disturbing her.
★ You will need a baby alarm installed in your baby's room, unless you live in a small flat. The type that can be plugged in wherever you are is the most flexible.

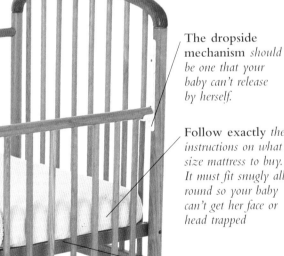

The dropside mechanism *should be one that your baby can't release by herself.*

Follow exactly *the instructions on what size mattress to buy. It must fit snugly all round so your baby can't get her face or head trapped*

The mattress base *should be at least 59.5cm (2ft) from the top edge of the cot, so your baby cannot climb out. You should be able to lower the base*

The spaces *between the bars should not be less than 2.5cm (1in), so she can't get an arm or leg stuck; and not more than 6cm (2½in), so she can't slip out feet first*

BABY MONITORS

Baby monitors have two separate units – one part is left close to the baby and the other goes with whoever is listening. A microphone means you can sit anywhere in the house and know your baby isn't crying. Many monitors now come with additional features such as adjustable volume on the parent unit, integrated nightlight, and remote digital room temperature display. Ranges can vary from around 75m (68ft) up to 300m (275ft), so it may be possible to sit in the back garden and still be in touch. As with any baby equipment, look for the BSI kite mark to show that goods are safety approved.

DAY- AND NIGHT-TIME SLEEP

Your newborn baby will sleep as much as she needs to; the only trouble is she may not take her sleep when you would like her to. In the early days she will sleep in short bursts randomly throughout the day and night. The chart below shows how her sleep pattern might develop: as the months pass, her longest period of sleep coincides more and more with the hours of night, and her wakeful times become longer. However, babies vary. Don't worry if yours takes longer than you expected (or hoped) to sleep through the night.

Emphasizing day and night

Right from the newborn stage, make a clear distinction between how you treat day- and night-time sleep, to help your baby learn which time is for play and which for sleep. During the day, put her to sleep in a carrycot, pram, or Moses basket: if you're using a cot already, save it for night-time only. A carrycot or pram can go out-side in a shady spot, always covered with an insect net and with the brakes on. Indoors, make sure pets can't get into the room where your baby is, but there is no need to keep the house especially quiet for her. When your baby cries, pick her up and make the most of her waking time: help her to associate the daylight hours with play and wakefulness.

At night, wrap your baby lightly so her jerking limbs won't wake her, and put her to sleep in her cot, if you're already using one. Keep the room dark. When she wakes and cries for a feed, pick her up and feed her quietly, talking as little as possible and only changing her nappy if she's very wet or dirty. She will gradually learn that night-time feeds are business only, not social times, and her sleep pattern will become more like yours as the weeks go by.

Your toddler's naps

From the age of about six months, bedtime will become a more and more important ritual in your baby's day, and she needs to be tired and ready for bed if she is to sleep through the night. She needs some daytime sleep to give her energy for her active life, and will go on needing it throughout toddlerhood, but don't let her nap for too long. Give her two hours at each nap (she may wake earlier), then wake her. She may be grumpy and confused if she was deeply asleep, so give her plenty of time before introducing the next activity.

"My ten-month-old wakes up at 6am and won't go to sleep again. Is there anything we can do?"

Early morning waking probably just means your baby has had enough sleep. Leave a few toys in his cot each night to occupy him for a while when he wakes, with a drink in a non-spill beaker in case he's thirsty. When he is tired of his toys and calls out for you, changing his nappy and offering some new toys in his cot may gain you an extra hour's sleep.

If early waking is a regular pattern, you could try adjusting his sleep times throughout the day so he has a later bedtime.

You could also try putting thick curtains up in your baby's bedroom so the sun won't wake him up too early in the morning.

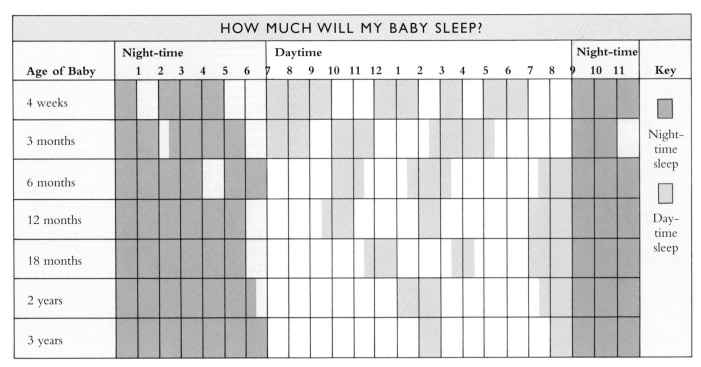

	HOW MUCH WILL MY BABY SLEEP?																						
Age of Baby	**Night-time**						**Daytime**														**Night-time**		**Key**
	1	2	3	4	5	6	7	8	9	10	11	12	1	2	3	4	5	6	7	8	9	10 11	
4 weeks																							Night-time sleep / Day-time sleep
3 months																							
6 months																							
12 months																							
18 months																							
2 years																							
3 years																							

GETTING THE TEMPERATURE RIGHT

The risk of cot death is increased when a baby is overwrapped or overheated, especially if he is feverish or unwell. And yet it is important not to let your baby become chilled. The ideal room temperature for the room where your baby sleeps is about 18°C (65°F) – a comfortable temperature for a lightly clothed adult. If the room is at this temperature, a baby who is wearing a sleep suit and a vest will also need to be covered by a sheet and three layers of blankets. Wrapping a very young baby snugly in a blanket stops his limbs jerking as he drops off to sleep and often helps him settle more easily. But there is a risk of overheating unless you remember that a baby who is wrapped like this will need fewer blankets to cover him. Duvets should not be used for babies under a year. Don't add extra bedding if your baby is unwell or feverish, or expose the baby to direct heat from a hot water bottle, electric blanket, or radiant heater.

SLEEPTIME SAFETY

* Never let your baby sleep with a pillow until at least two: it could smother her.
* Put your baby to sleep on her back. Doctors believe this is the safest position. Babies who sleep on their front seem to run an increased risk of cot death.
* Remove any polythene packaging from the mattress and don't use a plastic sheet.
* Don't let your baby get too hot or too cold.
* Don't smoke and keep your baby in a smoke-free atmosphere.
* Place your baby in the feet to foot position so she can't slip down beneath the covers.

Cot death A few babies each year die unexpectedly in their cots. There is no explanation for cot death, or Sudden Infant Death Syndrome, but doctors have suggested some safety precautions (see left) that can help to minimize the risk of cot death occurring. If you always put your baby to sleep on her back, make sure that she is not exposed to cigarette smoke, and are careful to see that she does not become overheated, you can greatly reduce the risk of cot death.

If you think your baby is unwell, consult your doctor straight away.

PUTTING YOUR BABY IN THE "FEET TO FOOT" POSITION

Place your baby's feet at the foot of the cot and tuck in the covers securely so they reach no higher than his shoulders and cannot slip up and cover his head. Babies whose heads are accidentally covered with bedding get too hot and run a greater risk of cot death.

Lay your baby *with his feet at the foot of the cot*

Putting a baby to bed
Babies regulate their body temperature by losing heat from their face and head. If a baby slips beneath the bedclothes so that his face and head are covered, heat can't be lost as easily. Make sure the bedding is arranged so that this can't happen. Unless the room is very cold, infants over one month should not wear hats indoors for sleeping.

Sleeping on his back
Doctors believe that the safest sleeping position for your baby is lying on his back – there is no evidence to suggest that babies tend to vomit and then choke in this position.

SETTLING FOR SLEEP

There will be times when your baby won't settle contentedly off to sleep after a feed. Gentle rocking, or a quiet period in your arms may help to relax her and send her off to sleep. But eventually you want her to learn to fall asleep on her own, so try to keep these soothing methods for times when she is really fretful so she does not become too dependent on them.

SOOTHING CONTACT

Rubbing your baby's stomach rhythmically may soothe her enough to send her to sleep. Don't alter the rhythm or you will disturb her, and don't stop until her eyelids have closed.

ROCKING

Rock your baby to and fro in your arms to lull her to sleep. You may have to keep it up for some time, and she may wake every time you stop to put her in her cot, but it's still a tried and tested way to send her to sleep.

SUCKING

Your baby will be soothed by sucking, and your clean little finger is ideal. He may suck his own fist. If you don't mind him having a dummy, use a natural-shaped one; you can limit its use to the first three months if you wish, he won't miss it at that age.

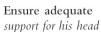

Ensure adequate support for his head

A SLING

If your baby wakes every time you put him down, try carrying him around in a sling: the motion of your body will keep him asleep (see page 85).

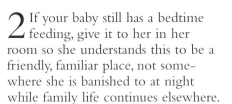

YOUR OLDER BABY'S BEDTIME ROUTINE

From about six months, your baby will settle down to sleep more happily if the whole process of going to bed takes place in exactly the same way – babies love routine and rituals. From now on she won't be quite so ready to go to sleep in strange surroundings, and her sleep patterns will be easily upset by a change in daily life, so try to impose the normal routine even if you're away from home. Make getting ready for bed as much fun as you can, so it's a pleasurable, but unde-manding, part of your baby's day.

WHAT TIME IS BEDTIME?

It's up to you and your partner to choose a time that fits in with your own routine – and one that you can stick to more or less every day. Make sure it's late enough that you're both home, and not so late that the routine takes up all your evening. Any time between 6 pm and 8 pm is suitable.

THE BEDTIME ROUTINE

1 Start the routine in the same way every evening. A bath is ideal, because it's both fun and relaxing. If she doesn't like being bathed, 20 minutes spent playing a gentle game together might help her unwind.

2 If your baby still has a bedtime feeding, give it to her in her room so she understands this to be a friendly, familiar place, not some-where she is banished to at night while family life continues elsewhere.

3 Put your baby into her cot with her favourite teddy or soft toys and her cuddly if she has one.

4 Now perhaps your partner could take over, so you're both involved in the bedtime routine. This last half hour or so needs to be always the same, to mark it clearly as the end of the day.

RHYTHMIC MOVEMENTS

Pushing your baby to and fro in her carrycot will often soothe her to sleep, although she may keep trying to look at you. When she does drop off, don't lift her out of the carrycot to put her in her cot, even if it is night-time.

A CAR RIDE

If you get desperate, try putting your baby in his car seat and going for a drive round the block: the motion will probably put him to sleep automatically. When you get home again, leave him undisturbed in his seat and carry both indoors. Cover him with a blanket to keep him warm.

A light blanket *is ideal for wrapping your baby*

WRAPPING

Some babies sleep more peacefully with their arms tucked in. Others will always work their arms loose even if you wrap them securely (but not tightly). It doesn't matter if his arms are left free; he won't catch cold.

OTHER METHODS

Lullabies, as you rock your baby to and fro, are an age-old method of soothing her to sleep. Your baby won't mind if you can't sing in tune.
Taped music playing softly in her room may help your baby to drop off to sleep. For difficult sleepers, a **soother tape** of the sounds she would have heard in the womb may work.

5 Read a story with your baby to relax her and help her wind down. Don't give up if you think she isn't paying attention: she will be tired and won't respond to the pictures with her usual lively interest, but that doesn't mean she isn't listening.

6 Tuck your baby up with her favourite toy or cuddly and kiss her good night. Turn the light down, or switch a nightlight on. Spend a moment or two pottering around the room before you go.

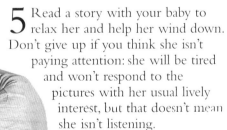

"Is it a good idea to take my baby into bed with me?"

Night feeds can be easier if you take your baby into bed, and provided neither you nor your partner has taken drugs or drunk alcohol, there's no risk of lying on him. Put him in the middle so you can't push him out. As he gets older, it's up to you to set the rules, although you will all sleep better in your own beds. Sleeping with you can become a habit, which may later be hard to break.

OVERCOMING SLEEPING PROBLEMS

NIGHT FEEDS	NIGHT WAKING	UNSETTLED BEDTIME

By the time your baby is six months old, she can go until morning without food; but she may well settle into a pattern of waking for a feed. If you want to wean her off these night-time feeds, start by reducing the feeds gradually, then stop the feeds but go in to her and offer reassurance for as long as she cries.

The tactics below provide a way of reassuring your older baby when she wakes in the night that all is well and you have not abandoned her, while conveying the message that she is only going to get the minimum of attention from you during these hours. If she is not sleeping through within a week, ask your health visitor's advice.

From the age of about nine months, establish a method of handling bed-time, then stick to it. If your baby gets into a pattern of not settling when you put her to bed, a week of resolutely following the tactics below should break it. She will soon get the message that you will always come to her if she cries, but you won't get her up again.

At her bedtime feed, try not to let your baby fall asleep with the breast or bottle in her mouth: she needs to learn to fall asleep on her own, not rely on sucking to relax. As soon as her eyelids droop, take her off the nipple or teat. Tuck her up in her cot.

⬇

For a few nights, give her a feed when she wakes, but reduce the amount. Put her back in her cot, asleep or not, kiss her, and leave.

⬇

If you are breast-feeding, your partner will have to take over at this point as your baby will smell your milk and want to carry on feeding. If she continues to cry, wait five minutes, then pop back in to give her a pat and rub her back to reassure her. Then go back to bed, even if she's still crying.

⬇

Continue to pop back every five minutes. Only pick her up if she is beside herself with crying; when her sobs subside, put her back in her cot and leave for a few minutes more. You may have a couple of hours of this, but persevere.

⬇

For the next few nights, stop offering the feed; instead adopt the tactics for night waking for as long as it takes to teach your baby to sleep through the night.

If your baby whimpers in the night, wait a few minutes to see if she goes back to sleep again.

⬇

If she cries properly, go in to check nothing is wrong. If not, soothe her and calm her down: rubbing her back may be enough, but you may need to pick her up and cuddle her. When the crying has subsided into sniffles, put her back into her cot, tuck her up so she is snug and warm, and kiss her good night. Then go back to bed yourself.

⬇

If the crying continues, or increases in intensity again, call out to her reassuringly from your own bed, but wait five minutes before going in to settle her down again.

⬇

When you do go back, just reassure her by patting and rubbing her back – don't get her up unless she is really beside herself – then tuck her up and leave her.

⬇

Continue going back in this way at five-minute intervals for as long as it takes her to fall back to sleep. After half an hour increase the intervals between visits to ten minutes, but never leave her crying for more than 15. A week of gentle firmness on your part should be enough to establish a more sociable sleeping pattern.

Keep to a bedtime routine, making it fun for your baby but relaxing and loving as well. If she cries when you leave her after tucking her up for the night, go back and give her a reassuring kiss, but don't pick her up, and don't stay more than a moment or two.

⬇

If she cries again, call out to her reassuringly, but wait five minutes before going in again.

⬇

When you do go in, check that there's nothing wrong, such as a wet nappy or something chafing. If not, pat her back to soothe her, kiss her good night again, and tuck her up. Be cheerful but firm, and then go. Don't hesitate – your baby's will is stronger than yours at this point, and you'll be easily persuaded to stay.

⬇

If she goes on crying, continue popping in for a brief look at five-minute intervals. After half an hour of that, start to increase the intervals between visits, but never leave your baby crying for longer than a quarter of an hour.

⬇

Eventually she will realize that the brief reward of you popping in at intervals isn't worth all the effort that she's putting in, and will drop off to sleep.

Your newborn baby can't keep herself awake – and once asleep, nothing will disturb her until she's had as much sleep as she needs.

CLOTHES AND DRESSING

In the early weeks, your baby may need clean clothes as often as he needs a clean nappy, so you will need plenty of first-size clothes. Ask your friends or relatives if they can let you have any cast-offs. As your child turns into an active toddler, you will need to have clothes that are comfortable and unrestricting – and you'll need far fewer. Your child is growing so fast that an extensive wardrobe or shoes and clothes "for best" don't make much sense – his clothes will be outgrown long before they are outworn. Choose them carefully: easy-to-manage fastenings and elasticated trousers, for example, will all help him as he learns to dress and undress himself. Choose clothes that are easy to care for, and machine-washable – keeping neat, still, and clean shouldn't have to figure in your child's life at all. He shouldn't have to worry about his clothes, and nor should you.

BUYING CLOTHES FOR YOUR BABY

Clothes for a young baby should be easy to put-on, machine-washable, and if possible made from natural fibres, which allow your baby to regulate his own temperature as well as he can. Don't use any biological powders or fabric conditioners to wash your baby's clothes, they may irritate his skin. The basic item of clothing now and throughout the first six months is the all-in-one stretchsuit.

Look for suits *with a large cotton content*

Simple cuffs *are best; if your suit has scratch mitts, don't use them*

Envelope neck *stretches wide*

Vest

Vest with poppers

Vest
Look for a wide or an envelope neck to help you get it over your baby's head, wide sleeves, and 100% cotton or wool.

Stretchsuit
Look for poppers up the front and round the crotch – this type is easiest to put on. Avoid scratch mitts, your baby needs to learn about his hands. A tight stretch-suit can deform his soft bones, so always dress him in one that is baggy all over.

Woolly hat

Mittens

Sun hat

On a cold day, your baby needs a **woolly hat** that ties under his chin and tie-on-**mittens** to stop him losing heat. In hot weather, he needs a **sun hat**.

Cardigan
Avoid mohair or fluffy wool, and any knit with large holes that could catch fingers.

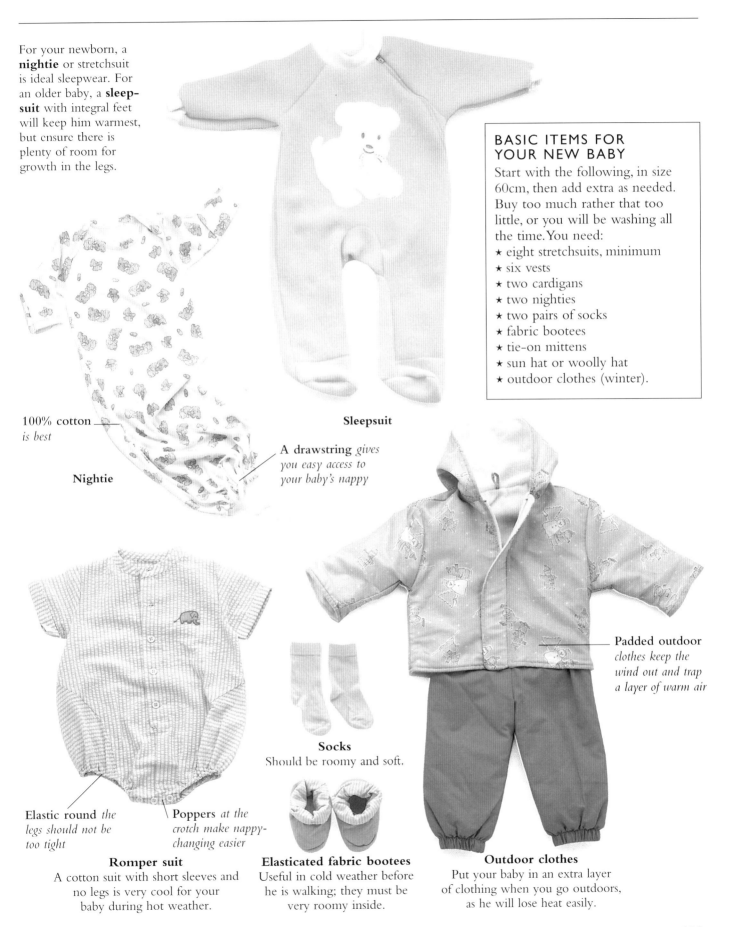

For your newborn, a **nightie** or stretchsuit is ideal sleepwear. For an older baby, a **sleep-suit** with integral feet will keep him warmest, but ensure there is plenty of room for growth in the legs.

Sleepsuit

100% cotton *is best*

Nightie

A drawstring *gives you easy access to your baby's nappy*

Padded outdoor *clothes keep the wind out and trap a layer of warm air*

Socks
Should be roomy and soft.

Elastic round *the legs should not be too tight*

Poppers *at the crotch make nappy-changing easier*

Romper suit
A cotton suit with short sleeves and no legs is very cool for your baby during hot weather.

Elasticated fabric bootees
Useful in cold weather before he is walking; they must be very roomy inside.

Outdoor clothes
Put your baby in an extra layer of clothing when you go outdoors, as he will lose heat easily.

HOW TO DRESS YOUR BABY

Dressing and undressing your baby is a lovely opportunity to let him learn about his own body by stroking and caressing his soft skin. He may hate being dressed, but you can make it pleasurable with lots of nuzzling, cuddles, kisses, and chat; be especially gentle, too. Gather up the clothes you need and undo all the poppers. Lay your baby on his changing mat.

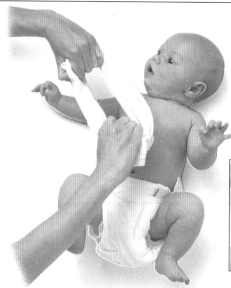

PUTTING ON A VEST

1 Hold the vest with the front facing you and gather it into your hands. Put the back edge at your baby's crown.

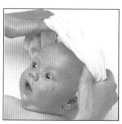

Position the back edge at the top of his head

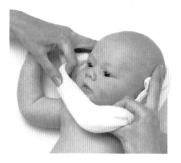

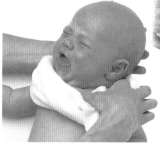

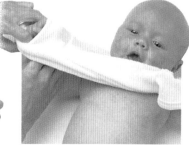

2 With one swift, gentle movement bring the front edge of the vest down to your baby's chin. Hold all the fabric gathered up together and stretch it as wide as you can, so that none of it drags on his face and upsets him.

3 Gently lift your baby's head and upper body and pull the back of the vest down so it is round his neck and lying behind his shoulders. Lower him to the mat without jolting or letting his head flop.

4 If your baby's vest has sleeves, put the fingers of one hand down through the first sleeve and stretch it wide, then with the other hand guide his fist into your fingers.

5 Hold your baby's hand with your first hand, and ease the sleeve over his arm with the other. Pull the vest down below his arm. Do the same with the other sleeve, pulling the vest, not your baby.

PUTTING ON A STRETCHSUIT

1 Pick your baby up while you lay the clean stretchsuit out flat on the changing mat, the front upwards and all the poppers undone. Lay your baby on top, his neck in line with the stretchsuit's.

Lay the stretchsuit out flat

6 Pull the vest over his tummy. Lift his lower body by his ankles and pull the back down. Do up the poppers at the crotch.

A vest *underneath the stretchsuit is essential in anything but the hottest weather*

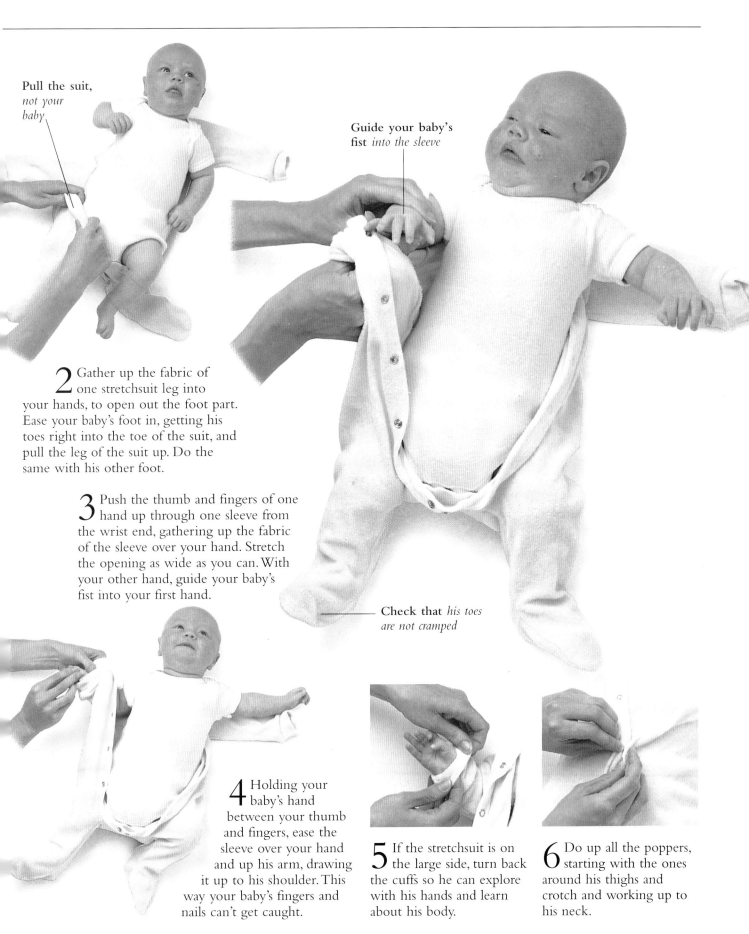

Pull the suit, *not your baby*

Guide your baby's fist *into the sleeve*

2 Gather up the fabric of one stretchsuit leg into your hands, to open out the foot part. Ease your baby's foot in, getting his toes right into the toe of the suit, and pull the leg of the suit up. Do the same with his other foot.

3 Push the thumb and fingers of one hand up through one sleeve from the wrist end, gathering up the fabric of the sleeve over your hand. Stretch the opening as wide as you can. With your other hand, guide your baby's fist into your first hand.

Check that *his toes are not cramped*

4 Holding your baby's hand between your thumb and fingers, ease the sleeve over your hand and up his arm, drawing it up to his shoulder. This way your baby's fingers and nails can't get caught.

5 If the stretchsuit is on the large side, turn back the cuffs so he can explore with his hands and learn about his body.

6 Do up all the poppers, starting with the ones around his thighs and crotch and working up to his neck.

131

UNDRESSING YOUR BABY

Your baby may be un-nerved by the feel of cold air against his skin as you undress him, so nuzzle his bare tummy, and make the most of this opportunity for skin-to-skin contact. Have a towel on hand to wrap your baby in when you've undressed him, or dress him again quickly. Lay your baby on his changing mat.

TAKING OFF A STRETCHSUIT

1 Undo the stretchsuit poppers. Hold one ankle inside the suit and pull the suit leg off. Do the same with the other.

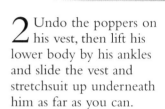

Hold his ankle *while you pull the leg of the suit off*

2 Undo the poppers on his vest, then lift his lower body by his ankles and slide the vest and stretchsuit up underneath him as far as you can.

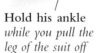

Be gentle *as you undress your baby*

Support *your baby's head*

3 Put your hand inside the sleeve and hold his elbow. Grasp the cuff and pull the sleeve off; then repeat on the other arm.

4 Slide your hand underneath your baby's head and neck and lift his upper body so you can remove the stretchsuit.

TAKING OFF A VEST

1 Hold his elbow inside the vest with one hand and ease all the fabric over his fist. Do the same on the other side.

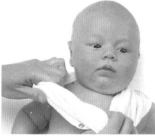

2 Gather up all the vest in your hands, so there is no spare fabric that might drag over your baby's face as you take it off.

3 Stretch the opening as wide as you can, then with one swift movement take it up and over your baby's face to his crown.

4 Slide your hand underneath your baby's head and neck and lift his upper body so you can slide out the vest.

HOW YOUR CHILD LEARNS TO DRESS HIMSELF

By about two years your child will probably manage to pull off his own socks or T-shirt, and the majority of children will begin to dress themselves by the age of about three. You can encourage this new independence by buying clothes that are easy for your child to manage, and by letting him dress and undress as much as he can himself.

WAYS TO HELP

★ Allow plenty of time – if you're not in a rush, you won't get too irritated by his slowness.
★ Lay out his clothes in the order he needs to put them on.
★ Buy trousers or skirts with elasticated waistbands. Avoid zip flies for a pre-school boy in case he gets his penis caught.
★ Look for clothes with large buttons, toggles, or Velcro fastenings.
★ Teach him to start doing buttons up from the bottom upwards.
★ Let him choose his "favourite" foot, then mark his shoe so he can get it on the correct foot.
★ Avoid anoraks with slot-in zippers.
★ When you have to help, make a game of getting dressed, playing "peep-bo" as you pop garments over his head.
★ Once he's dressed, let him stay dressed – even if he gets grubby.

CHOOSING SHOES

Bare feet are best for babies who are learning to walk. They make it easier to balance, and walking barefoot makes for healthy feet. Once your child is ready to walk out of doors he will need shoes, but even then, let him go barefoot as much as possible. Shoes are necessary only to protect feet, not to "support" them – the muscles give all the support the foot needs. Buy shoes from a specialist children's fitter, who will measure the length *and* the width of the foot. Have the fit checked every three months. Buy new socks at the same time as new shoes: too-small socks can be just as deforming as shoes.

What sort of shoes should I buy?

Any leather or canvas shoe is suitable *provided* your child's feet have been properly measured and the shoes fit in length *and* width. In practice, you may find that cheaper shoes like canvas sneakers aren't available in half-sizes and different width fittings. Wellington boots aren't usually available in half-sizes, but they're still essential for wet weather walks. Buy them on the large side, and fit an insole.

Avoid all plastic shoes: plastic doesn't mould itself to the shape of your child's foot like leather, so instead his foot will have to mould itself to the shoe.

What to look for in your child's shoes

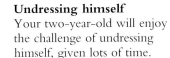

The space between *your child's big toe and the end of the shoe should be 0.5– 1.25 cm ($\frac{1}{4}$ to $\frac{1}{2}$ in) – no more and no less*

Wide toes *are important to give your child's toes room to splay out inside*

The fastening *should hold your child's foot snugly: buckles or Velcro are easiest for your child to manage*

The seams *must be smoothly finished, so nothing can rub your child's skin*

T-bar with buckle   **Open-toed sandal**

Undressing himself
Your two-year-old will enjoy the challenge of undressing himself, given lots of time.

BATHING AND WASHING YOUR BABY

A large part of taking care of your new baby day-to-day will be keeping him clean. His skin is delicate and soft, and even his own bodily functions – sweating, urinating, dribbling – will irritate it and make it sore. As your baby grows, his bathing needs change: he will be pushing food into his hair, exploring the world with his hands, helping you with his nappy changes, and generally getting himself grubby. So from a hygiene point of view, be vigilant about washing off urine, faeces, and sweat as well as milk and food. You don't have to give your baby a daily bath: topping and tailing or sponge bathing is quite adequate to keep him clean. But in all likelihood your baby will quickly come to love being bathed, and it will become an important part of your daily routine together.

EQUIPMENT FOR BATHING AND WASHING

There are plenty of products available designed to make bathtime easier for you, but make sure that you only buy products intended for use on babies. Adult shampoos, soaps, lotions, and creams contain too many additives and chemicals to be safe for your baby's delicate skin.

EQUIPMENT FOR BATHING

Baby bath
Until your baby is ready to go into an adult bath (between three and six months), a proper baby bath will make bathtime easy for you. Place it at a convenient height on a worktop, or put it on the floor. If you buy a special bath stand, make sure it puts the bath at the right height for you.

Small bowl of boiled water   **Cotton wool**

You will need cooled boiled water and plenty of cotton wool to wash your baby's eyes, ears, and face.

A rubber bath mat *stops your baby slipping down*

Waterproof apron
A cotton fabric with waterproof backing will feel softer to your baby than PVC.

Rubber bath mat
Once your baby moves into the big bath, a suctioned rubber bath mat is a must to stop him from sliding on the bottom of the tub.

BABY TOILETRIES

Bath liquid   **Lotion**   **Oil**   **Moisturizer**   **Powder**   **Shampoo**   **Soap**   **Cotton buds**

Fluoride toothpaste

Baby bath liquid is an excellent alternative to both soap and shampoo.
Baby lotion is useful for cleaning your baby's nappy area, particularly if his skin is very dry.
Baby oil is a good moisturizer when your baby's skin is dry or scaly.

Baby moisturizer can be used instead of baby oil.
Baby powder will absorb any dampness left on your baby's skin. Use only a little, putting the talc on your hands and then rubbing it on the baby. Don't shake it over the baby; he might inhale it.

Baby shampoo may be needed once a week.
Baby soap need only be used if you don't use bath liquid. With a young baby, soap him all over on your lap, then rinse the soap off in the baby bath – but remember his body will be very slippery, so hold him firmly.

Cotton wool buds are useful for cleaning between your baby's fingers and toes, but never push them into his ears, nose, eyes, or bottom.
Toothpaste can be an adult brand. Try not to let your child eat it – if he does, avoid using it until he's old enough not to eat it (see page 144).

HAIR, NAILS, AND TEETH

Hairbrush This should have soft bristles and be small enough for your child to brush his own hair from about eighteen months.
Comb Choose a small comb with rounded teeth.
Baby nail scissors These have rounded ends and short blades, so there's no danger of jabbing your baby.

Baby hairbrush and comb

Nail scissors

Toothbrush

Toothbrush This must have a small head so it can reach into the corners of his mouth, and soft, rounded bristles. Nylon or bristle is equally good. Let your baby play with a baby size brush, but use a child's size brush to clean his teeth. Change his brush regularly, and check with your dentist that it is cleaning adequately.

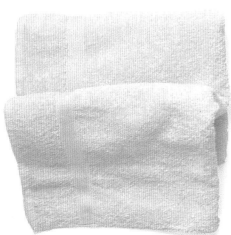

Towel

Keep a large, very soft towel for your baby's use only. Warm it on a radiator before you begin. Some towels have a corner piece that makes a hood.

Natural sponge

Flannel

Keep a new flannel or sponge for your baby's use only, and wash the flannel regularly. Don't let an older baby eat the sponge.

TIPS FOR WASHING YOUR YOUNG BABY

★ Until your baby is six months old, always use cooled boiled water to wash hs eyes, ears, mouth, and face. Boiling kills off any bacteria in the water.
★ Only clean the parts you can see – do not try to clean right inside your baby's nose or ears, just wipe away any visible mucus or wax with damp cotton wool. Otherwise you may push the dirt back up into the nose or ear.
★ With a baby girl, never try to separate her vaginal lips to clean inside them. You will hinder the natural flow of mucus that washes bacteria out.

★ With a baby boy, never try to push back his foreskin to clean under it: you may hurt him, or tear or damage the foreskin.
★ Always wipe from front to back when you are cleaning a baby girl's nappy area. This prevents germs from spreading from the anus into the vagina and causing infection.
★ When wiping your baby's eyes and ears, use a fresh piece of cotton wool for each one, or you may spread minor infections.
★ Always leave cleaning your baby's bottom until last, and use a fresh piece of cotton wool for each wipe. Dip in warm tap water.

TOPPING AND TAILING

Topping and tailing simply means cleaning only the parts of your baby that really need cleaning – her hands, face, neck, and nappy area. Top and tail your baby as part of your morning or bedtime routine – it's an excellent alternative to a bath, particularly during the first six weeks, when neither you nor your baby will feel very sure of bathing in the baby bath. Make sure the room is warm. Boil some water for washing your baby's face and pour it into a small bowl to cool. Wash your hands. Lay your baby on her changing mat and undress her down to her vest.

YOU WILL NEED
Small bowl of cooled boiled water for your baby's face
Bowl of warm tap water
Pieces of cotton wool
Tissues
Warm towel
Nappy-changing equipment
Clean clothes

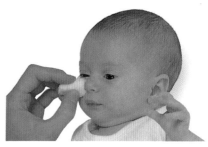

1 Wipe each eye from the nose outwards with cotton wool dipped in the boiled water. Use a fresh piece for each wipe, and for each eye. Dry gently with a tissue.

Wipe away *dirt and fluff behind her ears*

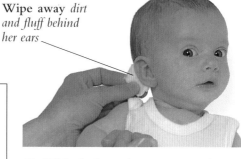

5 Uncurl her fingers *gently to wipe her hands*

2 With fresh moist cotton wool, wipe each ear. Don't try to wipe inside: just wipe over and behind it. Use a fresh piece of cotton wool for each ear, and dry with the towel.

CLEANING YOUR BABY'S CORD STUMP

The shrivelled up stump of your baby's umbilical cord will probably have dropped off by the time he is a week old. Until it drops off, your midwife will call every day to clean it, or you will be taught how. Careful cleaning makes sure infection cannot set it, and helps the cord to separate. She will advise you to dry the stump with cotton wool after bathing your baby.

Once the stump of cord has dropped off, you will need to clean the navel every day as part of your topping and tailing routine until it is fully healed.

Consult your midwife or health visitor as soon as possible if the navel looks red, swollen, inflamed, or starts to weep. A small amount of bleeding is normal, and usually nothing to worry about.

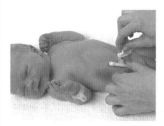

1 Using cotton wool moistened with surgical spirit, wipe carefully in the skin creases around the stump. (After two weeks you can use cooled boiled water.)

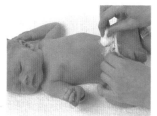

2 Dry with fresh cotton wool. Dust a little baby powder on a piece of cotton wool and dab it over the navel like a powder puff to absorb remaining moisture.

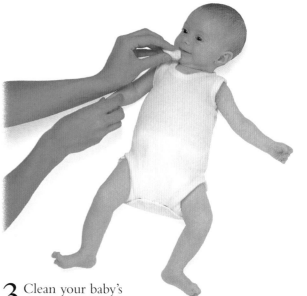

3 Clean your baby's face of milk and dribble by wiping around her mouth and nose, then, wipe over her cheeks and forehead. Dry with the towel.

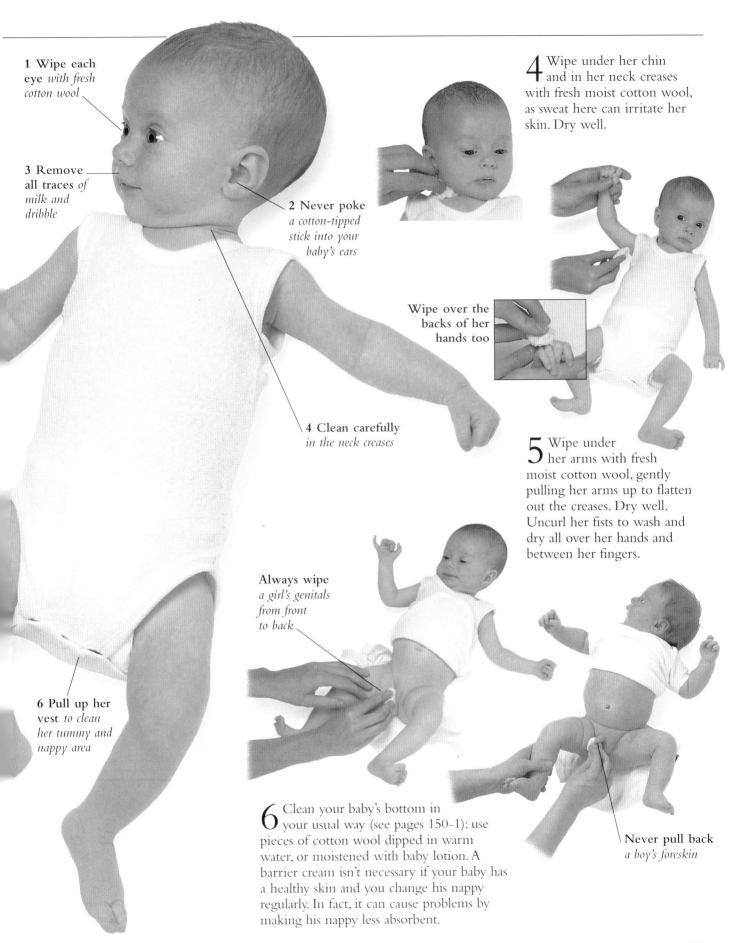

1 Wipe each eye *with fresh cotton wool*

3 Remove all traces *of milk and dribble*

2 Never poke *a cotton-tipped stick into your baby's ears*

4 Clean carefully *in the neck creases*

6 Pull up her vest *to clean her tummy and nappy area*

4 Wipe under her chin and in her neck creases with fresh moist cotton wool, as sweat here can irritate her skin. Dry well.

Wipe over the backs of her hands too

5 Wipe under her arms with fresh moist cotton wool, gently pulling her arms up to flatten out the creases. Dry well. Uncurl her fists to wash and dry all over her hands and between her fingers.

Always wipe *a girl's genitals from front to back*

6 Clean your baby's bottom in your usual way (see pages 150-1): use pieces of cotton wool dipped in warm water, or moistened with baby lotion. A barrier cream isn't necessary if your baby has a healthy skin and you change his nappy regularly. In fact, it can cause problems by making his nappy less absorbent.

Never pull back *a boy's foreskin*

137

BATHING YOUR YOUNG BABY

Most babies come to love the sensation of being bathed; but in the early days you and your baby will probably both have mixed feelings. A new baby often dislikes the feeling of being "unwrapped", and you may feel nervous of holding your baby's small, slippery body. In the first weeks, you can simply top and tail your baby to keep her fresh and clean; practise with a full bath once a week, and a hair wash every two weeks. Make sure the room is warm enough. You can kneel, sit, or stand to bath your baby, but make sure your back doesn't start to ache.

YOU WILL NEED
Baby bath
Changing mat
Your baby's bath towel
Hairwashing towel, if you're washing her hair
Waterproof apron
Bowl of cooled boiled water for washing her face
Pieces of cotton wool
Baby bath liquid (optional)
Nappy-changing equipment
Baby powder (optional)
Clean clothes

GETTING READY FOR THE BATH

1 Put in cold water, add hot and mix. Test with your elbow: the water should feel just warm, and be 10cm (4in) deep. Add bath liquid, if used.

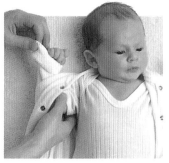

2 Lay the bath towel on the changing mat and undress your baby on it down to her nappy.

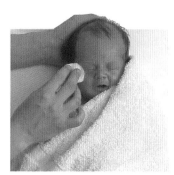

3 Wrap her up snugly and wipe her eyes and face in cotton wool dipped in boiled water.

"My four-week-old baby has ugly crusty patches on his scalp. What should I do about them?"

This is a harmless form of dandruff known as cradle cap. Rub your baby's scalp with baby oil and leave for 24 hours. Comb very gently, then wash the crusts off. If the cradle cap doesn't improve, ask your doctor or health visitor for advice.

WASHING YOUR BABY'S HAIR

1 Cradle her head in one hand, her back along your forearm, and tuck her legs under your elbow. Gently pour water from the bath over her head with a cupped hand. With most brands of bath liquid you don't need to rinse her hair in fresh water.

Avoid splashing *water over her face*

2 Bring your baby back to your lap to pat her head dry gently with a second towel.

CLEANING HER BOTTOM
Lay her on her mat. Take off her nappy and clean her bottom (see pages 150-1).

PUTTING YOUR BABY IN THE BATH

One wrist *supports her head, the other her nearest thigh*

Hold *her far shoulder all the time*

1 Unwrap her on your lap, then lift her in: support her head and neck on your forearm, your hand holding her firmly round her far shoulder and upper arm. Put your other hand under her bottom and thighs.

2 Smile and talk to your baby all the time, as you use her free hand to splash water gently over her body. Take it very slowly if she doesn't seem relaxed.

Let her kick *her arms and legs and enjoy the freedom of being naked*

LIFTING HER OUT AND DRYING HER

1 Two or three minutes in the water is enough for a very young baby. Lift her out of the water by sliding your free hand under her bottom: she will be slippery, so hold her firmly.

Support her head *so it can't flop*

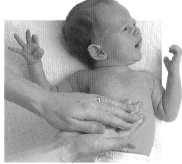

2 Wrap her in the towel on your lap and cuddle her dry. Put her on her mat and dry all her skin creases. Put on a clean nappy.

3 If you use talcum powder, sprinkle it on your hands and rub them together. Rub your hands gently over her skin.

BATHING IN THE BIG BATH

Your baby will probably be ready to graduate to the exciting territory of the big bath at the age of three or four months – and some babies are ready for the experience even earlier. If your baby hasn't yet learnt to enjoy bathtime, don't rush the change – give him a few more weeks of being bathed in his baby bath, until he really is too big for it, or is more confident. To bath your three-month-old, arrange everything you will need beside the bath. Make sure the room is warm. Put the rubber mat on the floor of the bath and run in cold water, then hot, so that the water is just warm. Put your baby on his changing mat to wash his face, eyes, and ears, using cooled boiled water. Then, undress him carefully and clean his bottom thoroughly before placing him gently in the bath.

YOU WILL NEED
Rubber bath mat
Waterproof apron
Baby bath liquid, or baby soap and baby shampoo (shampoo not needed every time)
Large soft towel
Baby's own sponge or facecloth
Equipment for washing your baby's face
Nappy-changing equipment
Pouring and other toys for an older baby
Toothbrush for an older child
Clean clothes

WASHING YOUR BABY

1 Lay your baby in the bath on a rubber mat. Keep his head and shoulders supported on your arm, his ears clear of the water.

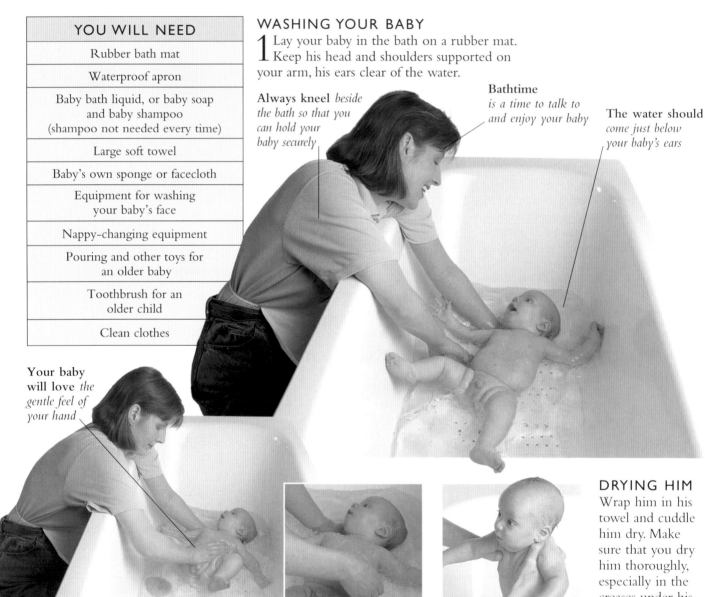

Always kneel *beside the bath so that you can hold your baby securely*

Bathtime *is a time to talk to and enjoy your baby*

The water should *come just below your baby's ears*

Your baby will love *the gentle feel of your hand*

2 If you are using soap, roll the bar in your free hand, then run your hand over his body. If you've put bath liquid in the water, just splash the water over him.

3 Rinse the soap off by splashing water gently over him. Bath liquid does not need to be rinsed off.

LIFTING HIM OUT

Put your hands under your baby's armpits to lift him out. Take care, he will be slippery.

DRYING HIM

Wrap him in his towel and cuddle him dry. Make sure that you dry him thoroughly, especially in the creases under his armpits, at the top of his thighs, and around the neck region. Between the fingers and toes also need careful attention.

WASHING YOUR BABY'S HAIR

 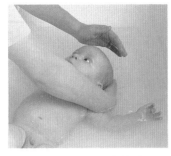 

1 It is only necessary to wash your baby's hair about once a week. Wet the hair first. If using a baby shampoo, slide your supporting hand forwards and pour a small amount into the palm.

2 Support your baby's head with your free hand. Rub shampoo gently over his hair. Be careful not to get the shampoo in his eyes. If you have bath liquid in the water, just wash the water over his hair.

3 Swap hands again and rinse the shampoo off with a wet, well squeezed out sponge or facecloth.

Take your cue *from him – he might enjoy a teasing game*

BATHTIME SAFETY

Always follow these few rules:
* Never leave a baby or small child alone in the bath, or move out of easy reach, even for a second. It takes no time for a child to slip and drown, even in very shallow water.
* Never let your child pull himself to standing in the bath even when he can stand steadily, and even though you have a rubber mat in the bath.
* Even when your baby can sit steadily, keep a hand ready to support him if he slips.
* A rubber mat in the bottom of the bath is essential.
* Never top up with hot water while your child is in the bath. If any topping up is necessary, mix hot and cold water in a jug so it's just warm, then pour it in.
* Make sure the thermostat on your water heater is not set too high.
* If the tap gets hot, tie a face cloth round it so your child can't burn himself on it.
* If you bath with your baby, have the water cooler than you would usually have it.

MAKING BATHTIME FUN

Once your baby can sit steadily, bathtime becomes a wonderful playtime – not just a way of getting him clean. Search out some bath toys: things that pour, like plastic beakers and funnels, sandcastle buckets with holes in, even plastic colanders, will fascinate him; and floating toys like boats or ducks are ideal too. About once a week use a pouring toy to wash her hair, but don't let water run over his face – he will probably hate it.

Always supervise bathtime, *and never leave your child alone in the bath*

BABIES WHO HATE WATER AND WASHING

BABIES WHO HATE BATHING

Some babies are frightened by bathtime – and often a baby or toddler may suddenly take a dislike to bathing. If this happens, give up baths all together for a short time: daily topping and tailing will keep a small baby clean, though a mobile baby will need an all-over sponge bath on your lap (see below). After two or three weeks, try having a bath with your baby to help him overcome his fear of the water.

Playing with water

Sit you baby beside a bowl of water on the kitchen floor and let him splash and play. Pouring beakers and floating toys can often persuade a child that water can be fun.

BABIES WHO HATE WASHING

Even if your child hates having his hands washed, it's important to do so before and after every meal. Make it more fun by washing his hands between your own wet and soapy ones.

BABIES WHO HATE HAIRWASHING

Babies and young children often particularly dislike having their hair washed, even if they love bathtime – around two-and-a-half to three years is often the most difficult time. If your child doesn't like having his hair washed, abandon it for a couple of weeks. Respect his dislike, but help him to be more reasonable about it: for example, go out together in the rain and show him how pleasurable raindrops feel on his face.

Reintroduce hair-washing at bathtime gradually. It may help to give him a facecloth to hold over his eyes and face: often it's the feel of water on their faces that children hate most. If your child will wear one, you could try putting a plastic "halo" round his hairline to keep the water off his face.

Sponging her hair

You can keep your child's hair clean by sponging out any bits of food and dirt with a damp facecloth or sponge.

GIVING YOUR BABY A SPONGE BATH

If your baby doesn't like water, there is no need to bath him: once he can hold his head up, a daily sponge bath on your lap is enough. First, lay him on his mat and wipe his eyes, face, and ears with clean pieces of cotton wool. Sit him on your lap with everything you need within reach.

YOU WILL NEED
Large bowl of warm water, with a little baby bath liquid added
Small bowl of cooled boiled water and cotton wool for your baby's face
Waterproof apron
Your baby's own sponge or facecloth
Warm towel
Nappy-changing equipment

TOP HALF

1 Take off the top half of your baby's clothing. Wet the sponge, squeeze it out well, and wash his neck. Dry well with the towel.

Wear an apron *that covers your upper body*

2 Dip the sponge in the water again, squeeze it out so it doesn't dribble, then wash all over his chest and tummy. Dry him well with the towel.

Put the towel *over your lap before you begin*

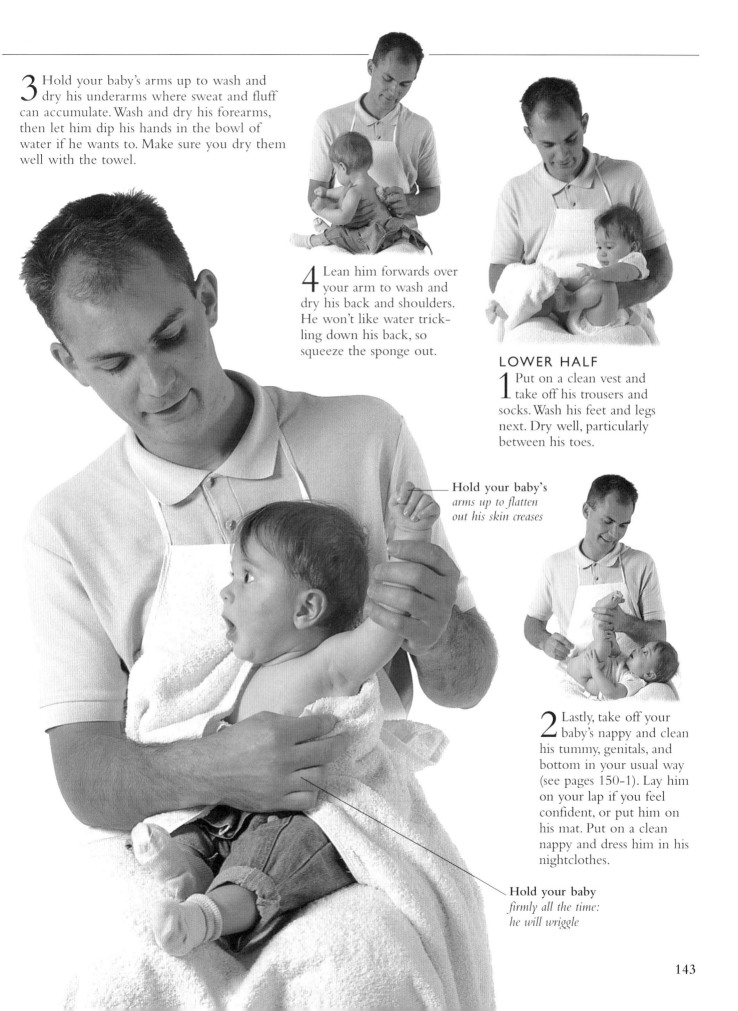

3 Hold your baby's arms up to wash and dry his underarms where sweat and fluff can accumulate. Wash and dry his forearms, then let him dip his hands in the bowl of water if he wants to. Make sure you dry them well with the towel.

4 Lean him forwards over your arm to wash and dry his back and shoulders. He won't like water trickling down his back, so squeeze the sponge out.

LOWER HALF

1 Put on a clean vest and take off his trousers and socks. Wash his feet and legs next. Dry well, particularly between his toes.

Hold your baby's *arms up to flatten out his skin creases*

2 Lastly, take off your baby's nappy and clean his tummy, genitals, and bottom in your usual way (see pages 150–1). Lay him on your lap if you feel confident, or put him on his mat. Put on a clean nappy and dress him in his nightclothes.

Hold your baby *firmly all the time: he will wriggle*

143

CARING FOR YOUR CHILD'S TEETH

It's never too early to start looking after your child's teeth. Once your baby has two or more teeth, wipe his teeth and gums over each evening with a wetted handkerchief. Twelve months is a good age to introduce him to a baby-size toothbrush: clean his teeth for him (see below) after breakfast and at bedtime, but let him play with a brush himself at bathtime too. Taking care of the first, or "milk", teeth helps to ensure that when the permanent teeth come through at around six years old, they will be correctly positioned and in healthy gums – and you will be establishing good, lifelong, habits in your child.

At any age, the more of a game teeth cleaning seems, the more your child will be encouraged to co-operate. Playing dentists, cleaning your own teeth with him, and spitting out messily into the washbasin will all help.

CLEANING YOUR BABY'S TEETH

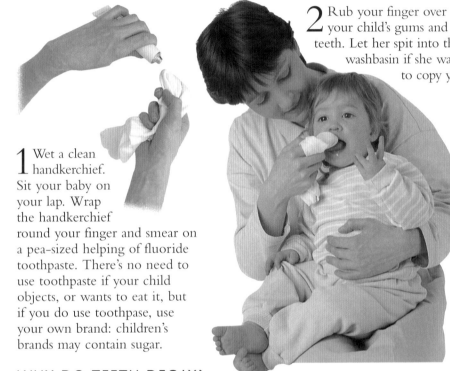

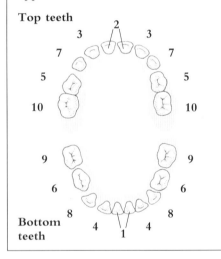

2 Rub your finger over your child's gums and teeth. Let her spit into the washbasin if she wants to copy you.

1 Wet a clean handkerchief. Sit your baby on your lap. Wrap the handkerchief round your finger and smear on a pea-sized helping of fluoride toothpaste. There's no need to use toothpaste if your child objects, or wants to eat it, but if you do use toothpase, use your own brand: children's brands may contain sugar.

HOW THE TEETH COME IN

Your baby might cut his first tooth at any time during the first year, and he will be teething into his third year. Babies' teeth usually appear in the same order.

Top teeth

Bottom teeth

WHY DO TEETH DECAY?

Teeth decay because bacteria in the mouth react with sugar to form acid, which eats through the hard enamel covering the teeth. Sweets and sugary foods and drinks increase the risk of tooth decay, particularly if they're eaten between meals because the teeth are bathed in sugar most of the time. So try to confine sweets to mealtimes, brush your child's teeth afterwards, and give him snacks that don't contain a lot of sugar (see page 116).

Fluoride

Children can have their teeth protected with fluoride, a chemical that hardens tooth enamel, and even heals small breaches in it. Twice daily brushing with a fluoride tooth-paste will help protect your child's teeth from decay, particularly if you leave it to linger in his mouth. Fluoride is present in some water sup-plies, or is given in drops or tablets: your health visitor can advise you.

Too much fluoride?

You needn't worry if your child swallows a little toothpaste as you brush his teeth, but he might love the taste so much that he wants to eat it from the tube. Don't let him. If he's getting fluoride from water or supplements, the extra in the toothpaste might be excessive.

VISITING THE DENTIST

It's sensible to get your child used to seeing the dentist before he is likely to need any treatment. He can go to the dentist even before he has a full set of teeth. If he seems frightened, sit him on your lap in the chair and show him what the equipment does. By the time he is about two and a half he should have regular dental check-ups every six months. Your dentist will have treatments available to prevent tooth decay, and he will be able to advise you about fluoride supplements – so see him even if you are sure your child's teeth are healthy. If there are any cavities, it's vital that they are spotted in good time.

HOW TO CLEAN YOUR CHILD'S TEETH

From the age of 18 months, start cleaning your child's teeth for him with a wetted toothbrush and a pea-sized helping of fluoride toothpaste. Brush them for him for as long as he will let you; he will probably want to brush his teeth himself from the age of about two. Always supervise your child – he needs to brush his teeth correctly. Teach him by standing behind him in front of a mirror, and, holding his hand, showing him the correct movements.

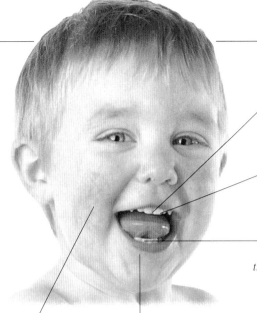

Top teeth: *brush downwards, away from the gums*

All biting surfaces: *brush to and fro along the flat tops of the teeth, all round the mouth*

Bottom teeth *brush upwards, away from the gums*

Get the brush *right to the back of your child's mouth*

Brush the gums *with a circular motion, both on the outsides and inside by the tongue*

Making a game of teeth cleaning
Have a game at bathtime to encourage your child to copy you; clean his teeth properly afterwards.

Cleaning your child's teeth
Stand your child on a step at the washbasin, with you behind her and to one side. Hold her head back so you can see into her mouth as you brush. Let her rinse and spit out – that's most of the fun.

CUTTING NAILS

YOUR NEWBORN BABY

Make sure that you keep your newborn baby's fingernails quite short so that there's no chance of him injuring himself by scratching his skin.

In the first few months, the fingernails are very soft, but don't feel tempted to trim them by biting them off yourself. Instead, use special baby scissors, designed for the purpose. They have blunt ends and are the saftest option for cutting your baby's fingernails.

Make sure that you always cut the fingernails straight across, otherwise the side edges might grow into the skin. So as you cut your baby's nails, it is best to follow the shape of his fingertips. When you have finished, check for any sharp points.

If your baby wriggles while you are trying to cut his fingernails, don't try to fight him. Instead, trim them while he is sleeping peacefully.

YOUR OLDER BABY

Sit your baby on your lap, with him facing forwards. Hold one finger at a time and cut his nails with special baby scissors.

CUTTING TOENAILS

Lay a young baby on his mat; sit an older baby on your lap. Hold his foot firmly, as he will try to kick you.

NAPPIES AND NAPPY CARE

The first few weeks of your newborn baby's life will probably seem a constant round of nappy-changing. Because your baby's bladder is small, she wets often, so at the very least you need to change her after a feed, soon after she wakes, and before she goes to bed, and in the early weeks, often after a night feed too. In fact, change her whenever her nappy is wet or dirty, because leaving her in it makes it more likely she will get nappy rash. Changing her isn't always your first priority: when she wakes in the morning she will be hungry, so take her wet nappy off, wrap her in a towel, and give her some milk before you change her. Nappy-changing need not be a chore: it's a time for games and cuddles, and an important way to show your baby that you love her. But as the months go by, you'll notice that her nappy needs changing less and less often. By around the age of two your child will start to recognize the feeling of a full bladder, and will be approaching readiness for giving up nappies altogether.

THE CONTENTS OF YOUR BABY'S NAPPY

All these are common sights on a baby's nappy:

★ **greenish-black, sticky tar (first two or three days only):** this is meconium, which fills the bowels before birth and must be passed before digestion begins

★ **greeny-brown or bright green semi-fluid stools, full of curds (first week only):** "changing stools" show that your baby is adapting to feeding through her digestive system

★ **orange-yellow, mustard-like stools, watery with bits of milk curd in them, often very copious:** the settled stools of a breast-fed baby

★ **pale brown, solid, formed, and smelly stools:** the settled stools of a bottle-fed baby

★ **green, or green-streaked, stools:** quite normal, but small green stools over several days may be a sign of under-feeding.

Consult your doctor if:

★ the stools are very watery and smelly, and your baby is vomiting and off food: diarrhoea is life-threatening in a young baby

★ you see blood on the diaper

★ anything at all worries you.

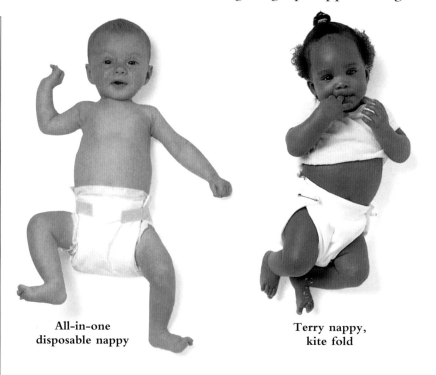

All-in-one disposable nappy

Terry nappy, kite fold

TYPES OF NAPPY

Your baby won't much mind whether you use disposable or fabric nappies, provided the nappy fits snugly and she's not left in a wet or dirty one. Disposables give your baby a neat, slim-line appearance. Terry nappies are bulkier, and the clothes you buy your baby may need to be a few centimetres larger to accommodate the nappy. But terries support your baby's hips well, an advantage if your doctor suspects a loose hip joint.

The raised edge *on the mat won't stop your baby rolling off*

CHANGING YOUR BABY'S NAPPY

Since you will be changing your baby's nappy so frequently, make your changing area a pleasant place for both of you: a mobile above your baby's head, a teddy nearby, transfer motifs stuck to the walls or furniture will all amuse your baby – and encourage her to lie still for you. A changing mat is cheap and convenient, and your baby will be safe if you put the mat on a clean and dry floor. A specially designed changing table may be useful for storing clean nappies and toiletries, but your baby can fall off a table – she can't fall off the floor. If you do put the mat on a raised surface, whether a changing table, worktop, chest-of-drawers, or your bed, never turn your back on your baby even for a second.

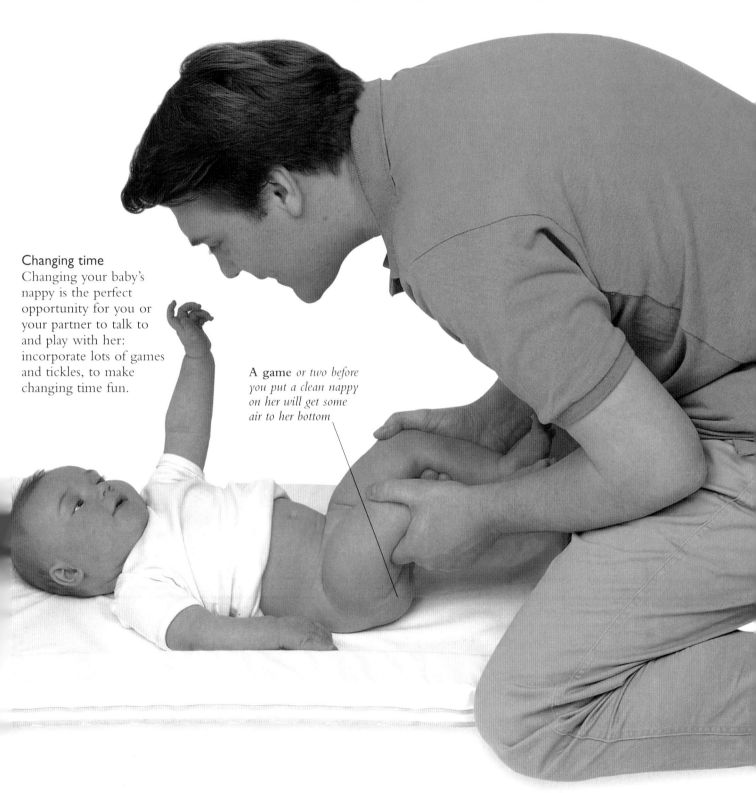

Changing time
Changing your baby's nappy is the perfect opportunity for you or your partner to talk to and play with her: incorporate lots of games and tickles, to make changing time fun.

A game *or two before you put a clean nappy on her will get some air to her bottom*

EQUIPMENT FOR CHANGING YOUR BABY'S NAPPY

Although it may seem to be a daunting array of equipment at first, keeping everything you will need together in one place will make nappy-changing seem that much easier. Make it easy for yourself too by keeping a full set of everything you need in one place; if you live in a house, put a duplicate set of equipment downstairs for the first few weeks. Flush used tissues, nappy liners, and wipes down the lavatory, but put cotton wool and disposable nappies, folded up and sealed, in a bin lined with a plastic bag. Drop terry nappies into the appropriate bucket, filled with sterilizing solution, before washing and rinsing them thoroughly (see page 153).

EQUIPMENT FOR CLEANING YOUR BABY'S BOTTOM

Changing mat
A padded, wipe-clean mat with raised edges is invaluable. In warm weather, put a fabric nappy under your baby's head: the plastic may make her sweaty.

Cotton wool
Buy in a roll or pleats, and break off several pieces before you start the nappy change so you don't have to put a dirty hand into the bag.

Flannels
Use some wet flannels, then some dry ones, to clean her bottom.

Tissues
Needed to wipe away faeces and to dry your baby's bottom.

Barrier cream
Use barrier cream sparingly, and only if your baby's bottom is sore. Be careful not to get any cream on to disposable nappies as the tapes will not stick.

Clean the mat *with a mild solution of disinfectant whenever it gets dirty*

Baby wipes
These are useful for cleaning your baby's bottom, but if used regularly they may contribute to nappy rash.

A few drops of **baby bath liquid** added to the bowl of warm water is a good alternative to water alone for cleaning your baby's bottom. A little **baby lotion** on cotton wool is also effective.

Baby oil

Baby lotion

WHAT KIND OF NAPPIES SHOULD YOU USE?

In a few months time you will be practised enough to change a nappy in a matter of moments, and almost in your sleep, but to begin with, nappies and nappy-changing may seem to take up a disproportionate amount of your day. When you are deciding whether to use terry or disposable nappies, you will be thinking about cost, convenience, and comfort for your baby. Perhaps you're concerned about the environmental aspect too – in the first few weeks you may be changing your baby ten times a day, and have 70 non-biodegradable nappies to dispose of.

Most parents choose disposables if they can afford them. Because they are nappy, liner, and plastic pants all in one they make changing quick and easy, and are just as comfortable for your baby as a conventional terry. Worth considering too is the all-in-one washable nappy.

Terries are the cheapest option. The all-in-one washable is more expensive, though still cheaper than disposables. However, you have to take into account laundry costs, including your own time and labour.

DISPOSABLE NAPPIES

Disposable nappies are sized according to your baby's weight. When you are happy with a brand, buy in bulk. "Ultra" or "High Performance" nappies are very absorbent, and will effectively keep the wetness away from your baby's skin. Some disposables have an outer cover that is breathable, allowing air to circulate next to the skin. "Standard" nappies are cheaper and bulkier, but you will have to change your baby more often. Nappies for boys have more padding at the front, those for girls have more padding underneath.

You will also need:
Plastic bag or bucket with a bin liner inside: drop the used nappies in this; when the bag is full, seal it and put it in the dustbin.
A dozen cloth nappies: for general mopping up around your baby.

Always buy non-chlorine-bleached *nappies if you can*

Elastic round *the legs protects against leaks*

Experiment until *you find a brand with reliable adhesive tapes and good absorbency*

Sticky tape or nappy pins *For when the tapes won't stick, or you need to reseal the nappy.*

Disposable nappy

FABRIC NAPPIES

Muslin nappies are very soft on your baby's skin, so are good for a newborn baby. They are less bulky too, and can be folded small enough to fit a premature baby. They are also good for mopping up. After she is about 6 weeks old your baby will need the extra absorbency of terry nappies. Whichever you use, you will need a one-way liner next to your baby's skin and a pair of plastic pants over the top.

ALL-IN-ONE RE-USABLE NAPPY

The all-in-one re-usable nappy has velcro fastenings, a soft cotton lining with an inner absorbent pad, and a built-in outer waterproof layer that makes for very easy changing, just like a disposable. It comes in two sizes and you will need to buy at least 18 of each size.

Terry nappies

Muslin nappies

Safety nappy pins
The hood locks the pin shut. You may find nappy clips easier and quicker.

Nappy liners
These liners are used inside a fabric nappy to allow moisture to seep through to the nappy.

Pants
These prevent leaks, but also encourage nappy rash.

NAPPY-WASHING EQUIPMENT

Two nappy buckets
Choose buckets of different colours, or with different lids: one is for wet nappies, one for dirty. Every morning fill with sterilizing solution (see page 153). Keep nappy buckets out of the reach of young children.

Tongs

Gloves

Nappy cleaning powder
Used to sterilize the nappies and rid them of bacteria that will give your baby nappy rash. Don't use biological washing powders for washing your baby's nappies, or fabric softener: either might irritate your baby's skin.

Sterilant contains bleach, so don't get it on your skin: use **tongs** or **rubber gloves** to handle the nappies.

CLEANING A GIRL

Clean your baby's bottom thoroughly at every nappy change, otherwise she will soon get red and sore. Wash your hands first. Put your baby on her mat, and undo her clothing and nappy. If she's wearing a fabric nappy, use a clean corner to wipe off most of any faeces. With a disposable, open the nappy out: wipe off the worst of the faeces with tissues and drop them into the nappy. Then lift your baby's legs and fold the nappy down under her.

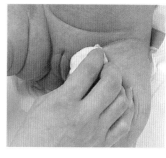

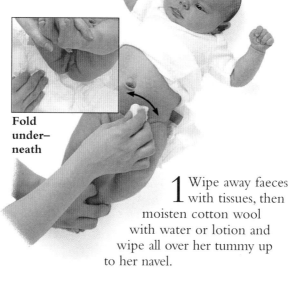

Fold under-neath

1 Wipe away faeces with tissues, then moisten cotton wool with water or lotion and wipe all over her tummy up to her navel.

2 Using fresh cotton wool clean inside all the creases at the tops of your baby's legs, wiping downwards and away from her body.

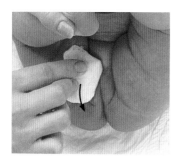

Dry the skin creases well

3 Lift her legs up with a finger between her ankles and clean her genitals next: always wipe from front to back to prevent germs from the anus entering the vagina. Do not try to clean inside the vaginal lips.

4 With fresh cotton wool, clean her anus, then her buttocks and thighs, working inwards towards the anus. When she's clean, remove the disposable nappy, seal the tapes over the front, and drop in the bin. Wipe your hands.

5 Dry her nappy area with tissues, then let her kick for a while without a nappy so that her bottom is open to the air.

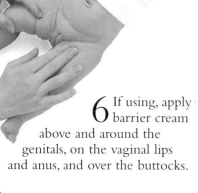

6 If using, apply barrier cream above and around the genitals, on the vaginal lips and anus, and over the buttocks.

NAPPY RASH

All babies get a red or sore bottom from time to time. Consult your doctor if the rash won't clear up.

To avoid nappy rash:
★ change your baby's nappy frequently
★ clean and dry her bottom and skin creases thoroughly, using warm water
★ avoid baby wipes
★ leave your baby without a nappy as often as possible
★ if using fabric nappies, buy tie-on or popper plastic pants, as these allow air to circulate
★ wash and rinse all fabric nappies thoroughly.

At the first signs of redness:
★ change nappies more frequently
★ use a healing nappy rash cream
★ leave your baby without a nappy for as much of the day as possible
★ if using fabric nappies, try a more absorbent type of liner
★ stop using plastic pants: they make nappy rash worse because they help keep urine close to the skin. If you don't like the leaks, switch to disposables for a while.

CLEANING A BOY

Your baby boy's urine will go everywhere, so you need to clean his bottom very thoroughly at every nappy change to guard against a sore bottom. Wash your hands. Put your baby on his mat and undo his clothing and his nappy. If he's wearing a fabric nappy, wipe off the worst of any faeces with a clean corner. With a disposable, undo the tapes, then pause (see right).

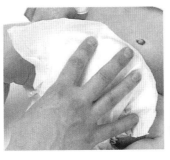

1 Your boy baby will often urinate just as you take his nappy off, so wait a couple of seconds with the nappy held over his penis to avoid urine going everywhere.

2 Open the nappy out. Wipe off faeces with tissues and drop them into the nappy, then fold it down under him. Moisten cotton wool with water or lotion to clean him: start by wiping his tummy up to his navel.

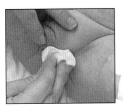

Clean carefully under his testicles

3 With fresh cotton wool, clean thoroughly in the creases at the tops of his legs and at the base of his genitals, wiping away from his body. Hold his testicles out of the way while you wipe underneath them.

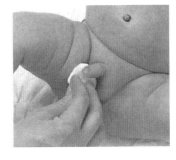

4 With fresh cotton wool, wipe all over your baby's testicles, including under his penis, as there may be traces of urine or faeces here. Hold his penis out of the way if necessary, but take care not to drag the skin.

5 Clean his penis, wiping away from the body: do not pull the foreskin back to clean underneath, this will keep itself clean.

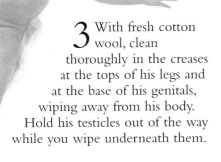

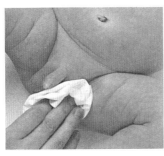

6 Lift your baby's legs to clean his anus and buttocks, keeping a finger between his ankles. Wipe over the back of his thighs too. When he's clean, remove the nappy.

7 Wipe your hands, then dry his nappy area with tissues. Let him kick for a while if he has a sore bottom, with tissues to hand just in case he urinates.

Put barrier cream over his lower tummy to protect against nappy rash

8 If using, apply barrier cream sparingly above the penis (but not on it), around the testicles and anus, and over the buttocks.

PUTTING ON AN ALL-IN-ONE DISPOSABLE NAPPY

Before you put on a new nappy, make sure that you clean your baby's bottom thoroughly and if using, apply a barrier cream. Wipe your hands well on a tissue, as the nappy's adhesive tapes won't stick very well if you get grease on them or on the front of the nappy.

1 Open up the nappy with the tapes at the top. Lift your baby by her ankles with one finger between them and slide the nappy under her, until the top edge lines up with her waist.

Bring the nappy *straight up: don't twist it to one side*

Spread the nappy *taut over your baby's tummy*

2 Bring the front up, pointing the boy's penis towards his feet (or he may urinate into the waistband).

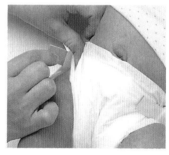

3 Hold one corner in position and, with the other hand, unpeel the tape and pull it forwards to stick to the front, parallel with the top edge of the nappy.

4 Do the same with the other side, making sure the nappy is snug round your baby's legs, and not twisted round to one side.

"How can I make my 15-month-old son lie still while I change his nappy? He wriggles so much I can't clean him properly or pin the nappy on".

No self-respecting toddler will lie patiently and quietly while you change his nappy – but you must still be able to get his bottom thoroughly cleaned. First of all, switch from fabric to disposable nappies. You can fit disposables very easily and quickly, and they have no awkward pins to worry about. Remember to make changing time fun, with tickling games. You can also try giving him some interesting toys to hold. If he's very dirty, it will be easier to clean him by standing him in the bath on a non-slip mat and hosing his bottom down with warm water from the shower attachment. Dry him well.

Fold the waistband *over if it is so high it could chafe your baby's tummy button*

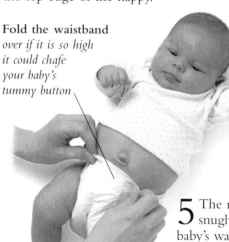

5 The nappy should fit snugly round your baby's waist – just room enough for one of your fingers. Check the fit, and if it's too loose unpeel the tapes and reposition them.

FOLDING FABRIC NAPPIES

TRIPLE ABSORBENT FOLD

The triple absorbent fold is very useful for newborn or small babies: it is small and neat when on, and gives several layers of fabric between your baby's legs, making it extra absorbent. It's good with muslin nappies too.

1 Fold a nappy in four. Put the folded edges nearest you and to the left.

2 Pick up the top layer by the right-hand corner, and pull it out.

3 Make a triangle, with all the edges meeting neatly at the top.

4 Turn the nappy over carefully, and straighten the edges again.

5 Pick up the vertical edge and fold into the middle by one third.

6 Fold these layers over again to make a thick central panel.

7 Put a nappy liner in position, folding one end up if necessary.

KITE FOLD

This way of folding the nappy is good for your growing baby: you can use it from the age of two or three months until your baby is out of nappies completely. As your baby gets bigger, adjust the size by varying the depth of your fold at step 3.

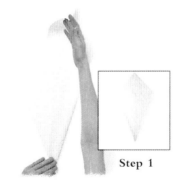  

Step 1

Ready for putting on

1 Lay the nappy out flat. Fold the two edges into the middle until they meet.

2 Fold the top point down, adjusting to make neat top corners.

3 Fold the bottom point up and put a nappy liner in position.

YOUR NAPPY-WASHING ROUTINE

Fabric nappies must be sterilized, washed, and rinsed very thoroughly, because any traces of urine left on them will irritate your baby's skin and cause nappy rash. See page 149 for the equipment you need.

★ Each morning, fill two plastic buckets with fresh cold water and nappy sterilizer.

★ During the day, drop wet nappies into the wet nappy bucket.

★ With dirty nappies, scrape the worst off into the lavatory. Drop into the dirty nappy bucket.

★ At night, put any nappies into a plastic bag or third bucket – the nappies need to soak for at least six hours, so they must go into the morning's fresh solution.

★ In the morning, put nappies from the wet nappy bucket into the washing machine and set it to rinse only.

★ Wash the nappies from the dirty nappy bucket on a hot programme; give them an extra rinse cycle.

★ Rinse out the buckets and fill with cold water and sterilizer. Drop in the nappies changed overnight.

★ Dry all fabric nappies away from direct heat, and air thoroughly.

★ Wash plastic pants in warm water with a little washing-up liquid added. Pat dry and leave to air.

PUTTING ON A TRIPLE ABSORBENT FOLD FABRIC NAPPY

Have all your clean fabric nappies ready folded with liners in position, so you don't have to fold one every time. Clean your baby's bottom thoroughly and, if using, apply barrier cream. Always put the soiled nappy well out of your baby's inquisitive reach, and deal with it when you've finished changing your baby.

1 Lift your baby's legs by the ankles and slide the nappy under her. Align the top edge with her waist.

2 Bring the nappy up between her legs (tuck a boy's penis downwards to prevent leakage around the waist), and hold it there while you turn up one long edge a short way.

Position the thick central *panel under her bottom*

3 Bring that corner up round your baby's waist, pulling slightly on the nappy to get it taut. Hold it in position while you fold up the other long edge.

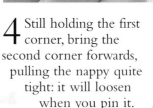

4 Still holding the first corner, bring the second corner forwards, pulling the nappy quite tight: it will loosen when you pin it.

Fold up the long edge *by about four centimetres first to give a good fit round her legs.*

5 Slide your fingers between the nappy and her tummy so you can't jab her, then pin all layers together. Put the pin in horizontally, and clip it shut.

Tuck the plastic pants *in round her waist and legs to protect her clothes from leaks*

6 A good nappy will fit snugly round waist and legs: test with your finger. Fabric nappies always loosen as your baby wriggles, so if the nappy is baggy already, take the pin out and start again.

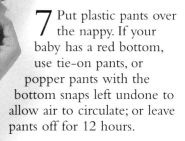

7 Put plastic pants over the nappy. If your baby has a red bottom, use tie-on pants, or popper pants with the bottom snaps left undone to allow air to circulate; or leave pants off for 12 hours.

PUTTING ON A KITE FOLD FABRIC NAPPY

To make nappy changing more efficient, try to have all your clean fabric nappies ready folded with their liners in position. Thoroughly clean your baby's bottom and, if using, apply barrier cream. Once your baby is broader around the tummy, the two corners of the nappy will no longer overlap in the front, so it will be necessary to fasten the nappy with two pins.

SMALL BABY

1 Lift your baby's legs gently by the ankles and slide the nappy under her. Then, fold the two long edges in by approximately four centimetres.

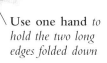

Hold the nappy *tightly – don't let it loosen*

2 Bring the short edge up between your baby's legs as far as it will go; tuck a boy's penis downwards. Hold the nappy there with one hand while you bring one side corner forwards and over the top.

Use one hand *to hold the two long edges folded down*

Align the top edge *of the nappy with her waist*

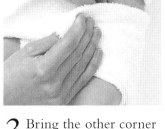

Pull the nappy taut *as you bring each corner forwards*

3 Bring the other corner forwards and over the first, pulling on the fabric as you do so to get a snug fit.

4 Without letting the nappy loosen, put your fingers inside the nappy and pin horizontally.

LARGE BABY
Repeat step 1, then bring the nappy up between your baby's legs as far as it will go, tucking a boy's penis down-wards. Take one front corner round his waist, pull the back corner of the nappy forwards tightly, and pin horizontally. Do the same on the other side, pulling the nappy firmly round your baby's waist. Put the second pin in. Check for bagginess around his legs, tucking excess fabric in, then put plastic pants on.

Pinning the second corner

A good fit *round the legs is essential to avoid leaks*

5 Check you have a good fit – re-pin the nappy if it looks baggy – then put plastic pants on your baby.

GIVING UP NAPPIES

Achieving control over his bowel and bladder functions is a big step in your toddler's development. At some time in the second year, usually around the age of two, your child will start to recognize the feeling of a full rectum and a full bladder. The next step is knowing that a movement is on its way, and once your child grasps this, he will quickly train himself to get to the potty in time if it is easily accessible to him. Progress will probably be uneven: he may gain control over his bowels before his bladder, or vice versa, so puddles or messes will be frequent once he's in pants. But however slowly he learns, trying to "train" him before his body is ready is a waste of your time.

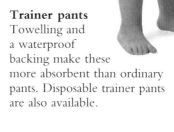

Trainer pants
Towelling and a waterproof backing make these more absorbent than ordinary pants. Disposable trainer pants are also available.

TIPS TO HELP
Remember, too much pressure from you can be confusing, as your child struggles to understand and do what you want.
★ Choose a time for potty-training when your child's life is relatively free of new situations, *and* when you can approach it with a relaxed attitude.
★ Set the situation up so he is more likely to succeed in getting his functions in the potty than fail – if he thinks he always fails, he will stop trying.
★ When he's successful, be pleased with him, but not over-enthusiastic.
★ When he has an accident, be sympathetic about it.

Your child's potty
He will soon understand what it's for, and be proud of himself for learning a new skill.

ACHIEVING DAYTIME CONTROL

1

Wait until your child is ready
Your child is ready to learn to use the potty if he:
★ is aged two to two-and-a-half (boys may not be ready until the age of three)
★ recognizes that he's done something in his nappy, perhaps by pointing and shouting
★ is often dry after a nap.

2

Introduce the potty
Show him a potty and tell him what it's for. Put it in the bathroom for a few days before doing anything further, so he gets used to it. Show him how to sit on it, but with his nappy on for now.

3

Set aside a suitable time
The ideal arrangement for potty training is to set aside two weeks during the summer, when you can stay at home most of the time with your child playing outside in the garden. If you can't organize it this way, it can still be a good idea to have two weeks of concentrated effort, during which a few accidents won't disrupt the household. *Don't* start when your routines are already upset: a holiday away from home, for example, is not a good time.

4

Put him in pants, and remind him often to use the potty
For these two weeks, let your child wear pants or trainer pants, which will absorb at least a little of the urine. Have the potty nearby, and suggest he sits on it after a meal, a drink, a snack, or a nap, and whenever he shows any signs of needing it.

5

Help him to use the potty
Be encouraging about sitting on the potty, but not pressuring. Pull down his pants and help him to sit down on it, tucking a boy's penis in. If he's managed to tell you he needs it, thank him.

If your child jumps up immediately
Suggest he sits there a little longer – about five minutes – and distract him with a toy or a book. If nothing happens, let him get up and carry on playing.

When he does go in the potty
When he does use the potty, always praise him and tell him what a good boy he is. Wipe off any drips of urine with lavatory paper or clean his bottom quickly (wipe a girl from front to back). Hold the potty steady as he stands up, and pull up his pants for him. Don't show disgust at the contents of the potty, just flush them down the lavatory, wipe the potty clean, then rinse it with disinfectant. Wash your hands.

6

When your child has an accident, don't scold him
You can't expect him to remember to use the potty at this stage. If he wets or dirties his pants, don't scold him – it's really your fault for not reminding him to sit on the potty often enough. Clean his bottom with a sympathetic air and put fresh pants on him.

If he doesn't get the hang of it
If after two weeks your child is showing no signs of understanding, and is not telling you he needs the potty on at least some occasions, he's not ready to give up nappies yet. Put him back in them for a few more weeks, then try again – you may have several two-week training stints before he gets himself to the potty on most occasions when he needs to.

7

Leave a nappy off during naps
Once your child is using the potty fairly reliably during the daytime, and his nappy has been dry after a nap for about a week, you can leave his nappy off – he may even ask you to leave it off. Suggest he sits on the potty after he wakes from his nap. Napping without nappies will help him towards staying dry at night.

8

When you go out
Until your child is fairly reliable, put a nappy on him when you go out, but try to make sure, without forcing him, that he uses his potty beforehand. If you're going on a car journey, put him in a nappy unless you will be able to stop easily. Take a potty, spare clothes, and an old towel in case of accidents.

9

Suggest using the toilet
After a few weeks of using the potty during the day, suggest that he might try being like you and use the lavatory. Clip a child's seat on it to give him confidence that he won't fall in, and put a step in front so he can climb up. Help him the first few times, until he gets the hang of it. If he just wants to urinate, lift the seat and lid and show him how to aim his penis. Otherwise help him pull his pants down and climb up to sit on the seat; do the same for a girl. Stay nearby until he's finished, wipe his bottom, and help him down; he won't be able to wipe his own bottom until at least four. He will probably want to flush the lavatory afterwards – that's part of the fun; then wash his and your hands.

ACHIEVING NIGHT-TIME CONTROL

1

Wait until your child is already dry at night
If you have taken a dry nappy off your child in the morning for about a week, you can start leaving his nappy off at night.

2

Let him sleep without anything on his bottom at all
For the first week, put him to bed without a nappy, pants, or pyjama trousers, and protect the bed with a waterproof sheet if you want to. Make sure he uses the lavatory before bed. He should sleep through without any problems. If he doesn't, and wets the bed, he's simply not ready to give up night-time nappies yet.

3

If he lapses into bedwetting
If your child starts to wet his bed, after being dry at night for weeks or months, it's probably because he has suffered some sort of upheaval in his life. Never scold or punish him for bedwetting. If he wakes up wet in the night, quickly and sympathetically dry him and put him in clean pyjamas with a clean sheet on the bed. If it happens more than once, put him back in nappies until he's more settled, and you have taken off a dry one for seven consecutive mornings. He may not be dry at night until five or six, but this is not unusual. Withholding a bedtime drink won't help him.

A clip-on lavatory seat
This makes the hole in the adult seat smaller, so gives your child more confidence.

GETTING OUT AND ABOUT

Some form of pram or push-chair, and a car seat, are essential items for your new baby. Other useful items are a sling or a backpack carrier if your baby is older. You will also need a sun-blind to fix to the window on the sunny side of the car. A changing bag with detachable changing mat is convenient for outings: pack it with disposable nappies, changing equipment, spare clothes, and feeding equipment. It's a good idea to take a bottle or beaker of diluted juice or boiled water, and don't forget her favourite toy or her cuddly. Your older baby will derive great enjoyment from your outings. Everything is fascinating to her – traffic jams, shop windows, other people – so try to look at the world through her eyes, answer her questions, and don't dismiss her when she points excitedly at something that to you seems trivial or mundane.

METHODS OF TRANSPORT

Choosing a method of transporting your baby can be bewildering. In a nutshell, an ideal and practical choice is a carrycot on a chassis that can later convert into a pushchair. Your newborn needs protection from draughts and fumes, and a pushchair can't provide this even if you can arrange it so that your baby faces you. Once she is older, a sturdy, rigid-backed pushchair is a good choice.

PRAM *from birth*
- ☑ Gives your young baby good protection from draughts and fumes.
- ☑ Gives your baby a comfortable ride.
- ☑ Can be used up to about one year.
- ☒ Can't be used on public transport.
- ☒ You need ample storage space.

CARRYCOT ON A CHASSIS
from birth
- ☑ Gives your young baby good protection from draughts and fumes.
- ☑ Your young baby can sleep in it day and night.
- ☑ Your baby can be snug under a carrycot duvet.
- ☑ Some types convert to take a pushchair seat.
- ☑ Chassis folds flat.
- ☒ Can be awkard to take on public transport.

FLAT-FOLDING PUSHCHAIR
from three months
- ☑ Your baby can face you, or forwards.
- ☑ Rigid seat-back gives your baby good support.
- ☑ Can be free-standing when folded flat.
- ☑ Light, and easy to manoeuvre.
- ☒ Your young baby cannot lie flat.
- ☒ Gives your young baby no protection from draughts and fumes.
- ☒ You will have to dress your baby in extra clothes, or buy a fitted padded covering.
- ☒ Plastic hood for wet weather protection is often an extra.

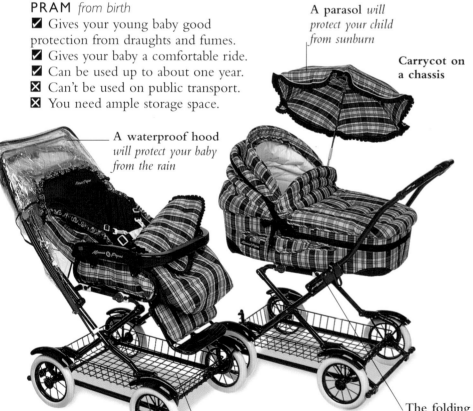

A parasol will protect your child from sunburn

Carrycot on a chassis

A waterproof hood *will protect your baby from the rain*

Flat-folding pushchair

A large tray *is useful for shopping and changing equipment*

The folding mechanism *should be easy to use*

UMBRELLA-FOLDING PUSHCHAIR
from six months

☑ Folds up neatly, so is good on public transport and if storage space is limited.

☑ The cheapest option; also the lightest.

☒ Soft seat-back gives poor support, so not suitable for babies under six months.

☒ No shopping tray.

WHEN YOUR CHILD IS WALKING

Reins are the ideal way to keep your child from wandering off, and give her more freedom than holding your hand. Take the pushchair with you for when she tires.

CAR TRAVEL

You can help to protect your child from injury by **always** restraining her on car journeys as described below. Although the car safety equipment may seem expensive, it's very cheap compared to the cost of running a car. It can be hired, but choose a reputable agency who will maintain the equipment properly.

IN-CAR ENTERTAINMENT

Make long car journeys as enjoyable as possible:

★ play her own cassettes of stories and songs

★ join in singing songs and reciting rhymes with her

★ point out animals, houses, and lorries to her

★ take toys such as finger puppets or an activity centre

★ take snacks and drinks

★ stop frequently.

BIRTH TO SIX OR NINE MONTHS

Safest: A rearward-facing infant seat on the back seat, held in place as the manufacturer recommends with the adult seat belt, or on the front seat, provided your car has no air bags (see also page 236). Strap your baby in with a harness. The car seat must conform to British Standard number BSAU202.

Next best: A carrycot, *with* its storm cover securely fastened on, strapped to the back seat with proper carrycot restraints. Your baby's head should point towards the middle of the car.

The carrycot restraints must conform to British Standard number BSAU186. Even so, your baby can be thrown out.

UP TO FOUR YEARS

Safest: Forward-facing child car seat fitted in the back seat with a purpose-designed anchorage kit: the middle of the back seat is preferable. Strap your child in with a harness. Some seats can be held with the rear seat belt. The seat must conform to British Standard number BS3254.

Last resort: Strap your child in with the rear adult seat belt. Never let a child travel in the front seat of a car with air bags.

WHEN YOU HAVE TO LEAVE YOUR CHILD

During your first few days or weeks with your new baby you may feel that you will never have the time to do anything but care for the baby ever again. So, the first time that you leave your baby, even if it is just for an hour or two's shopping, a trip to the gym, or a visit to the cinema, is a real milestone for you. Leaving your precious new baby in the care of even the most trusted friend, grandparent, or baby-sitter is a real wrench. You may even feel a bit guilty because it suddenly seems such a relief to be free, albeit briefly, from the feeling of total responsibility that you have for your tiny infant.

GETTING YOUR CHILD USED TO OTHER PEOPLE

BABYSITTERS

Nothing is more important during your baby's early months than your loving closeness. And yet eventually he has to learn to lead a separate existence independently of you. His eventual transition to school will be easier and his confidence will grow if he has opportunities to explore the world outside his immediate family, to be independent of you, and to make close relationships with other people – grandparents, babysitters, and friends.

So it isn't frivolous and it isn't selfish to get your baby used to a regular babysitter when he is very young. And if you plan to go back to work within the next year or so, then it is essential that they get used to the idea that someone else besides you can be relied on to love and care for him. There are several things you can do to make babysitting easier both for the sitter and the baby.

★ Always tell your baby what's going to happen, even if he is too young to understand.

★ If you go out in the evening, make sure he knows the babysitter, so that if he wakes he won't be terrified at seeing a stranger.

★ Don't introduce any new baby-sitting arrangement when your baby is tired, hungry, or sick. Pick a time of day when you think he'll be at his most alert and happiest.

★ If you have a new babysitter, don't rush to go out even if you are in a hurry. Spend some time holding him and letting him size up this new person. Let the baby see that you like the babysitter.

★ Show the babysitter which are his favourite toys and how to play the games he likes to play.

★ If the babysitter has to put your child to bed, make sure they know every detail of his bedtime routine so that your child will go to bed happily.

SEPARATION ANXIETY

At some time, usually between seven months and a year, your baby may start to seem reluctant even to let you out of his sight for a second. He'll cling when you try to put him down, or cry inconsolably if he is left with anyone else. Don't worry about such behaviour. This "separation anxiety" is quite normal and means that he recognizes you as separate from him and realizes how essential you are to him. Even the most clingy baby will eventually become independent. But meanwhile, accept his utter dependence on you lovingly and patiently. If you have to go out, always tell him – don't just sneak out to avoid a scene. Tell him where you are going and reassure him that you will be coming back.

New faces
Getting to know other people is a vital part of your baby's learning experience.

CUDDLIES AND SECURITY BLANKETS

By eight or nine months most children form a strong attachment to a favourite soft toy, blanket, or a special object. This powerful need for something cuddly grows even stronger after the first birthday. The child may carry it around continually during the day, take it to bed at night, cuddling or sucking it for comfort. Eventually it becomes a kind of talisman, something the child turns to for comfort whenever they are sad, frightened, or frustrated. Your child's cuddly will become grubby, shabby, and eventually probably unsanitary, because the child will be reluctant to let you wash it as its smell is part of its comfortable familiarity. Don't try to persuade them to give it up. It fulfils a real need. Keep it handy, make sure babysitters know about it, and try to forestall the disaster of losing it by keeping a duplicate somewhere safe.

CHILDCARE OPTIONS

GOING BACK TO WORK

Whether you are going back to work because you love your job or whether it is a matter of financial necessity, going back to work is bound to be stressful at first. How smoothly it goes depends almost entirely on the childcare arrangements you make. It will take a little while for everything to settle down, so don't worry too much if the first few days are difficult. Children are pretty adaptable, and most settle down quickly under a new routine. But keep a careful eye on your child during the first few weeks you are back at work. If his behaviour deteriorates or if he seems generally unhappy, you may need to re-think your childcare plans.

Grandparent care

This may be an ideal arrangement provided that the grandparent is willing. It is important that they know and respect your views on childcare – and vice versa. Problems may arise if you feel that your baby is being "taken over".

Shared care with a friend or relative

If you intend to work part-time, and have a good friend or close relative who also has small children, this may be a workable solution. It's important to formalize the arrangement and stick to it, so that neither party feels they are being taken advantage of.

Childminder

This is one of the least expensive childcare options. Only use a childminder registered with your local authority. A registered childminder may look after three children under 5 years and another three under 8 years (including her own), in her own home.

A childminder's home is checked by the local authority for suitability and police checks are carried out on other members of their household over 16. But you also need to talk to the minder yourself, to make sure that she is the kind of person you want to care for your child. It may be difficult to find a place for a very young baby.

Nursery care

Private nurseries offer full day care, usually from around 7.0am to 6.0pm, and usually stay open during holiday periods. Nursery care is expensive, but there is usually a fairly high ratio of staff to children and a stimulating environment. Most have a separate baby area for children under the age of two.

Nanny care

This is the most expensive option but you may be able to split the cost by sharing with another family. Having a nanny means your child has one to one care in his or her own home. A qualified nanny will have a childcare qualification such as an NNEB diploma. Always ask to see registration documents and childcare qualification certificates, and always check references before offering a job.

N.B. An au pair is a mother-helper, not a mother-substitute. Au pairs are untrained and will have little or no childcare experience. He or she is not a suitable person to take sole charge of a baby or young child.

Adapting well
Your child will soon get used to someone else looking after him.

GROWING AND LEARNING

Watching your child grow and learn is a rewarding experience. Every stage brings something new: at first it's rolling over, using his hands, sitting, crawling, walking. Once he's mastered those he will learn to talk, and will refine his co-ordination and dexterity. Even though you might think there's nothing so thrilling as watching him take his first steps, the next year will bring some subtler achievements that will fill you with pride.

Throughout these pre-school years, your child needs your help. He needs your stimulation and responsiveness, and he needs you to structure his play, too. Everything he knows about the way things behave, colours and shapes, cause and effect, he learns through playing with toys and everyday objects. To your child everything is a wonderful game. Getting dressed, unpacking the shopping, laying the table – it's all a chance to participate and learn.

THE FIRST SIX MONTHS

During these months you will see your baby develop into a real personality, able to reward you with lots of enchanting smiles and gurgles. Although there are a lot of toys aimed at this age group, he needs – and loves – your company most of all. When he's wakeful, take the time to talk and smile to him. Plenty of stimulation in the form of things to look at, sounds to hear, and textures to explore is vital too. You don't need expensive toys: old postcards and photographs, rattles, non-glass mirrors, will all do just as well.

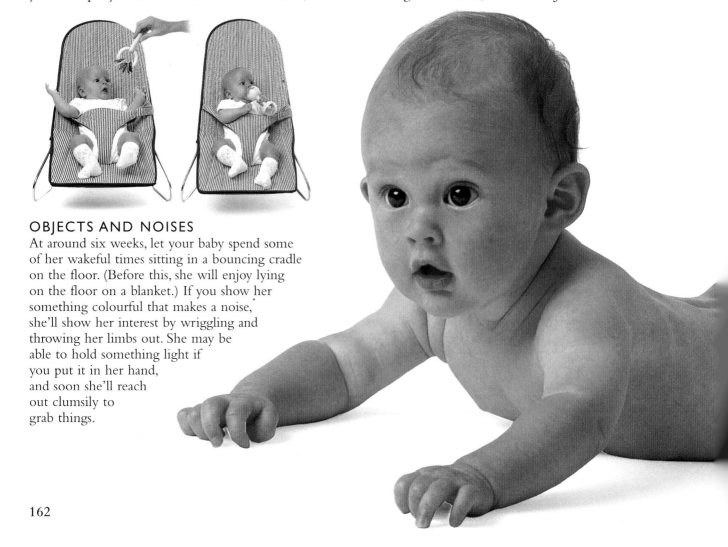

OBJECTS AND NOISES
At around six weeks, let your baby spend some of her wakeful times sitting in a bouncing cradle on the floor. (Before this, she will enjoy lying on the floor on a blanket.) If you show her something colourful that makes a noise, she'll show her interest by wriggling and throwing her limbs out. She may be able to hold something light if you put it in her hand, and soon she'll reach out clumsily to grab things.

LEARNING ABOUT EACH OTHER

During the first couple of months of life, your baby can't focus beyond about 25cm (10in), so bring your face close when you talk to her, and exaggerate your expressions and smiles. It's this eye contact that helps your baby become a person, and shows her what building a loving relationship is all about.

ROLLING

Sometime during this six months, your baby will learn to roll over, from front to back first, then from back to front. It will give him a great sense of achievement: he's beginning to make his body move for him. Remember that even before he's learnt to roll he can fall off things, so never leave him unattended on a high surface, not even the bed.

LEARNING TO SIT

As your baby gets more control over his body, help him learn to sit by surrounding him with cushions. They will help him balance, and protect him if he topples over.

PREMATURE BABIES

Your premature baby will probably reach all his developmental milestones rather later than other babies. Remember that in reality he has two "birthdays": one is the day he was born, but the more important one for the first few months is the date on which he was expected to be born. If you take those missing weeks in the womb into account, you will almost certainly find that his progress is not slow at all. Take him to the clinic for regular monitoring; he should have caught up with other children born at the same time by the age of two.

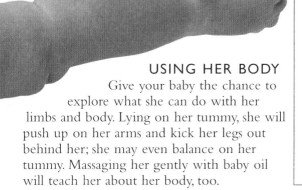

USING HER BODY

Give your baby the chance to explore what she can do with her limbs and body. Lying on her tummy, she will push up on her arms and kick her legs out behind her; she may even balance on her tummy. Massaging her gently with baby oil will teach her about her body, too.

STEPPING STONES CHART

Babies don't all develop at the same rate, or learn a particular skill at a particular time. But because everything they learn acts as a "stepping stone" to the next stage of development, they do acquire skills in the same order. The chart below shows the "stepping stones" in various areas of your child's development – physical skills, manual dexterity, sight, hearing and speech, and social behaviour and play. Your child may learn to do something either sooner or later than the average age given in the chart, and he may acquire skills more slowly in one area than another. This is unimportant – all that matters is that he makes steady progress, at his own pace, from one stepping stone to the next.

STEPPING STONES IN CHILD DEVELOPMENT				
Age	Physical Movements	Manual Dexterity	Hearing, Vision, and Speech	Social Behaviour and Play
One Month	Lies on back with head to one side. Held sitting, head falls forwards with back in one complete curve. Held standing on hard surface, presses down feet, straightens body, and often makes reflex "stepping" movements.	Hands normally closed, but if open will grasp a finger if it touches his palm.	Startled by loud noises. Turns head and eyes towards light. Eyes will follow dangling toy held 6–8 inches away and moved slowly from side to side.	Stops crying when picked up and spoken to. Looks at mother's face intently when she feeds or talks to him.
Three Months	Lies on back with head in mid-line. Kicks vigorously. Held sitting, can hold head erect and steady for several seconds. Placed face down, lifts head and upper chest well up. Held standing with feet on hard surface, sags at knees.	Watches movements of own hands and begins to clasp and unclasp hands. Holds rattle placed in his hands for a few moments, but can't look at it at the same time.	Very alert. Interested in people's faces. Moves head to look around. Eyes converge as a toy held above his face is moved nearer. Smiles at mother's voice. Vocalizes when spoken to or pleased. Turns head and eyes towards a sound.	Smiles at 5–6 weeks. Recognizes and begins to react to preparations for bath, feeds, etc, by smiles, coos, excited movements. Responds with obvious pleasure to friendly handling, tickling, being talked or sung to.
Six Months	Raises head when lying on back. Sits with support. When hands are grasped, can pull himself up. Rolls over, front to back. Placed face down, lifts head and chest up. Held standing on hard surface, takes his weight and bounces.	Stretches out both hands to grasp interesting object. Usually uses both hands to scoop up an object, occasionally uses just one hand. Shakes rattle deliberately, and often looks at it at the same time. Takes everything to mouth.	"Sings" and chats to himself using single and double syllables, e.g. ka, muh. Turns immediately to mother's voice across room. Screams when annoyed. Recognizes and responds to different emotional tones of mother's voice.	Laughs, chuckles, and squeals aloud in play. Still friendly with strangers, but sometimes shows some anxiety, especially if mother is out of sight. When he drops a toy he'll forget about it.
Nine Months	Sits alone for 10–15 minutes on floor. Progresses on floor by rolling or squirming Tries to crawl on all fours. Pulls self to standing with support but can't lower himself. Held standing, steps purposefully on alternate feet.	Examines objects by passing them from one hand to the other. Stretches out one hand to grasp small objects. Will hold out toy to adult, but can't yet let go unless pressing against hard surface. Grasps spoon while being fed.	Shouts to attract attention, listens and shouts again. Babbles tunefully, using long strings of syllables e.g. dad-dad. Understands "no" and "bye-bye". Imitates adult noises – cough, brrr etc. Watches people and activities with interest.	Looks after toys falling over edge of pram or table. Can find partially hidden toy. Plays "peek-a-boo." May be wary of strangers, clinging to known adult and hiding face.

Age	Physical Movements	Manual Dexterity	Hearing, Vision, and Speech	Social Behaviour and Play
Twelve Months	Sits well for indefinite time. Crawls rapidly. Can pull self to standing. Walks round furniture stepping sideways. Walks with one or both hands held. May stand alone for a few moments. May walk alone.	Can pick up small objects with thumb and index finger. Points at objects he wants or which interest him. Holds spoon but usually cannot use it alone. Drinks from cup with little assistance.	Knows and responds to own name. Babbles loudly and incessantly. Shows by behaviour that he understands several familiar words and also commands associated with gestures "clap hands," etc.	Shows affection to familiar people. Tries to help with dressing. Throws toys deliberately and watches them fall to ground. Waves bye-bye and claps hands in imitation. Puts wooden cubes in and out of box.
Fifteen Months	Walks unsteadily with feet wide apart. Goes from standing to sitting by collapsing backwards with a bump, or falling forwards on hands. Crawls upstairs. May be able to bend over to pick up toys from floor.	Builds tower of two cubes after being shown. Grasps crayon and imitates scribble. Brings spoon to mouth to lick, but can't stop it turning over. Holds cup when given it, and gives it back.	Speaks 2–6 recognisable words and understands many more. Understands and obeys simple commands, eg. shut the door, bring me your shoes. Looks with interest at pictures in book and pats page.	Helps more constructively with dressing. May easily get upset or frustrated. Very dependent on mother's reassuring presence. Can push large wheeled toy on level ground.
Eighteen Months	Walks well. Runs stiffly, but can't run round obstacles. Carries large toys while walking. Walks upstairs with helping hand. Creeps backwards downstairs. May sit on stairs and bump down a few steps.	Can pick up tiny objects with delicate pincer grasp. Preference for one hand more obvious. Scribbles with crayon, using preferred hand. Builds tower of three cubes after demonstration.	Jabbers to himself. Uses 6–20 words and understands many more. Sings and tries to join in nursery rhymes. Enjoys picture books, often recognizing and pointing out coloured items. Turns pages two at a time.	Takes off shoes, socks, and hat. No longer takes toys to mouth. Plays contentedly alone, but likes to be near adult. Emotionally still very dependent on familiar adults, especially mother.
Two Years	Runs safely. Walks backwards. Pulls wheeled toy. Climbs on and off furniture. Goes up and down stairs holding rail, two feet to a step. Throws small ball. Sits on wheeled toy and moves forwards with feet.	Builds tower of six cubes or more. Draws spontaneous circle and dots. Can imitate vertical line. Recognizes familiar adults in photograph after having been shown once. Hand preference becoming obvious.	Turns pages one by one. Uses 50 plus recognizable words. Puts two or more words together to make simple sentences. Refers to himself by name. Constantly asking names of objects. Joins in nursery rhymes and songs.	Follows mother around house and copies what she does. Plays simple make-believe games. Plays near other children but not with them. Tantrums when frustrated, but easily distracted.
Two and a Half Years	Walks upstairs alone, but downstairs holding rail, two feet to a step. Can climb easy climbing frame. Jumps with two feet together. Can kick large ball. Sits on tricycle and steers, but can't yet pedal.	Can build tower of seven or more cubes and line up blocks to form a "train". Can draw a horizontal line and circle when shown how. Eats skilfully with spoon and may use a fork.	Uses 200 plus words. Knows full name. Uses "I", "me" and "you". Always asking questions beginning "what?" and "where?" Can say a few nursery rhymes. Recognizes self in photo, once shown.	Rebellious and throws violent tantrums if frustrated and is less easily distracted. Enjoys make-believe play. Likes to watch other children at play and may join in for a few minutes. Still has little idea of sharing toys.
Three Years	Walks alone upstairs with alternating feet, downstairs with two feet to step. Climbs with agility. Rides tricycle. Can walk on tiptoes. Can stand on one foot for a moment. Sits with feet crossed at ankle.	Eats well with fork and spoon. Can wash hands. Can pull pants down and up. Can build tower of nine blocks or more. Can draw man with head and some features. Paints "pictures" with large brush. Uses scissors.	Can give full name, sex, and sometimes age. Can carry on simple conversations and talk about past experiences. Listens eagerly to stories and demands favourites over and over. Can match 2–3 primary colours.	Less prone to tantrums. Affectionate. Likes to help with adult's activities. Enjoys floor play with bricks, cars, etc. Plays with other children. Understands about taking turns. Affectionate towards younger siblings.

THE SECOND SIX MONTHS

Your baby will cram a great deal into these months. He will sit up unsupported, he may crawl and even stand or walk by his first birthday. It won't be steady progress, and not every child goes through each stage. Don't be surprised if your child never crawls, for example: it won't hinder his walking development. This is the age when he learns to explore every new thing by putting it in his mouth – so finger foods are ideal. From now until around two years old, make sure your child never gets hold of anything sharp or toxic, or so small that he could swallow it.

EXPLORING BOXES
Don't be surprised if the baby finds the boxes her toys arrive in just as fascinating as the toys. Check for and remove any staples.

MAKING NOISES
A wooden spoon and a saucepan make a perfect drum – your baby will love banging away and listening to the loud noise.

SITTING UP
Your baby will lean forwards and splay her legs out wide and straight when she first learns to balance sitting up. (Put a cushion behind her until she's really steady.) Now she has both hands free to explore. A board book is easy to handle, and even more fun if you look at it with her and point out the action, objects, and characters.

CRAWLING
Getting about on all fours is a great achievement. She may not use each leg in the same way: a lop-sided shuffle with one knee and the other foot are quite normal.

'PAT-A-CAKE'

Give your baby a small cube in each hand, and clap your hands together as he claps his.

WATER PLAY

Show your baby how water behaves and feels on her hands. Sieves and plastic jugs make good substitutes for toy buckets.

BOXES AND OBJECTS

Give your older baby a box and some empty cotton reels, and he will happily take them out one by one, then put them back in again.

INTRODUCING A BALL

At seven months your baby may be fascinated to see a ball rolling around, but surprised when she accidentally makes it move. By a year, she may be able to pick it up, throw it, and roll it – she's learnt how a ball behaves.

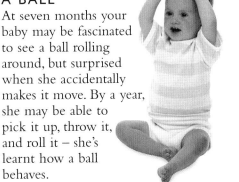

PULLING UP AND CRUISING

At ten months, your child may be able to co-ordinate his arms and legs well enough to pull himself up on furniture (clear away anything unstable). The next stage is to start shuffling sideways holding on – known as cruising. He will probably sit down with a heavy bump.

CLIMBING STAIRS

As soon as your child shows interest in the stairs, for his own safety teach him how to go up *and* down on all fours, facing into the stairs. Fit a stair gate for when you're not watching.

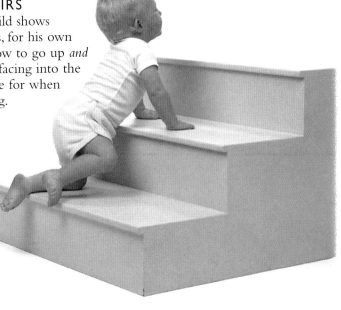

PLAYPENS AND BABYWALKER

A **playpen** can be a useful safe place if you have to leave your mobile child alone for a few moments – to answer the door, for example. Never leave him in it for more than a few minutes, he will get frustrated and bored. A **babywalker** is a chair on wheels that your baby can propel around using his feet. It may delay learning to walk by weakening his incentive to get around himself. **Never** leave your baby alone in a walker. It will tip easily, particularly on shallow steps down between rooms.

THE SECOND YEAR

First steps and first words will probably be your child's most exciting and significant achievements during his second year. New worlds open up for him once he can get about as you do, and communicate with you in word. Handedness becomes apparent around the middle of this year: he will show a definite preference for one hand, and once he starts to draw and paint this will become more marked. Although he will amuse himself for short periods, you're still his essential and most-valued playmate, and his most effective teacher too.

First steps will be unsteady

USING STAIRS
Towards the end of this year, your child may grow confident and skilful enough to go up and down stairs upright and facing forwards.

LEARNING TO WALK
Once your child has taken her first hesitant steps unsupported, it will only be a few days before she's waddling about enthusiastically, if unsteadily. She'll keep her feet wide apart and her arms out for balance. Let her go barefoot as often as possible: she only needs shoes for walking about out of doors.

BUILDING A TOWER
From about 18 months, your child will be able to build a tower of four or even five bricks.

WALKING SKILLS
A pull-along toy will help his sense of balance.

IMITATING YOU
Copying you is how your child learns – and "helping" is always a favourite game. Toy tools make it easy for him to join in.

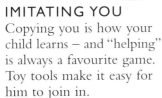

GREATER MOBILITY
At around 18 months, a simple, stable, ride-on toy will improve co-ordination and confidence, and provide a new challenge.

USING CRAYONS
Introduce non-toxic crayons during the second half of this year. She'll just scribble now; soon she'll make up and down strokes.

LEARNING SHAPES
Sorting shapes into their correct holes is an absorbing and challenging lesson. Give plenty of praise when he gets one right.

PRACTISING SPEECH
A telephone and doll are two invaluable toys for practising the art of communication by copying what you do.

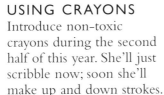

LEARNING ABOUT HIMSELF
Teach your child to point to his eyes, nose, and ears, and see if he can point to yours too. It will expand his vocabulary, and help him learn to see himself as a person in his own right.

LEARNING TO TALK
Your child's first word – probably "dada" or "mama" – will appear some time around his first birthday, and from then on he may acquire roughly two or three new words a month. By the age of two he may be able to string two words together – "me go", say – and will have about 200 words in all. Help him learn and improve:
★ Talk to him.
★ Continue to include picture books and rhymes in your playtimes.
★ Listen to him, be interested in what he's saying, and try to understand.
★ Don't interrupt him to make him repeat things "properly". He won't always get the pronunciation right at first.
★ Use adult language when you talk back to him, so he can hear the words spoken correctly.
★ Be clear and direct: "Put the brick on the top" is less muddling than "Let's see if we can get this nice red brick on top of the other one."

THE THIRD YEAR

This year, your child may surprise you with a burgeoning imagination that can make an absorbing game out of anything. Don't waste money on expensive kits and toys that can only stifle his creativity. A big cardboard box makes a house, a car, a boat, a spaceship – then when it gets tatty, you can throw it away and get another one (remove any staples). A sheet draped over two chairs is a haven, a tent, a house – anything he can think of. Towards the end of this year your child might join a playgroup, and start to play with other children in a constructive way; and you'll notice that he's becoming open to suggestion and reason when you want him to do things.

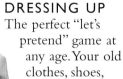

DRESSING UP

The perfect "let's pretend" game at any age. Your old clothes, shoes, handbags, and hats are all ideal items for a dressing-up box, and much more fun to play with than the special childsize outfits in the toyshops.

IRREGULAR SHAPES

Jigsaws demand concentration, dexterity, and visual understanding. If he gives up quickly, try giving him a simpler one.

COLOUR AND PAINT

Painting is a good way to learn about colour and texture. Give him thick brushes and non-spill pots, and protect his clothes.

IMAGINARY FRIENDS

Dolls and teddies will become friends to your girl or boy, and she will want to control their lives in the way you control hers.

USING HIS HANDS

Help your child refine his hand movements. He can screw and unscrew small objects now, and will enjoy using pastry cutters to make shapes out of play dough or your pastry.

JUMPING AND RUNNING

Learning to jump, run, and balance are new physical challenges. Jump with him to show him how to bend his knees as he lands.

PLAYING TOGETHER

A sandpit is always fun. Show your child how to use buckets and shovels, and teach her not to throw sand. She will soon find her own level of creativity. Cover the pit when not in use to stop dogs and cats fouling it.

SHARING AND PLAYING

It takes time for children to learn to take turns and share toys. Some time around the age of two- and-a-half to three, your child will start to play *with* other children for the first time, sharing his toys amicably and joining in a common project. This is the ideal age to introduce him to a playgroup: the more your child is with others of his own age, the more quickly and easily he will learn to join in – and to fit in.

You can provide plenty of good play opportunities yourself: a sandpit, a paddling pool, inter-locking plastic bricks, dressing up, making Christmas decorations – all these are excellent ways for children to learn to play together constructively. Your supervision is vital, though, throughout the pre-school years, to keep a check on safety or to step in if tempers start to fray.

GAMES TO PLAY WITH YOUR BABY

Most parents realize how important it is to talk to their baby. But not everyone finds it easy to do this without feeling embarrassed or self-conscious. That's one reason why the games that parents traditionally play with their babies are so important. They provide a natural way for you to interact with your baby. Many of them involve simple repetitive rhymes and songs that even a baby quickly learns to recognize and that will help to stimulate his own language development. Here are some favourite games to play with your young child.

PLAYING CATCH

All children seem to love a game of simple catch. Sit down on the floor, with your baby directly opposite you, and gently roll a soft ball or wheeled toy towards him. He may pick the toy up and want to return it to you. Alternatively, he may simply want to hold the toy and examine or even chew it. He may even puzzle you by holding out the toy for you to take and then pulling it back again. This is quite common – although he's learned to grasp something, he may not yet have learnt to let it go. Don't try to pull the toy away from him. Just tell him what a nice toy it is and keep on chatting to him.

ACTIVITY GAMES

Games that involve riding and bouncing on a parents knee, such as "Ride a cock horse", "This is the way the ladies ride", and "Ride a horse to Boston", can be as boisterous or as gentle as the baby's own age and temperament dictate. Your baby will very quickly learn to indicate when he wants to do it again – and when he has had enough.

HIDING AND FINDING GAMES

Search and find games can be fascinating right from babyhood to the "Hunt the thimble" type games of the primary school child. A baby's first "treasure hunt" is to see you hide one of his toys under a blanket or towel right in front of him, and then, when you say "Where did the toy go?" make the discovery that the hidden toy is actually still there, under the blanket. You can step up the excitement by using three towels – which one is the toy under? To find it the baby has to follow rudimentary rules – the toy is under a towel, not somewhere else quite different – and to remember under which towel his toy has gone.

"Peek-a-boo" is an immensely popular variation on this. The surprise of seeing your face dip out of sight and then come back into view can send a little one squealing with pleasure. You can try playing it with your baby in a "bouncer": as he twirls around, you'll disappear, then he'll shout delightedly as he bounces

around to face you again. And even if your baby loved it when he was only six months old, he will still enjoy variations on this search and find game later on. As he grows older he'll imitate you and may "hide" from you behind his hands or under a towel. He'll pass through a stage where he thinks you can't see him simply because he can't see you. This is normal and can be fun when you turn it into a game.

TICKLING AND TOUCHING GAMES

Games that involve you lovingly handling his body are fun for your baby, and you will be surprised at how soon he will learn to understand and respond when you start to play one of them. When you sing "The wheels on the bus", you can involve his whole body, his legs becoming the wheels, his arms the opening and closing doors and the wipers. He will enjoy having his toes wiggled in "This little piggy", and having you lightly run your fingers from his toes to his head for "all the way home". In games like "Round and round the garden", and "There was a little mouse that lived just there", he will be overcome with excitement at anticipation of the tickly ending.

SINGING AND LANGUAGE GAMES

Nursery rhymes and songs are part of your child's heritage. A few of the many excellent tapes of music and songs for small children are invaluable on car journeys. Best of all though, is to sing to your baby yourself. All babies seem to love being sung to. Singing lullabies to your baby such as "Twinkle, twinkle little star", and "Rock-a-bye Baby", can help soothe him. He will enjoy the rhythm and rhymes of these and other lullabies. In finger play songs such as "Incy Wincy Spider", the action of your hands can reinforce the meaning of the songs and help your baby to remember them.

Songs are one of the best ways to encourage your baby's language development and help him to understand and identify the world around him. "This little piggy" for example, explores the concepts of going and coming and opposites ("went to market", "stayed at home", "had roast beef", "had none". "Old McDonald had a farm", will teach him about animals and animal noises.

In his third and fourth years, your child will start to appreciate rhyming and nonsense rhymes. You can reduce him to helpless laughter with your own nonsense variation on a song he knows well ("Hickory dickory dee, The mouse ran up the tree...") and you will find he will very soon start imitating you and making up his own versions.

READING

Your baby will like to have you read to him long before he has any idea of what reading is all about. He'll enjoy the physical closeness as he sits on your knee and is cuddled. He'll like the sound of your voice as you talk to him about the pictures in the book. He'll like the bright colours of the pictures themselves. To begin with, reading is just another opportunity for you to spend time with your baby and talk to him. But eventually he will even understand what it is you are talking about.

BECOMING A PERSON

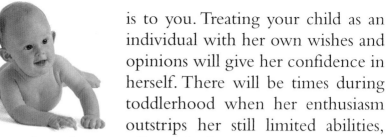

You will quickly become familiar with your baby's own particular temperament. She may be placid and "easy", she may cry a lot and be hard to comfort, or she may have a rather suspicious attitude towards anything new. Those characteristics will tend to persist as she gets older, but her personality is also shaped by what happens to her, and the way others behave towards her – particularly you and your partner. You can help her to be secure, confident, and out-going by showing her, right from the beginning, how special she is to you. Treating your child as an individual with her own wishes and opinions will give her confidence in herself. There will be times during toddlerhood when her enthusiasm outstrips her still limited abilities, and you will need all your tact to help her succeed without letting her think that you're taking over. But if you are able to think yourself into your baby's shoes and understand her frustrations, the pre-school years should be a time of tremendous enjoyment and discovery for both of you.

GETTING ALONG TOGETHER

Learning to get along well together in the pre-school years is a process of adjustment for both of you. Your child has to learn the boundaries of acceptable behaviour, while you may have to adapt your own natural style as a parent, which may not always make you tolerant, consistent, and fair. Your child needs you to show her, not just tell her, how to behave well. Kindness, politeness, thoughtfulness – all this she will only learn by copying you when you show the same behaviour to her.

Learning for himself
Give your child help when he needs it, but don't take over – it's his toy, and he needs to feel he can succeed.

How to handle your child
Your child will respond best to you and do as you say more willingly if you can be both affectionate and firm. It isn't easy to get the balance right.
★ Be consistent in what you say and do. If your child is smacked when she is naughty, she will hit other children when she's cross with them.
★ "Do's" work better than "Don'ts". "Hang your coat up so no one will tread on it," elicits a more positive response than "Don't drop your coat on the floor."
★ Say please – and thank you – when you ask her to do something.
★ Agree with your partner what you will allow, and back each other up.
★ Try to persuade rather than coerce. If she's in the middle of some absorbing activity, try "Let's finish this and then it'll be time to go to bed," rather than "Clear away those toys now it's bedtime."
★ Don't be too restrictive. Try listening to the way you talk to your child. Do you find you're nearly always issuing orders – "Stop that, Do as you're told, Don't touch"?
★ If you were unreasonable over something, say so, and apologize.
★ Don't assert your authority un-necessarily – avoid a clash of wills.
★ Always explain *why* she mustn't do something as well as *what* it is she mustn't do, even if she's too young to understand fully.

Rules to keep your child safe
Until your child has reached at least two-and-a-half, you can't expect her to understand reasons for not doing things, nor to remember what she mustn't do. It's your responsibility to make sure her curiosity can't lead her into much danger, and that the important rules are enforced.

For example, "You must never go out of the garden on your own" is an abstract rule that your toddler cannot comprehend, much less remember when she's busy playing or absorbed in her toys. You can only keep an eye on her and *make sure* – with a secure catch on the garden gate – that she doesn't stray out.

Childproof your home to minimize any dangers and so that you don't have to keep reprimanding her – otherwise her curiosity will lead the two of you into conflict (see pages 234-6). Move the television out of her reach, don't let flexes trail, use a fireguard, put child-resistant locks on drawers, cupboards, and fridge, and put socket covers over electric sockets. Sometimes keeping her out of the way is the only answer: a stair gate across the kitchen door may be the best way to keep her safe when you're cooking.

Loving and spoiling

You may worry that the normal affection you give your child will spoil her. It won't. She needs your love, combined with plenty of attention. But you *can* spoil her by being over-lenient in the face of bad behaviour. Letting her get her own way through tears and tantrums will not help her in her relations with friends and adults.

If you go out to work, you may find yourself "making up" to your child for not being there by lavishing toys on her. Toys can't take your place, and you may be giving her unrealistic expectations of what you can afford. Instead, when you *can* be around give her your time, your love, and plenty of affection.

Showing your love
Your child will prefer your love and attention to any toys. Don't worry about spoiling him with love, you can't.

DEVELOPING A SENSE OF IDENTITY

At around the age of 18 months or so, your child begins to realize that he is a separate person. He will start to refer to himself by name, and he'll enjoy looking at photos of himself too. From now on, he'll want to take charge of his own life more and more, and assert his own wishes and personality. You can help to foster this burgeoning sense of identity and determination to do things for himself.

Encouraging independence

★ Make things easy. From two on, organize his possessions so that he can do as much as possible for himself. Buy clothes that are easy to manage, so he can dress and undress himself as far as possible; put a step by the washbasin so he can wash his hands without your help; and fix a low peg so he can hang up his own coat.
★ Encourage him to help you. "Helping" is a game at the moment, not a chore. Simple jobs, such as unpacking the shopping, laying the table, or sweeping the kitchen floor, make your child feel he's achieved something, and show him that helping is part of family life.
★ Let him make decisions. The opportunity to make simple decisions gives your child the feeling that he has some control over his own life. So let him choose which T-shirt he wants to wear, or how his room is arranged, or where he'd like to go for a walk.

Helping your child to feel special

Your child, just like every child, needs to feel that he's special – that you love him and that he is worth loving. It's this message that helps to make him emotionally strong and able to cope away from the security of home. There are plenty of little ways you can show how special he is to you:
★ Don't forget to say you love him, or be too busy to give a hug or a cuddle when he wants one.
★ Respect his feelings and respond to his needs. When he's miserable, he needs to cry and be comforted. Saying "Don't be a crybaby" is denying him the right to feel sad.
★ Praise him and be enthusiastic about each fresh achievement.
★ Listen and show interest when he talks to you.

Becoming a person

Try to appreciate your toddler for the lively, fascinating, and independent individual he is fast becoming.

GOOD AND BAD BEHAVIOUR

When they are well and happy, children usually behave acceptably. But every child has off-days, and every child wants to test her limits – and yours – by seeing how far she can go. Bad behaviour is often an effective way of gaining your attention, too. The time of greatest conflict will probably come at some stage during her thrid year: tears and tantrums often go hand in hand with being two years old.

Dealing with bad behaviour

Act quickly and remove the source of the trouble or pick your child up and remove her with a firm "NO". At the same time, distract her attention with some other activity or toy.

Some types of bad behaviour, whinging and whining, for example, are best simply ignored. If your child never manages to elicit a response from you, and is *never* allowed to win any arguments by such behaviour, she will soon stop. Even tantrums are best ignored. Just be calm and carry on as normal. If necessary, put her outside the room until she calms down.

Rewards for good behaviour

It's very easy to give your child more attention when she behaves badly and least when she behaves well, and you feel you can relax. But rewarding your child with praise, affection, or a story on your lap when she behaves well is much more effective. You will encourage the behaviour you want, and teach her a very useful lesson – that being nice to people works much better than being nasty in life.

Punishments

Whatever punishment you give, it has to be *immediate*. Threats of future action, perhaps the withdrawal of treats and privileges to come, are useless and unfair for young children – your child won't understand why she is having this delayed punishment.

An immediate punishment that your child *will* understand is to be isolated for a short while to cool off. A quarter of an hour spent somewhere safe but alone – the hall is often suitable – will be long enough for her to forget whatever it was she wanted to do, and give you time to cool down.

Should I smack my child?

Smacking is often a sign that you have reached the end of your tether. It's not a good way to deal with bad behaviour and it doesn't deter your child from doing the same thing again. What is more, you are teaching her that physical force is an acceptable way to make people do what you want.

How to avoid getting to the end of your tether

However clever you become at managing your child, there will be days when her behaviour seems completely unbearable and you know you are close to losing control.

The solution is simple: take your child out. Whatever the weather, a trip to the park, the shops, or a friend will distract both of you from your

Being firm

You needn't be angry or upset when you discipline your child, just consistent, so your child gets the clear message that she's never allowed to behave in that way.

respective moods and help you recover your sanity and sense of humour.

Dealing with aggressive children

All small children fight occasionally, especially when they are bored or tired, and boys are often more aggressive than girls. When fights get out of hand, step in quickly:
★ separate the fighting children
★ divert them by introducing some other game or change of scene
★ don't take sides – it's nearly always impossible to work out the rights and wrongs of any situation.
If your child bites another child:
★ give all your attention and concern to the bitten child
★ remove the biter straight away and put her somewhere else, safe but alone, for a quarter of an hour.

Your child is bound to snatch and grab when she first starts to play with other children, but with help from you she will soon learn to share. It helps to get your child used to being with other children from an early age, so ask your health visitor about local toddler groups. A few children will continue to be very rough and aggressive, and their behaviour will eventually make them unpopular. For your child's sake, help her to be gentle with others:
★ give her a good model to follow by always trying to be gentle, patient, and loving towards her
★ make it clear through the way you act that it's your child's *behaviour* you dislike, not her
★ always step in and stop your child immediately if she starts to hit another child. Be firm, but don't shout or be aggressive yourself
★ never let her get her own way by behaving aggressively or unpleasantly.

If your child's behaviour continues to worry you, and you can't seem to find a way to deal with it, seek advice from your doctor or health visitor.

CHILDHOOD HABITS

Many small children develop habits such as thumb-sucking, head-banging, or breath-holding, which they resort to usually when they are angry, frustrated, bored, or simply in need of comfort. These habits are common and harmless, but they often worry parents. Although the child usually grows out of them by the time they are four, sometimes they can be hard to break.

Thumb-sucking and dummies

About half of all three year olds suck their thumbs, and a few are still doing so when they are 6 or 7. Persistent thumb-suckers may gradually push their front teeth forwards. Continually sucking a cuddly or blanket may have the same effect. However, unless the habit continues continues after the age of 6, when the second set of teeth come in, the distortion won't be permanent. Sucking a dummy is less likely to distort the teeth, so if your baby shows signs of being a habitual thumb-sucker, it might be worth offering him a dummy. You may be able to encourage a persistent thumb- or dummy-sucker to give up the habit by offering a small reward.

Head-banging, rolling, and rocking

Sometime in their first year many children develop a habit of rocking rhythmically on all fours in their cot, rolling their heads from side to side, or banging their heads on the head-board. Usually they'll do this as they are going off to sleep or as they wake up and often the rocking is violent enough to move the cot across the floor. Although this is alarming to watch, and to listen to, you really do not need to worry about it. Infants and young toddlers who do this seldom hurt themselves, though they may damage the furniture. These rhythmic behaviours nearly always disappear by the time the child is 3 or 4.

Some toddlers develop an equally worrying habit of banging their head on a hard surface during the day, usually to express frustration or boredom. Again, the child won't hurt himself, apart from the odd bruise. It's usually best to take no notice, though you may want to offer the child a pillow to soften the impact. If you ignore the habit, it will eventually disappear.

Head-banging or rocking that starts in older children, or persists after the age of 4, needs to be taken more seriously. Discuss with your doctor; it may mean that your child has some emotional problem.

Breath holding attacks

A few young children deal with pain or frustration by holding their breath. They may do this for up to half a minute, and sometimes they will even pass out. Immediately this happens, the child will automatically start to breathe again, and no harm is done, but the child quickly discovers this is a splendid way to gain attention. Ignore the attacks as much as possible, and they will probably have stopped by the time your child is four.

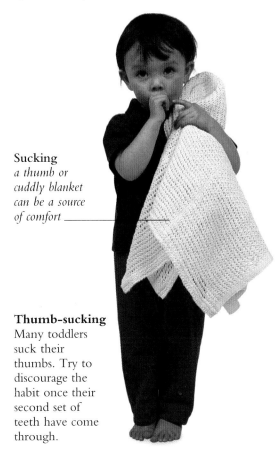

Sucking
a thumb or cuddly blanket can be a source of comfort

Thumb-sucking
Many toddlers suck their thumbs. Try to discourage the habit once their second set of teeth have come through.

"BAD DREAMS" AND NIGHT TERRORS

Even a child as young as one may have nightmares about something that has frightened him during the day, even though he doesn't yet understand what a dream is and certainly couldn't tell you about it. If a very young child wakes from a nightmare, simply cuddle and comfort him till he calms down.

By the time he is two years old, he may try to tell you about it and you can reassure him that it was "only a dream", though he won't yet really understand this concept. By three or four he will have a much better idea of what is "real" and "not real". But he will still need you to soothe his fears and make it clear that you won't let anything bad happen to him. It may reassure him to have a nightlight in his room, and for the door to be left open.

A few children, however, have night terrors, which are quite different from nightmares. Nightmares usually occur in the second half of the night when the child is sleeping lightly and dreams are at their most plentiful. A night terror will start much earlier, usually between one and four hours after the child has gone to sleep, and is sleeping very deeply. You will hear your child screaming or moaning as if in terror, but when you rush into her she won't seem to recognize you, may push you away, and scream even more if you try to hold her. This is because she is not properly awake, and if left alone will quite quickly go back to sleep. So don't try to wake her or even hold her. Simply wait beside her so that you are there if she does wake. In the morning she will have no memory of what happened and be none the worse for it.

YOUR CHILD'S HEALTH

Everything you need to know to recognize and treat common childhood illnesses, plus a guide to first aid.

THE FIRST THREE MONTHS

It is difficult to know when a baby is ill. If he is contented, and feeding normally, he is probably perfectly healthy. But babies can become ill quite quickly and any infection may be dangerous, so for the first three months you should be overcautious and call your doctor straight away if you think your baby is ill. If you notice any signs of illness, look at the symptoms listed here. These are the most common health problems for babies under three months old. This symptoms guide directs you to the relevant section on pages 182–5, but is not intended as a definite medical diagnosis – only a doctor can give that. If you can't find your baby's symptoms here, look at the pages 186–7, which covers illnesses for children of all ages. Babies are born with a natural immunity to many infections, since antibodies (which destroy germs) are passed to them from their mother's blood. Breast fed babies also receive antibodies from their mother's milk. This immunity lasts for about six months and will give them some protection against disease.

EMERGENCY SIGNS

Call for an ambulance immediately or go to the nearest Hospital Casualty Department if your baby:
* brings up green vomit
* has a temperature over 39°C (102.2°F) for more than half an hour
* vomits AND cries uncontrollably as if in great pain
* is breathing very noisily or rapidly

Fontanelle

* has a taut, bulging fontanelle when he isn't crying
* purplish spots on skin that do not fade if a glass is pressed against it.
* passes stools containing blood and mucus, which resemble red-currant jelly.

CALL THE DOCTOR

Don't wait to call your doctor if your baby seems unwell or:
* cries more than usual, or his crying sounds different from usual over a period of about an hour
* seems abnormally quiet, drowsy, or listless
* refuses two successive feeds, or does not demand a feed for six hours
* seems particularly irritable or restless.

Crying

If you fail to calm your baby after an hour or so, or if his crying sounds unusual, **don't wait to call your doctor.** If your baby cries inconsolably for two or three hours at about the same time each day, but shows no other signs of illness, he might have colic (see page 118). This may continue for several weeks, but there is no treatment for it.

Loss of appetite

If your baby does not want to feed, but seems generally well and contented, there is no need to worry. If he refuses two feeds in succession, or does not demand a feed for six hours, **call your doctor now.**

Slow weight gain

If your baby does not seem to be gaining weight at the normal rate (see charts on pages 254–7), consult your doctor or health visitor. Occasionally an underlying illness can make a baby grow more slowly than normal.

PREMATURE BABIES

Babies who were very small at birth, or who were born a month or more before their due date, are very vulnerable to infections during their first weeks. Until your baby is older and has put on weight, keep him away from anyone who has a cough or cold, and don't take him into public places where he might pick up an infection.

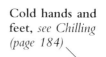

Cold hands and feet, *see Chilling (page 184)*

Areas of dry, flaking skin *mean that your baby's skin needs moisturizing, so rub a little baby oil or baby moisturizer gently into the dry areas*

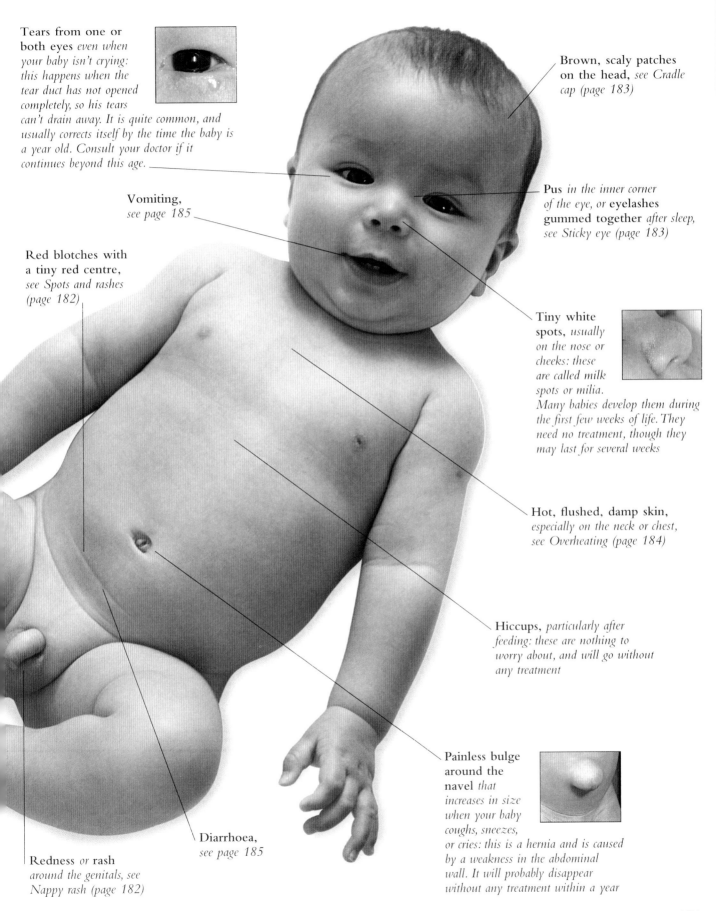

Tears from one or both eyes *even when your baby isn't crying: this happens when the tear duct has not opened completely, so his tears can't drain away. It is quite common, and usually corrects itself by the time the baby is a year old. Consult your doctor if it continues beyond this age.*

Vomiting, *see page 185*

Red blotches with a tiny red centre, *see Spots and rashes (page 182)*

Brown, scaly patches on the head, *see Cradle cap (page 183)*

Pus *in the inner corner of the eye, or* eyelashes gummed together *after sleep, see Sticky eye (page 183)*

Tiny white spots, *usually on the nose or cheeks: these are called milk spots or milia. Many babies develop them during the first few weeks of life. They need no treatment, though they may last for several weeks*

Hot, flushed, damp skin, *especially on the neck or chest, see Overheating (page 184)*

Hiccups, *particularly after feeding: these are nothing to worry about, and will go without any treatment*

Painless bulge around the navel *that increases in size when your baby coughs, sneezes, or cries: this is a hernia and is caused by a weakness in the abdominal wall. It will probably disappear without any treatment within a year*

Diarrhoea, *see page 185*

Redness *or* rash *around the genitals, see Nappy rash (page 182)*

SPOTS AND RASHES

What are they?

Many newborn babies go through a spotty stage in the first few weeks, so don't worry unnecessarily if your baby develops a few spots – they don't usually mean that he is ill in any way. One of the most common rashes in young babies is called newborn urticaria. Newborn urticaria usually appears during the first week of your baby's life, and will generally disappear without any treatment.

What can I do?

If your baby has newborn urticaria (see symptoms box), simply ignore the spots. Unlike urticaria in older children, which may require treatment, newborn urticaria will disappear on its own within about two or three days, so it is not necessary to put any lotions or creams on the spots. Don't be tempted to alter your baby's feeds in any way – the spots are not due to milk disagreeing with him.

SYMPTOMS

* Red blotches with a tiny red centre, which come and go on different parts of the baby's body, and last only a few hours.

GET HELP

Call your doctor now if the spots are flat and dark red or purplish (a petechial rash). Consult your doctor as soon as possible if:
* a spot has developed a pus-filled centre
* you think a spot has become infected.

NAPPY RASH

What is it?

Nappy rash is an inflammation of the skin on a baby's bottom. It may occur if your baby has been left in a dirty nappy for too long, because as urine and faeces are broken down, ammonia is released, which burns and irritates his skin. It can also be due to an allergy to soap powder used when washing fabric nappies. A similar-looking rash may be caused by thrush, which normally starts in the mouth (see page 213), but can spread through the body and affect the skin around the anus.

SYMPTOMS

* Red, spotty, sore-looking skin in the nappy area
* smell of ammonia from your baby's nappy.

What can I do?

1 Change your baby's nappy frequently, and clean and dry her bottom thoroughly at each change (see pages 150–1). Inside fabric nappies, use an extra-absorbent type of liner.

2 Whenever possible, let your baby lie on a nappy with her bottom exposed to the air. Don't use plastic pants over fabric nappies until the rash subsides, since these prevent air circulating to her bottom.

3 Look for white patches inside your baby's mouth. If you see any, she may have thrush (see page 213).

Spread the cream *evenly all over your baby's nappy area*

4 Don't use biological powder or fabric conditioner to wash her nappies, as they can trigger an allergy. Rinse her nappies thoroughly.

5 Buy a nappy rash cream (available at most chemists) and apply it when you change her nappy, to soothe and heal the skin.

GET HELP

Consult your doctor or health visitor as soon as possible if:
* the rash lasts longer than two days
* you think your baby has thrush.

What might the doctor do?

The doctor may prescribe an antibiotic cream if the rash has become infected, or an anti-fungal cream if your baby has thrush.

CRADLE CAP

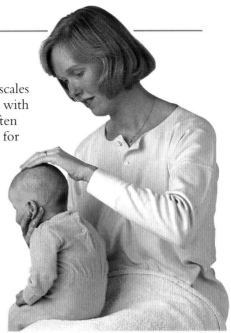

What is it?
Thick, brownish, crusty patches on a baby's scalp are known as cradle cap. Sometimes it may spread to the baby's face, body, or nappy area, producing a red scaly rash. Cradle cap may appear during the first few months of life, and generally clears up by the age of about two years. Although it looks irritating and unsightly, cradle cap is harmless and doesn't seem to distress the baby.

What can I do?
1 Rub the cradle cap scales on your baby's head with baby or olive oil to soften them. Leave the oil on for 12 to 24 hours, then comb your baby's hair gently to loosen the scales. Finally, wash his hair – most of the scales should simply wash away.

SYMPTOMS

★ Brownish, scaly patches on the scalp.

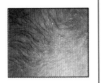

GET HELP

Consult your doctor as soon as possible if the rash spreads and:
★ seems to irritate the baby
★ looks infected or begins to ooze
★ does not clear up after five days.

2 If the rash spreads, keep the affected areas clean and dry. Don't use soap, baby lotion, or baby bath liquid – ask your chemist for an emulsifying ointment instead.

What might the doctor do?
If the condition proves obstinate, or if the rash looks infected or starts to ooze, your doctor may prescribe a cream to be rubbed gently on the area.

STICKY EYE

What is it?
This is a very common mild eye infection caused by blood or fluid getting into your baby's eye during birth. If your baby develops any of these symptoms after she is two days old, she probably has conjunctivitis (see page 209).

What can I do?
Clean your baby's eyes twice a day with cotton wool dipped in warm boiled water. Wipe outwards from the inner corner of her eye, and use a fresh piece of cotton wool for each eye.

SYMPTOMS

★ Eyelashes gummed together after sleep
★ pus in the inner corner of the eye.

GET HELP

Call your doctor now if your baby has a bad discharge of yellow pus. Consult your doctor as soon as possible if:
★ your baby develops symptoms of sticky eye after the first two days of life
★ sticky eye does not clear up after three days.

What might the doctor do?
If the doctor thinks your baby has conjunctivitis, he will probably prescribe antibiotic eye drops.

To give the eye drops, swaddle your baby in a blanket and hold her eyes open very gently, then squeeze in the drops. If necessary, ask another adult to hold her head still.

CHILLING

Why are babies at risk?
For the first few weeks of his life, your baby will be unable to regulate his body temperature very efficiently. If he becomes too cold, his body temperature will drop and he may become dangerously chilled quite quickly. Babies who were born prematurely are particularly vulnerable to serious chilling.

What can I do?

1 Warm your baby up by taking him into a heated room and feeding him. Once he has become chilled, it doesn't help just to pile on extra clothes or blankets.

2 Take your baby's temperature (see page 193) If it is below 35°C (96°F), he is dangerously chilled, so **call your doctor now.**

SYMPTOMS

First signs
★ Crying and restless behaviour
★ cold hands and feet.

Signs of serious chilling
★ Quiet, listless behaviour as the baby gets colder
★ cool skin on the chest and stomach
★ pink, flushed face, hands, and feet.

How can I prevent chilling?
Keep the room your baby sleeps in at about 16–20°C (65–68°F). When you undress and bathe him, the room should be warmer still. Be sensible about taking him out in cold weather – wrap him up well and don't stay out for too long. Never leave him to sleep outside in his pram on a cold day.

GET HELP
Call your doctor now if your baby:
★ shows signs of serious chilling
★ has a temperature below 35°C (96°F).

Put a bonnet *under the hood to keep his head warm*

In cold weather, dress your baby in an all-in-one outdoor suit, or wrap a shawl over his other clothes and use mittens and bootees.

OVERHEATING

Why are babies at risk?
Overheating is as dangerous for young babies as chilling, especially if they are feverish or unwell. Overwrapping of babies at night is thought to be one of the factors that contributes to cot death (see page 123).

What can I do?
1 Take your baby to a cooler place and remove a layer of clothing.

2 Take your baby's temperature (see page 193) and, if it is raised, try to reduce it by sponging her with tepid water (see page 194).

SYMPTOMS
★ Restless behaviour
★ hot, sweaty skin
★ raised temperature.

How can I prevent overheating?
Dress your baby according to the weather – on very hot days, she can sleep in just a nappy and a vest, but always remember the danger of chilling (see above). Never leave her to sleep in the sun, her skin will burn easily. Provide shade of some sort, and check her frequently as the sun moves round.

GET HELP
Call your doctor if your baby's temperature does not return to normal within one hour.

VOMITING

Why do babies vomit?

All babies regurgitate a small amount of milk during or just after a feed, usually due to wind. This "possetting" is perfectly normal, and does not mean that your baby is ill, but until you are used to it, you may think that she is vomiting. If your baby vomits, she will bring up most of her feed. This is unlikely to happen in a breast-fed baby.

Frequent vomiting in a bottle-fed baby, especially if she also has diarrhoea, may be caused by gastro-enteritis (see page 222). This is very serious in a young baby because it can make her dehydrated very quickly.

FORCEFUL VOMITING

Sometimes a baby vomits with great force, so that the vomit shoots across the room. If your baby does this at two successive feeds, **consult your doctor as soon as possible.**

The most likely reason is that she has brought back part of her feed with a large burp of wind. However, if it happens after every feed, especially if she is hungry all the time, she may have a condition call pyloric stenosis, in which the outlet from the stomach becomes blocked. This condition runs in families, and usually develops when the baby is two to eight weeks old. If your baby has this, she will need a simple operation.

What can I do?

1 Stop bottle-feeding for 24 hours. To replace fluids lost through vomiting, give your baby frequent drinks of either cooled boiled water or glucose solution (dissolve three level teaspoons of glucose in 200ml (7fl oz) cooled boiled water, or ask your chemist for oral rehydration powder). She needs at least $\frac{1}{2}$ litre (1 pint) a day.

2 Give you baby diluted feeds for the next three days, made up as described below. To make sure that she has enough to drink, offer her a small amount every hour.
Day 1 Use a quarter of the usual amount of powder formula to the normal amount of water.
Day 2 Use half the normal amount of powder formula to make up a feed.
Day 3 Make up your baby's feeds to the normal strength once again.

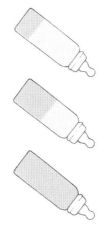

EMERGENCY SIGNS

Call for emergency help immediately if your baby:
★ vomits all feeds in an eight-hour period
★ has a dry mouth
★ brings up green vomit
★ has sunken eyes or a sunken fontanelle
★ has a dry nappy for more than six hours
★ is abnormally drowsy.

GET HELP

Call your doctor now if:
★ your baby vomits and shows any other signs of illness
★ your baby vomits the whole of two successive feeds.

What might the doctor do?

The doctor may prescribe a powder to be mixed with water for your baby to drink. If your baby has lost a lot of body fluid, the doctor might send her to hospital, where she may be given liquid through a drip.

How can I prevent an upset stomach?

If you are bottle-feeding your baby, sterilize all feeding equipment and throw away any unfinished feeds. When you make up feeds, cool them quickly under cold running water and store in the fridge. Never keep a feed warm for a long period.

DIARRHOEA

What is it?

Until babies start eating solid food, they will usually pass fairly runny stools a few times a day. If your baby passes very watery, greenish stools more often than usual, he has diarrhoea. Diarrhoea is serious in a young baby, since there is a danger that he may become dehydrated quite quickly.

What can I do?

It is important to prevent your baby from becoming dehydrated, so make sure that he has plenty to drink. If you are breast-feeding, offer your baby cooled boiled water between his normal feeds. If you are bottle-feeding your baby, make up diluted feeds for a few days, as for vomiting (see above).

GET HELP

Call the doctor now if your baby also has a fever or if there is blood in the diarrhoea, or if she has had diarrhoea for six hours AND has any other symptoms, or if the diarrhoea continues for more than 24 hours.

DIAGNOSIS GUIDE

If your child is unwell, try to identify her symptoms in the guide below. If she has more than one symptom, look up the most severe one. This gives you a possible diagnosis and refers you to a section covering the complaint. As well as giving a more detailed list of symptoms, the section contains a brief explanation of the nature of the illness, with information about how you can help your child, and advice on whether you need to call a doctor. Bear in mind that the guide is not intended to give an accurate diagnosis, only a doctor can do that, and that your child may not develop all the symptoms listed for an illness. If your baby is under three months old, look also at the guide on pages 180–1, which covers special health risks for young babies.

Raised temperature
A raised temperature (fever) may mean that your child has an infection, so you should check for other signs of illness. However, healthy children may get a slight fever during energetic play or in very hot weather, so check your child's temperature again after she has rested for about half an hour. If it is still over 38°C (100.4°F), she may have an infection.

Changed behaviour
If your child is less lively than usual, more irritable, whiny, or simply unhappy, she may be ill.

Unusual paleness
If your child looks much paler than usual, she may be ill.

Hot, flushed face
This may be a sign of a fever.

Loss of appetite
Although a child's appetite varies from meal to meal, a sudden loss of appetite may be a sign of illness. If your baby is under six months old and has refused two successive feeds, or has not demanded a feed for more than eight hours, **call your doctor now**. If your child goes off her food for more than 24 hours, look for other signs of illness (see page 189).

Eyes looking in different directions, *see Squint (page 210)*

Red, sore, or sticky eyes or eyelids, *see Eye problems (pages 209–10); if combined with a* **rash and fever**, *see Measles (page 204)*

Itchy eyes, *especially if accompanied by* **runny nose or sneezing**, *see Colds and flu (pages 200–1). Could also be hay fever, particularly if it occurs in summer – consult your doctor*

Aversion to bright light, *especially if accompanied by* **fever, headache, and stiff neck**, *see Meningitis and encephalitis (page 208)*

Runny or blocked nose, sneezing, *see Colds and flu (pages 200–1)*

Sore mouth, *see page 213*

Momentary lapses of attention, *see Absence attacks (page 233)*

Loss of consciousness, combined with stiffness and twitching movements, *see Major seizure (page 233)*

Itchy head or tiny white grains in the hair, *see Lice and nits (page 232)*

Earache, partial deafness, discharge from ears, itchy ears, *see Ear problems (pages 211–2)*

Puffy face, swollen glands, *at the angle of the jaw-bone and on the sides of the neck, see Mumps (page 206); swollen glands accompanied by* **sore throat**, *see Tonsillitis (page 214) and German measles (page 203)*

Stiff neck, *if accompanied by* **fever and headache**, *see Meningitis and encephalitis (page 208)*

Red lump, perhaps with pus-filled centre, *anywhere on the body, see Spots and boils (page 226)*

Red, raw skin, *see Chapped skin (page 229)*

Sore throat, *see Throat infections (page 214); if accompanied by* fever and general illness, *see Colds and flu (pages 200–1); if also accompanied by* a rash, *see German measles (page 203); if accompanied by* puffy face, *see Mumps (page 206)*

Spots or rash *anywhere on the body, if accompanied by* sore throat *or* fever, *see Infectious illnesses (pages 203–8); if without other symptoms, see Skin problems (pages 226–32) and Insect stings (page 252)*

Stomach pain, *see page 220; if accompanied by nausea, vomiting, or diarrhoea, see Gastro-enteritis (page 222)*

Abnormal-looking faeces, *see page 223*

Diarrhoea, *see page 223*

Constipation, *see page 221*

Intense itching around the anus, *see Threadworms (page 232)*

Pain when urinating, odd-coloured urine, frequent urination, *see Urinary system infections (page 224)*

Sore tip of penis, *see Genital problems in boys (page 225)*

Painless bulge in the groin or scrotum, *see Genital problems in boys (page 225)*

Vomiting with great force *in babies, see Forceful vomiting (page 185)*

Vomiting or nausea, *see page 222*

Sores around the mouth, *see Cold sores (page 230) and Impetigo (page 231)*

Faint red rash over the face or in skin creases, *see Heat rash (page 227)*

Cough, *see Coughs and chest infections (pages 215–9) and Whooping cough (page 207); if accompanied by a* rash, *see Measles (page 204)*

Breathing difficulty, wheezing, rapid breathing, *see Coughs and chest infections (pages 215–9)*

Areas of very itchy, dry, red, scaly skin *anywhere on the body, see Eczema (page 228)*

Red, tender skin *anywhere on the body, see Sunburn (page 229) or Burns and scalds (page 245)*

Dry, painless lump *anywhere on the body, see Warts and verrucas (page 230)*

Soreness, itching or redness around the vagina, vaginal discharge, *see Genital problems in girls (page 225)*

Intense itching around the vagina, *see Threadworms (page 232)*

White or brown lump on sole of foot, *see Warts and verrucas (page 230)*

FIRST SIGNS OF ILLNESS

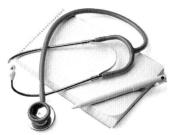

Even if your child has no definite symptoms, you will probably know when he is sickening for something. He may look pale, be more clingy than usual, cry or whine, or seem very irritable. He may be off his food. When your baby is teething, don't assume that all his symptoms are due to this. Although teething may make his gums sore, so that he is more dribbly and irritable than usual, it won't give him a temperature or make him ill. In a baby under a year old, all symptoms should be taken seriously – babies can become ill very quickly. If your child is over a year old, keep a check on how his symptoms progress over the next few hours.

Feeling unwell
Your child may become more clingy, and demand extra attention when she is ill.

CALLING THE DOCTOR

If you think you know what is wrong with your child, read the relevant section among complaints covered on pages 200–33. This advises you whether you need to call the doctor. As a general rule, the younger the child, the more quickly he should be seen by a doctor. If you are unsure what to do, phone your doctor and describe your child's symptoms to him and tell him his age. The doctor will tell you what to do and will know whether your child needs medical attention.

Degree of urgency

Whenever you are instructed to call the doctor, you will be told how quickly your child needs medical help.

★ **Call for emergency help immediately:** this is a life-threatening emergency. So call for an ambulance, or go to the nearest hospital emergency department.

★ **Call your doctor now:** your child needs medical help now, so contact your doctor straight away, even if it is the middle of the night. If he can't come now, call for emergency help immediately.

★ **Consult your doctor as soon as possible:** your child needs to be seen by a doctor within the next 24 hours.

★ **Consult your doctor:** your child should be seen by a doctor within the next few days.

SYMPTOMS

The most common early symptoms of illness in children are:
★ raised temperature – 38°C (100.4°F) or more
★ crying and irritability
★ vomiting or diarrhoea
★ refusal to eat or drink
★ sore or red throat
★ rash
★ swollen glands in the neck or behind the jaw.

EMERGENCY SIGNS

Call for emergency help immediately if your child:
★ is breathing very noisily, rapidly, or with difficulty
★ has a convulsion
★ loses consciousness after a fall
★ is in severe, persistent pain
★ has a fever and is unusually irritable or drowsy
★ has a rash of flat dark red or purplish blood-spots (petechial rash).
★ screams with pain and turns pale when he screams.

CHECKING FOR SYMPTOMS

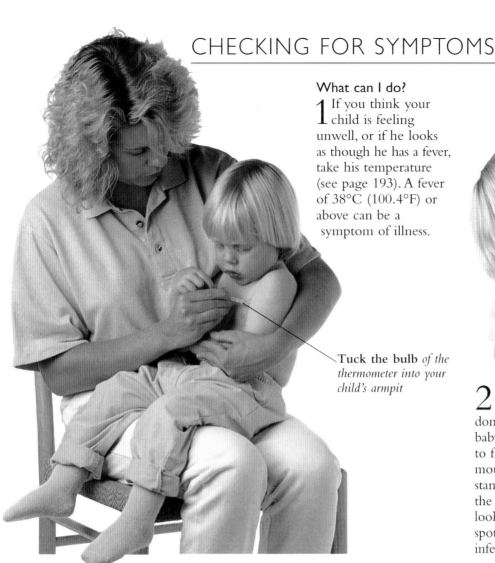

Tuck the bulb *of the thermometer into your child's armpit*

What can I do?

1 If you think your child is feeling unwell, or if he looks as though he has a fever, take his temperature (see page 193). A fever of 38°C (100.4°F) or above can be a symptom of illness.

2 Check whether your child's throat is inflamed or infected, but don't try to examine the throat of a baby under a year old. Ask your child to face a strong light and open his mouth. If he is old enough to understand, ask him to say "Aah" to open the back of his throat. If his throat looks red or you can see creamy spots, he has a sore throat (see Throat infections, page 214).

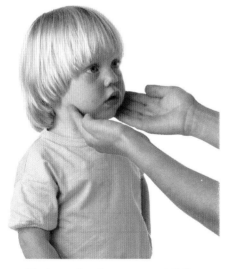

3 Feel gently along your child's jaw-bone and down either side of the back of his neck. If you can feel tiny lumps under the skin, or if any of these areas seem swollen or tender, your child has swollen glands, which is a common sign of illness.

4 Check to see whether your child has a rash, particularly on his chest and behind his ears – the most common areas for a rash to start. If he has a rash and a fever, he may have one of the common childhood infectious illnesses (see pages 203–8).

"Is my child in pain?"

If your baby is in pain, his crying may sound different from normal. When a baby or a small child cries or complains of pain, it can be difficult to discover where the pain is, let alone how bad it might be.

Serious pain will affect your child's behaviour, so watch him to find out how severe his pain is. Does it make him cry or stop him sleeping, eating, or playing? Does his face look drawn or his colour changed? Would you know that he had a pain even if he didn't tell you? If not, his pain isn't severe.

If your child is in pain give paracetamol elixir (not aspirin). Consult your doctor if the pain continues.

THE DOCTOR'S EXAMINATION

The doctor will ask you about any symptoms you have noticed in your child and how long he has had them, and will then examine your child. If your child is old enough to understand, explain what will happen when he visits the doctor. If the doctor suspects any particular illness, he may do other investigations as well as or instead of those shown below.

1 The doctor will feel the glands that lie along your child's jaw-bone, down the back of his neck, and in his armpits and groin. These may become swollen during an infectious illness.

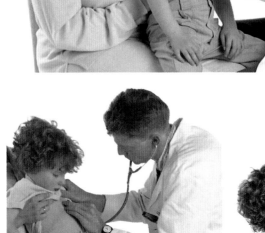

2 He will feel your child's pulse to check if his heart is beating faster than usual. This is often a sign of a raised temperature. The doctor may also take your child's temperature.

3 By listening to your child's chest and back through a stethoscope, and asking your child to breathe deeply, the doctor will check the health of his heart and lungs.

4 If your child has a sore or inflamed throat, the doctor will examine his throat using a small torch, pressing his tongue down with a spatula.

5 The doctor may ask your child to lie on the examining couch so that he can gently feel his abdomen. He will check for swelling or tenderness in any of the internal organs.

QUESTIONS TO ASK THE DOCTOR

Don't hesitate to ask the doctor about anything that is worrying you. In particular, find out:
★ how long your child may be ill, and what symptoms to expect
★ whether he is infectious, and whether you should isolate him, particularly from small babies and pregnant women
★ how you can make your child more comfortable while he is ill.

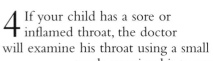

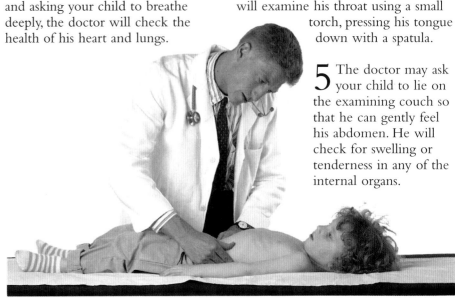

GOING TO HOSPITAL

Going into hospital is stressful for anyone. For a child who is too young to understand why he is there, it can be terrifying, especially if he is separated from his parents. While it helps to explain to your child what is happening, you can't do much to prepare him if he is under two – all he really needs at this age is your presence. If your child is over two, playing with a favourite toy may help: explain that teddy goes to hospital to be made better, not as a punishment, and soon teddy comes home again. Keep your explanations simple but truthful; your child will feel let-down and mistrustful if you promise something won't hurt, and then it does.

VISITING YOUR CHILD

Hospital staff know how important it is for a parent to be with a child to comfort and reassure him, and should make it easy for you to visit him at any time. Some even provide accommodation so that you can live in with your child – find out about this before his admission. He won't find the hospital so frightening if you continue to care for him as you would at home, so ask the nurses whether you can still bathe and feed him.

If you can't stay in hospital with your child, visit him as often as you can, and bring brothers and sisters to see him. Even if he cries when you leave, don't feel that he might settle better without your visits. It would only make him even more anxious, unhappy, and abandoned. Make a special effort to be with him for the first day or two, and when he has any unpleasant procedures such as injections, or having his stitches removed.

WHAT TO PACK

Your child will need the following things while she is in the hospital. Pack nappy changing equipment as well, if necessary. Label everything, particularly her toys.

Bib and feeding equipment

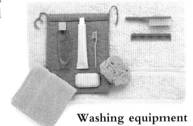

Washing equipment

Pack soap, a face flannel, a sponge, her toothbrush and toothpaste, her brush, comb, and a towel.

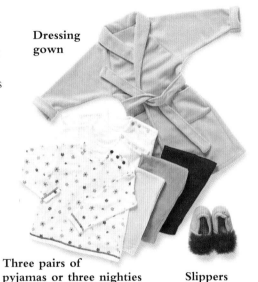

Dressing gown

Three pairs of pyjamas or three nighties

Slippers

Favourite toys

HAVING AN OPERATION

If your child is old enough to understand, it will help to explain what will happen on the day of his operation. Ask the doctor how the anaesthetic will be given (it may be injected or inhaled through a mask), and find out whether you will be allowed to stay with your child while he is given the anaesthetic. Try to be with him when he wakes up after the operation since he may be frightened.

1 Warn your child that he may not be allowed to eat or drink anything on the day of his operation.

2 Tell your child that he will be dressed up for the operation in a hospital gown, and will wear a bracelet with his name on it.

3 While he is still in the ward, your child will be given a "pre-med" to make him sleepy.

4 Your child will be wheeled in his bed to the anaesthetic room, where he will be given an anaesthetic. He will fall asleep quickly.

5 Warn your child that he may vomit when he wakes up.

6 If your child has stitches, discourage him from scratching them. It will hurt only momentarily when they are removed.

THE CHILD WITH A TEMPERATURE

In children, normal body temperature is between 36° and 37.5°C (96.8° and 99.5°F). A temperature above 38°C (100.4°F) may be a sign of illness. A child's temperature can shoot up alarmingly quickly when she is ill, but a slightly raised temperature is not a reliable guide to her health. Babies and children can be ill with a normal, or below normal, temperature, and some children can have a slight fever without being ill. So, if your child seems unwell, she may be ill even if her temperature is normal. Her temperature may rise temporarily if she has been playing actively, especially in hot weather. If it is still above 38°C (100.4°F) after she has rested for about half an hour, she may be ill, so check for other signs of illness.

Feel your child's forehead with your cheek if you think he has a fever – don't use your hand because, if it is cold, your child's skin will feel warm by comparison. If his forehead feels hot, take his temperature.

READING A THERMOMETER

Call your doctor now: *your child has become dangerously chilled*

Your child has a fever, *so take her temperature again after 20 minutes. If it is still raised, try to reduce it (see page 194)*

Normal temperature range

SIGNS OF A FEVER

Your child may have a fever if:
★ she complains of feeling unwell
★ she looks pale and feels cold and shivery
★ she looks flushed and her forehead feels hot.

CALL THE DOCTOR

Call the doctor now if your child:
★ has a fever over 39.4°C (103°F) – over 39C (102 F) if she is under a year old – and you can't bring it down
★ has a fever for 24 hours.

CHOOSING A THERMOMETER

The best thermometers for babies and young children are the easy-to-read mercury thermometer, the digital thermometer, and the temperature indicator strip. The easy-to-read thermometer contains mercury that, as it is warmed, expands up the tube alongside a temperature scale.

Safe and easy to use, the digital and ear thermometers give a quick and accurate reading. Although they are more expensive than other thermometers, they are ideal for young children. Always keep spare batteries.

Heat-sensitive panels on the temperature indicator strip glow in sequence and stop when they reach your child's temperature.

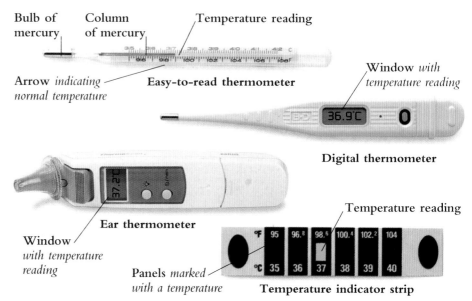

Bulb of mercury

Column of mercury

Temperature reading

Arrow *indicating normal temperature*

Easy-to-read thermometer

Window *with temperature reading*

36.9°C

Digital thermometer

Window *with temperature reading*

Ear thermometer

Panels *marked with a temperature*

Temperature reading

Temperature indicator strip

TAKING YOUR CHILD'S TEMPERATURE

When your child is unwell, take her temperature at least twice a day, morning and evening. One method is to place the thermometer under her arm, which gives a reading 1°F (0.6°C) lower than her true temperature. Never put a mercury thermometer into a young child's mouth, since it can break easily. The digital thermometer is not breakable so it is safe to put it into a young child's mouth, but if she can't hold it correctly under her tongue, place it in her armpit, as for a mercury thermometer. The ear thermometer is also suitable for young children. The temperature indicator strip is much the easiest way of taking a young child's temperature, but the reading is less accurate than that of a thermometer.

USING A MERCURY THERMOMETER

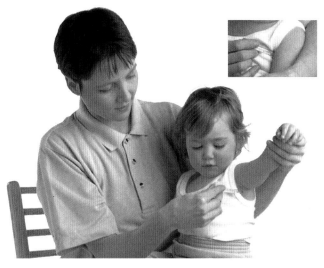

1 Hold the thermometer firmly and shake it sharply several times, with a downwards flick of your wrist, to shake the mercury back into the bulb. Then sit your child on your knee and lift her arm. Tuck the bulb end of the thermometer into her armpit.

2 Bring your child's arm down and fold it over her chest. Hold the thermometer firmly in place for the recommended time – usually about three minutes. Then remove the thermometer from under your child's arm.

The number *aligning with the top of the mercury column is your child's temperature*

3 Turn the thermometer round until you can see the column of mercury next to the scale. After use, wash it in cool water and store it out of your child's reach.

USING AN EAR THERMOMETER

Hold the thermometer *firmly in place*

Make sure a clean lens filter is in place. Pull the ear back and insert the thermometer until the ear canal is sealed off. Press the button on top of the thermometer for one second, then remove the thermometer and read your child's temperature.

USING A DIGITAL THERMOMETER

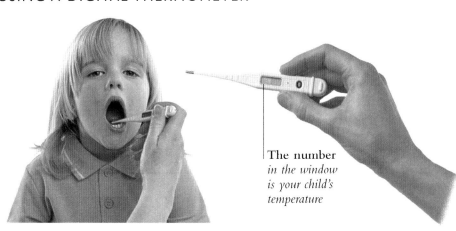

The number *in the window is your child's temperature*

1 Switch the thermometer on and ask your child to open her mouth. Place the thermometer under her tongue and ask her to close her mouth. Wait for about three minutes.

2 Remove the thermometer and read your child's temperature. Anything over 37.5°C (99.5°F) is a fever. Switch the thermometer off, then wash it in cool water and dry it.

USING AN INDICATOR STRIP

Hold the indicator strip on your child's forehead for about 15 seconds. The highest panel that glows indicates your child's temperature. Any reading over 37.5°C (99.5°F) is a fever.

BRINGING DOWN A FEVER

KEEPING HIM COMFORTABLE

If your child has a fever, try to bring down his temperature and make sure that he has plenty of fluids.

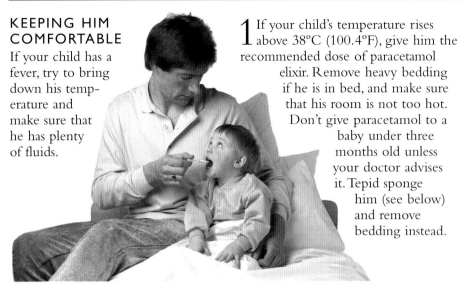

1 If your child's temperature rises above 38°C (100.4°F), give him the recommended dose of paracetamol elixir. Remove heavy bedding if he is in bed, and make sure that his room is not too hot. Don't give paracetamol to a baby under three months old unless your doctor advises it. Tepid sponge him (see below) and remove bedding instead.

2 Your child may sweat profusely as his temperature falls, so give him plenty to drink, to replace the lost fluid. Change his bedding and pyjamas when his temperature is normal again, to make him comfortable.

TEPID SPONGING

If your child's temperature rises above 39.4°C (103°F), try to reduce it by sponging with tepid water as well as treating her as shown above. If your baby is under three months, just tepid sponge her.

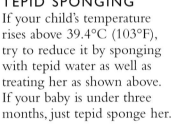

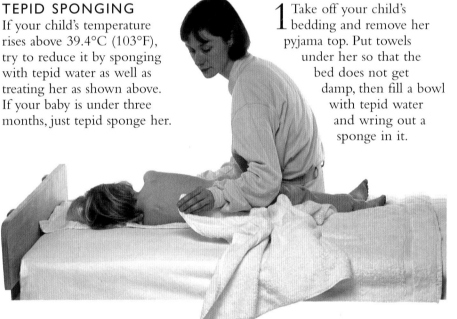

1 Take off your child's bedding and remove her pyjama top. Put towels under her so that the bed does not get damp, then fill a bowl with tepid water and wring out a sponge in it.

2 Gently wipe your child's face, neck, and arms. Remove her pyjama trousers and sponge her legs. Let her skin dry naturally. Continue for about half an hour, then take her temperature. If it is still above 39.4°C (103°F), **call your doctor now.**

FEVERISH CONVULSIONS

A rapid rise in temperature can cause a convulsion in a few children, making them lose consciousness and go rigid for a few seconds, then twitch uncontrollably.

What can I do?

Place your child carefully on the floor and stay with her, but do not try to restrain her in any way. Call your doctor as soon as the convulsions stop.

How can I prevent feverish convulsions?

If a tendency to have feverish convulsions runs in your family, keep your child's temperature as low as you can when she is ill. Follow the cooling methods shown above, and try not to let her temperature rise above 39°C (102.2°F). Your doctor may instruct you to give her a dose of paracetamol elixir when she shows the first signs of illness, to stop her getting a fever.

DELIRIOUS CHILDREN

Some children become delirious when they have a high fever. If your child is delirious, she will be very agitated, and may hallucinate and seem very frightened. This delirious state is alarming, but it isn't dangerous for your child. Stay with her to comfort her. When her temperature drops, she will probably fall asleep, and will be back to normal when she wakes up.

ALL ABOUT MEDICINES

Most minor illnesses get better on their own, with or without treatment. However, if a medicine is necessary, your doctor will tell you how often, and for how long, your child should take it. Follow the directions carefully. Always shake the bottle before pouring out the medicine, and measure the dose exactly. Never mix a medicine into your baby's feed or your child's drink, since he may not finish it. If your baby or child struggles when you give him medicine or try to put drops into his nose, ears, or eyes, ask another adult to hold him still while you give the medicine. You can prevent a baby wriggling by swaddling him firmly. If the doctor prescribes a course of antibiotics, your child must take the full course, even if he seems better before the medicine is finished; otherwise the infection may recur. However, antibiotics aren't effective against all illnesses, only those that are caused by bacteria, for example, chest and urinary infections. They don't affect viruses, so there is no real cure for viral illnesses such as colds, measles, mumps, and chicken pox. Many childhood viral illnesses can now be prevented by immunization, but once caught, they simply have to run their course.

GIVING MEDICINE TO BABIES

Sterilize all the equipment in boiling water before giving medicine to a baby under six months. If your baby cannot yet sit up, hold him as if you were going to feed him. If he can sit up, sit him on your lap and tuck one of his arms behind your back. Put your hand firmly on his other arm to prevent him from struggling. Keep some tissues handy.

Using two spoons
Measure the exact dose and pour half into a sterile teaspoon, so it won't spill easily.

MEDICINE SPOON

Measure your baby's dose and pour half into another spoon (see above). Keep both spoons nearby, then pick up your baby. Hold him so that he can't wriggle, then pick up one spoon and rest it on his lower lip. Let him suck the medicine off, then repeat with the rest of the dose.

MEDICINE DROPPER

Measure the dose in a measuring spoon, then suck some of it into a dropper. Put the dropper into your baby's mouth and squeeze the medicine in. Give the rest of the dose. Don't use a dropper for a young baby: she could choke. Don't use a glass dropper if your baby has teeth.

MEDICINE TUBE

Measure the correct dose and pour it into the medicine tube, then pick up your baby and rest the mouth-piece of the tube on his lower lip. Tilt the tube slightly so that the medicine runs into your baby's mouth, but don't tilt it too much, or the medicine will run out too quickly.

FINGERTIP

If your baby is reluctant to take her medicine, let her suck it off your finger. Measure the dose in a medicine spoon, then pick up your baby, keeping the spoon nearby. Dip your finger into it and let her suck the medicine off. Continue until she has taken the whole dose.

GIVING MEDICINES TO CHILDREN

Most medicines for children are made to taste fairly pleasant, but if your child dislikes the taste, the following tips may help.

★ Have your child's favourite drink ready to take away the taste of the medicine, and try bribery – a small treat or reward may help.

★ Tell your child to hold her nose so that she can't taste the medicine, but never do this forcibly for her.

★ If your child is old enough to understand, explain why she has to take the medicine – if she knows that it will make her feel better, she may be more inclined to take it.

★ If you really find it impossible to get the medicine into your child, ask your doctor if he can prescribe it with a different flavour or in a different form.

A taste tip
If your child dislikes the taste of the medicine, pour it onto the back of her tongue – it won't taste so strong, because her taste buds are at the front.

MEDICINE AND SAFETY

Make sure that your child can't help herself to any medicines in your home.

★ Keep all medications out of her reach, preferably in a locked cabinet.

★ Buy medicines with child-proof lids or packaging.

★ Don't pretend to your child that her medicine is a soft drink.

Medicine and tooth decay

Try to clean your child's teeth after giving her medicine. This is because many medicines for children contain sugar and may cause tooth decay. If your child has to take medicine over a long period, ask your doctor or pharmacist whether a sugar-free alternative is available.

WARNING

Never give aspirin to your child when she is ill; give her paracetamol elixir instead. A few children who have been given aspirin for a mild illness such as the flu have developed a rare, but very serious illness called Reye's syndrome. If your child suddenly vomits and develops a high fever while she is recovering from an illness, **call for emergency help immediately.**

GIVING NOSE DROPS

CHILDREN

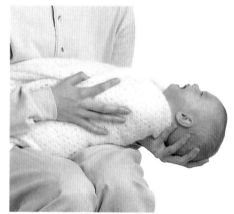

1 Place a small pillow or cushion on a bed and help your child to lie on her back with the pillow beneath her shoulders and her head dropped back. If your child is likely to wriggle as you give her the drops, ask another adult to help you by holding her head.

2 Put the tip of the dropper just above your child's nostril and squeeze out the prescribed number of drops. Don't let the dropper touch her nose – if it does, wash it before using it again. Keep your child lying down for about a minute.

BABIES

Wrap your baby in a blanket, then lay her on her back across your knee, so that her head falls back over your left thigh. Put your left hand beneath her head to support it, then give the drops as instructed for a child.

GIVING EAR DROPS

CHILDREN

1 Most children find ear drops too cold as they are squeezed into their ears, so ask your doctor whether you can warm them up (some medicines deteriorate if they are warmed). To warm the drops, place the bottle in a bowl of warm, not hot, water for a few minutes. Before giving to your child, check the temperature on the inside of your wrist.

2 Ask your child to lie on his side with the affected ear uppermost. Then place the dropper close to his ear and gently squeeze the prescribed number of drops into the ear canal. Keep your child lying down for approximately a minute and place a piece of cotton wool very lightly in his ear to prevent excess liquid running out down his neck.

BABIES

Wrap your baby and lay her on her side across your lap. Support her head with one hand, then give the ear drops as instructed for a child.

EYE DROPS

CHILDREN

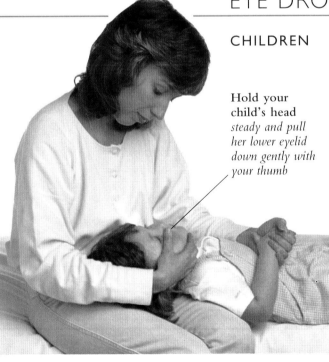

Hold your child's head *steady and pull her lower eyelid down gently with your thumb*

1 Bathe your child's affected eye with cotton wool dipped in warm boiled water, then ask your child to lie on her back across your knee or with her head in your lap. Put one arm round your child's head with your palm against her cheek, then tilt her head so that the affected eye is slightly lower than the other. Draw her lower eyelid gently down with your thumb.

2 Hold the dropper over the gap between the lower lid and the eye, angling it so that it is out of your child's sight. If necessary, ask someone to hold her head steady. Squeeze out the prescribed number of drops, being careful not to touch the eye or the lid. Even if she cries, enough of the medicine is likely to stay in her eye.

BABIES

Choose a time when your baby is relaxed, then swaddle her and lay her on a firm surface or across your knee. Give your drops as for a child.

EYE OINTMENT

If your child is prescribed eye ointment, squeeze a tiny amount into the outer corner of her eye.

CARING FOR A SICK CHILD

While your child is feeling ill, she may demand a great deal of attention, and may be irritable and easily bored. Most children become more babyish when they are ill, and need a lot of extra cuddling and reassurance. Keep your baby with you during the day, so that you can check on her frequently. Let your child lie down in the sitting room, so that she is near you. At night, sleep in the same room as your child if she is very unwell, so that you are nearby if she needs you. Many children vomit when they are ill, so keep a small bowl nearby. Vomiting is only rarely a serious symptom and, while it is often a sign of illness, it can also be brought on by emotional upset or excitement. Frequent or persistent vomiting can be a sign of a serious condition, and may lead to dehydration; see page 222 for when to call your doctor and how to prevent dehydration.

EATING AND DRINKING

Your child will probably have a smaller appetite than usual while she is ill. Don't worry if she doesn't want to eat much for a few days – it won't do her any harm. Allow her to choose her favourite food, and offer small helpings. Let her eat as much or as little as she wants: when she is feeling better, her appetite will return. Babies may demand feeds more frequently than usual, but take very little milk each time. Be patient if your baby behaves like this – she needs the comfort of feeling close to you as she suckles. Drink is much more important than food while your child is ill. Make sure that she has plenty to drink – about $1\frac{1}{2}$ liters (3 pints) a day, especially if she has a raised temperature, or has been vomiting or had diarrhoea – to make sure that she doesn't get dehydrated.

Giving your child a drink
Let your child choose her favourite drink – it doesn't matter whether this is a fizzy drink, fruit juice, milk, or water.

ENCOURAGING YOUR CHILD TO DRINK

If it is difficult to persuade your child to drink enough, make her drinks seem more appetizing by trying some of the ideas suggested below.

Small container
Offer frequent small drinks from a doll's cup or an egg cup, rather than giving large amounts.

Straws
Make drinks look appetizing and more fun by letting your child use a straw.

Teacher beaker
Offer drinks in a teacher beaker or bottle if your child has just grown out of either of these.

Ice cubes
For a child over a year, freeze diluted fruit juice into cubes, then let her suck the cubes.

Ice lolly
Your child may prefer an ice lolly – the "drink on a stick". Try to avoid ones with artificial colouring.

SICKNESS AND VOMITING

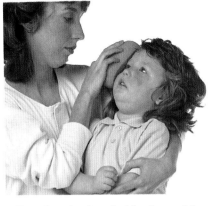

1 Hold your child while she is vomiting to comfort her. Support her head with one hand on her forehead, and put your other hand over her stomach, just below her rib cage.

2 After she has finished vomiting, do your best to reassure your child. Then sponge her face and wipe around her mouth. Give her a few sips of water, let her rinse her mouth out, or help her to clean her teeth, to take away any unpleasant taste that she may have.

3 Let your child rest quietly after vomiting; she may want to lie down and perhaps sleep for a while. Wash out the container and put it within easy reach, in case she vomits again. If your child vomits frequently, she may have gastro-enteritis (see page 222).

COMFORT AND ENTERTAINMENT

STAYING IN BED
There is no need to insist that your sick child stays in bed, though if he is feeling very ill, he will probably prefer to stay there. If he wants to get up, make sure that he is dressed warmly and that the room he is playing in isn't too drafty. However, your child may want to lie down and go to sleep during the day, even if it isn't his usual naptime. If he doesn't want to be left alone, let him snuggle up with a pillow and a duvet and his favourite cuddly toy on the sofa in the sitting room, or make up a bed for him wherever you are (a folding guestbed is ideal). In this way your child still feels like he is a part of the family and does not get too bored or lonely.

Playing in bed
If your child feels like staying in bed, but wants to sit up, prop him up with pillows. Make a bed-table by resting a large tray or board on piles of books.

ENTERTAINING YOUR CHILD
Try to keep your child occupied, so that he doesn't get too bored, but remember that he will probably act younger than his age while he is feeling unwell. He won't be able to concentrate for very long, and he won't want to do anything too demanding. Bring out an old favourite toy that he hasn't played with for a while. If you give him small presents to keep him entertained and cheer him up, don't be tempted to buy toys that are advanced for his age. Babies will enjoy a new mobile or a rattle that makes a new sound. Quiet activities such as interlocking building bricks, felt pictures, simple jigsaws, crayons or felt tip pens, a kaleidoscope, or Plasticine are ideal for sick toddlers and children. Protect the bedding with a towel if your child wants to play with something messy while he is in bed.

COLDS AND FLU

All children get occasional colds and bouts of flu and as soon as your child comes into contact with other children, he may get one cold after another. Both illnesses are caused by viruses; as your child grows older, he will develop resistance to many of the viruses.

Wiping your child's nose
If your child has a runny nose, dab it gently with a tissue to prevent it becoming sore from frequent wiping. Throw the tissue away immediately, to avoid spreading infection.

EMERGENCY SIGNS

Call for emergency help immediately if your child develops a rash of flat dark red or purplish blood-spots (petechial rash) that does not disappear when pressed.

CALL THE DOCTOR

Consult your doctor as soon as possible if your child is under a year old, or seems very miserable and unwell, or has any of the following symptoms:
★ a temperature over 39°C (102.2°F)
★ wheezy, fast, or laboured breathing
★ earache
★ a throat so sore that swallowing is painful
★ a severe cough
★ no improvement after three days.

COLDS

What are they?

Perhaps the most common of all illnesses, a cold is an infection that causes irritation in the nose and throat. Children don't catch a cold simply by being cold – for example, by going out without wearing a coat, or getting their feet wet. While it is not a severe illness, a cold should be taken more seriously in babies and children than in adults, because of the risk of a chest or ear infection developing. If your child develops a rash as well as the symptoms of a normal cold, she might have German measles or measles (see pages 203–04),

---

SYMPTOMS

★ Runny or blocked nose and sneezing
★ slightly raised temperature
★ sore throat
★ cough.

What can I do?

1 Take your child's temperature (see page 193), and give her paracetamol elixir, if necessary to bring it down. Make sure that she has plenty to drink, but don't force her to eat if she's not hungry. A drink before bedtime may help to keep her nose clear at night.

WHAT MIGHT THE DOCTOR DO?

If your baby has trouble feeding because her nose is blocked, your doctor may prescribe nose drops to be given just before a feed.

NOSE DROPS AND DECONGESTANTS

Use these only if your doctor has prescribed them, and never use them for more than three days because if over-used, they can increase mucus production, which will make your child's nose even more blocked.

SINUSITIS

The sinuses are air-filled cavities in the bones of the face. The lining of the nose extends into them, so they can easily become infected after a cold. This infection, sinusitis, causes facial pain. Children under the age of four rarely suffer from sinusitis because their sinuses have not yet fully developed.

FLU

What is it ?

Flu (also known as influenza) is a very infectious illness of the upper respiratory tract. It is caused by hundreds of related viruses, and can affect children of all ages. It tends to occur in epidemics every two or three years, when a new strain of the virus appears to which people have not yet developed immunity. If your child has caught the flu, he will develop symptoms a day or two later, and will probably be unwell for about three or four days. The symptoms usually clear completely within ten days. He may feel ill enough to want to stay in bed for some of the time, and could feel weak for several days after his temperature goes down. A few children develop a chest infection such as bronchitis or pneumonia (see pages 218–19) after having flu.

SYMPTOMS

★ Raised temperature
★ headache
★ aching all over the body
★ shivery feeling
★ runny nose
★ cough
★ sore throat.

What can I do?

Take your child's temperature (see page 193) and give him paracetamol elixir to reduce fever, if necessary. Keep your child in a warm, well-ventilated, humidified room. Make sure he drinks plenty of fluids, especially if his temperature is high. Offer your baby cooled water at frequent intervals.

"Should I have my child vaccinated against flu?"

If your child has a high risk of developing a chest infection after an attack of flu, or if he has a chronic disorder such as lung disease or any defect of the immunue system, an annual vaccination against influenza may be a good idea, so discuss it with your doctor. It will protect him from flu for about a year. However, since new strains of the virus develop every two or three years, the vaccine (which can only be made from existing forms of the virus) does not give life-long protection.

2 Smear a barrier cream, such as zinc and castor oil, under your child's nose and round her nostrils, if the area has become red and sore from a constantly runny nose or frequent wiping.

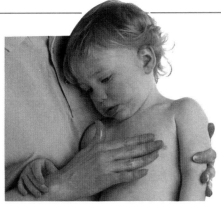

3 If your child is over a year old, rub a menthol chest rub on to her chest before she goes to bed.

4 Sprinkle one or two menthol drops on to your child's nightclothes or a hankerchief. Tuck the hankerchief next to the mattress at the top of the cot or bed.

5 If your baby has a cold, she will be able to breathe more easily if you raise the head of the cot mattress slightly. Put a small pillow or a folded towel underneath it, then lay your baby in her cot so that her head and chest are slightly raised.

Make sure that there are no gaps between the mattress and the head of the cot

6 Keep your child's room warm, but make sure that the air isn't too dry, since breathing very dry air can be uncom-fortable. Use a humidifier if you have one, or hang a wet towel near the heater in your child's room, to add moisture to the air.

HAVING YOUR CHILD IMMUNIZED

When your baby is about two months old, you should start the immunization programme that will protect her against most severe infectious diseases. When your baby is immunized, she is given a vaccine that contains harmless versions of the germ that causes the disease. The vaccine is too weak to cause the disease, but it makes the body produce special proteins (antibodies) that will protect your child from that disease in the future. You must continue with the immunization programme even if your child catches the disease.

Why should my baby be immunized?
Some parents decide against immunization because they are worried about possible risks or because they think that it is unnecessary. However, if fewer children are immunized, diseases can spread more quickly, leading to epidemics.

What are the risks?
Immunization is safe, although it may make your baby mildly unwell for a short time. However, if your baby has had a convulsion, or has a close relative with epilepsy, she has an increased risk of a serious reaction to the whooping cough vaccine, so discuss this with your doctor. Do not take her to be immunized if she has a feverish illness. However, there is no need to postpone immunization if she has some minor infection such as a cold, or is simply off-colour.

What are the after-effects?
Immunization may give your baby a slight fever, so keep a check on her temperature for 24 hours and, if it rises, give her the recommended dose of paracetamol elixir. Your baby may develop a small, hard lump at the injection site. This will go in a few weeks, and is nothing to worry about. The measles vaccine may give her a rash and a fever up to ten days later, and the mumps vaccine might make her face swell slightly three weeks later. If she develops any other symptoms, or if her crying sounds unusual or her temperature rises above 38°C (100.4°F), **call your doctor now.**

Having an injection
Hold your baby firmly while she has the injection, to comfort her and keep her still. The doctor may inject her in the top of her arm or in her bottom or thigh.

IMMUNIZATION PROGRAMME

Age	Vaccine	How given
2 months	Diphtheria Meningitis (Hib★) Tetanus Whooping cough (pertussis)	Injection
	Polio	By mouth
3 months	Diphtheria Meningitis (Hib★) Tetanus Whooping cough	Injection
	Polio	By mouth
4 months	Diphtheria Meningitis (Hib★) Tetanus Whooping cough	Injection
	Polio	By mouth
12–18 months	Measles Mumps German measles (rubella)	Injection (MMR)
3½–5 years, Pre-school booster	Diphtheria Tetanus MMR	Injection
	Polio	By mouth
10–14 years (sometimes shortly after birth)	BCG (tuberculosis)	Skin test followed by one injection if needed
School leavers	Diphtheria Tetanus	Injection
	Polio	By mouth

★Hib: *Haemophilis influenzae* type b, a bacterium that can cause one type of meningitis.

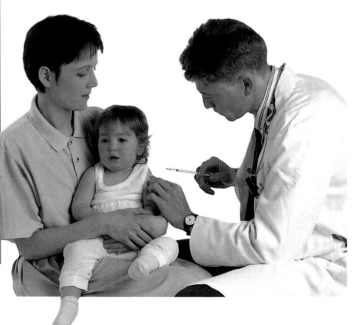

INFECTIOUS ILLNESSES

Now that most children are immunized, many of these diseases have become much less common. If your child catches one of them, he will probably be immune for the rest of his life. Since most of these infectious diseases are caused by viruses, there are no medicines to cure them, but most children recover quickly and uneventfully. There is little point in trying to isolate your child when he has an infectious illness, unless he has German measles (see below), but it is a good idea to inform the parents of any children he has recently contacted.

WARNING

If your child has a raised temperature while he is ill with one of these diseases, **DO NOT** give him aspirin to bring the fever down, since it can cause a very serious disease called Reye's syndrome (see page 196). Give him paracetamol elixir instead.

EMERGENCY SIGNS

Call for emergency help immediately if your child has an infectious disease and develops any of these signs:
* ★ unusual and increasing drowsiness
* ★ headache or stiff neck
* ★ convulsions
* ★ rash of flat dark red or purplish blood-spots.

GERMAN MEASLES

What is it?
German measles was once common but has become rare because of routine immunization (see page 202). It is a very mild illness, so your child may feel perfectly well and may not want to stay in bed. She will develop symptoms two to three weeks after she has been infected.

What can I do?
1 Take your child's temperature at least twice a day (see page 193) and, if necessary, give her paracetamol elixir to reduce her fever.

2 Make sure that your child has plenty to drink, especially if she has a raised temperature.

SYMPTOMS

Days 1 and 2
* ★ Symptoms of a mild cold
* ★ slightly sore throat
* ★ swollen glands behind the ears, on the sides of the neck, and on the nape of the neck.

Day 2 or 3
* ★ Blotchy rash of flat, pink spots appearing first on the face, then spreading down the body
* ★ slightly raised temperature.

Day 4 or 5
* ★ Fading rash, and general improvement.

Day 6
* ★ Your child is back to normal.

Day 9 or 10
* ★ Your child is no longer infectious.

CALL THE DOCTOR

Call for emergency help immediately if your child develops any of the emergency signs above. Consult your doctor as soon as possible if you think your child has German measles, but do not take her to the doctor's surgery in case she comes into contact with a pregnant woman.

What might the doctor do?
Your doctor will confirm that your child has German measles, but there is no treatment for it.

German measles and pregnancy
While your child is infectious, keep her away from any woman who might be pregnant. Although German measles is a mild disease, it can cause defects in a developing baby if a pregnant woman catches it.

MEASLES

What is it?
Measles is a very infectious illness that causes a rash, fever, and a cough, and sometimes more serious complications. It used to be common, but widespread immunization has made it a rare disease.

What can I do?
1 Try to bring down her temperature (see page 194) and give plenty of fluids. She may feel very miserable and want to stay in bed.

2 If her eyes are sore, bathe them with cotton wool dipped in cool water. Keep her room dark if this makes her more comfortable.

What the doctor might do
Your doctor will confirm the diagnosis and may want to keep a check on your child until she has recovered. He will treat any complications if they develop.

SYMPTOMS
Symptoms develop 10–14 days after infection.
Days 1 and 2
★ Runny nose, dry cough, and red watering eyes
★ steadily rising temperature.

Day 3
★ Tiny white spots, like grains of salt, in the mouth.

Days 4 and 5
★ Dull-red rash of slightly raised spots appears, first on the forehead and behind the ears, gradually spreading to the rest of the face and trunk. After two or three days, the rash fades and other symptoms disappear.

CALL THE DOCTOR
Call for emergency help immediately if your child develops any of the signs listed on page 203. Consult your doctor as soon as possible if you think your child has measles. Call him again if:
★ your child is no better three days after the rash develops
★ your child's temperature rises suddenly
★ her condition worsens after she seemed to be improving
★ your child has earache
★ your child's breathing is noisy or difficult.

ROSEOLA INFANTUM

What is it?
Roseola is a mild illness that is very common in early childhood. It is characterized by a high fever that lasts for about three days, followed by a rash of pink spots. Most children will have had it by the time they are two.

SYMPTOMS
Symptoms appear 5–15 days after infection
Days 1 to 4
★ High temperature
★ sometimes a mild cold or cough.

Days 4 to 8
★ Temperature suddenly returns to normal
★ rash of pink, slightly raised spots appears over head and trunk
★ rash fades and child is back to normal.

What can I do?
1 Call your doctor if your child's temperature is 39°C (102.2°F) or above.

2 Try to bring down the fever to make your child more comfortable (see page 194). Paracetamol may bring his temperature down briefly.

3 Make sure your child has plenty to drink.

CALL THE DOCTOR
Call for emergency help immediately if your child develops any of the emergency signs on page 203.

CHICKEN POX

What is it?

Chicken pox is a very infectious illness characterized by a rash of itchy spots that turn into fluid-filled blisters. It is usually accompanied by a slight fever. Your child may not feel very ill, but if she has a lot of spots, she may itch all over. Symptoms appear two to three weeks after your child has been infected. It is a very common childhood illness. In later life the chicken pox virus may be reactivated and cause shingles, so a child may catch chicken pox after contact with an adult who has shingles.

SYMPTOMS

Days 1 to 4
* Groups of small, red, very itchy spots with fluid-filled centres, appearing in batches first on the child's chest, abdomen, and back, later elsewhere on the body
* fluid within the spots becomes white and cloudy
* slight temperature.

Days 5 to 9
* The spots burst, leaving small craters
* scabs form over the spots and drop off after a few days.

Day 10
* Your child is back to normal.

Day 11 or 12
* Your child is no longer infectious.

CALL THE DOCTOR

Call for emergency help immediately if your child develops any of the signs listed on page 203. Consult your doctor as soon as possible if you think your child has chicken pox, and call him again if your child has any of these symptoms:
* very severe itching
* redness or swelling around any spots, or pus oozing from the spots – this means they have become infected.

What can I do?

1 Take your child's temperature (see page 193), and give her the recommended dose of paracetamol elixir to bring it down if it is raised. Give her plenty of fluids to drink if she has a fever. Though your child may not feel very ill try to make sure that she has plenty of rest as this will aid her recovery.

2 Try to discourage your child from scratching the spots, since it can infect them, and also cause scarring when they heal. Cut your child's fingernails short and keep them clean, so that the spots are less likely to become infected if she does scratch them. Put scratch mitts on her.

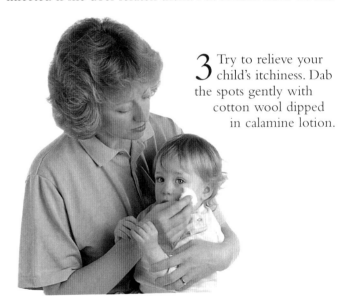

3 Try to relieve your child's itchiness. Dab the spots gently with cotton wool dipped in calamine lotion.

4 Give your child warm baths with a handful of bicarbonate of soda dissolved in the water, to help reduce the itching.

5 If your child is very itchy, she will probably find loose cotton clothes the most comfortable.

What the doctor might do

Your doctor will confirm the diagnosis and may prescribe an antihistamine cream or medicine to relieve your child's itching if it is very severe. If any of the spots have become infected, he may prescribe an antibiotic cream.

MUMPS

What is it?
Mumps is an infection that was common among children until routine immunization was introduced. It causes swollen glands, particularly the glands just in front of and below the ears. Occasionally mumps causes inflammation of the testicles, but this is rare in a boy before puberty.

SYMPTOMS

Symptoms appear 14–24 days after infection
★ Raised temperature
★ one or two days later the child develops painful swellings on one or both sides of the face. This lasts from 4–8 days.

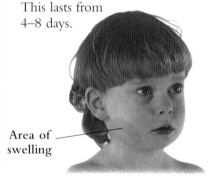

Area of swelling

What can I do?

1 Give paracetamol elixir to bring his temperature down.

2 Give plenty of cold drinks but avoid acidic drinks such as fruit juice. Let your child drink through a straw if it hurts to open his mouth.

3 If it hurts your child to swallow, give him liquid or semi-liquid foods such as ice-cream and soup.

CALL THE DOCTOR

Call for emergency help immediately if your child develops any of the signs on page 203. Consult your doctor as soon as possible if you think your child has mumps, and call him again if he develops bad stomach pain or a red testicle.

What the doctor might do
The doctor will confirm that your child has mumps and treat any complications if they develop.

ERYTHEMA INFECTIOSUM (SLAPPED CHEEK DISEASE)

What is it?
Erythema infectiosum is a mild, and mildly infectious, illness that usually occurs in small outbreaks in the spring, and mostly affects children over the age of two years. It is also sometimes called "fifth disease". The disease is characterized by a bright red rash that suddenly appears on both cheeks, hence its other name of "slapped cheek disease".

What can I do?
Give your child paracetamol elixir to reduce the fever. Make sure she drinks plenty of fluids. If your child has a blood disorder (for example, sickle cell anaemia or thalassaemia), consult your doctor. Erythema infectiosum can sometimes cause severe illness in such children. If your child has Erythema infectiosum, keep her away from anyone who might be pregnant. Although once the rash appears she is unlikely to be infectious, the disease can, in rare circumstances, lead to miscarriage if contracted during pregnancy.

SYMPTOMS

Symptoms appear 4–14 days after infection.

Day 1
★ Bright red cheeks, with a contrasting pale area around the mouth
★ mild fever.

Days 2–5
★ Blotchy, lace-like rash spreading over trunk and limbs.

Days 7–10
★ Rash fades. Your child is no longer infectious. The rash may recur over the next few weeks or months, particularly if your child gets hot or is exposed to sunlight.

WHOOPING COUGH

What is it?

One of the most serious childhood diseases, whooping cough (also known as pertussis) is a severe and persistent cough. It is caused by a bacterial infection. It is highly infectious, so keep your child away from babies and children who have not been immunized. Immunized children can get a mild form of the illness. A few children with whooping cough develop a secondary infection, such as bronchitis or pneumonia (see pages 218–19).

SYMPTOMS

Week 1
★ Symptoms of a normal cough and cold
★ slight temperature.

Week 2
★ Worsening cough, with frequent coughing fits lasting up to a minute, after which your child has to fight for breath
★ if your child is over 18 months, he may learn to force breath in with a "whooping" sound
★ vomiting after a coughing fit.

Weeks 3 to 10
★ Cough improves, but may worsen if your child gets a cold
★ your child is unlikely to be infectious after the third week.

What can I do?

1 Stay with your child during any coughing fits, since he may become very distressed. Sit him on your lap and support him gently as he leans slightly forwards. Keep a small bowl nearby so that he can spit out any phlegm that he coughs up, and in case he should vomit. Clean the bowl thoroughly with boiling water afterwards, to make sure that the infection doesn't spread to the rest of the family.

2 If your child often coughs and vomits after meals, offer him small meals at frequent intervals, if possible just after a coughing fit.

3 Keep your child entertained – he will have fewer coughing fits if his attention is distracted, but don't let him get too excited or over-tired since this may bring on a coughing fit.

EMERGENCY SIGNS

Call for emergency help immediately if your child turns blue during a coughing fit.

CALL THE DOCTOR

Consult your doctor as soon as possible if you suspect that your child has whooping cough.

4 Sleep in the same room as your child, so that you can be with him if he has a coughing fit at night.

5 Don't let anyone smoke near your child, and don't give him any cough medicines.

What might the doctor do?

The doctor may prescribe a cough suppressant and an antibiotic. Although the antibiotic won't cure your child's cough, it may reduce its severity and make your child less infectious. This is particularly important if you have a baby who is at risk of catching whooping cough from an older brother or sister who already has the disease. However, the antibiotic is only really effective if it is given right at the beginning of the infection.

NURSING A BABY

Whooping cough is dangerous in babies because they may not be able to draw breath properly after coughing. Your baby will need careful nursing and may be admitted to hospital. She may find feeding difficult if she vomits frequently, so abandon your regular feeding schedule, and offer a feed as soon as she has calmed down after coughing or vomiting.

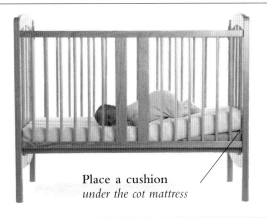

Place a cushion
under the cot mattress

Coughing fits

When your baby has a coughing fit, lay her in her cot on her stomach with the foot of her cot slightly raised, or face down across your lap. Stay with her until she has stopped coughing and is breathing normally again. Then cuddle her to comfort her and put her down to sleep on her back as usual.

MENINGITIS

What is it?

Meningitis is an inflammation of the tissues covering the brain. It can be caused by infection with bacteria or viruses. Viral meningitis is more common than bacterial meningitis, and is also less serious. It can be caused by several different viruses, and tends to occur in winter epidemics. Viral meningitis is more likely to affect children over 5 years old. Bacterial meningitis is quite rare, but it can be

The meninges

Three protective layers, known as the meninges, cover the brain and spinal cord. Meningitis occurs when the meninges become infected by viruses or bacteria.

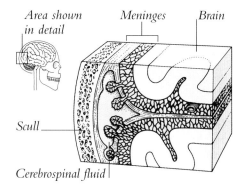

Area shown in detail   *Meninges*   *Brain*

Scull

Cerebrospinal fluid

life-threatening. In Britain, the Hib vaccination has wiped out one type of bacterial meningitis. Unfortunately there are others, of which the most common is called Group B meningococcal bacteria. Two other strains of these bacteria, Group A and Group C, also cause the disease, but are rarer. Although bacterial meningitis can occur at any age, it is most common in children under the age of 5.

The early symptoms of bacterial and viral meningitis are very similar, and can easily be mistaken for those of flu. However, the symptoms of bacterial meningitis are usually more severe. What makes bacterial meningitis so dangerous is that it can develop very rapidly, so that the child may become seriously ill within a few hours, with increasing drowsiness and sometimes loss of consciousness or convulsions.

Meningitis rash

Some children with meningitis develop a characteristic rash of tiny blood-spots under the skin, which can appear anywhere on the body. The spots are flat, pink, or purple,

look like pin-pricks at first, but if untreated grow bigger till they look like fresh bruises.

What can I do?

Call your doctor now, or take your child to the nearest hospital accident and emergency department if they seem abnormally drowsy or have any two of the symptoms listed in the emergency signs box below.

What might the doctor do?

The doctor may send your child to hospital for a lumbar puncture test to confirm the diagnosis.

If viral meningitis is diagnosed, no treatment is necessary except painkillers and your child will recover completely within a week or two.

Bacterial meningitis will be treated with antibiotics and, if convulsions occur, with anti-convulsant drugs. If the disease is picked up early and treated promptly, most children recover completely. Rarely, the disease may be fatal, and in a few children it may cause some brain damage, especially if treatment is delayed.

EMERGENCY SIGNS

Call for emergency help immediately if your child has two or more of the following symptoms:
★ Abnormal drowsiness
★ fever with cold hands and feet
★ vomiting
★ stiff neck
★ refusing feeds
★ restlessness and irritability
★ tense or bulging fontanelle
★ purple-red rash that does not fade when pressed

older children may also have:
★ severe headache
★ dislike of bright light and loud noise.

If your child has a dark, purplish rash, check to see whether it fades when pressed. To do this, press the side of a glass on to the rash. If the

rash is still visible through the glass, it may be a purpura rash, which requires immediate medical attention. Take your child to the nearest accident and emergency department.

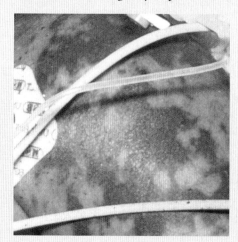

Purpura on dark skin

Purpura on light skin

EYE PROBLEMS

Most eye disorders clear up quickly with treatment but all problems affecting the eye should be taken seriously. Eye infections spread easily, so give your child her own face flannel and towel. Use a clean tissue to dry each eye. Keep your child's hands clean and try to stop her rubbing her eyes – this helps to prevent an infection, as well as stopping it spreading.

EMERGENCY SIGNS

Call for emergency help immediately if your child has any injury that has damaged her eye, or if she cannot see clearly after an injury.

BLEPHARITIS

What is it?
Blepharitis is an inflammation of the edges of the eyelids, which usually affects both eyes. Many children with dandruff get blepharitis.

SYMPTOMS

★ Red and scaly eyelids.

What can I do?
1 Dissolve a teaspoon of salt or sodium bicarbonate in a glass of warm boiled water, and use this to bathe your child's eyelids. Wash your hands before and afterwards, and use fresh cotton wool for each eye. Do this twice a day, making a fresh solution each time.

2 If your child has dandruff, wash her hair with an anti-dandruff shampoo. Use an anti-cradle cap shampoo for a baby.

CALL THE DOCTOR

Consult your doctor as soon as possible if:
★ your child's eyes are sticky
★ there is no improvement after about a week of home treatment.

What might the doctor do?
The doctor might prescribe a cream to soothe your child's eyelids, or an antibiotic ointment.

CONJUNCTIVITIS

What is it?
Also known as "pink eye", because the white of the eye may turn pink, conjunctivitis is an inflammation of the lining of the eye and eyelids. It can be caused by a virus or by bacteria, being milder when it is caused by a virus. If your child's eyelids are gummed together with pus when she wakes up, she probably has bacterial, rather than viral, conjunctivitis. If your baby develops any of these symptoms in the first day or two of life, see Sticky eye, page 183.

SYMPTOMS

★ Bloodshot eye
★ gritty, sore eye
★ discharge of pus
★ eyelids gummed together after sleep.

CALL THE DOCTOR

Consult your doctor as soon as possible if you think your child has conjunctivitis or if her eyes are bloodshot and sore.

What can I do?
1 Try to find out whether your child's symptoms might be caused by something other than conjunctivitis. She might have an allergy such as hayfever, or she may have a speck of dust or an eyelash in her eye. If she has an allergy, her eyes may be itchy and watering as well as red and sore.

2 If you think she has conjunctivitis, dissolve a teaspoon of salt in a glass of warm boiled water, and dip a piece of cotton wool in this. Bathe both of her eyes, using fresh cotton wool for each one. Start with the infected one, and wipe from the outside corner to the inside. Wash your hands before and afterwards.

What might the doctor do?
The doctor may prescribe antibiotic drops or ointment for a bacterial infection, which will cure it quickly. Viral conjunctivitis needs no treatment, but may last a few weeks.

STYE

What is it?

A stye is a painful, pus-filled swelling on the upper or lower eyelid. It is caused by an infection, usually bacterial, at the base of an eyelash.

Some styes simply dry up, but most come to a head and burst within about a week, relieving the pain. Styes are not serious and you can treat them at home. Try to stop your child from touching the stye to prevent the infection from spreading.

SYMPTOMS

* Red, painful swelling on the eyelid
* pus-filled centre appearing in the swelling.

CALL THE DOCTOR

Consult your doctor as soon as possible if:
* the stye does not improve after about a week
* your child's whole eyelid is swollen
* the skin all around your child's eye turns red
* your child also has blepharitis.

What can I do?

1 Dip some cotton wool in hot, but not boiling, water, squeeze it out, and press it gently onto your child's stye. This will help to bring the stye to a head more quickly and encourage the release of pus. Repeat this for two or three minutes, three times a day until the stye bursts.

2 When the stye bursts and releases the pus, the pain is relieved. Wash the pus away very gently with cotton wool that has been dipped in warm boiled water. The swelling will soon go down.

SQUINT

What is it?

Normally, both eyes look in the same direction at the same time, but in a child with a squint, one eye focuses on an object, while the other does not follow it properly.

A newborn baby's eyes do not always work together correctly, so intermittent squinting is common. This is nothing to worry about. But if your baby's eyes don't move together by the time he is three months old, talk to your health visitor. He may have a squint.

Squinting may be constant, but in some children it comes and goes. However, children do not grow out of a squint, so it is essential to have it treated. The younger the child, the more successful the treatment.

SYMPTOMS

* Eyes looking in different directions.

CALL THE DOCTOR

Consult your doctor if you think your child has a squint.

How can I check for a squint?

When your baby is about three months old, hold a toy 20cm (8in) from his face and move it slowly from side to side. Check that his eyes work together to follow the moving object.

What might the doctor do?

The doctor will check your child's vision and may give him a patch to wear over his stronger eye for several hours each day, so that he is forced to use his weak or lazy eye. A toddler may need to wear glasses. If your child is under two, this treatment will probably cure his squint in a few months. If your child has a severe squint caused by muscle weakness, he may need to have an operation on one of the muscles in his weak eye, to correct the defect and straighten his eyes.

EAR PROBLEMS

Most ear problems in small children arise from an infection of the outer or middle ear, or because the tube connecting the ear and throat becomes blocked. Ear infections should be taken seriously but are dangerous only if they are not treated promptly: pus may build up behind the ear-drum, causing it to burst, or infection may spread into a bone behind the ear (mastoidtis).

Anatomy of the ear
Each ear consists of three parts. From the outer ear (the only visible part) a slightly curved canal leads to the ear-drum. Behind this is a cavity, the middle ear, in which lie three small bones, which transmit sound vibrations to the inner ear, the part of the ear that contains the structures concerned with hearing and balance.

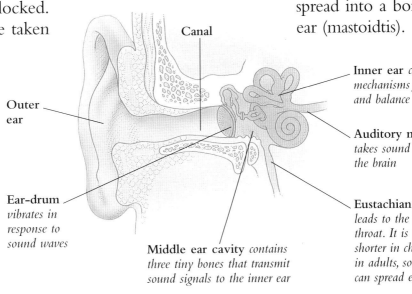

Canal

Outer ear

Ear-drum *vibrates in response to sound waves*

Middle ear cavity *contains three tiny bones that transmit sound signals to the inner ear*

Inner ear *contains the mechanisms for hearing and balance*

Auditory nerve *takes sound signals to the brain*

Eustachian tube *leads to the back of the throat. It is much shorter in children than in adults, so infection can spread easily*

OUTER EAR INFECTION

What is it?
The skin lining the outer ear canal becomes inflamed when your child has an outer ear infection. This may happen if he swims a lot in chlorinated water, or because he has poked or scratched his ear and it has become infected. Children with eczema are especially prone to such infections if they get water in their ears.

What can I do?
1 Give your child the recommended dose of paracetamol elixir to relieve the pain.

2 Make sure that water doesn't get into the affected ear at bathtime, and just sponge his hair clean. Don't let your child go swimming until the infection clears up.

What might the doctor do?
Your doctor will probably prescribe antibiotic or anti-inflammatory ear drops to clear the infection.

SYMPTOMS

★ Pain in the ear that is worse when the child touches his ear or lies on it
★ redness in the ear canal
★ discharge from the ear
★ itchiness inside the ear.

CALL THE DOCTOR

Consult your doctor as soon as possible if you think your child has an outer ear infection.

WAX IN THE EAR

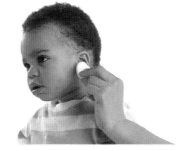

Wax sometimes accumulates in the ear, giving a feeling of fullness or partial deafness. If your child has a lot of ear wax, very gently wipe away any visible wax with cotton wool, but don't poke anything into the ear. If this doesn't help, consult your doctor.

To give the ear drops, ask your child to lie on his side and keep still while you squeeze drops into the affected ear. Keep him in this position for about a minute afterwards.

MIDDLE EAR INFECTION

What is it?
Earache is commonly caused by an infection of the middle ear. If your child has a middle ear infection, the cavity behind his ear-drum becomes infected or inflamed, usually because an infection has spread from the throat. The tube that runs from the throat to the ear is very short and narrow in a child, allowing infection to spread easily. Generally only one ear is infected.

By the time your child is seven or eight years old, the eustachian tube will have increased in width, making your child much less prone to these infections.

What can I do?
1 Try to relieve your child's earache. Fill a hot water bottle with warm, not hot, water and wrap it in a towel, then let him rest his ear against it. Don't give a hot water bottle to a baby who is too young to push it away if it is too hot – heat a soft cloth and hold it against the baby's ear instead.

2 If your child's ear is very painful and is causing him a lot of discomfort, try giving the recommended dose of paracetamol elixir. This should relieve the pain.

SYMPTOMS

★ Very painful ear, which may stop your child sleeping
★ crying and rubbing or tugging at the ear, if your child can't yet talk well enough to complain of earache
★ crying, loss of appetite, and general signs of illness in young babies, especially after a cold
★ raised temperature
★ partial deafness.

---

3 If you notice a discharge, don't clear it away or probe his ear – just put a clean handkerchief over his ear. Encourage him to rest his head on the affected side, so that any discharge can drain away.

How can I prevent ear infection?
In cold weather, keep your child's ears warm. Use menthol drops or a menthol rub whenever he has a cold (see page 201). These help to clear your child's nasal passages, which reduces the chances of infection spreading to the ear.

CALL THE DOCTOR

Consult your doctor as soon as possible if your child's ear is infected or has a discharge.

What might the doctor do?
Your doctor will examine your child's ears and may prescribe an antibiotic. If pus has built up behind the ear-drum, the doctor may prescribe a drug to help it drain away. If this is not effective, your child may need a small operation.

GLUE EAR

What is it?
Repeated middle ear infections can lead to glue ear, an accumulation of sticky fluid in the middle ear.

SYMPTOMS

★ Partial deafness after repeated middle ear infections.

CALL THE DOCTOR

Consult your doctor as soon as possible if you think your child has glue ear.

What can I do?
If you smoke, try to stop. Children of parents who smoke seem to be more prone than others to suffer glue ear.

What might the doctor do?
Your doctor may prescribe a decongestant, but a simple operation may be necessary. Under anaesthetic, a hole is made in the ear-drum and a tiny tube (a grommet) is inserted. The grommet is not uncomfortable, and will not affect your child's hearing, but he must not go swimming while it is in place. After several months it will fall out, the hole will heal, and his hearing will be back to normal.

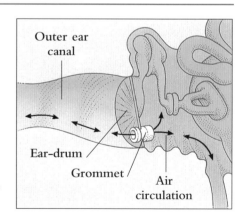

The grommet is implanted in the ear-drum, to equalize air pressure on either side of the ear-drum and to allow the ear to dry out.

MOUTH INFECTIONS

Ababy or child with a mouth infection will have a very sore mouth, so that feeding is painful. Thrush is the most common mouth affliction in babies. Children over one are prone to cold sores (see page 230), usually around the lips, but sometimes inside the mouth.

Helping the child with a sore mouth
If your child's mouth is sore, try to make eating and drinking as painless as you can. Allow warm meals to get cool before giving them to your child, since hot food generally hurts more than cold, and offer her plenty of very cold drinks. If she is reluctant to eat or drink, try some of the suggestions given here.

Let your child drink through a straw or
use a teacher beaker, since this may be less painful than drinking from a cup.

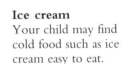

Soup
This is nourishing and easy to eat, and can be served cold. Alternatively, liquidize food, or chop it very small.

Cold drinks
Serve drinks very cold; avoid fruit juice, since it is too acidic.

Ice cream
Your child may find cold food such as ice cream easy to eat.

Water

Cheese
Encourage you child to finish meals with cheese and a drink of water to help keep her teeth clean without brushing.

THRUSH

What is it?
Thrush is an infection caused by a yeast that lives in the mouth and intestines. The yeast is normally kept under control by bacteria, but sometimes it multiplies out of control, producing a sore, irritating rash. Occasionally, it spreads through the intestines and causes a rash round the anus. It is not a serious infection and, although it does not respond to home remedies, it usually clears up quickly with medical treatment.

SYMPTOMS

★ Creamy yellow, slightly raised patches on the inside of the cheeks, tongue, or the roof of the mouth, which do not come away easily if you try to wipe them off
★ in babies, a rash around the anus that looks like nappy rash
★ reluctance to eat due to a sore mouth.

CALL THE DOCTOR

Consult your doctor as soon as possible if you think your baby or child has thrush.

What can I do?
1 Wipe the patches in your child's mouth very gently with a clean handkerchief. If they don't come off easily, she probably has thrush. Don't rub them hard, because if you scrape them off they will leave a sore, bleeding patch underneath.

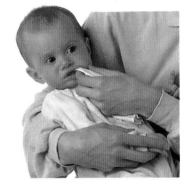

2 Give your child food that is easy to eat (see above). If you are bottle-feeding, buy a special soft teat and clean it carefully, then sterilize it after each feed.

3 If you are breast-feeding, continue to feed as normal, but take extra care with nipple hygiene to prevent your nipples becoming infected. Wash them in water only, not soap, after every feed, and don't wear breast pads. If they are sore or develop white spots, consult your doctor.

What might the doctor do?
Your doctor may prescribe a medicine to be dropped into your baby's mouth just before a feed, or, for a child over about two, lozenges to suck. If you are breast-feeding, the doctor may prescribe an antifungal cream for your nipples.

THROAT INFECTIONS

Sore throats are common in children, and often accompany another illness such as a cold or flu. Most mild sore throats clear up in a few days, but a more severe infection, particularly if his tonsils are affected, may give him a fever and make swallowing difficult and painful.

CALL THE DOCTOR

Consult your doctor as soon as possible if your child:
★ has such a sore throat that swallowing is painful
★ seems generally unwell and has a fever or rash
★ has infected tonsils
★ has not been immunized against diphtheria.

SORE THROAT

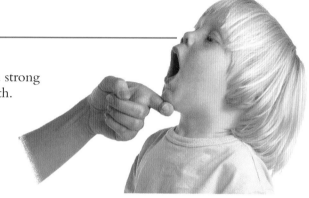

What is it?
A sore throat is an infection of the throat that makes the area sore and red. It may be part of a cold or flu (see pages 200–01), or one of the first signs of German measles or mumps (see pages 203 and 206). Children are prone to earache when they have a throat infection (see pages 211–12).

SYMPTOMS

★ Reluctance to eat, because it hurts to swallow
★ red, raw-looking throat
★ earache (see pages 211–12))
★ slightly raised temperature
★ swollen glands
★ stomach ache in young children.

What can I do?
1 Ask your child to face a strong light and open his mouth. Examine the back of his throat carefully (see page 189). If it is sore, it will look red and raw and you may be able to see creamy spots.

2 Gently feel down each side of your child's neck and just below the angle of his jaw-bone, to check whether his glands are swollen (see page 189).

3 Give your child plenty of cold drinks, and liquidize food if it hurts him to swallow. He may find very cold food such as ice cream less painful to eat than warm food.

4 Take your child's temperature (see page 193), and if it is above normal, give him the recommended dose of paracetamol elixir to bring his fever down.

What might the doctor do?
Most mild sore throats need no treatment, but if the doctor suspects that the infection is caused by bacteria, he may prescribe an antibiotic.

TONSILLITIS

SYMPTOMS

★ Very sore throat
★ red and enlarged tonsils, possibly covered with creamy spots
★ temperature over 38°C (100.4°F)
★ swollen glands on the neck.

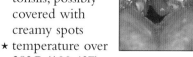

What is it?
Tonsillitis is an inflammation of the tonsils, causing a very sore throat and other symptoms of illness. The tonsils are glands at the back of the throat, one on either side, which trap infection and prevent it spreading.

What can I do?
1 Examine your child's tonsils and feel his glands (see page 189). If infected, his tonsils will be large and red, and may have creamy spots.

2 Take his temperature (see page 193) and give him paracetamol elixir to bring it down, if necessary.

3 Encourage your child to have plenty to drink, especially if he has a fever. Offer him cold drinks and liquid or semi-liquid foods.

What might the doctor do?
Your doctor will examine your child's throat, and may take a throat swab by wiping a sterile swab across it. He may prescribe an antibiotic to clear the infection up quickly.

If your child frequently has such severe tonsillitis that his general health suffers, your doctor may recommend that he has his tonsils removed. However, this operation is rarely done before a child is four.

COUGHS AND CHEST INFECTIONS

Most coughs in small children are a symptom of a cold or flu (see pages 200–01), which produces a dry, tickly cough. A cough may also be a symptom of a chest infection (see pages 216–19) or an early sign of measles (see page 204). A severe, persistent cough might be whooping cough (see page 207). Your child may get a chest infection after having a cold or flu. In this case, he will have other symptoms as well as a cough: he may find breathing difficult, and might cough up some phlegm. However, slightly wheezy breathing is normal for a small child with a cold or flu: his airways are very narrow and become even narrower if they are swollen when he is ill, so this symptom on its own isn't a sign of an infection. Occassionally, a chest infection develops as a complication of measles or whooping cough.

EMERGENCY SIGNS

Call for emergency help immediately if your child:
* has a bluish tinge round his face, mouth, and tongue
* is breathing very rapidly
* is breathing so noisily that it can be heard across the room
* seems to be fighting for breath
* deteriorates suddenly when he has a cold or flu
* is abnormally drowsy
* is unable to speak or make sounds as usual.

FREQUENT CHEST INFECTIONS

Babies under a year old and children with a long-term chest disorder such as asthma (see page 218) are prone to chest infections. If you smoke, your children are much more likely to develop chest infections than are the children of non-smoking parents.

If your child has frequent chest infections, your doctor may arrange for tests to find the cause.

Breathing

When your child breathes in, air is sucked down his windpipe and bronchi (the airways) into his lungs, where oxygen is absorbed into his bloodstream. His blood then carries the oxygen all round his body.

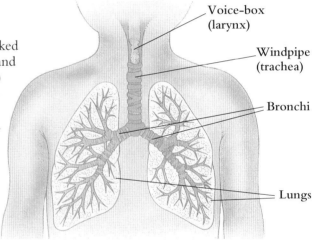

Voice-box (larynx)

Windpipe (trachea)

Bronchi

Lungs

CROUP

What is it?

Croup is an inflammation of the voice-box, which makes it swell, so that your child finds it difficult to breathe. Attacks of croup tend to occur at night, and usually last about two hours.

SYMPTOMS

* Breathing difficulty
* loud, crowing sound as breath is drawn in
* barking cough.

What can I do?

1 Keep calm, and reassure your child. He is likely to be very frightened, but if he panics, it will be even harder for him to breathe.

2 Create a steamy atmosphere by keeping a kettle boiling or taking your child into the bathroom and turning on the hot taps. The moist air will soothe his air passages and help him to breath more easily.

3 Prop your child up on pillows, or hold him sitting on your lap – he will be able to breathe more easily in either of these positions.

CALL THE DOCTOR

Call your doctor now if your child has difficulty breathing, or if you think he has croup.

What might the doctor do?

The doctor will reassure you and tell you what to do if the croup recurs. He might give a medicated inhalation to help ease your child's breathing if he has another attack. If the attack is severe, the doctor might send him to hospital. It may take a few days for a child to recover from a severe attack.

COUGH

What is it?

A cough is a protective reflex action that helps to clear any irritants or blockages from the airways. It can be either a reaction to irritation in the throat or windpipe, or the result of an infection of the respiratory tract. It may also be caused by an obstruction in the airways. A cough will generally disappear of its own accord.

A dry, ticklish cough, without sputum, is rarely serious. It probably means that your child's throat or windpipe is irritated, which may be a by-product of a cold, because mucus dribbles down the throat and irritates it. Her throat might also be irritated if she is with adults who smoke. An ear infection can also cause a dry cough. If your child has a moist sounding cough, particularly if she coughs up any phlegm, then she probably has a minor respiratory infection. While most coughs like this are not serious, they can be a symptom of bronchiolitis, bronchitis, or pneumonia (see pages 217–219).

What might the doctor do?

The doctor will examine your child and listen to his breathing.

If your child has a dry cough, the doctor may prescribe a cough suppressant medicine to soothe his throat.

If the cough is particularly chesty, the doctor may carry out some diagnostic tests. He may prescribe antibiotics and perhaps a cough medicine to make the phlegm easier to cough up.

CALL THE DOCTOR

Consult your doctor as soon as possible if:
* ★ your baby is under six months
* ★ the cough prevents your child sleeping
* ★ the cough does not improve in three days
* ★ your child has a recurrent cough.

What can I do?

1 If your child has a sudden attack of coughing, check whether she might have inhaled a small object such as a sweet or a button. If she has, try to remove it (see Choking, page 242), but don't put your fingers down her throat to try to hook it out.

2 If your child has a chesty cough, help her to clear the phlegm from her chest when she is coughing. Support her as she leans forwards. Hold a small bowl and encourage her to spit out any phegm that she coughs up.

Keep your child's head *slightly tipped down*

3 If your child has a dry cough, a warm drink at bedtime will ease her throat. Ask your chemist for a soothing cough linctus that is suitable for children.

4 Make sure that your child's bedroom is not overheated because this will dry out the air. If the air becomes too dry, it will aggravate her cough.

5 Moisten the air in her bedroom at night by hanging a wet towel near to a radiator.

6 Don't allow anyone to smoke around your child.

Extra pillows *will prevent mucus dribbling down her throat at night.*

BRONCHIOLITIS

What is it?

Bronchiolitis is a common and usually mild viral illness that causes inflammation of the smallest airways in the lungs, called bronchioles. It occurs in epidemics during the winter. Those most commonly affected are babies under a year old. The risk of a child getting bronchiolitis increases if his parents are smokers or if he lives in overcrowded accommodation in which viral infections spread more easily.

Your baby may have a runny nose for a day or two, and then suddenly seem much worse, with a fever, dry rasping cough, and rapid or difficult breathing. Mild bronchiolitis usually improves within about a week.

What can I do?

1 Give your baby plenty of drinks to make sure that he is getting enough fluids.

2 No drug will alter the course of the illness, but liquid paracetamol will help bring down his temperature.

3 You may be able to loosen the thick mucus in his lungs by lying him face down across your lap and slapping him gently on the back.

4 Increase the humidity in your child's bedroom by hanging a wet towel near to a source of heat, such as the radiator. This will help to relieve your child's breathing.

What might the doctor do?

For a mild attack your doctor may prescribe a bronchodilator drug to make breathing easier.

In more severe cases your baby may be admitted to hospital where oxygen can be given and the baby can be fed through a tube inserted through the nose and into the stomach or, sometimes, intravenously. Most children are able to return home in 3–10 days, when they are able to feed normally.

The cough may persist for a few weeks longer. Though there are no lasting after-effects, for the next few years many children who have had bronchiolitis tend to suffer from wheezing whenever they have a cold.

SYMPTOMS

* ★ Runny nose
* ★ fever
* ★ dry, rasping cough
* ★ rapid or difficult breathing
* ★ wheezing
* ★ feeding difficulties.

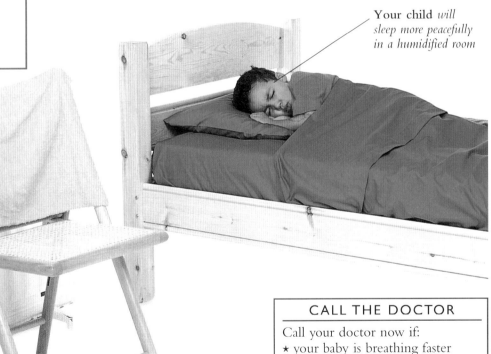

Your child *will sleep more peacefully in a humidified room*

Hang a wet towel *next to the radiator*

CALL THE DOCTOR

Call your doctor now if:
* ★ your baby is breathing faster than usual or his breathing is laboured or wheezy
* ★ your baby is having difficulty feeding
* ★ your baby looks bluish around the lips.

BRONCHITIS

What is it?

Bronchitis is an inflammation of the lining of the bronchi (the main air passages leading to the lungs). It usually follows a viral infection such as a cold, flu, or a sore throat because the infection has spread downwards, but it may also be caused by a bacterial infection.

Your child probably won't feel particularly ill, but he may have difficulty sleeping if his cough tends to be worse at night.

SYMPTOMS
★ Rattly cough
★ slight wheeziness
★ slight temperature
★ runny nose.

What can I do?

1 Help to relieve wheezy breathing and clear your child's lungs when he has a coughing fit. Support your child as he lean forwards and pat his back.

2 Take your child's temperature and, if it is raised, give him paracetamol elixir. Also give your child plenty to drink.

3 Put a pillow under the head of your baby's cot mattress, so that it is raised slightly. When your older child goes to bed, try to prop him up in bed with extra pillows (see page 216).

4 Until your child is feeling better, make sure that he is kept indoors in a warm, though not too hot or stuffy, room.

CALL THE DOCTOR
Call for emergency help immediately if your child shows any of the emergency signs on page 215. Consult your doctor as soon as possible if you think your child may have bronchitis, and call him again if he:
★ shows no sign of improvement after two days
★ coughs up greenish-yellow coloured phlegm.

What might the doctor do?

Your doctor might prescribe a cough suppressant to help your child sleep. If he thinks your child has a secondary infection, he might also prescribe an antibiotic to eliminate it.

ASTHMA

What is it?

Asthma is recurrent episodes of narrowing of the tiny airways leading to the lungs, which makes breathing, especially breathing out, difficult. It may be caused by an allergy, particularly if other people in your family have asthma, eczema, or hayfever. Mild asthma is common, and your child will probably grow out of it.

SYMPTOMS
★ Coughing, particularly at night or after exercise
★ slight wheeziness and breathlessness, especially during a cold
★ attacks of severe breathlessness, when breathing is shallow and difficult
★ feeling of suffocation during an asthma attack
★ pale, sweaty skin during an attack
★ bluish tinge round the lips during a severe attack.

What can I do?

1 Keep calm and reassure your child. If he has had previous attacks, give him whatever medicine the doctor has prescribed. If this has no effect, **call for emergency help.**

2 Sit your child on your lap and help him to lean slightly forwards – this makes it easier for him to breathe. Don't hold him tightly – let him settle into the most comfortable position.

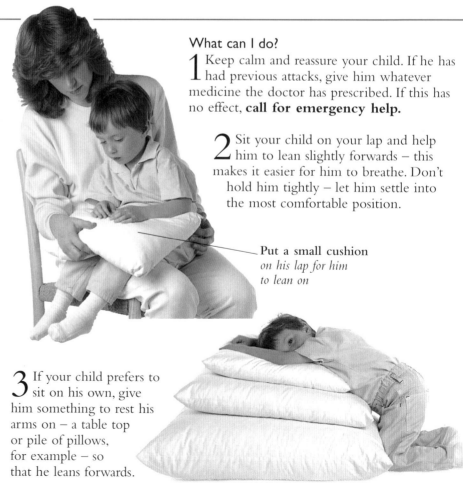

Put a small cushion *on his lap for him to lean on*

3 If your child prefers to sit on his own, give him something to rest his arms on – a table top or pile of pillows, for example – so that he leans forwards.

PNEUMONIA

What is it?
Pneumonia is an inflammation of the lungs, which causes breathing difficulty. Usually only a proportion of one lung is affected but in severe cases both lungs may be affected.

In young children pneumonia is nearly always due to the spread of an upper respiratory tract infection such as a cold or flu, and is usually caused by a virus, not bacteria.

Occasionally pneumonia is the result of a tiny amount of food being inhaled into the lungs and causing a small patch of inflammation and infection.

Pneumonia is most common in babies under a year. Although it is a serious disease, most babies who are otherwise healthy will usually recover completely in about a week, and it will not result in any long-term damage to the lung tissue.

SYMPTOMS
★ Deterioration in a sick child
★ raised temperature
★ dry cough
★ rapid breathing
★ difficult or noisy breathing.

CALL THE DOCTOR
Call for emergency help immediately if your child develops any of the emergency signs on page 215. Call your doctor now if you think your child has pneumonia.

What can I do?
1 Prop your child up with extra pillows in bed, so that he can breathe more easily. For a baby, put a pillow under the head of the mattress.

2 Take your child's temperature and, if it is raised, try to reduce it by giving him the recommended dose of paracetamol elixir or tepid sponging him (see page 194).

3 Make sure that your child has plenty to drink, especially if his temperature is high. Offer your baby cooled boiled water.

What might the doctor do?
The doctor will advise you how to nurse your child, and, if the infection is bacterial, he may prescribe an antibiotic. If your child is very ill, he might need to be treated in hospital.

PREVENTING ASTHMA ATTACKS
Try to find out what causes your child's asthma attacks by keeping a record of when they occur. Vigorous exercise and over-excitement can bring on an attack. Some other common triggers are shown here.

Feather-filled cushions or duvets
Change these for ones with a synthetic filling and air regularly.

Dust
Reduce house dust by vacuuming and damp sponging, rather than sweeping and dusting. Cover your child's mattress with a plastic sheet. Consider buying special bedding that reduces dust levels.

Animal fur
If you have a pet, let it stay somewhere else for a while, and note whether your child has fewer attacks.

Pollen, especially from grass and trees
Discourage your child from playing in long grass, and keep him inside when the pollen count is high.

Cigarette smoke
Don't let people smoke near your child.

EMERGENCY SIGNS
Call for emergency help immediately if your child:
★ has a bluish tinge on his tongue or round his lips
★ is severely breathless
★ does not start to breathe more easily ten minutes after taking his medicine
★ becomes unresponsive.

CALL THE DOCTOR
Call your doctor now if this is your child's first asthma attack. Consult your doctor as soon as possible if you think your child may have asthma.

What might the doctor do?
If your child's asthma is mild, the doctor may prescribe a bronchodilator drug that he can inhale during an attack. In severe cases, a drug to prevent attacks may be prescribed.

STOMACH PAIN

Stomach pain can be a symptom of many disorders, including gastro-enteritis and urinary tract infections. It may also be caused by vomiting, and can accompany illnesses such as tonsillitis and measles. Your child may complain of a tummy ache if he feels generally unwell, knows he is about to be sick, or if he has a pain elsewhere but can't quite describe its location.

DEALING WITH A TUMMY ACHE

What causes stomach pain?

Many children have recurrent bouts of stomach pain when something makes them feel anxious or insecure. Provided that your child's pain is not severe and lasts for only an hour or two, you needn't worry; try to find out what is bothering him, and reassure him.

However, if your child is in severe pain for a few hours, you should take it seriously. He might have appendicitis, though this is extremely rare in children under three. Typically, appendicitis pain is felt around the navel for a few hours, then moves to the lower right part of the abdomen.

Waves of severe stomach pain at intervals of about 15 to 20 minutes in a baby or toddler may mean that his bowel has become blocked.

What can I do?

1 Take your child's temperature. If it is slightly raised, he may have appendicitis, especially if the stomach pain is severe or seems to be located around his navel. Don't give him a painkiller to ease it, or anything to reduce his temperature.

2 If you think your child may have appendicitis, don't give him anything to eat or drink. Otherwise, give him some water if he is thirsty, but don't let him eat anything.

3 Comfort your child by giving him cuddles and extra attention.

4 If you don't suspect appendicitis, fill a hot water bottle with warm, not hot, water and wrap it in a towel. Let your child lie down with this held against his stomach.

Wrap the hot water bottle *securely in a towel*

EMERGENCY SIGNS

Call for emergency help immediately if your baby or child:
* screams with pain at intervals of about 15 to 20 minutes, and goes pale when he screams
* passes dark red stools that resemble redcurrant jelly
* has severe stomach pain for longer than three hours
* has severe stomach pain combined with a raised temperature.

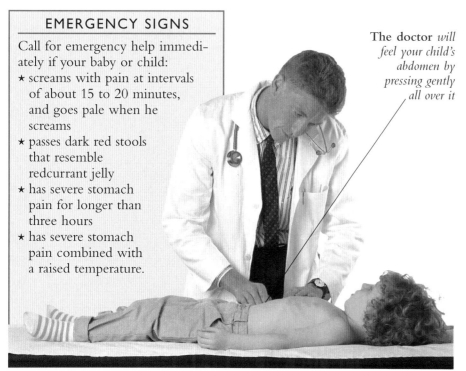

The doctor *will feel your child's abdomen by pressing gently all over it*

CALL THE DOCTOR

Call your doctor now if your child:
* develops any other symptoms
* has stomach pain for longer than three hours.

Consult your doctor if your child has frequent stomach pain.

What the doctor might do

The doctor will examine your child to try to find out the cause of his stomach pain. The treatment will depend on his diagnosis, but stomach pain often needs no treatment. If the doctor suspects appendicitis or a blocked bowel, he will arrange for your child to go to the hospital for an emergency operation.

CONSTIPATION, VOMITING, AND DIARRHOEA

A minor change in diet can cause temporary constipation or diarrhoea. Vomiting or diarrhoea may accompany almost any illness, and can also be caused by excitement or anxiety. Frequent vomiting or severe diarrhoea can quickly make a baby or young child dehydrated. This is a serious condition and must be treated promptly (see page 222).

CONSTIPATION

What is it?
If your child has constipation, she passes stools less frequently than usual, and they are harder than normal. Children's bowel habits vary greatly: some children have a bowel movement twice a day, others go only once every two or three days. Whatever your child's regular pattern, it is quite normal – don't tamper with it. Babies often become slightly constipated when they learn to sit up or crawl, and before they can walk.

CALL THE DOCTOR
Consult your doctor as soon as possible if your child:
★ cries or complains of pain when moving her bowels
★ has streaks of blood in her stools or on her nappy or pants
★ has constipation for more than three days.

What can I do?
1 Don't worry if your child is temporarily constipated, it won't do her any harm. Don't give her a laxative, since this will upset the normal action of her bowels, and don't add sugar to her bottle.

2 Give your child plenty of fluids to drink, especially if the weather is hot – this will help to soften her stools. Fruit juice will help to ease her constipation. Too much milk tends to make constipation worse. Don't let your child drink more than 500ml a day.

3 Don't hurry your child when she is sitting on the potty, but, on the other hand, don't let her remain there for too long.

4 Try to include more fibre in your child's diet (see below). This provides the bulk that helps the bowel to grip and move its contents along.

What the doctor might do
The doctor may prescribe a mild laxative and give you some advice on your child's diet. If your child has streaks of blood in her stool, she could have a small tear in the lining of her anus, so the doctor may lubricate the area very gently.

GOOD SOURCES OF FIBRE
Some examples of foods rich in fibre are shown here. Fresh foods are always best. Wash vegetables and fruit thoroughly, remove pips and strings, and peel for a child under one year. Purée the food for a baby under eight months (see pages 110–11).

Fresh fruit Offer your child a variety of fruit such as slices of peeled pear, peach, and banana.

Wholemeal bread **Wholemeal breakfast cereal**

Dried fruit Prunes and apricots are ideal for young children.

Fresh vegetables Mashed potato and lightly cooked broccoli are high in fibre. Celery and carrots can be served raw.

VOMITING

What is it?
When your child vomits, she will bring up most of the contents of her stomach. Most cases clear up within 24 hours but young children and babies can dehydrate rapidly so make sure your child drinks plenty of fluids.

Babies under about six months old often regurgitate a small amount of their feeds. This is known as "posseting" and is perfectly normal – your baby is not vomiting.

CALL THE DOCTOR

Call your doctor now if your child:
* vomits and seems abnormally drowsy
* throws up greenish-yellow vomit
* has vomited repeatedly for more than six hours
* shows any signs of dehydration.

What can I do?
1 Hold your child over a bowl and comfort her while she is vomiting (see page 199). Wipe her face afterwards and give her some sips of water.

2 Make sure that your child has plenty to drink – she needs 1 to 1½ litres (2–3 pints) a day. Make a glucose and salt drink (see Dehydration, below) and offer her a little every hour. If your baby won't take a bottle, try using a teaspoon or a medicine dropper (see page 195).

What might the doctor do?
The doctor will examine your child to find out what is making her vomit, and will then treat her according to the diagnosis.

If she shows signs of dehydration, the doctor may prescribe a powder to be added to her drinks. If she is very dehydrated, the doctor might arrange for her to be admitted to hospital, where she can be given liquid through a drip.

IDENTIFYING AND TREATING DEHYDRATION

Your child may be dehydrated if she shows one or more of the symptoms listed below:
* dry mouth and lips
* dark, concentrated urine
* no urine passed for six hours
* sunken eyes
* sunken fontanelle
* abnormal drowsiness or lethargy.

If your child is dehydrated, or is in danger of becoming so, buy a ready-mixed oral rehydration powder from your chemist. If you are breastfeeding, give the rehydration solution before the breast-feed. You can make up your own solution by adding 2 level teaspoons of sugar to 200 ml (7fl oz) of cooled boiled water.

GASTRO-ENTERITIS

What is it?
Gastro-enteritis is an infection in the stomach and intestines that can be caused by contaminated food. It is serious in babies, since it can dehydrate them very quickly, but it is rare in breast-fed babies. A mild attack in a child over two is not serious.

SYMPTOMS

* Vomiting and nausea
* diarrhoea
* stomach cramps
* loss of appetite
* raised temperature.

What can I do?
1 Make sure that your child drinks about 1 to 1 litres (2-3 pints) a day. A glucose drink, made as described above, is best.

2 Don't give your child anything to eat until he stops vomiting, then introduce bland foods. Give your baby diluted feeds (see page 185).

3 Take your child's temperature and, if it is raised, give him a dose of paracetamol elixir to reduce it.

4 Let your child wear a nappy again if he has just grown out of them.

5 Make sure that your child washes his hands after using his potty and before eating. Wash your own hands after changing his nappy and before preparing his food. Sterilize all his feeding equipment.

DIARRHOEA

What is it?
Episodes of diarrhoea are common in early childhood. If your child has diarrhoea, she will pass watery stools more frequently than normal. This may be the result of eating food that is too rich for her or that contains more fibre than she is used to. It is important to give your child plenty of fluids to prevent dehydration.

CALL THE DOCTOR
Call your doctor now if your child:
★ has had diarrhoea for more than 24 hours
★ has blood in her stools
★ shows any signs of dehydration (see page 222).

What can I do?
1 Make sure that your child has plenty to drink. A glucose drink made as described for vomiting (see Dehydration, page 222) is ideal for a child with diarrhoea.

2 Put your child in a nappy again if she has just grown out of them. This will prevent any unnecessary soiling.

3 Pay careful attention to hygiene: wash your hands after changing your baby's nappy and before preparing her food, and make sure that your child always washes her hands after using the potty and before eating.

What might the doctor do?
The doctor will examine your child to find out the cause of her diarrhoea, and will treat her according to the diagnosis. If your child has become dehydrated, the doctor may prescribe an oral rehydration powder to be added to her drinks. If she is very dehydrated, he might arrange for her to be admitted to hospital, where she can be given the extra liquid she needs through a drip.

ABNORMAL-LOOKING FAECES
Changes in the colour of your child's faeces are probably caused by a change in her diet, so check whether she has eaten anything unusual. Sometimes, though, an underlying illness accounts for the different appearance.
★ **Very pale, bulky faeces** that smell very offensive and float when you try to flush them away may mean that your child cannot properly digest gluten, a protein found in cereals (coeliac disease). Consult your doctor.
★ **Frothy, acid faeces** may indicate that your child can't digest milk properly (lactose intolerance). Consult your doctor.

CALL THE DOCTOR
Call your doctor now if your child:
★ is under two and may have gastro-enteritis
★ is over two and has had symptoms of gastro-enteritis for more than two days.

What might the doctor do?
The doctor will probably treat your child for dehydration and may advise you to give him only liquids for a few days. He may ask for a sample of your child's faeces.

Q&A "What steps can I take to prevent gastro-enteritis?"
Sterilize all your baby's feeding equipment for as long as he drinks milk from a bottle (see pages 100–1). Store made-up feeds in the main compartment of the fridge – never keep them warm in a vacuum flask, since bacteria thrive in warm conditions.

Be scrupulous about personal hygiene, and pay particular attention to hygiene when preparing food. If you store any cooked food, keep it in the fridge for no longer than two days, and make sure it is pipping hot when you reheat it, because heat kills the bacteria that could give your child gastro-enteritis.

Wash your child's feeding bowls and beakers in very hot water. Dry them on kitchen paper, not a teatowel.

If you are travelling abroad, ask your doctor or health visitor about any precautions you should take, particularly with regard to water, fruit, and salads. Always take an oral rehydration powder with you – this will help to prevent dehyradation.

BLADDER, KIDNEY, AND GENITAL PROBLEMS

Most urinary system infections are due to bacteria entering the urethra and spreading up into the bladder. They are quite common in young children, and are usually not serious. Some children are born with minor abnor- malities of the urinary system, which make them prone to such infections. Minor infec- tions of the genitals are also quite common, and in babies and young children they are often part of the symptoms of nappy rash (see page 182).

The urinary system
Your child has two kidneys that filter his blood. The clean blood returns to his bloodstream, while the waste product (the urine) drains into his bladder, where it collects until he is ready to urinate.

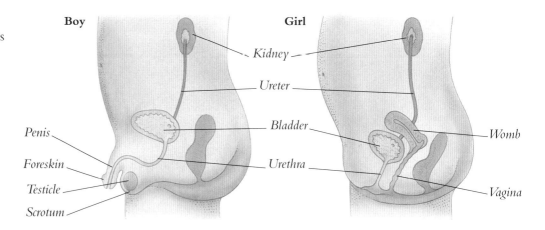

Boy

Penis

Foreskin

Testicle

Scrotum

Girl

Kidney

Ureter

Bladder

Urethra

Womb

Vagina

URINARY SYSTEM INFECTIONS

What are they?
Any part of the urinary system – the kidneys, the bladder, and the connecting tubes – can become infected with bacteria. Infections are more common in girls, because the tube from the bladder (the urethra) is shorter in a girl than in a boy, and its opening is nearer to the anus, so germs can spread to it more easily.

What can I do?
1 If your child seems unwell, check to see whether her urine looks pink or cloudy. Note whether she is urinating more frequently than usual and whether it seems to hurt her to pass urine. If your child is still in nappies, you probably won't be able to tell that urination is frequent or painful, but you will probably notice a change in odour.

2 Make sure that your child has plenty to drink, to keep her kidneys flushed out.

3 Take your child's temperature and, if it is raised, give her the recom- mended dose of paracetamol elixir to reduce it.

SYMPTOMS

★ Urinating more often than usual
★ pain when urinating
★ pink, red, or cloudy urine
★ change in odour of the urine
★ raised temperature
★ listlessness
★ loss of appetite
★ abdominal pain.

CALL THE DOCTOR

Consult your doctor as soon as possible if you think your child has a urinary system infection.

What might the doctor do?
The doctor will examine your child and may ask you to take a sample of her urine (ask your doctor how you should collect this). If your child has an infection the doctor may prescribe an antibiotic. He may also arrange for your child to have special tests or investigations to check her kidneys and urinary tract.

GENITAL PROBLEMS IN GIRLS

What can go wrong?
A little girl's vagina can become sore due to nappy rash (see page 182), an infection such as thrush (see page 213), or threadworms (see page 232).

If your daughter has a blood-stained or smelly discharge from her vagina, she may have pushed something into it. Newborn girls often produce a white or blood-stained discharge for a few days, and this is nothing to worry about. After this age until just before puberty, a discharge is abnormal and should be investigated by a doctor.

What can I do?
1 If your daughter's bottom is sore or red, don't use soap when you wash it as this may irritate it even more – just use water, and dry it thoroughly. Always wipe from the front to back, so that germs can't spread forwards from her anus.

2 Allow your child to go without a nappy for as long as possible each day, and don't put plastic pants over her nappies as they prevent air circulating to her bottom.

3 If your daughter has a discharge from her vagina, check whether she might have pushed something into it. If she has, **consult your doctor as soon as possible**.

What might the doctor do?
The doctor will examine your daughter and may take a sample of the discharge. If she has something lodged in her vagina, he will remove it gently. If she has an infection, he may prescribe antibiotics to be taken by mouth, or a cream to be applied to the affected area, depending on the cause of her symptoms.

SYMPTOMS

* ★ Soreness or itching in or around the vagina
* ★ redness around the vagina
* ★ discharge from the vagina.

CALL THE DOCTOR

Consult your doctor as soon as possible if your daughter:
* ★ has a discharge from her vagina
* ★ still has symptoms after two days of home treatment
* ★ has pushed something into her vagina.

GENITAL PROBLEMS IN BOYS

What can go wrong?
The foreskin, which covers the tip of the penis, can become inflamed or infected (balanitis), often as part of nappy rash (see page 182).

If a swelling develops in your son's groin or scrotum, he may have a hernia (a loop of the intestines bulging through a weak area in the wall of the abdomen).

What can I do?
Wash and dry his foreskin carefully at each nappy change, and let him go without a nappy for as long as possible each day. Use an enzyme free washing powder and rinse nappies and pants well.

How can I prevent inflammation?
Don't try to pull your son's foreskin back – it won't retract until he is at least four. If you try to force it, you may make his foreskin inflamed.

SYMPTOMS

Inflamed foreskin
* ★ Red, swollen foreskin
* ★ discharge of pus from the penis.

Hernia
* ★ Soft, painless bulge in the groin or scrotum, which may disappear when your child lies down and get bigger when he coughs, sneezes, or cries.

What might the doctor do?
If your son's foreskin is inflamed, the doctor may prescribe an antibiotic cream. If your son has a hernia, your doctor will recommend that he has an operation to repair it. If the hernia is painful or tender, the doctor may send him to hospital straight away for emergency surgery.

CALL THE DOCTOR

Consult your doctor as soon as possible if:
* ★ your son's foreskin looks red or swollen, or if there is any discharge
* ★ your son's hernia becomes painful, or changes in any other way.
Consult your doctor if you think your son may have a hernia.

CIRCUMCISION
This is an operation to remove the foreskin. If you are thinking of having your son circumcised, discuss it with your doctor. Like any operation, it carries a small risk, so it is usually done only for religious or medical reasons.

SKIN PROBLEMS

Minor skin problems are common in childhood. Most clear up quickly, but some are very contagious, and must be treated promptly.

If your child has a rash combined with other signs of illness, he may have an infectious illness (see pages 203–8). For other problems, see below.

QUICK DIAGNOSIS GUIDE
One or more red spots, or a rash, see Spots and boils, Hives, Heat rash (below and opposite), Insect stings (page 252) or, if dry and scaly, see Eczema (page 228).
Raw, cracked areas, usually on or around the lips, or on the cheeks and hands, see Chapped skin (page 229).
Small blisters or crusty patches on or around the mouth, see Cold sores and Impetigo (pages 230–31).
Hard lump of skin, usually on the hands or feet, see Warts and verrucas (page 230).
Itchy head, see Lice and nits (page 232).
Intense itching around the anus, see Threadworms (page 232).

DEALING WITH ITCHING
Many skin problems cause itching, and since scratching can make the skin infected, it is important to relieve your child's itchiness.
★ Dress him in cotton clothes, since cotton is less irritating to the skin than wool or other fabrics.
★ Gently dab the area with cotton wool soaked in calamine lotion, to soothe inflamed or irritated skin.
★ Dissolve a handful of bicarbonate of soda in your child's bath.
★ Buy cotton scratch mitts for him to wear in bed.

SPOTS AND BOILS

What are they?
A spot is a small red swelling, usually on the face. A boil is an infection in the skin that causes a large, painful lump, which then festers to produce a head of pus in the middle. Boils are most likely to occur on the face or on pressure points such as the buttocks, but they can appear anywhere on the body.

Don't worry if your child gets occasional spots, but recurrent boils may be a sign of illness.

SYMPTOMS

Spot
★ Small, red, painless lump.

Boil
★ Painful, red lump that gradually gets larger
★ white or yellow centre of pus appearing after a day or two.

CALL THE DOCTOR

Consult your doctor as soon as possible if:
★ your child has a spot that looks inflamed
★ your child has a boil in an awkward or painful place
★ the centre of pus does not appear three days after the boil first developed
★ red streaks spread out from the boil.
Consult your doctor if your child often gets boils.

What can I do?
1 If your child gets occasional spots, simply ignore them. They will clear up in a few days without treatment. If she tends to dribble, and the spots appear round her mouth, smear a barrier cream over the area.

2 If your child has a boil, or a spot that looks inflamed, gently clean it, and the skin around it, with cotton wool dipped in antiseptic.

3 Cover it with sticking plaster. If it is rubbed by clothing, or is in a painful place such as on the buttocks, pad it with plenty of cotton wool then put sticking plaster over it.

4 The boil will come to a head and burst of its own accord in a few days. Don't squeeze it – this may spread the infection. After it has burst, clean it gently with cotton wool dipped in antiseptic, and keep it covered with sticking plaster until it has healed.

What might the doctor do?
The doctor may lance the boil and drain away the pus, to reduce the pain and swelling, and might prescribe a cream. If your child has a lot of boils, or if they keep recurring, the doctor may prescribe a course of antibiotics.

HIVES

What is it?
Hives (also known as nettle rash or urticaria) is an intensely itchy rash of red patches. The patches usually fade after a few hours, but new ones may appear. A nettle sting is the most common cause, but it can be caused by strong sunshine or by an allergy to certain foods (for example, milk or a citrus fruit) or drugs (for instance, penicillin).

SYMPTOMS

* Itchy rash of raised red patches (weals), sometimes with a pale centre
* welts varying in length from 1mm to 1cm ($\frac{1}{16}$ to $\frac{1}{2}$ in)
* larger weals joining together.

What can I do?
1 Dab your child's rash with cotton wool dipped in calamine lotion.

2 If the rash is caused by an allergy, try to find out what your child is allergic to, so that you can help her avoid it in future. The rash usually develops a few hours after contact with an allergen, so try to remember whether, for example, she has recently eaten a new food.

CALL THE DOCTOR
Call your doctor now if your child's face, tongue, or throat is swollen. Consult your doctor as soon as possible if:
* the rash does not disappear within four hours
* your child has frequent attacks of hives.

What the doctor might do
The doctor may prescribe an antihistamine cream or medication. He might also carry out tests to discover the cause of your child's allergy. If your child's face, tongue, or throat is swollen, she might need an injection to reduce the swelling.

HEAT RASH

What is it?
Heat rash is a faint rash caused by overheating. It is more common in babies than in children, and usually appears on the face or in skin creases, where sweat can gather. It is not a serious disorder, and you can treat it yourself at home.

SYMPTOMS

* Pink rash on the face or in skin creases.

CALL THE DOCTOR
Consult your doctor as soon as possible if the rash has not faded 12 hours after your child cools down.

What can I do?
1 Take off any heavy bedding and remove a layer of your baby's clothing. Let him sleep dressed in just a vest and nappy.

2 Give him a bath in luke-warm water. Pat his skin dry gently, leaving it slightly damp so that he cools down as his skin dries. When he is dry, apply a little baby powder to absorb new sweat.

3 Take your baby's temperature and, if it is raised, give him the recommended dose of paracetamol elixir or tepid sponge him (see page 194).

How can I prevent heat rash?
Dress your baby in light clothes when the weather is hot, with cotton next to his skin, rather than wool or a man-made fibre. Keep him in the shade, or put a sun canopy over him.

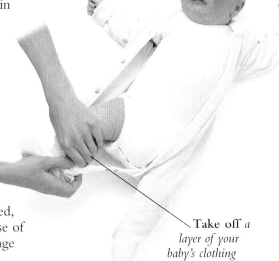

Take off *a layer of your baby's clothing*

What the doctor might do
The doctor will check that the rash is just a heat rash. If it is, your baby needs no medical treatment. If the rash has another cause, the doctor will treat that.

ECZEMA

What is it?
Eczema is an allergy causing areas of inflamed, itchy, red, scaly skin. It most commonly affects the face and skin creases such as the inside of the elbows and the back of the knees, although it can appear anywhere on the body.

It usually first appears between the ages of three months and two years, then improves as the child grows older. About half of all children with eczema grow out of it by the age of six, and nearly all of them grow out of it by puberty. Your child is more likely to develop eczema if other members of the family suffer from eczema or from an other allergic complaint such as asthma or hayfever.

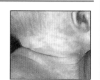

SYMPTOMS
★ Itchy, red, scaly, dry patches, usually on the face or in skin creases
★ clear fluid oozing from the affected areas.

What can I do?
1 When you give your child a bath, clean the affected areas by wiping them with baby oil, a glycerine and water cream, or emulsifying ointment, rather than washing with soap. Rinse well with water.

Use cotton wool *to apply the baby oil*

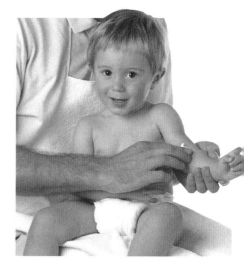

2 After a bath, apply an unscented moisturizing cream to your child's skin, since it may be very dry. Babies' brands are ideal.

3 Dress your child in cotton, rather than wool. In cold weather, put cotton clothing under warmer layers.

4 Try to stop your child scratching the affected areas – put scratch mitts on him at night if this seems to help, and keep his fingernails short.

5 Try to discover the cause of the allergy. Common allergens include foods (especially dairy produce and wheat), animal fur, woollen clothes, and washing powder. Anxiety can trigger eczema, so find out if anything is worrying your child.

6 When your child's eczema is bad, keep him away from anyone with chicken pox or a cold sore.

CALL THE DOCTOR
Consult your doctor as soon as possible if:
★ your child's eczema is very widespread or very itchy
★ fluid is weeping from the eczema.
Consult your doctor if you think your child has eczema.

What might the doctor do?
The doctor may prescribe a cream, and if the area is infected, an antibiotic. If your child is allergic to a particular food, your doctor or health visitor can advise you how to give him a balanced diet while avoiding that food.

SUNBURN

What is it?
Sunburn is sore or reddened skin caused by over-exposure to ultra-violet rays from the sun. The skin becomes hot and tender and may blister if badly burnt. Babies and young children, especially those with fair hair and blue eyes, are particularly vulnerable to it. Too much exposure to the sun increases the risk of skin cancer in later life.

SYMPTOMS

* ★ Red, sore areas of skin
* ★ blisters appearing on badly affected areas
* ★ flaking or peeling skin a day or two later.

What can I do?

1 Take your child inside or into the shade as soon as her skin begins to look red. Bear in mind that the worst symptoms of sunburn are likely to be delayed for a few hours.

2 Cool down any reddened area of skin with cold water, then apply a soothing after-sun lotion or dab on some calamine lotion.

PREVENTING SUNBURN
Never leave your baby to sleep in the sun, and try to minimize the amount of time an older child spends playing in the sun. Make sure that your child wears protective clothing at all times. An old T-shirt can be worn over a bathing suit while swimming. In particular, your child should always wear a hat. Apply Factor 15 sunscreen **before** your child goes outdoors in the sun, making sure that every part of the body is covered. Re-apply the sunscreen every hour, and always after she been has playing in the water.

CALL THE DOCTOR

Consult your doctor as soon as possible if:
* ★ your child has a fever and seems unwell
* ★ blisters appear over a large area.

What might the doctor do?
The doctor may prescribe a soothing and healing cream.

CHAPPED SKIN

What is it?
Chaps are small cracks in the skin that occur when the skin becomes dry after being exposed to cold or hot, dry air. Chapping is not serious, but it can be painful.

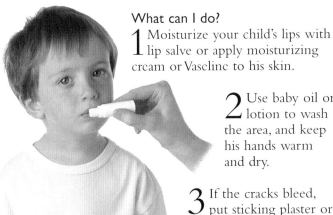

What can I do?
1 Moisturize your child's lips with lip salve or apply moisturizing cream or Vaseline to his skin.

2 Use baby oil or lotion to wash the area, and keep his hands warm and dry.

3 If the cracks bleed, put sticking plaster or surgical tape over them.

SYMPTOMS

* ★ Tiny cracks in the skin, usually on or around the lips or on the cheeks or hands
* ★ bleeding if the cracks are deep.

CALL THE DOCTOR

Consult your doctor as soon as possible if:
* ★ the cracks do not heal after three days
* ★ the cracks become red and sore, or pus-filled.

What might the doctor do?
The doctor might suggest a moisturizer or, if the area is infected, prescribe an antibiotic.

COLD SORES

What are they?

Cold sores are small blisters, usually on or around the lips, but they sometimes develop inside the mouth or elsewhere on the face.

They are caused by a strain of the herpes simplex virus that, once it has infected a child, lies dormant in the skin and tends to flare up occasionally. So, if your child has had a cold sore, he is liable to get others in the future. Strong sunlight or cold winds can trigger a recurrence, and so can a minor illness, such as a cold (which is why they are known as cold sores). Anxiety or emotional stress may also reactivate the virus.

<table>
<tr><td colspan="2">SYMPTOMS</td></tr>
<tr><td>
★ Raised, red area that tingles or itches, usually around the mouth
★ small, painful yellow blisters forming about a day later
★ blisters crusting over after a day or two
★ fever and general illness during the first attack.
</td><td></td></tr>
</table>

What can I do?

1 At the first sign of a cold sore, hold an ice cube against the affected area for 10 minutes. This may prevent the blister developing.

Wrap an ice cube *in a cloth and hold it against your child's lip*

2 If your child develops a blister, apply a soothing cream such as Vaseline.

3 Keep his hands clean, and stop him touching the sore, as he could spread the infection to his eyes.

4 Since cold sores are very contagious, don't let your child kiss other people and, if he tends to put toys into his mouth, don't let him share them with other children until the sore has gone.

5 If your child has ever had a cold sore, protect his lips from strong sunlight with a sunscreen, because sunlight can trigger a recurrence.

<table>
<tr><td>CALL THE DOCTOR</td></tr>
<tr><td>
Consult your doctor as soon as possible if:
★ your child has a cold sore for the first time
★ your child's cold sore starts to weep or spread
★ your child has a cold sore near his eyes.
</td></tr>
</table>

What might the doctor do?

The doctor might prescribe an anti-viral cream, which you can apply at the first sign of an attack, and make it less severe.

WARTS AND VERRUCAS

What are they?

A wart is a lump of hard, dry skin; a verruca is a wart on the sole of the foot. They are caused by a virus that invades the skin and are contagious. Almost all children get occasional warts or veruccas. Warts are not painful, and disappear spontaneously, usually after a few months, so treatment is not necessary. Veruccas tend to be painful because of the pressure put on them whenever the child walks or wears shoes, so they should be treated promptly.

<table>
<tr><td colspan="2">SYMPTOMS</td></tr>
<tr><td>
Wart
★ Hard lump of dry skin.
</td><td></td></tr>
<tr><td>
Verruca
★ Hard, painful area on the sole of the foot, perhaps with a tiny black centre.
</td><td>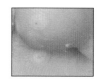</td></tr>
</table>

What can I do?

1 If your child has a wart, simply ignore it, unless it is on his genitals or by his anus. It will disappear on its own probably after a few months, although some last for a year or more.

IMPETIGO

What is it?

Impetigo is a bacterial skin infection that may develop when a rash such as eczema or a cold sore becomes infected, although healthy skin can sometimes become infected with impetigo. It most often affects young children, especially babies.

It usually affects the skin around the mouth and nose, and the nappy area in babies, but it can occur anywhere on the body. Impetigo isn't a serious disorder in children, but in a young baby it can spread over a large area and make him quite ill. It is highly contagious, so it is important to have it treated promptly.

What can I do?

1 Keep your child's face flannel and towel separate from those of the rest of the family, and wash them frequently, so the infection doesn't spread.

2 Try to keep your child from touching the affected area – don't let him suck his thumb or pick his nose, as this could spread the infection.

3 If your doctor has prescribed a cream, remove the crusts each day before applying it, by wiping them with damp cotton wool. Don't rub hard, but persevere until the crusts loosen.

Wipe the crusts gently
with cotton wool dipped in warm, soapy water

4 Pat the area dry with a tissue or paper towel and throw it away immediately, so that the infection can't spread.

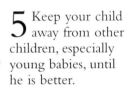

5 Keep your child away from other children, especially young babies, until he is better.

CALL THE DOCTOR

Call your doctor now if your baby is under three months old and suddenly develops widespread impetigo. Consult your doctor as soon as possible if you think your child has impetigo.

What might the doctor do?

The doctor may prescribe a cream and tell you to wipe away the crusts (see left) before applying it. If the infection is widespread, he may prescribe an antibiotic.

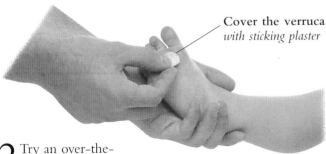

Cover the verruca
with sticking plaster

2 Try an over-the-counter remedy from your chemist. Remove dead skin from the surface of a verucca by rubbing with a pumice stone. Cover a verucca with sticking plaster if your child goes swimming.

CALL THE DOCTOR

Consult your doctor if:
★ your child's warts multiply
★ your child has a wart on his genitals or anus
★ your child has a verruca.

What might the doctor do?

If home treatment is not successful, your doctor may refer your child to the out-patients' department at hospital, where the wart can be burnt or frozen off under local anaesthetic. Warts sometimes recur even after they have been treated.

LICE AND NITS

What are they?
Lice are tiny insects that infest the hair, and make the child's head itchy. Their minute white eggs (nits) cling to their hair roots. Lice spread very easily from one head to another, so treat the whole family if your child picks up lice. Tell your friends to check their children's heads, and tell the staff at your child's toddler group or nursery toddler group, or nursery school. Keep him at home until he is free of nits.

Use *cotton wool to apply the lotion*

SYMPTOMS

* Itchy head
* tiny white grains firmly attached to the hairs near the roots
* red bite marks under the hair.

What can I do?
1 Wash the hair in the normal way. Put on plenty of conditioner. This makes the hair slippery and the lice easier to remove.

2 Comb the wet hair from the roots, using a special fine tooth nit comb. Wipe the comb with a tissue between each stroke to remove lice. Repeat this treatment every 3 or 4 days for two weeks to eradicate all the lice.

3 Seal your child's hats, brush, and comb in a plastic bag and leave for at least ten days – the nits will die.

4 As an alternative to wet-combing, ask your health visitor to suggest a lotion you can use that will kill the lice and nits. You can then comb them off. If you use this method it is important to follow the instructions carefully. You can also use the lotion to clean your child's brush and comb.

THREADWORMS

What are they?
Threadworms are tiny, white thread-like worms, about 1cm ($\frac{1}{2}$in) long. They can enter the body in contaminated food, and then live in the bowels, coming out at night to lay eggs around the anus, and causing intense itchiness. They are common in children, and are harmless, though the itching may be extremely uncomfortable. In little girls, the worms may crawl forwards to the vagina.

SYMPTOMS

* Intense itching around the anus, which is usually worse at night
* intense itching around the vagina
* tiny white worms in the faeces.

What can I do?
1 Try to prevent your child scratching, because she might inflame the skin around her anus or vagina.

2 Keep her fingernails short so that if she scratches, she doesn't pick up any eggs under her nails, which could reinfect her or other people.

3 Make sure that the whole family washes their hands thoroughly after going to the lavatory and before eating. Use a nail brush to clean the nails properly.

CALL THE DOCTOR

Consult your doctor as soon as possible if you think your child has threadworms.

4 If your child no longer wears nappies, make sure she wears pyjamas, or cotton pants under a nightgown. Change her pants and pyjama trousers every day and sterilize them in boiling water to kill any worms or eggs on them. Change her bed-linen every day and wash and rinse it thoroughly in very hot water.

5 When she feels itchy, lay her across her lap and look for tiny white worms near her anus. Remove any you see with damp cotton wool and flush them down the lavatory.

What might the doctor do?
The doctor will probably prescribe a medicine for the whole family, which will kill the worms. He may also prescribe a cream for your child to soothe any inflammation around the anus or vagina.

EPILEPSY

Epilepsy, which causes recurrent convulsions, affects about one in 200 people. A seizure is caused by excessive electrical discharges by brain cells. The most common cause of convulsion in children is a high fever (see page 194), but this is not normally a form of epilepsy. A single seizure does not mean your child has epilepsy.

EPILEPSY

What is it?
Epilepsy is a tendency to have seizures (also called fits or convulsions), which are bursts of abnormal electrical activity in the brain. With treatment, most children grow out of it by adolescence. There are several different types of epilepsy; two common forms in childhood are absence attacks and major seizures (see symptoms box).

What can I do?
1 Put your child on her side on the floor during a seizure. Stay with her to make sure she doesn't injure herself, but don't try to restrain her.

2 After a major seizure, put your child into the recovery position (see page 241). Don't wake her if she falls asleep, but make sure that she is breathing properly (see page 238).

3 Try to avoid letting your child get into situations that could be dangerous if she has a seizure – for example, put a guard at the top of the stairs, and don't leave her alone in the bath. But don't be over-protective – she shouldn't feel that her epilepsy makes her abnormal.

What might the doctor do?
The doctor may send your child to hospital for tests. He may also prescribe a drug to help control the seizures; if so, tell the doctor if your child's behaviour changes in any way, but don't stop giving her the drug.

The recovery position
If your child has a convulsion, place her in the recovery position and ensure that she is breathing properly. Leave her in this position until she regains consciousness. If she falls asleep, let her wake naturally.

SYMPTOMS

Absence attacks (petit mal convulsions)
* Sudden lack of movement
* dazed expression
* complete recovery in a few seconds.

Major seizures (grand mal convulsions)
* Sudden unconsciousness, so your child falls down
* stiff arms and legs
* twitching or jerky movements
* urination
* sleeping, or gradual return to consciousness, when the twitching movements stop.

CALL THE DOCTOR

Call your doctor now if your child has:
* a major seizure for the first time
* a major seizure lasting more than three minutes
* a series of seizures in rapid succession.
Consult your doctor if you think your child has absence attacks.

As you roll *the child over, keep her hand held against her cheek*

Bend the top *knee at a right angle*

YOUR CHILD'S SAFETY

About a quarter of all the accidents that happen in the home involve children under four, but there are a number of ways you can make your home safer. Best of all, keep your child under your own watchful eye. The chances of an accident happening are greatest when your child is tired, hungry, or unwell, or when you are busy or worried. The risks are also high when you are away from home. Make sure that the equipment you buy conforms to the safety rules established by the British Safety Institute, and use it only for the age of child it is designed for. Buy new if possible. Second-hand items may not comply with safety regulations or have been damaged or worn beyond safe limits, and instructions about their use may be missing.

SAFETY IN YOUR HOME

All children are accident prone, because their desire to explore and experiment far outstrips their common sense and forethought. Many accidents can easily be prevented, and it is your responsibility to make sure that your child can't injure himself. However, keeping him safe should not mean restricting his activities, but simply making sure that his world is safe for him to play in and explore.

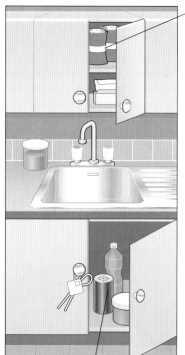

Store *polythene bags and plastic wrap out of your child's reach*

Buy *coiled flexes or make sure your flexes are short*

Push *hot drinks to the back of kitchen surfaces*

Keep sharp *utensils such as kitchen knives in a drawer with a child-resistant catch*

Fit a guard *round your hob and turn your saucepan handles away from the front. Use the back rings rather than the front ones*

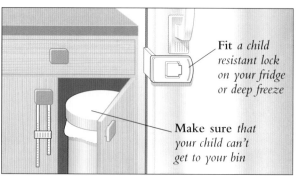

Fit *a child resistant lock on your fridge or deep freeze*

Make sure *that your child can't get to your bin*

Keep all *household cleaners and bleaches in a cupboard with a child-resistant catch*

Don't let *your child touch the oven door while it is hot*

KITCHEN

Your kitchen is full of potential hazards for a child and these dangers are increased if you are busy. Keep him away from the cooking area when you are cooking – a bouncing cradle or a playpen is ideal. Don't forget that cooker rings, kettles, and irons stay hot long after you have switched them off. At mealtimes, keep hot food near the centre of the table, so that your child can't grab them. Don't use a table cloth, since he could pull it and spill hot things over himself.

KEEPING YOUR BABY SAFE

With each new skill he develops, your baby will find ways of running into danger, so you must think ahead to avoid hazards. He will learn to roll over when he is very young, so if you need to lay him down for even a moment, put him on the floor. He will soon grab things so make sure that anything he can reach is safe to handle and too large to swallow or choke on. Don't eat, drink, carry anything hot, or smoke while you are holding your baby. Never leave him alone with a bottle – he could choke. Always use safety straps on his pram and high-chair. Don't put him in a bouncing cradle on a high surface – it could easily fall off. Don't leave a young child alone with your baby: he might pick him up and drop him, or give him dangerous objects to play with.

BEDROOM

Your child will spend a lot of time in his bedroom, so make sure it is safe. Don't put a pillow in his cot until he is at least two, and don't use loose plastic sheeting as a waterproof mattress cover. Never attach his toys to the cot with cords – they might wind round his neck. Keep large toys out of the cot – your child could use them as stepping stones to climb out – and don't string toys across the cot once he can stand. His toys should be non-toxic and non-flammable, and must have no sharp edges or pieces small enough to swallow.

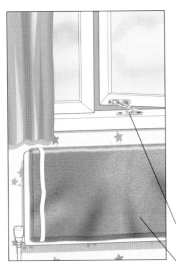

Fix *catches on the windows, so that they can be opened only a little way. Open sash windows from the top*

Cover *hot radiators with a towel*

Store *toys in a low cupboard or shelf, so your child can reach them without climbing*

Make *sure that your furniture is sturdy and has rounded edges. You can buy corner pieces to fix on to sharp edges*

Keep *nappy changing materials in a box with a lid*

Change *your baby's nappy on the floor*

Use flame-resistant *bedding and sleepwear*

Set *the cot mattress to its lowest position before your baby can pull himself to standing*

BATHROOM

Never leave a child under four alone in the bath, or in the bathroom if the bathtub is full, even for a few seconds. Use a non-slip bath mat. Set your water heater lower than 55°C (130°F), and run the cold water into your child's bath first. Test the temperature before putting your child in. Other accidents that may occur in the bathroom can easily be prevented:
★ Keep all medicines out of your child's reach in a cabinet with a lock or a child-resistant catch.
★ Put razors and cosmetics out of your child's reach.
★ Cover any heated towel rails with towels.

★ If you have an electric heater, it should be wall-mounted, and have a pull-string switch.
★ Keep cleaning fluids and the toilet brush in a cupboard with a child-resistant catch.
★ If you have a shower with a glass screen, replace the screen with a curtain or install safety glass.

Keep *all your pond covered with wire netting or surround it with a sturdy fence. Children can drown in a few centimetres of water*

The *sand in your child's sandpit should be too shallow for him to bury himself. Teach him not to throw sand. Cover the sandpit when not in use, as dogs and cats could foul the sand, which is a hygiene risk.*

GARDEN

Keep an eye on your child when he is playing in the garden, and if you leave your baby to sleep outside, put a net over the pram. Never let your child play in or near a paddling pool without supervision, and empty the pool after use. If you have a pond, cover or fence it securely. Make sure that the plants in your garden aren't poisonous. Teach your child not to eat any berries. Fix child-resistant locks on all gates Don't let your child play in an area where you have recently used pesticide, weed-killer, or fertilizer.

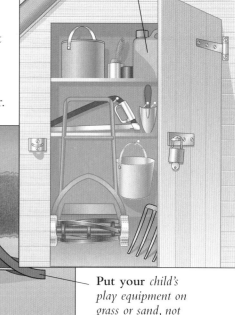

Lock away *all your gardening and DIY tools, and any weed-killer, fertilizer, and pesticide*

Put your *child's play equipment on grass or sand, not on a hard surface*

LIVING ROOM

When you buy upholstered furniture, make sure that it will not give off toxic fumes if you have a fire. Fix a guard round all fires. Keep the television out of your child's reach, so that he can't touch the back.

Don't leave cigarettes, matches, alcohol, sewing equipment, or coins lying around. Keep indoor plants out of his reach, as some are poisonous.

If you have low glass panels in doors or windows, use toughened, laminated, or wire-net glass or apply a transparent safety film, or put coloured stickers on them, so that your child can see where the glass is. Avoid glass-topped tables.

HALL AND STAIRS

Fix safety gates at the top and bottom of the stairs before your child can crawl or climb. Make sure that the hall, stairs, and landings are well lit, and that your banisters aren't so wide apart that your child could fall through. Make sure that the front door latch is out of his reach. Install a smoke detector. Repair

ELECTRICITY

Electric shocks from the mains can be very serious, so minimize the chance of your child receiving a shock:
★ Switch off electrical appliances when you are not using them.
★ Never leave a socket switched on with nothing plugged into it.
★ Cover unused sockets with dummy socket covers, or mask them with heavy insulating tape.
★ Check all flexes regularly, and renew those with bare wires.
★ Don't let your child play with toys powered from the mains until he is at least four.

loose tiles or tears in rugs. On polished wooden floors, don't let your child wear socks without shoes.

CARS

Your child should always travel in a car seat that is officially approved for his age and weight. Not all car seats fit all cars, so check your vehicle manufacturer's handbook to see if it will take a "Universal" child seat, which most seats are. Children should never travel in the front seat of a car with air bags. Use child-proof locks on the doors, and don't let your child lean out of the window or put his hand out while you are travelling.

Don't leave your child by himself in the car for more than a few moments, and when he is alone, make sure the handbrake is on, take the keys out of the ignition, and leave the car in gear.

Check where your child is before closing the door or reversing.

FIRST AID

If your child is injured, always treat the most serious injury first. If he is unconscious, check his breathing, and resuscitate if necessary before giving first aid for any other injury. If he is breathing, first treat anything that might prevent him breathing properly, then control any heavy bleeding. If your child is badly injured or in shock, he will need urgent medical treatment, but you should give first aid before calling for medical help. This chapter will help you to cope with various injuries and tell you when help is necessary. If you need to get your child to hospital quickly, it may be faster to take him there yourself, rather than to call for an ambulance, but see below for occasions when you must call an ambulance.

GETTING YOUR CHILD TO HOSPITAL
Call for an ambulance, or ask someone else to phone if:
★ you think your child might have a spinal injury
★ you think he needs special treatment while travelling
★ you have no suitable transport of your own.
If you take your child to hospital yourself, try to get someone else to drive while you sit in the back with your child and continue to give first aid.

If you need an ambulance and your child is unconscious, don't leave him alone for more than a minute or so and, if you can, keep him in sight while you call for help. If he is not breathing, resuscitate him before phoning for an ambulance. Don't stop until he is breathing again, but shout to other people between breaths if necessary.

WARNING
If there is a chance that your child has injured his neck or spine – for example, after a bad fall – don't move him unless it is absolutely essential. Leave him in whatever position you found him while you check whether he is breathing. If you need to perform artificial respiration, get someone to help you if possible. Turn your child on to his back very gently without twisting his spine, try to hold his head, shoulders, and hips, so that his body turns as a single unit.

FIRST AID KIT
Keep a supply of first aid equipment in a clean, dry container, and replace anything you use as soon as possible. Take some antiseptic wipes with you on outings, to clean cuts and grazes.

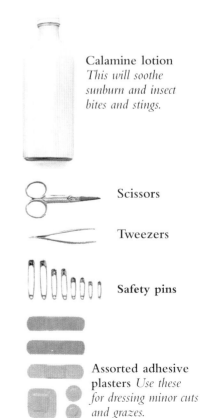

Surgical tape *This is useful for sticking on dressings, and drawing together the edges of large cuts.*

Calamine lotion *This will soothe sunburn and insect bites and stings.*

Non-adherent, absorbent, sterile wound dressings *These peel easily off a wound.*

One crepe bandage

Triangular bandage *This can be used to make a sling or secure a dressing.*

Scissors

Tweezers

Safety pins

Two gauze bandages

Prepared wound dressings *These consist of a pad attached to a bandage, and are easy to put on.*

Assorted adhesive plasters *Use these for dressing minor cuts and grazes.*

LIFE-SAVING TECHNIQUES

Familiarize yourself with these life-saving instructions so that you can act quickly in an emergency. Every second counts. If your child appears to be unconscious, follow these procedures before treating any injuries. If he has stopped breathing, it is vital to get air into his lungs quickly, so that he doesn't suffer brain damage. By breathing your own air into his lungs, you can prevent this. If his heart has stopped beating, you can pump it manually to keep his blood circulating round his body. Don't give up – children have revived after several hours of resuscitation.

EMERGENCY

+ Call for emergency help if your baby or child becomes unconscious, even if this is only for a few seconds.

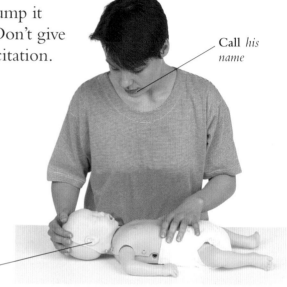

Call *his name*

Assess *your baby's condition*

CHECKING FOR UNCONSCIOUSNESS

Unconsciousness is a potentially life-threatening condition that requires immediate medical assistance. To assess whether your child is unconscious, tap or flick the soles of your baby's or child's feet, and call out his name loudly. If he does not move, or if his eyes remain closed, it is likely that he is unconscious.
Do not shake a baby, since this could worsen any injuries he may have.

+ If he doesn't respond, he is unconscious, so check immediately that he is breathing.

+ If he responds, check for injury and treat any he may have (see pages 242–53).

OPEN AIRWAY AND CHECK BREATHING

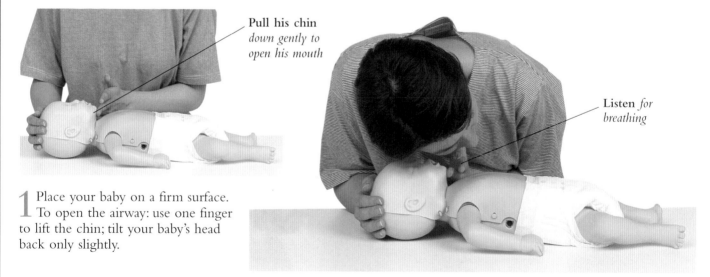

Pull his chin *down gently to open his mouth*

Listen *for breathing*

1 Place your baby on a firm surface. To open the airway: use one finger to lift the chin; tilt your baby's head back only slightly.

2 Look inside the mouth and then sweep one finger round inside his mouth to clear any obvious obstruction that might be blocking his breathing, but be very careful not to push anything down his throat. Check for any signs of breathing.

3 Place your ear close to his mouth and nose, looking towards his feet. To check for breathing: listen for any sounds of breathing; feel for breath on your cheek; look along the chest for movement; check for ten seconds before deciding breathing is absent.

+ If there are no signs of breathing, start artificial respiration straight away (see opposite).

+ If breathing, put your child on his side, or hold your baby, in the recovery position (see page 241) and call for emergency help immediately.

ARTIFICIAL RESPIRATION FOR A BABY

2 Seal your lips tightly around his mouth and nose. Breathe gently into the lungs until the chest rises.

3 Remove your lips and allow the baby's chest to fall back.

1 Place your baby on his back on a firm surface. Ensure that the airway is still open by keeping the chin lifted and the head tilted back.

✚ **If his chest doesn't rise,** he probably has something blocking his windpipe. Treat him for choking (see page 242), then continue with artificial respiration if necessary.

✚ **If his chest rises** remove your mouth from his face and let his chest fall. Give two quick, gentle breaths, then check for signs of circulation (see next page).

ARTIFICIAL RESPIRATION FOR A CHILD

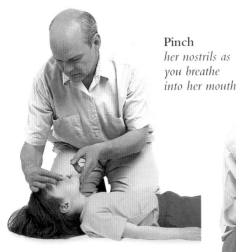

Pinch
her nostrils as you breathe into her mouth

2 Pinch her nostrils closed. Seal your lips round her open mouth. Breathe into the lungs until you see the chest rise. If your child is still very small, seal your mouth over her mouth and nose, as for a baby (see above).

3 Remove your mouth and let the chest fall. Keep the nostrils pinched.

1 Place your child on her back on a firm surface. Lift the point of her chin using two fingers and tilt her head back. Remove any obvious obstruction from her mouth.

✚ **If her chest doesn't rise,** she probably has something blocking her windpipe. Treat her for choking (see page 242), then continue with artificial respiration if necessary.

✚ **If her chest rises** remove your mouth from her face and let her chest fall. Give two quick, gentle breaths, then check for signs of circulation (see next page).

LIFE-SAVING TECHNIQUES *continued*

CHECKING FOR (SIGNS OF) CIRCULATION

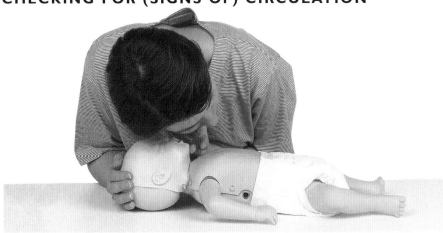

Look for signs of circulation in the baby or child, such as breathing (see page 238), any movement, a return of colour to the skin, swallowing or coughing. Carry out these checks for up to 10 seconds.

FOR A BABY OR A CHILD

✚ **If there are no signs of circulation,** his heart may have stopped. Start external chest compression immediately (see below).

✚ **If there are signs of circulation** (for example, the skin retains its normal colour), but the casualty is not breathing, continue breathing gently into his lungs at a rate of about one breath every three seconds, until he starts to breathe on his own, or until emergency help arrives. As soon as he starts to breathe again, turn him on his side in the recovery position (see opposite).

CARDIOPULMONARY RESUSCITATION (CPR)

FOR A BABY

1 Place your baby on a firm surface. With one hand on the baby's head, position the tips of two fingers on the lower breastbone just below the nipple line.

2 Press down sharply to no more than one third of the depth of the chest. Do this five times at a rate of 100 compressions per minute.

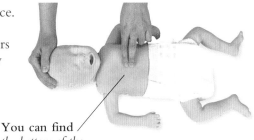

You can find *the bottom of the breastbone by feeling where the rib cage forms an inverted V-shape*

3 Give one full breath of artificial ventilation. Continue the cycle of five chest compressions to one breath of artificial ventilation for about a minute, checking for signs of circulation between each cycle.

4 Once the cycle has been continued for about a minute, call an ambulance, and continue giving CPR until help arrives.

FOR A CHILD OVER TWO

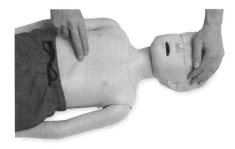

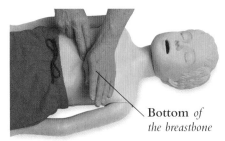

Bottom *of the breastbone*

1 Place your child on her back on a firm surface. Tilt the head back slightly. Find the point on the chest where the ribs meet to form an inverted V-shape. Put your middle finger on the bottom of the breastbone, and your index finger on the bone above.

2 Slide the heel of your other hand down the breastbone until it meets your two fingers. Using the heel of the top hand only, press down sharply at this point to no more than one third of the depth of the chest. Do this five times at a rate of 100 compressions a minute.

3 Give one full breath of artificial ventilation. Continue the cycles of five chest compressions to one breath for about a minute, checking for signs of circulation between each cycle. Then call an ambulance. Continue giving CPR until the child recovers or the ambulance arrives.

THE RECOVERY POSITION

Put your child into this position if he is unconscious, but breathing. This is the safest position because it prevents his tongue falling back into his throat and obstructing his airway, and avoids the risk of him choking if he vomits. For a baby, see right.

WARNING
Do not use the recovery position if there is a possibility that your child's neck or spine is damaged, for example, after a car accident.

RECOVERY POSITION FOR A BABY
A baby or child under the age of two should be cradled in your arms with his head tilted down to avoid obstruction of his airway.

FOR A CHILD OVER TWO

1 Kneel beside your child. Tilt her head back and lift her chin forwards. This keeps her air passages open while you put her in the recovery position.

Her head *must be tilted well back with the chin jutting forwards*

2 If necessary, straighten her legs. Bend the arm nearest to you so that it makes a right angle and lay it on the ground, with the palm of the hand upwards.

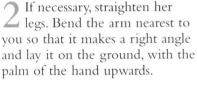

3 Bring her other arm across her chest. Hold the back of her hand against her opposite cheek.

Move *furthest arm across her chest and bend it*

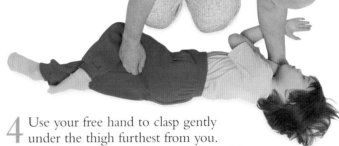

4 Use your free hand to clasp gently under the thigh furthest from you. Leaving the foot flat on the ground, carefully pull the knee up to bend the leg. Keeping your child's hand against her cheek to support her head, pull on the thigh of the bent leg to roll her towards you and onto her side.

Bend *top leg into a right angle to prevent her rolling forwards*

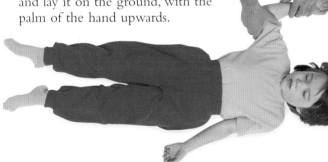

5 Adjust her arm and leg so she cannot fall forwards, and tilt her head. Call an ambulance.

CHOKING

This happens when a small object or piece of food gets lodged in the windpipe, causing a coughing fit. It is important to dislodge the object quickly, so that your child can breathe properly again. Choking is common in very young children, who tend to put everything they get hold of into their mouths.

HELPING A BABY

1 Hold your baby face down with his head low along your forearm. Support his head and shoulders on your hand. Give five sharp slaps to the upper part of his back.

Keep his *head low and give five sharp slaps on the back*

2 Turn him face up along your other arm. Look in his mouth and remove any obvious obstruction with one finger. **Do not** feel blindly down the baby's throat.

Turn him *on to his back along your other arm*

3 If back slaps fail, place two fingers on the lower half of his breastbone and give five sharp downwards thursts at a rate of one every three seconds. These act as artificial coughs. Check the mouth again.

4 If the blockage hasn't cleared, repeat steps 1–3 three times. Take your baby with you and call an ambulance.

HELPING A CHILD

1 Your child may be able to cough up the object on his own. Encourage him to do this, but do not waste time. If this fails, make him bend forwards. Give him five sharp slaps between the shoulder blades.

2 Check his mouth. Put your finger on the tongue for a clear view. Remove any object you can see.

3 If the back slaps fail, give chest thrusts. Make a fist and place it over the lower breastbone. Hold the fist with your other hand. Pull sharply inwards up to five time at a rate of one every three seconds. Check the mouth again.

Give *five sharp slaps on the back*

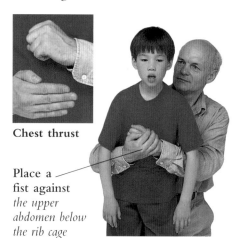

Chest thrust

Place a fist against *the upper abdomen below the rib cage*

4 If chest thrusts fail, give abdominal thrusts. Place a fist in the middle of the upper abdomen below the rib cage. Hold your other hand over it. Give five upward thrusts. Check the mouth.

5 If the abdominal thrusts fail, repeat steps 1–4 three times. If you are still unsuccessful, call an ambulance, but continue the above cycle.

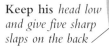

SUFFOCATION

Anything that is lying across your child's face may block his mouth and nose, and prevent him from breathing.

WHAT CAN I DO?

1 Remove whatever is covering your child's face.

2 Check to see if your child is conscious and breathing (see page 238).

EMERGENCY

✚ Call for emergency help immediately if your child:
★ becomes unconscious
★ stops breathing, even if only for a few seconds
★ shows any worrying symptoms.

✚ **If he is not breathing,** start artificial respiration immediately (see page 239) and ask someone to call for emergency help.

✚ **If he is breathing but unconscious,** place him in the recovery position (see page 241), then call for emergency help.

✚ **If he is conscious,** simply comfort and reassure him.

DROWNING

Babies and children can drown in very shallow water. When a young child's face is submerged, her automatic reaction is to take a deep breath to scream, rather than to lift her face up out of the water.

WHAT CAN I DO?

Make sure that your child is conscious and breathing (see page 238). If she is coughing, choking, or vomiting, she is still breathing. If there is any chance that she has injured her neck or back, lift her very gently and make sure that you don't twist her spine.

✚ **If she is not breathing,** clear any debris, such as seaweed, from her mouth and start artificial respiration (see page 239) right away – if possible while she is still being carried from the water and **call for emergency help.** Continue artificial respiration until help arrives or until she starts to breathe again. When she starts to breathe again, put her in the recovery position (see page 241).

Tilt her head *back and begin artificial respiration*

EMERGENCY

✚ Call for emergency help immediately if your child was rescued from drowning, even if she didn't become unconscious.

✚ **If she is conscious,** simply comfort and reassure her, and make sure she keeps warm.

✚ **If she is breathing but unconscious,** place your child in the recovery position (see page 241) so that water can drain from her mouth and lungs, and **call for emergency help immediately.** Cover her with a towel, coat, or blanket to keep her warm. Get her to a warm room as soon as you can, because she may have become dangerously chilled after even a short period of immersion in cold water.

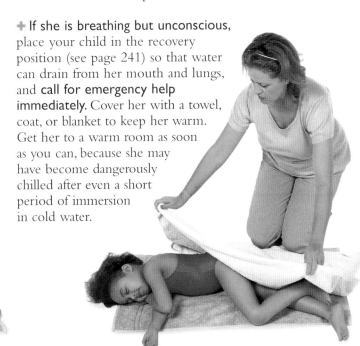

SHOCK

Shock is a condition in which blood pressure suddenly drops, depriving the body's vital organs of oxygen. It can occur as a reaction to any severe injury, especially heavy bleeding or severe burns.

SYMPTOMS

* ★ Pale, cold, sweaty skin
* ★ blue or greyish tinge inside the lips or under the fingernails
* ★ rapid and shallow breathing
* ★ restlessness
* ★ drowsiness or confusion
* ★ unconsciousness.

EMERGENCY

✚ Call for emergency help immediately if your child is in shock.

WHAT CAN I DO?

1 Lay your child down on his back. Turn his head to one side, then raise his feet about 20cm (8in) and rest them on something, such as a pile of clothes or a bag. **Do not** raise his legs if he has a broken leg or a poisonous bite on his leg.

2 Cover him with a blanket or coat, or cuddle him, to keep him warm. **Do not** try to warm him up with a hot water bottle or an electric blanket – this only draws blood away from the vital body organs to the skin.

3 If he complains of thirst, moisten his lips with a damp cloth. **Do not** give him anything to eat or drink unless he has been badly burned. In this case, give sips of water.

4 If he becomes unconscious, check his breathing (see page 238).

✚ **If the child is not breathing,** start artificial respiration immediately (see page 239).

✚ **If the child is breathing,** put him into the recovery position (see page 241).

POISONING

Children tend to be curious, so it is vital to keep poisonous substances out of reach. It is one of the most common emergencies in young children.

SYMPTOMS

Your child's symptoms will depend on the type of poison he has swallowed. You may notice any of these signs:
* ★ stomach pain
* ★ vomiting
* ★ symptoms of shock (see above)
* ★ convulsions
* ★ drowsiness
* ★ unconsciousness
* ★ burns or discoloration around the mouth if your child has swallowed a corrosive poison
* ★ poison or empty container nearby.

WHAT CAN I DO?

1 If your child is unconscious, check her breathing (see page 238).

✚ **If she is not breathing,** start artificial respiration immediately (see page 239), but wipe her face first (see above) or place a fine cloth over her mouth and breathe through that, to avoid getting any poison into your own mouth.

✚ **If she is breathing,** put her into the recovery position (see page 241).

EMERGENCY

✚ Call for emergency help immediately if you think your child has swallowed something poisonous.

2 If you see signs of burning around your child's mouth, or have any other reason to think she may have swallowed a chemical product, wash her skin and lips with water. If she is conscious, give her some milk or water to drink.

3 Try to find out what she has taken, how much of it, and how long ago. Inform the doctor or ambulance staff and, if possible, give them a sample of the poison or its container.

4 If your child vomits, keep a small sample of the vomit and give it to the doctor or ambulance staff. **Do not** try to induce your child to vomit.

BURNS AND SCALDS

A burn that causes reddening of the skin over an area of about 2–3cm (1in) is a minor burn, and can safely be treated at home. A burn that affects an area greater than this is a major burn, and is dangerous, since fluid is lost from the damaged area and infection can enter it.

EMERGENCY

✚ Get your child professional medical help as soon as you have given first aid if:
  ★ the burn covers an area of more than about 2–3cm (1in).
  ★ the burn was caused by an electric shock (see page 251).

MINOR BURNS
WHAT CAN I DO?

1 Cool the burn immediately, by holding it under cold, slowly running water until the pain decreases. This will help to prevent blisters from developing.

2 If a blister develops, put a pad of clean, non-fluffy material over it and hold it in place with sticking plaster or surgical tape.
Do not burst the blister – it protects the damaged area underneath while the new skin is growing.
Do not put any cream or lotion on the burn.

BURNING CLOTHES
WHAT CAN I DO?

1 Stop the child moving as movement will fan the flames. Drop him to the floor to stop burning his face and airway.

2 Wrap the child in a non-flammable coat or blanket to help smother the flames.

3 Roll the child on the ground. This will help to put out the fire.

4 If water is available, lay him down burning side uppermost, and dowse him with water or a non-flammable liquid. **Do not** let the child run about in panic; movement will fan the flames.

MAJOR BURNS
WHAT CAN I DO?

1 To stop the burning process and relieve pain, cool the burn with cold water for at least ten minutes before removing any clothing that may be sticking to the burned area.
Do not immerse young children in cold water as this can cause hypothermia.

2 Once cooled, remove clothing from the burned area and, if the pain persists, cool again. Cut around any material sticking to the skin. Remove restrictive clothing from the area of the burn before it begins to swell. **Do not** touch the burn or burst any blisters.

3 Cover the burn with clean, non-fluffy material (such as a pillow case) to protect it from infection. The dressing does not need to be secured. **Do not** apply lotions, fat, or ointment. Ensure that the child remains warm to prevent the onset of hypothermia. **Do not** give her anything to eat or drink and watch for signs of shock (see page 244).

HEAVY BLEEDING

If blood spurts from a wound or if bleeding continues for five minutes or more, try to stem the flow so that the blood has a chance to clot.

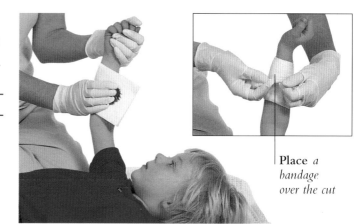

Place *a bandage over the cut*

EMERGENCY

✚ Get your child to hospital as soon as you have given first aid if he has been bleeding heavily.

WHAT CAN I DO?

1 Raise the injured part above the level of your child's heart, to reduce the amount of blood flowing through it. Check for embedded objects in the wound; if there are any, treat as below.

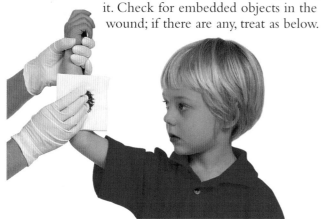

2 Lay your child down. Place a pad of clean, non-fluffy material over the wound – a clean tea towel is ideal – then press hard on it for about ten minutes. If there is no clean material available, press with your fingers, drawing the edges of the cut firmly together.

3 Leaving the original pad in place, bind a clean pad or dressing firmly over the wound so that the pressure is maintained. If this becomes soaked with blood, don't remove it, just bandage another pad over it, maintaining the pressure all the time.

4 Check for symptoms of shock (see page 244), and treat your child for this if necessary.

EMBEDDED OBJECTS

Small pieces of dirt in a cut will be washed out by bleeding. However, if your child has a foreign object embedded in a wound, do not attempt to remove it. Try to stop the bleeding, bandage, and take your child to hospital.

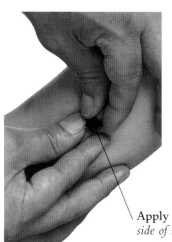

Apply *pressure either side of the wound*

EMERGENCY

✚ Take your child to hospital as soon as you have given first aid if he has something embedded in a wound.

WHAT CAN I DO?

1 Help your child to rest. Apply pressure on either side of the object and raise the injured part above the level of your child's heart. **Do not** try to remove any objects that are embedded in a wound as you may cause further damage and bleeding.

2 Place a piece of gauze over the wound and object to minimize the risk of infection.

3 Use spare bandage rolls to build up padding to the same height as the embedded object.

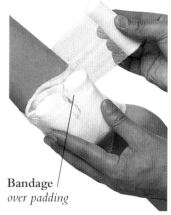

Bandage *over padding*

4 Secure the padding by bandaging over it, being careful not to press on the embedded object. Take your child to hospital.

CUTS AND SCRAPES

Cuts and scrapes are common throughout childhood, and you can treat most of them yourself. Make sure that you keep your child's tetanus injections up to date. Treat an animal bite as a cut, but if your child receives a poisonous bite or sting, see page 252.

EMERGENCY

✚ Take your child to hospital as soon as you have given first aid if:
   ★ the cut is large or deep
   ★ the cut is jagged or gapes open
   ★ your child has cut his face badly
   ★ the cut or scrape is very dirty
   ★ your child has a puncture wound (a deep cut with only a small opening in the skin) caused by something dirty such as a rusty nail or an animal's tooth.

CALL THE DOCTOR

☎ Consult your doctor as soon as possible if the area around the wound later becomes tender and red – it may be infected.

WHAT CAN I DO?

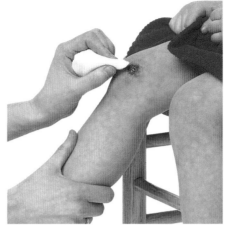

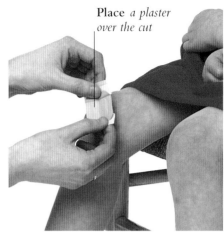

Place *a plaster over the cut*

1 Wash your hands first. Clean the cut by holding it under running water, or wiping gently around it with an antiseptic wipe or cotton wool soaked in warm water. Use a clean piece of cotton wool for each stroke. **Do not** remove anything that is embedded in the cut (see opposite).

✚ **If your child has been bitten by an animal,** wash the wound thoroughly with soap and water.

2 If the cut is still bleeding after five minutes, press a pad such as a clean handkerchief firmly on it for a few minutes.

3 Put a plaster or dressing over the cut, to help protect the wound and keep it clean. **Do not** put any antiseptic ointment on your child's cut.

4 Keep the cut covered with sticking plaster or a dressing until it has completely healed. This ensures that the area remains moist, and helps the cut heal more quickly. Change the plaster or dressing every day – soak sticking plaster in water to remove it easily.

NOSE BLEEDS

Nose bleeds can result from a bump on the nose, nose-picking, or excessive nose-blowing. A few children seem prone to nose bleeds, probably because they have fragile blood vessels in their noses.

CALL THE DOCTOR

☎ Call your doctor now if your child's nose is still bleeding just as badly after half an hour. Consult your doctor if your child has frequent, severe nose bleeds.

WHAT CAN I DO?

1 If you child experiences a nosebleed, you will need to apply direct pressure on the nose. To do this, help your child to lean forwards over a bowl or washbasin, and pinch her nostrils firmly together. Keep this pressure on for about ten minutes. Try to stop your child from sniffing or swallowing the blood – encourage her to spit it out instead.

Pinch *your child's nostrils firmly*

2 If her nose is still bleeding, hold a cloth wrung out in very cold water, or an ice pack wrapped in a cloth, over her nose for about two minutes, then pinch her nose again.

3 Don't have your child blow her nose for about four hours after the bleeding has stopped.

HEAD AND FACE INJURY

Bumps on the head are common in young children, but are seldom serious. A cut on the forehead or scalp, even a small one, is likely to bleed profusely. If your child has had a severe blow to her head, she may have concussion, which results when the brain is shaken within the skull, or from bleeding inside the skull – this may not be apparent for some hours.

WHAT CAN I DO?

1 If your child's head is bruised, hold a cloth wrung out in very cold water, or an ice pack wrapped in a damp cloth, over the bruise. This may stop it from swelling up. Check the skin underneath the pack every minute, and remove the pack if a red patch with a white waxy centre develops.

2 If your child's head is bleeding, place a clean cloth over the cut and press on the wound, just as you would for bleeding anywhere else on the body (see page 246).

EMERGENCY

✚ Call for emergency help immediately if your child has injured her head and shows any unusual behaviour or has any of these symptoms up to 24 hours later:
  ★ unconsciousness, however brief
  ★ vomiting
  ★ noisy breathing or snoring, if your child doesn't normally snore
  ★ difficulty in waking, or abnormal drowsiness
  ★ discharge of clear or blood-stained fluid from her nose or ear
  ★ unusual crying
  ★ severe headache
  ★ dislike of bright light.

3 Watch your child carefully for the next 24 hours, in case she develops any of the emergency signs listed above. If she bumped her head badly, wake her every three hours – **if she won't wake up, call for emergency help immediately.**

If a discharge of clear or blood-stained fluid trickles from your child's nose or ear, put her into the recovery position with a pad of clean material placed under her nose or ear. If she deteriorates or loses consciousness, assess her condition (see page 238). Be prepared to resuscitate (see page 239). If breathing, place her in the recovery position (see page 241). **Call an ambulance.**

BROKEN TEETH
If your child has broken a tooth, or one has become dislodged, cover the tooth or broken piece with milk, and take your child and her tooth to your dentist or to hospital immediately.

Put *your child in the recovery position*

BRUISES AND SWELLING

A bruise appears when a fall or blow causes bleeding into the tissues beneath the skin, which produces swelling and discoloration.

CRUSHED FINGERS AND TOES
If your child has crushed his fingers in a door or window, or dropped something heavy on his foot, hold the injured area under cold running water for a few minutes. If it is very swollen, or still painful after about half an hour, take your child to hospital.

WHAT CAN I DO?

1 Hold a pad wrung out in very cold water, or an ice pack wrapped in a damp cloth, over the bruise for about half an hour. This should help to reduce pain and swelling.

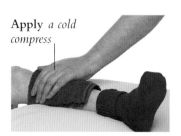

Apply *a cold compress*

2 If your child seems to be in great pain or if it hurts him to use a bruised limb, especially if the swelling is severe, check for any signs of a sprained joint or a broken bone (see opposite).

SPRAINED JOINTS

When a joint is sprained, the ligaments are damaged. This can cause symptoms very like those of a broken bone: if you are not sure which it is, treat it as a broken bone (see below).

WHAT CAN I DO?

1 Taking care not to pull or twist the injured joint, gently take off your child's shoe and sock, or any other items that might constrict swelling around the injury.

2 Support the injured joint in the most comfortable position for your child, then hold a cloth wrung out in ice-cold water, or an ice pack wrapped in a damp cloth, on the joint, to reduce swelling and pain.

3 Wrap a thick layer of cotton wool round the joint, then bandage it firmly, but not so tightly that the beds of her toenails (or fingernails if you have bandaged her wrist or elbow) turn white or pale blue.

SYMPTOMS

★ Pain in the injured area
★ swelling and, later, bruising
★ difficulty moving the joint.

FRACTURES AND DISLOCATED JOINTS

Broken bones are unusual in young children – their bones have not hardened, so they are flexible and tend to bend rather than break. Sometimes there may be a partial break, which mends easily. A joint is dislocated if one or more bones slip out of place.

SYMPTOMS

★ Severe pain in the injured area
★ swelling and, later, bruising
★ difficulty moving the injured part
★ misshapen appearance to the injured part – a limb may be bent in an odd way, or may look shorter than the uninjured limb.

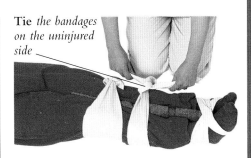

Tie *the bandages on the uninjured side*

For a broken leg or ankle, lay your child down and put padding round the injured area and between his knees and ankles. Bandage the injured leg to the uninjured one, securing it above and below the injury. Put some padding under the knots.

WHAT CAN I DO?

1 Gently take off your child's shoe and sock, or anything else that might constrict swelling around the injured area. Do not move him unless it is absolutely essential.

2 Support the injured part in the most comfortable position for your child. For a broken wrist, arm, or collar-bone, put padding round the injured area and, if your child will let you, gently fold his arm across his chest, then support it in an arm sling, fastening the bandage with a reef knot tied just below the shoulder.

Arm sling   **Elevation sling**

Don't try to force his arm into this position. If there is bleeding or swelling that needs to be reduced, the arm should be raised in an elevation sling. The fingertips are brought up to the level of the opposite shoulder, the sling is wrapped around the arm, passed from the elbow across the back, and then tied at the shoulder.

3 Check for symptoms of shock and treat him for this if necessary (see page 244). If you think he has a broken leg, don't raise his legs.

FOREIGN BODY IN THE EYE

Eyelashes or particles of dust can easily get into the eye. If your child's eye seems irritated but you can't see anything in it, she may have an eye infection (see page 209).

(see page 209)

SYMPTOMS

* Pain in the eye
* red, watering eye
* your child may rub her eye.

CHEMICALS IN THE EYE

If your child has splashed any chemicals or corrosive fluids in her eyes, wash her eyes out immediately under cold running water, keeping her eyelids apart with your fingers. If only one eye is affected, tilt her head so that the injured eye is lower, and the chemical cannot wash over into the uninjured one. Then cover the eye with a pad and take your child to a hospital. If possible, take the chemical bottle with you.

WHAT CAN I DO?

1 Wait a few minutes to see if the natural watering of the eye washes the foreign body away. Try to stop your child from rubbing her eye.

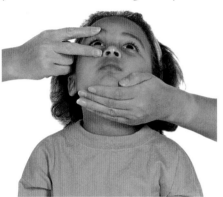

2 Sit your child down, facing the light. Separate the eyelids. Ask her to look right, left, up, and down. Make sure that you examine all of the eye.

3 If you can see the foreign body, wash it out using a jug of clean water. Aim for the inner corner so that water will wash over the eye. Or, use a damp swab or hankerchief to lift it off.

4 If an object is under the eyelid, you can ask an older child to clear it by lifting the upper eyelid over the lower. You will need to do this for a younger child; wrap her in a towel first to stop her grabbing your arms. If the eye is still red or sore once the object has been removed, take her to hospital.

A FOREIGN BODY THAT CANNOT BE REMOVED

Cover the eye with a sterile dressing. Reassure the child and take her to the hospital.

FOREIGN BODY IN THE EAR

Insects may crawl into your child's ear, and children may push small objects into their ears. Don't let your child play with beads or similar small objects until he is old enough to understand that they should not be put into his ears.

SYMPTOMS

* Tickling in the ear
* partial deafness
* your child may rub or tug at his ear.

WHAT CAN I DO?

1 If your child has an insect in her ear, she may be very alarmed. Sit her down and support her head with the affected ear uppermost. Gently flood the ear with tepid water so that the insect floats out. If you can't remove the insect, take your child to hospital.

2 Children often push things into their ears. A hard object may become stuck. This may result in pain and temporary deafness; it may damage the ear drum. Do not attempt to remove the object, even if you can see it. Reassure your child and ask her what she put into her ear. Take your child to hospital.

Tip the container *very gently, so just a few drops go into her ear.*

FOREIGN BODY IN THE NOSE

Children sometimes stuff small pieces of food or other objects such as beads or marbles up their noses.

SYMPTOMS

★ Smelly, blood-stained discharge from the nose.

WHAT CAN I DO?
If your child can blow his nose, help him to blow it, one nostril at a time. If this does not dislodge the object, don't try to remove it yourself – take your child to hospital straight away.

ELECTRIC SHOCK

A mild electrical shock gives only a brief pins and needles sensation. A severe one can knock your child down, render her unconscious and stop both breathing and heartbeat. Electric current can also burn.

EMERGENCY

✚ Get your child to the hospital as soon as you have given first aid if:
★ she was unconscious, even if only for a few seconds
★ she has any electrical burns.

WHAT CAN I DO?
1 Switch off the current, at the mains if possible.

✚ **If you can't do this,** stand on an insulating material – such as a rubber mat or a pile of dry newspaper. Separate your child from the electrical source by pushing the cable or your child away, using some dry, non-conducting object such as a wooden chair or broom handle.

✚ **If nothing is available,** drag your child away, insulating your hand as much as you can by wrapping it in a dry cloth or newspaper. Grasp your child's clothes, and avoid touching her skin.

ELECTRICAL BURNS

Electricity can burn where the current enters the body and where it leaves, so your child may have burns where she touched the electrical source and anywhere that was in contact with the ground. Although these burns may look small, they are often very deep.

2 Check to see if your child is conscious (see page 238).

✚ **If she is unconscious,** check her breathing: start artificial respiration immediately if necessary (see page 239). If she is breathing, put her in the recovery position (see page 241).

✚ **If she is conscious,** comfort and reassure her. Look for symptoms of shock (see page 244).

3 Examine her for any burns: check areas that were in contact with the electrical source or the ground (burns will look red or scorched, and may swell up). If you find any, treat them as major burns (see page 245).

Move *the cable rather than your child's arm*

251

MINOR BITES AND STINGS

While they may be painful and uncomfortable, most bites and stings from plants, insects, and jellyfish are not usually life-threatening for your child. However, a few people develop a serious allergic reaction to stings, and therefore need urgent medical treatment.

EMERGENCY

✚ Get your child to a hospital emergency room as soon as you have given first aid if he:
★ has difficulty breathing
★ develops a widespread rash with weals
★ feels dizzy or faints
★ develops symptoms of shock (see page 244)
★ has a sting inside his mouth.

SYMPTOMS

★ Sharp pain
★ redness
★ slight swelling
★ itching.

WHAT CAN I DO?

1 If your child has been stung by a bee, check whether the sting has been left in the skin. Scrape it off with a knife or fingernail, or pull it out with tweezers, taking care not to squeeze the tiny sac of poison.

2 Hold a cloth wrung out in ice-cold water over the sting.

3 Soothe the area around the sting, which will quickly become red, swollen, and itchy, by dabbing it gently with cotton wool dipped in calamine lotion or surgical spirit, or by applying a little antihistamine ointment around the sting.

✚ If your child has been stung in his mouth, give him a cold drink or, if your child is over two, let him suck an ice cube. This will help to reduce any swelling.

SNAKE AND SPIDER BITES, SCORPION STINGS

Bites from snakes and poisonous spiders, and scorpion stings are always serious for young children. Snake bites carry a risk of tetanus, but your child can be vaccinated against this. The only poisonous snake in Britain is the adder.

SYMPTOMS

Your child's symptoms will depend on what has bitten or stung him; some symptoms may not appear for a few hours:
★ severe pain
★ one or two puncture marks
★ swelling
★ nausea or vomiting
★ difficulty breathing
★ shock (see page 244)
★ convulsions
★ drowsiness
★ unconsciousness.

Reassure *the child and keep her still*

EMERGENCY

✚ Get your child to a hospital as soon as you have given first aid if she has been bitten by a snake or spider, or stung by a scorpion.

WHAT CAN I DO?

1 Calm your child, and help her to sit down. Keep the bitten or stung part still, and position it below the level of her heart.

2 Wash thoroughly around the area, but do not suck out any poison.

3 Carefully place a clean, sterile dressing over the affected area.

4 Place a conforming bandage around the affected limb.

5 Immobilize the limb with padding. If the hand or foot feels numb or cold, loosen the bandages.

6 Reassure her. Keep her still to stop the venom spreading through her body.

SEVERE JELLYFISH STINGS

In Europe, the only jellyfish that gives a severe sting is the Portuguese Man-of-War. It is found throughout Europe, and looks like a pale blue translucent sac floating in the water. A child stung by one will need medical attention.

EMERGENCY

✚ Get your child to hospital as soon as you have given first aid if she has a severe jellyfish sting.

WHAT CAN I DO?

1 Pour some vinegar over the affected area.

2 Dust a dry powder, such as talcum powder, over the skin around the injury.

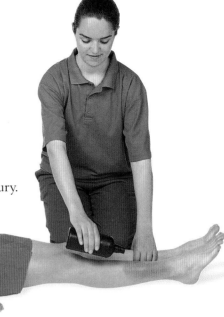

SYMPTOMS

★ Burning pain
★ redness
★ shortness of breath
★ fainting.

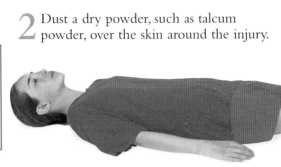

THORNS AND SPLINTERS

Thorns or tiny splinters will often become embedded in a child's hands or feet. Splinters in the fingers tips will hurt more than those on the feet.

CALL THE DOCTOR

☎ Consult your doctor as soon as possible if:
★ the area around a splinter becomes red, swollen, or tender up to 48 hours later
★ you cannot remove a large or painful splinter
★ your child has a splinter of glass or metal.

WHAT CAN I DO?

1 If the end of the splinter is sticking out, sterilize a pair of tweezers in a flame, then pull the splinter straight out gently. Wash the area thoroughly with soap and water.

2 If there is no loose end, but you can see the splinter clearly, it is probably lying just below the surface of the skin. Sterilize a needle in a flame and let it cool. Then, starting where the splinter entered, gently tear the skin a little way along the line of the splinter. Carefully lift up the end of the splinter with the needle point and pull it out with tweezers, then wash the area thoroughly with soap and water.

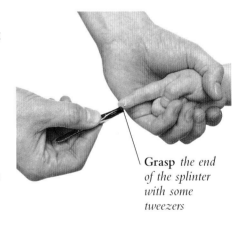

Grasp *the end of the splinter with some tweezers*

3 If a small thorn or splinter has gone straight down into the skin, and is not painful, it is best to leave it alone. It will probably work its own way out.

BLISTERS

Blisters form when burns, scalds, or friction damage the skin. The fluid-filled blister protects the new skin forming underneath.

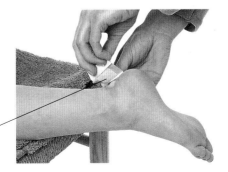

Cover the blister *with a sticking plaster to prevent your child's shoe from rubbing it*

WHAT CAN I DO?

1 Don't burst or prick the blister or try to remove the top layer of skin. This will leave the raw skin open to infection. Dress your child in clothes that will not rub against it.

2 If the blister bursts, cover with a plaster with a large enough pad to cover the whole blister.

GROWTH CHARTS: GIRLS

The charts below show average growth in children (the solid line), and the range of normal measurements. You can check your baby's progress by weighing and measuring her regularly and marking in her own growth curves on the charts. The shape of her curve should match closely the shape of the "average" curve: this shows a healthy rate of growth.

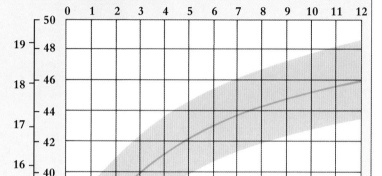

GIRL BABY'S HEAD CIRCUMFERENCE

HEAD CIRCUMFERENCE
Your health visitor or doctor will pass a tape measure round the largest part of your baby's head, just above her eyebrows and ears (see page 81). During the first year of life, head circumference is an easier yardstick of healthy growth to measure than length.

ROUGH GUIDE TO CLOTHES SIZES

Size		Weight
0–3 months,	60cm	up to 4.5kg (10lbs)
3–6 months	70cm	up to 6.5kg (14½lbs)
6–12 months	80cm	up to 8.5kg (19lbs)
12–18 months	85–90cm	
18–24 months	90–100cm	

/ average

▨ range of measurements likely in a normal child; 94% of girls fall within this area

GIRL CHILDS HEIGHT

YOUR CHILD'S HEIGHT
About every six months measure your child against the same patch of wall. She should stand close to it, without shoes and with feet together. Use a ruler at right angles to the wall to mark her height, then measure the distance from mark to floor. Don't worry if your child has periods of slow growth interspersed with spurts; but if two consecutive measurements seem very low, consult your doctor.

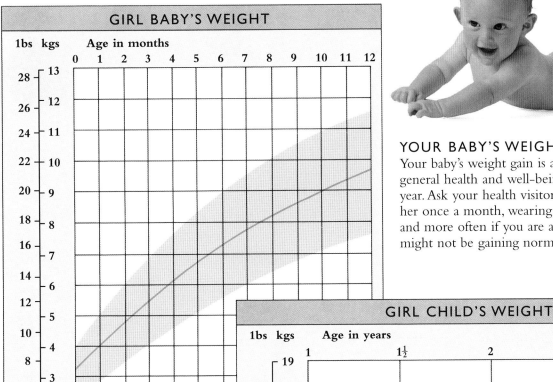

GIRL BABY'S WEIGHT

1bs kgs — Age in months

YOUR BABY'S WEIGHT

Your baby's weight gain is a vital indicator of her general health and well-being throughout the first year. Ask your health visitor or doctor to weigh her once a month, wearing just a clean nappy, and more often if you are at all worried that she might not be gaining normally.

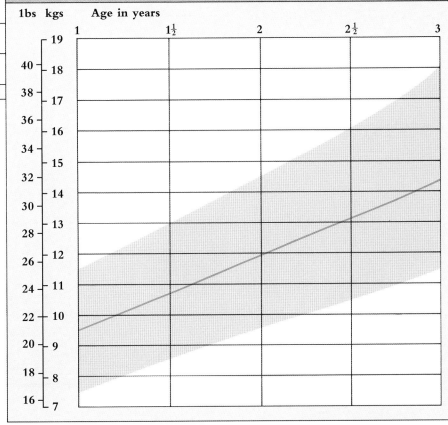

GIRL CHILD'S WEIGHT

1bs kgs — Age in years

YOUR CHILD'S WEIGHT

After her first birthday, weigh your child in a clean nappy or naked about every six months. She won't put weight on steadily, but the periods of slow and rapid growth should balance out. She shouldn't lose weight: even if she is very fat, she only needs to mark time until her height catches up. Ask your doctor's advice if her weight drops, or if two consecutive measurements are less than you would expect.

GROWTH CHARTS: BOYS

The charts below show average growth in children (the solid line), and the range of normal measurements. You can check your baby's progress by weighing and measuring him regularly and marking in his own growth curves on the charts. The shape of his curve should match closely the shape of the "average" curve: this shows a healthy rate of growth.

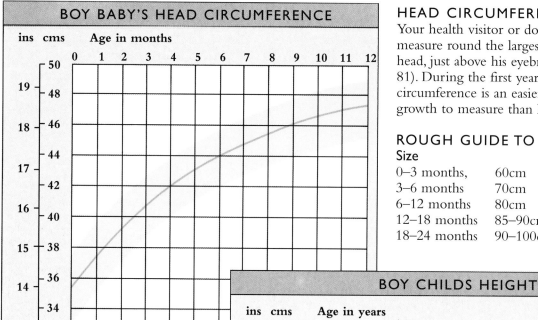

BOY BABY'S HEAD CIRCUMFERENCE

ins cms — Age in months

HEAD CIRCUMFERENCE

Your health visitor or doctor will pass a tape measure round the largest part of your baby's head, just above his eyebrows and ears (see page 81). During the first year of life, head circumference is an easier yardstick of healthy growth to measure than length.

ROUGH GUIDE TO CLOTHES SIZES

Size		Weight
0–3 months,	60cm	up to 4.5kg (10lbs)
3–6 months	70cm	up to 6.5kg (14½ lbs)
6–12 months	80cm	up to 8.5kg (19lbs)
12–18 months	85–90cm	
18–24 months	90–100cm	

—— average

range of measurements likely in a normal child; 94% of boys fall within this area

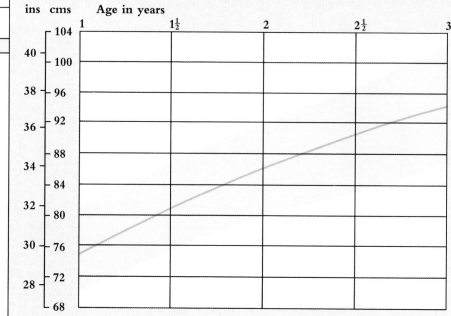

BOY CHILDS HEIGHT

ins cms — Age in years

YOUR CHILD'S HEIGHT

About every six months measure your child against the same patch of wall. He should stand close to it, without shoes and with feet together. Use a ruler at right angles to the wall to mark his height, then measure the distance from mark to floor. Don't worry if your child has periods of slow growth interspersed with spurts; but if two consecutive measurements seem very low, consult your doctor.

BOY BABY'S WEIGHT

1bs	kgs	Age in months

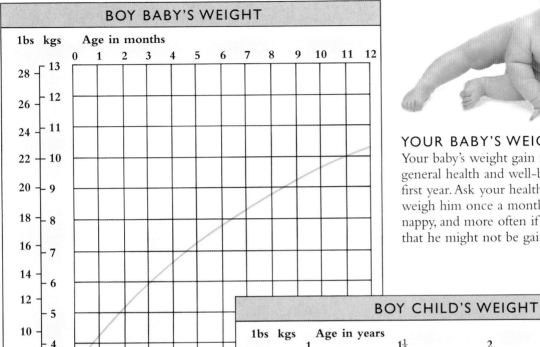

YOUR BABY'S WEIGHT

Your baby's weight gain is a vital indicator of his general health and well-being throughout the first year. Ask your health visitor or doctor to weigh him once a month, wearing just a clean nappy, and more often if you are at all worried that he might not be gaining normally.

BOY CHILD'S WEIGHT

1bs	kgs	Age in years

YOUR CHILD'S WEIGHT

After his first birthday, weigh your child in a clean nappy or naked about every six months. He won't put weight on steadily, but the periods of slow and rapid growth should balance out. He shouldn't lose weight: even if he is very fat, he only needs to mark time until his height catches up. Ask your doctor's advice if his weight drops, or if two consecutive measurements are less than you would expect.

USEFUL ADDRESSES

ANTENATAL SUPPORT

AIMS (Association for Improvements in the Maternity Services)
Tel: 020 8723 4356
Web: www.aims.org.uk

APEC (Action on Pre-eclampsia)
84–88 Pinner Road
Harrow
Middx
HA1 4HZ
Tel: 020 8863 3271

ARC (Antenatal Results and Choices)
73–75 Charlotte Street
London
W1T 4PN
Tel: 020 7631 0285

The Independent Midwives Association
1 The Great Quarry
Guildford
Surrey
GU1 3XN
Web: www.independentmidwives.org.uk

POSTNATAL SUPPORT

Association of Breastfeeding Mothers
PO Box 207
Bridgwater
TA6 7YT
Tel: 020 7813 1481
Web: http://home/clara.net/abm/

Association for Postnatal Illness
25 Jerdan Place
Fulham
London
SW6 1BE
Tel: 020 7386 0868

Caesarian Support
Yvonne Williams
55 Cooli Drive
Douglas
Isle of Man
Tel: 01624 661269 (after 6pm)

Family Planning Association
2–12 Pentonville Road
London
N1 9FP
Tel: 020 7837 5432
Web: www.fpa.org.uk

Health Visitors Association
40 Bermondsey Street
London
SE1 3UD
Tel: 020 7939 7000
Web: www.msfcphva.org

MAMA (Meet-a-Mum Association)
Waterside Centre
26 Avenue Road
South Norwood
London
SE25 4DX
Tel: 020 8771 5995 (office)
Helpline: 020 8768 0123
Web: www.MAMA.org.uk
For isolated or depressed mothers

National Childbirth Trust
Alexandra House
Oldham Terrace
Acton
London
W3 6NH
Tel: 0870 444 8707
Web:www.nct:online.org

VBAC (Vaginal Birth After Caesarian)
Linda Howes
8 Wren Way
Farnborough
Hants
Tel: 01252 543250

PARENTS' GROUPS

BLISS (Baby Life Support Systems)
2nd Floor
Camelford House
89 Albert Embankment
London
SE1 7TP
Tel: 020 7820 9471
Web: www.bliss.org.uk

CRY-SIS Support Group
BM Cry-Sis
London
WC1N 3XX
Tel: 020 7404 5011
Advice on babies who cry excessively

Foundation for the Study of Infant Death
Artillery House
11–19 Artillery Row
London
SW1P 1RT
General enquiries: 020 7222 8001
Helpline: 020 7233 2090
Web: www.sids.org.uk/fsid/

Gingerbread
7 Sovereign Court
Sovereign Close
London
E1W 3HW
Tel: 020 7488 9300
Web: www.gingerbread.org.uk
For one-parent families

La Leche League
Tel: 0207 242 1278
Web: www.laleche.org.uk

The Miscarriage Association
c/o Clayton Hospital
Northgate
Wakefield
West Yorkshire
WF1 3JS
Tel: 01924 298834
Web: www.miscarriageassociation.org.uk
For advice, information, and support

Multiple Births Foundation
Level 4
Hammersmith House
Queen Charlotte's and Chelsea Hospital
Du Cane Road
London
W12 0HS
Tel: 020 8383 3041
Web: www.multiplebirth.org.uk

National Council for One-Parent Families
255 Kentish Town Road
London
NW5 2LX
Tel: 0800 018 5026
Web: www.oneparentfamilies.org.uk
Support for those raising a family on their own

Parentline Plus
520 Highgate Studios
53–79 Highgate Road
London
NW5 1TL
Tel: 020 7284 5500
Helpline: 0808 800 2222
Web: www.parentlineplus.org.uk

SANDS (Stillbirth and Neonatal Death Society)
28 Portland Place
London
W1N 4DE
Tel: 020 7436 5881
Web: www.uk-sands.org
Helpline for bereaved parents

TAMBA (Twins and Multiple Birth Association)
Harnott House
309 Chester Road
Little Sutton
Elsemere Port
CH66 1QQ
Tel: 0151 348 0020
Helpline: 01732 868000
Web:www.tamba.org.uk
Support for families with twins or higher multiples, also local clubs

Vegetarian Society
Parkdale
Dunham Road
Altrincham
Cheshire
WA14 4QG
Tel: 0161 928 0793
Web: www.vegsoc.org

CARE AND EDUCATION

British Association for Early Childhood Education (Early Education)
136 Cavell Street
London
E1 2JA
Tel: 020 7539 5400
Web: www.early-education.org.uk

National Childminding Association
8 Masons Hill
Bromley
Kent
BR2 9EY
Tel: 020 8464 6164
Web: www.ncma.org.uk

Preschool Learning Alliance (previously known as Preschool Playgroups Association)
69 King's Cross Road
London
WC1X 9LL
Tel: 020 7833 0991
Web: www.pre-school.org.uk

FIRST AID AND SAFETY

British Red Cross
9 Grosvenor Crescent
London
SW1X 7EJ
Tel: 020 7235 5454
Web: www. redcross.org.uk

British Standards Institute
389 Chiswick High Road
London
W4 4AL
Tel: 020 8996 9000
Web: www.bsi-global.com

Child Accident Prevention Trust
18–20 Farringdon Lane
London
EC1R 3HA
Tel: 020 7608 3828

Royal Society for the Prevention of Accidents (RoSPA)
Edgbaston Park
353 Bristol Road
Edgbaston
Birmingham
B5 7ST
Tel: 0121 248 2000
Web: www.rospa.co.uk

CHILDREN WITH SPECIAL NEEDS

Association for Spina Bifida and Hydrocephalus (ASBAH)
Asbah House
42 Park Road
Peterborough
PE1 2UQ
Tel: 01733 555988
Web: www.asbah.org

Contact-a-Family
170 Tottenham Court Road
London
W1T 7HA
Tel: 020 7383 3555
Web: www.cafamily.org.uk
Supports parents of children with special needs

Down's Syndrome Association
155 Mitcham Road
London
SW17 9PG
Tel: 020 8682 4001
Web: www.downs-syndrome.org.uk

Hyperactive Children's Support Group
71 Whyke Lane
Chichester
West Sussex
PO19 2LD
Tel: 01903 725182
Web: www.hacsg.org.uk

MENCAP (The Royal Society for Mentally Handicapped Children and Adults)
Mencap National Centre
123 Golden Lane
London
EC1Y 0RT
Tel: 020 7454 0454
Web: www.mencap.org.uk
For people with learning disabilities

INDEX

ACKNOWLEDGMENTS

DORLING KINDERSLEY would like to thank Elizabeth Fenwick, the author of the English edition, for all the work she put into writing the book; and the following for their design and editorial work on the original edition: Rowena Alsey, Carole Ash, Tina Hill, Tanya Hines, Claire Le Bas, Sarah Pearce, and Daphne Razazan.

Special photography
(Abbreviations key: t=top, b=bottom, r=right, l=left, c=centre)

Andy Crawford assisted by Gary Ombler: 192bc, 197tl;
Antonia Deutsch assisted by Pamela Cowan: 6cl, 17, 19t, 21, 27b, 29b, 37–42, 43t, 44–49, 56t and br, 57–61, 64, 67, 71t, 72–73, 90tr and br, 91tl, tc, and cr, 92bl and br, 94, 95tr, tl and cr, 97;
Trish Gant: 55c and b, 82b, 86cl, 95br, 100cr and c, 121br, 123, 160t, 161b, 191cr, 201b, 216t, 243b, 246cl and tr, 247b, 249b, 250c and cl, 251;
Steve Gorton: 145cr;
Dave King: 4: 1st column pictures 2–4, 2nd column pictures 1–4; 6: 2nd column t and lower c, 7: 1st column, 2nd column all except bl, 50–52, 53b, 54 tr and c, 55 tl, tr and c, 76–81, 88tl, 95bl, 98, 99t, l and tc, 100tl, 101, 104, 105 all except bl, 108 all except t, br, bl and cr, 109br, 110–111, 112tl, 114–16, 117t, 2nd row r, 121 all except t and tl, 124bl, 125tr and b, 128–33, 134t, 138–41, 145t and cl, 146t, 149cl, bl and bc, 154, 159, 162–63, 166–71, 171–73, 175, 180t and l, 182b, 183tr, cr and br, 182–202 all except 197tl, 204r, cr and b, 205tr and br, 206–7, 209br, 210tr and b, 211–12, 213tl, tr, and cr, 214t, 216b, 218–23, 225, 226c and r, 227t and bl, 228cl, cr, and b, 229 tl, tr and bl, 230tl and cr, 231tl, cr and b, 232c and r, 234t, 237, 254b, 255b, 256–57;
Ray Moller: 6: 2nd column upper cr, 99b, 100t, b, 106cl, cr, bl and br, 107, 136t, cr, and br, 137 all except br, 142bl and br, 143, 146bl, 181c;
Stephen Oliver: 4: 1st column pictures 1 and 5; 10, 15, 54l and b, 55tr, 56bl, 99bc and br, 103, 105bl, 108t, 120br, 121t and tl, 125tl, 134 all except t, 135, 148, 149tr, box tr, cl and cr, 153, 155, 156
Susanna Price: 6: 2nd column upper cl and b, 7: 2nd column bl, 68–69, 84, 86

all except cl, 87, 88bl and br, 90tl and c, 91tr and bl, 92tl and tr, 93, 112tr, c and br, 117 2nd row l, 3rd row l and r, 4th row l, c and r, 120t, 124 all except bl, 125c, 127, 136bl and bc, 137br, 142tl, 144, bc, and br, 150–52, 158t, 174, 254t, 255t;
Steve Shott: 2: 2nd column picture 5; 157, 158t, 159.

Picture credits
Picture researcher: Anna Grapes
Picture librarians: Melanie Simmonds, Marcus Scott

The publisher would like to thank the following for their kind permission to reproduce their photographs:

(Abbreviations key: t=top, b=bottom, r=right, l=left, c=centre)

Jacket images: **Image Bank/Sandy King;** all other images @ Dorling Kindersley. For further information see: www.dkimages.com.

Sue Ford, Western Ophthalmic Hospital: 181tr, 183bl, 209r; **Genesis Film Productions Ltd/Neil Bromhall:** 23; **Getty Images:** 1 (Dennis O'Clair), 11 (Neil Harding); **Lesley Howling:** 43b; **Meningitis Research Foundation:** 208; **Mother and Baby Picture Library/Emap Esprit:** 31; 74–75 main picture, 89, 178–179 main picture (Ian Hooton), 2–3 main picture, 8–9 main picture (Paul Mitchell), 12–13,12t, 16, 18, 20, 22, 24, 26, 28, 30 (Steve Shott); **National Medical Slide Bank:** 181br, 204tr, 209tl, 213bl, 226l, 227cl, 232l; **St. John's Institute of Dermatology:** 228tl, 231tr; **St. Mary's Hospital:** 183tl, 205tl, 205bl; **Science Photo Library:** 70 (Hank Morgan), 206br (Dr. H. C. Robinson); **Tony Stone:** 1 (Dennis O'Clair), 11 (Neil Harding); **Ron Sutherland:** 67c; **Dr. I. Williams:** 180br, 181cr, 182t and cr, 203r, 210l, 214b, 227bl, 229br, 230t, bc and b.

Loan or supply of props
Baby B's, Fulham, London, England; Diana Dolls Fashions Inc., Stoney Creek, Ontario; The Nursery Collection, Watford, England; Porter Nash Medical, London, England; Seward Ltd., London, England.

Special thanks to: Mary Snyder at Snugli, Inc.; Gerry Baby Products Company, Denver, Colorado; Judi's Originals, Scottsdale, Arizona.

Illustrators
Coral Mula: all line artwork except p.14t; Nick Hall: 14t; Kevin Jones Associates: 234, 235, 236; Richard Tibbitts: 14, 16, 18, 20, 22, 24, 28, 30.

Consultants
Dorling Kindersley acknowledges the contribution of the following consultants to the original edition.
Professor R. W. Taylor, MD, FRCOG, Head of Department of Gynecology, The United Medical Schools of Guy's and St Thomas's Hospitals, London; Professor Jon Scopes, MB, PhD, FRCP, Department of Pediatrics, St Thomas's Hospital, London; Christine Williams, RGN, HV, FWT, Health Visitor and Family Planning Nurse; Janice Leighton, RGN, RM, Community Midwife; Alan McLaughlin, RGN, Department of Clinical Neurology, St Thomas's Hospital, London.

Indexing Specialists
Milla Hills, Indexing Specialists, 202 Church Road, Hove, East Sussex, BN3 2DJ, UK.Tel: 01273 738299. Fax: 01273 323309. e.mail: richard@indexing.co.uk Website:http://www.indexing.co.uk